ROLL OUT THE CARPET

101 SEASONS OF WEST VIRGINIA UNIVERSITY BASKETBALL

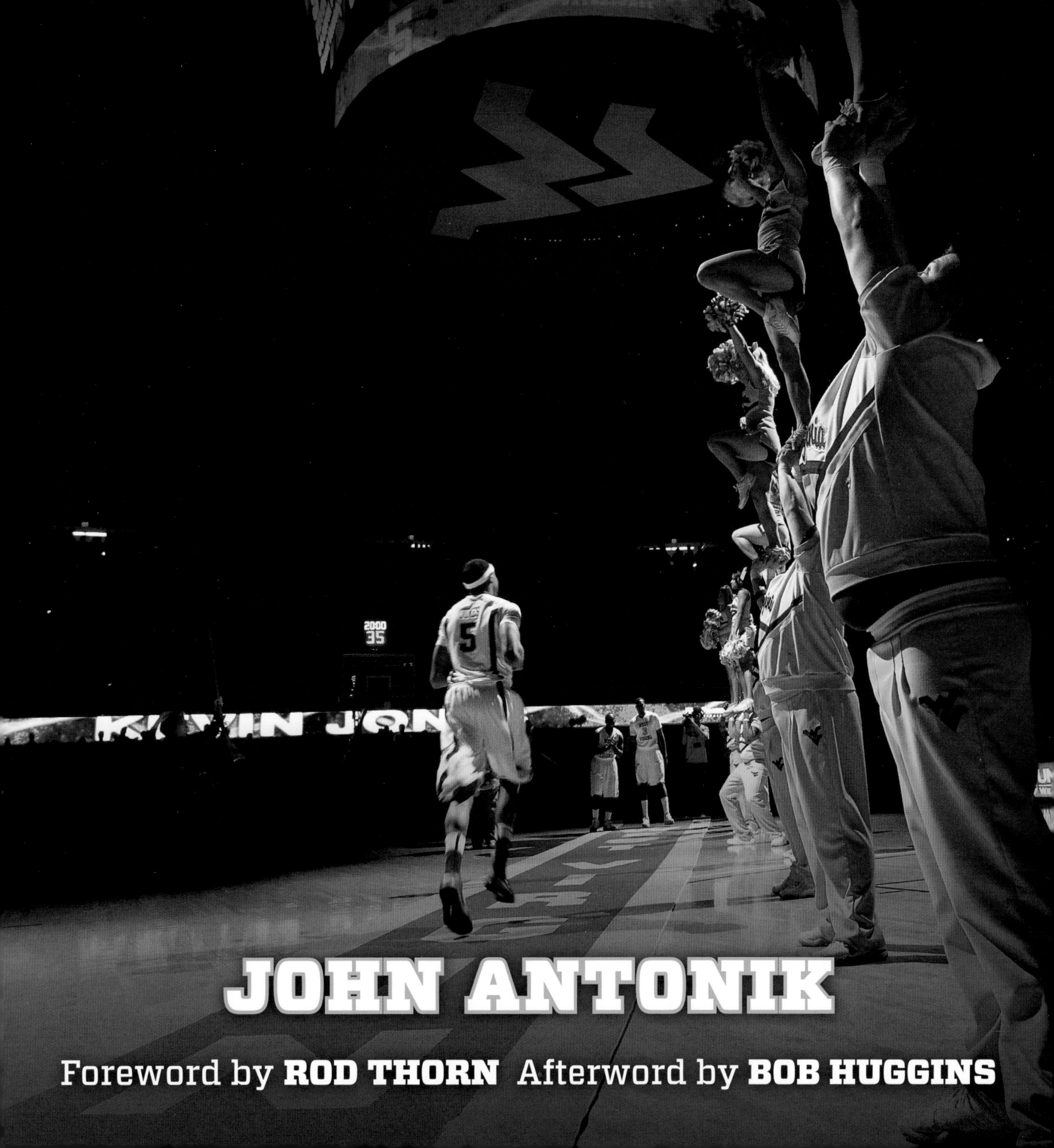

JOHN ANTONIK

Foreword by **ROD THORN** Afterword by **BOB HUGGINS**

West Virginia University Press, Morgantown 26506

First edition published 2010 by

West Virginia University Press

Printed in the United States of America

18 17 16 15 14 13 12 11 10   1 2 3 4 5 6 7 8 9

ISBN-10: 1-933202-66-1

ISBN-13: 978-1-933202-66-2 (alk. paper)

Library of Congress

Cataloguing-in-Publication Data Pending

Library of Congress Control Number: 2010021921

Photo credits: WVU Sports Communications, West Virginia and Regional History Collection, WVU Alumni Association, University of California, Manhattan College, Virginia Tech, University of Pittsburgh/Sam Scuillo, Rich Schmitt, Van Slider, Brent Kepner, Big East Conference, All-Pro Photography/Dale Sparks, *Blue and Gold News*/Greg Hunter, Kevin Kinder, and Allison Toffle, WVU Photographic Services/Brian Persinger, M. G. Ellis, Dan Friend, and Scott Lituchy

Book design by Than Saffel/West Virginia University Press.

Jacket design by Than Saffel

with production assistance from Jessica Russo/Blaine Turner Advertising, Inc.

Edited by Danielle Zahoran/West Virginia University Press.

Contents

EBANKS
3

Foreword

Rod Thorn, former president and general manager of the NBA's New Jersey Nets, spent more than 45 years in the NBA as a player, coach and league executive. While serving as general manager of the Chicago Bulls, Thorn was instrumental in the selection of Michael Jordan in the 1984 draft. From 1986–2000, Thorn was the NBA's Executive Vice President of Basketball Operations.

The unbridled legacy of West Virginia University basketball has been one of accomplishment and achievement for decades and has served to warm the hearts of Mountaineer fans everywhere on many a cold and dreary night.

I can still vividly recall the dulcet tones of the great Jack Fleming as he described the machinations of Becker, Isner and Holmes those many years ago. His play-calling was magical and made you feel as if you were courtside.

Growing up in Princeton during the Golden Age of West Virginia basketball was a thrilling experience to say the least. Rod Hundley's incredible charisma and ahead-of-his-time talent, Jerry West's unparalleled greatness in all aspects of the game, the heartbreaking loss to California in the 1959 title game and Fred Schaus's bigger-than-life persona and leadership qualities. When he spoke at the Princeton High Banquet after my junior year, you could have heard a pin drop. West Virginia basketball was a big part of the national scene, and Mountaineers everywhere were invigorated as never before. Every game was an important event.

During my time at the university, several memories are still clear: the fantastic student and fan support, the respect WVU basketball engendered every place we played, the confidence the uniform gave to our players and the tremendous home-court advantage the old Field House gave us. In fact, many teams were defeated before the game ever started. No opposing team had an easy time on Beechurst Avenue! We took a great deal of pride in representing the state and in showing the basketball world that West Virginia could compete with anyone, anytime, anywhere.

There have been a host of great coaches through the years—Brown, Catlett, Schaus, Beilein and Huggins to name a few—men who set a standard of excellence and maintained it over time.

Outstanding players have also matriculated at the university and lived up to their press clippings: Workman, Sharrar, Hundley, West, Williams, Robinson, Jones, Pittsnogle, Gansey and Butler are but a few who have distinguished themselves and brought honor and fame to the state and to themselves.

I have spent more than 45 years in professional basketball on many different levels and have observed countless collegiate programs up close. West Virginia's is in the upper tier, and now that it plays in the Big East—the premier league in the country— I am sure it will remain there for years to come.

The lessons learned on the playgrounds in Princeton and honed at West Virginia University have proven invaluable in helping me compete at the highest levels in both the corporate and sporting worlds. I am forever thankful that I had the opportunity to grow and learn in such a nurturing environment. Go Mountaineers!!!

MSNsportsNET.com
WEST 3 VIRGINIA
WEST 42 VIRGINIA
WEST 33 VIRGINIA
WEST 25 VIRGINIA
WEST 41 VIRGINIA
MEGA MILLIONS

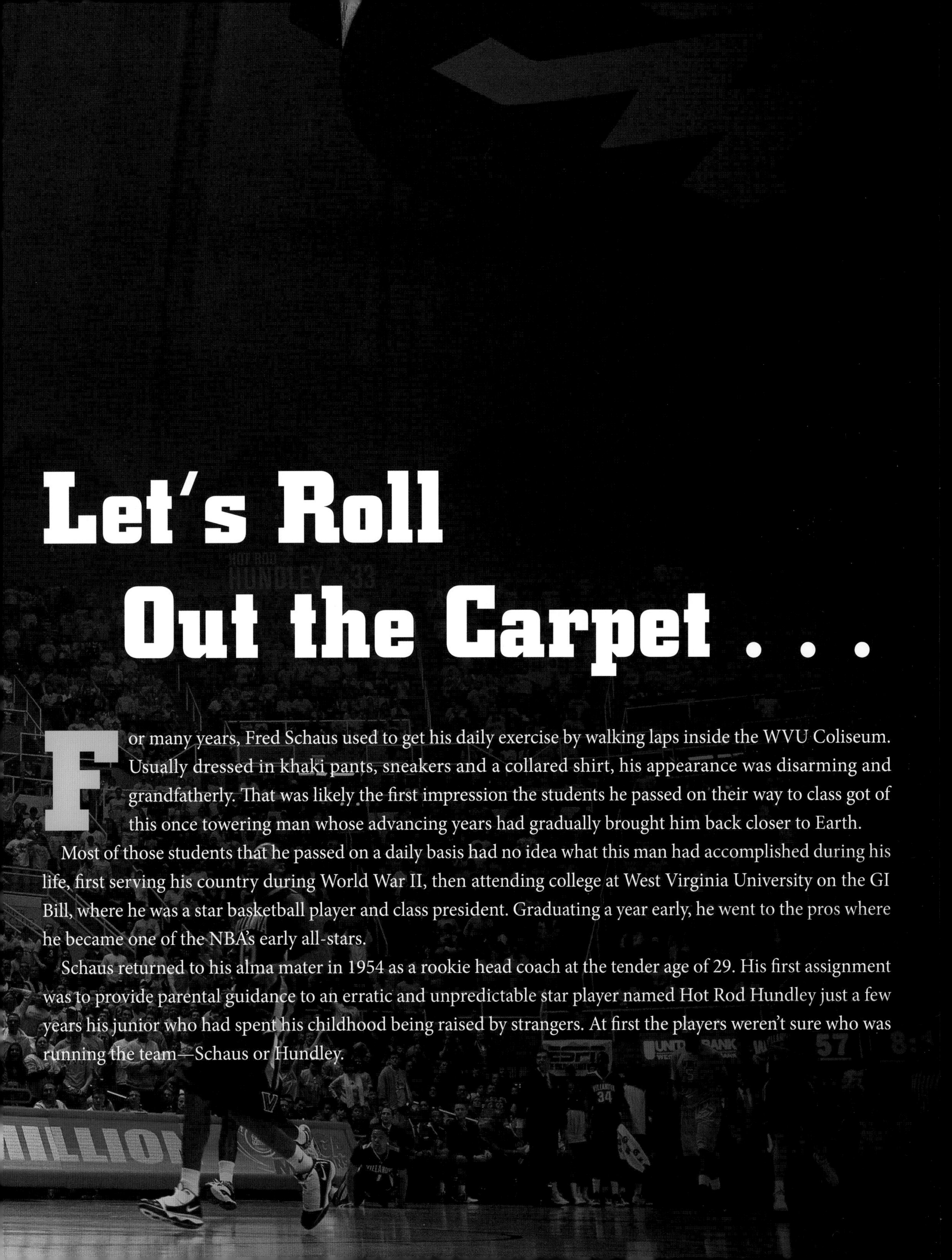

Let's Roll Out the Carpet . . .

For many years, Fred Schaus used to get his daily exercise by walking laps inside the WVU Coliseum. Usually dressed in khaki pants, sneakers and a collared shirt, his appearance was disarming and grandfatherly. That was likely the first impression the students he passed on their way to class got of this once towering man whose advancing years had gradually brought him back closer to Earth.

Most of those students that he passed on a daily basis had no idea what this man had accomplished during his life, first serving his country during World War II, then attending college at West Virginia University on the GI Bill, where he was a star basketball player and class president. Graduating a year early, he went to the pros where he became one of the NBA's early all-stars.

Schaus returned to his alma mater in 1954 as a rookie head coach at the tender age of 29. His first assignment was to provide parental guidance to an erratic and unpredictable star player named Hot Rod Hundley just a few years his junior who had spent his childhood being raised by strangers. At first the players weren't sure who was running the team—Schaus or Hundley.

But Schaus conquered that and all other obstacles to build West Virginia University into one of the most envied basketball programs in the country. His teams won the conference championship and advanced to the NCAA tournament all six years he coached at WVU.

In the summer of 1960, Schaus left West Virginia for the Los Angeles Lakers, where he led them to seven consecutive playoff appearances, including four Western Conference titles during a five-year span. Later as general manager of the Lakers, he helped construct one of the best teams in professional basketball history, which won a record 33 consecutive games and the NBA title in 1972.

Schaus returned to college basketball at Purdue in 1973 and then turned to athletic administration in 1979. Two years after that, he was asked to help extract the WVU athletic department from a substantial financial crisis as its new athletic director. Not coincidentally, it was around the time of Schaus's homecoming that the WVU basketball program experienced a revival under Gale Catlett, who Schaus had recruited to the university in 1959.

A decade after his retirement in 1989, those mornings when I came to work and observed the ex-coach/GM/athletic director amiably walking the hallways, I began to wonder why no one had ever written a book about those great Fred Schaus basketball teams of the late 1950s. For that matter, why hadn't a thorough history of Mountaineer basketball ever been attempted? For one, anniversaries are often forgotten, and two, there is some pretty heavy lifting involved. Not to diminish the accomplishments of West Virginia's earlier teams, but the great history of Mountaineer basketball really begins in 1942 with Dyke Raese leading a roster full of West Virginians to an improbable NIT championship in New York City. Before that, basketball was just a little more than a winter diversion for WVU sports fans anxiously waiting for another football season to begin. In the early days there were no scholarships given to basketball players and the school's most successful coach before Raese—Francis Stadsvold—was a lawyer by trade who spent his summers in his native Minnesota. Some of the best of those early teams were simply the

Fred Schaus brought great success to West Virginia University, first as a player in the 1940s, then as a coach in the 1950s, and later, as a director of athletics in the 1980s.

WVU SPORTS COMMUNICATIONS PHOTO

result of having an abundance of great football and baseball players such as Homer Martin, Little Sleepy Glenn, Joe Stydahar and Babe Barna.

But that changed when Raese arrived, and after a few passes of the baton, Lee Patton in the late 1940s continued what Raese had started. Soon young boys everywhere in West Virginia were attaching metal hoops to sycamore trees, nailing the backs of ping-pong tables to telephone poles, clearing off fields, redirecting traffic on side streets and playing basketball. From that era was born a staggering array of homegrown talent, as good as anywhere in the country on a per capita basis, some would say. Scotty Hamilton (Grafton), Leland Byrd (Matoaka), Mark Workman (Charleston by way of Logan), Hot Rod Hundley (Charleston), Jerry West (Chelyan), Rod Thorn (Princeton), Fritz Williams (Weirton)—and many, many years later, Kevin Pittsnogle (Martinsburg)—all became All-America players raised on West Virginia University basketball.

When the Mountaineers became a national sensation in the late 1950s and early 1960s, West Virginia fans would frequently drive to the nearest mountaintop to pick up Wheeling's WWVA, straining to hear Jack Fleming's completely biased but always enthusiastic description of the games through the nighttime crackles and pops. That's how Jerry West came to love the Mountaineers—curled up with a radio in his bed underneath the covers with the volume turned down just low enough for his mother to think he was asleep.

There was Dr. Lowell Schwab, whose love affair with the Mountaineers became a personal

Roy McHugh, sports editor of the *Pittsburgh Press*, wrote of Jerry West in 1967, "The Jerry Wests of this world don't come in pairs."

ALL-PRO PHOTOGRAPHY/DALE SPARKS.

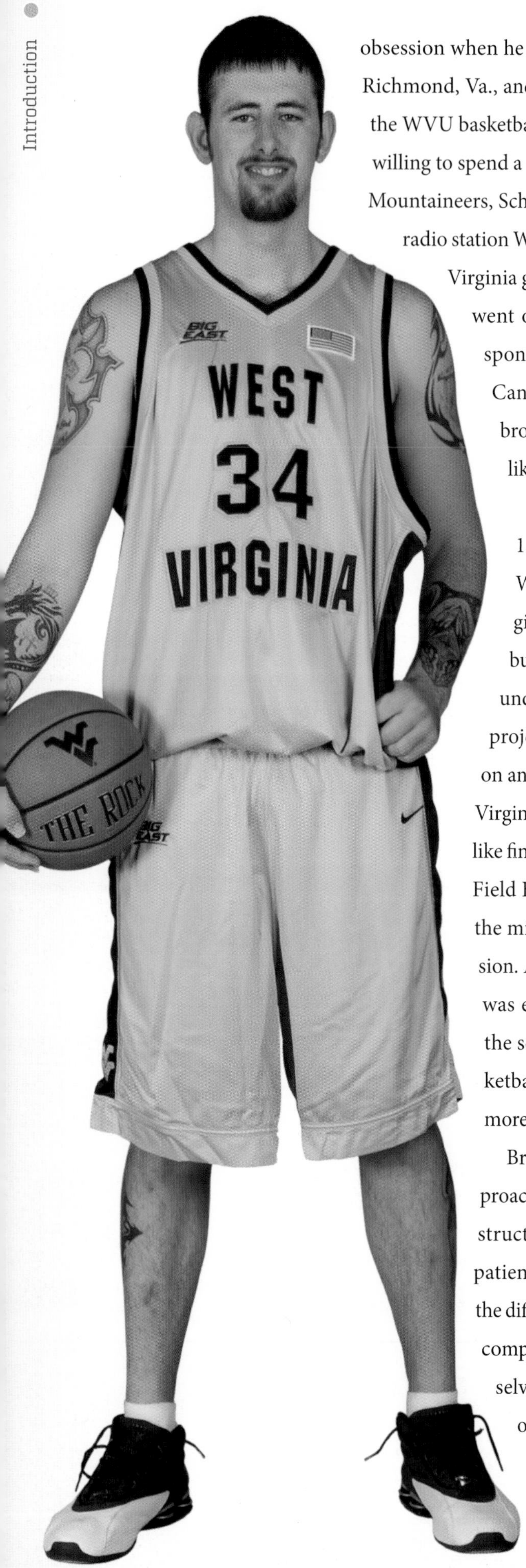

obsession when he went to medical school in Richmond, Va., and could no longer listen to the WVU basketball games on the radio. Unwilling to spend a winter without his beloved Mountaineers, Schwab convinced Richmond radio station WRVA in 1962 to carry West Virginia games that season. He even went out and personally sold a sponsorship (Old Dominion Candy) to help pay for the broadcast. How could a story like that go untold?

There was Red Brown's 13-year crusade to build the WVU Coliseum. West Virginia University's other great builder—Harry Stansbury—understood that construction projects many times can take on an evolutionary pace in West Virginia, so he instituted a Ponzi-like financing scheme to build the Field House in just two years in the middle of the Great Depression. All of the outstanding debt was eventually paid back, and the school had a first-rate basketball Field House that lasted more than 40 years.

Brown used a different approach to get the Coliseum constructed in the late 1960s. He patiently bided his time, letting the different political factions and competing interests sort themselves out before seizing his opportunity when he sensed

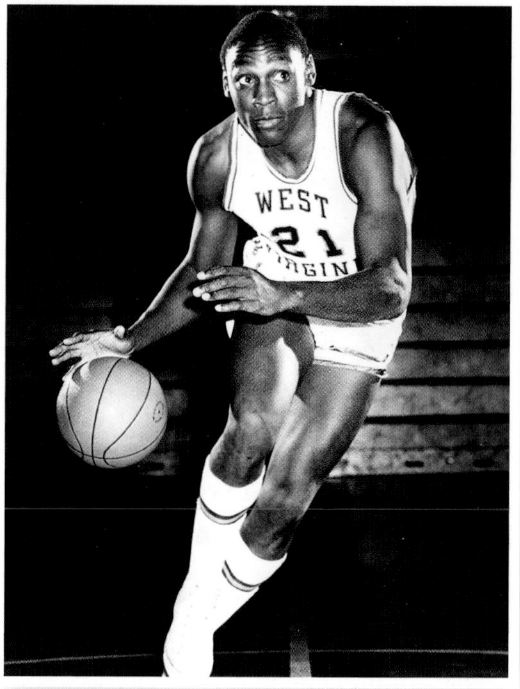

the time was finally ripe. Completed in time for the 1971 season, the WVU Coliseum was the grandest thing anyone in West Virginia had ever dreamed of building. Even today, it is hard to imagine another facility the magnitude of the WVU Coliseum ever being built again in West Virginia.

There was George King unknowingly integrating the Southern Conference in 1965. The courage and grace that Ron Williams, Jim Lewis, Ed Harvard, Norman Holmes (and a year later, Carl Head) displayed in the mid-1960s made WVU's transition to a multicultural campus a smooth one at a time when nothing seemed to be going smoothly on college campuses around the country.

And today, just like Schaus, Patton and Raese before him, Bob Huggins has a similar blend of charisma, savvy and intelligence that is creating a whole new generation of Mountaineer basketball fans. Whenever

Mountain State natives have always played a prominent role in West Virginia University basketball history, from Kevin Pittsnogle (left) to Ron "Fritz" Williams (above) to Bob Huggins (right).
PHOTOS: WVU SPORTS COMMUNICATIONS, *BLUE AND GOLD NEWS* /KEVIN KINDER, AND ALL-PRO PHOTOGRAPHY/DALE SPARKS

Huggins walks into a room, all eyes immediately train on him. I imagine that was also the case some 50 years ago when Fred Schaus made an entrance.

Huggins has West Virginia basketball primed for another renaissance—at least that's what I frequently hear from the old-timers who were around a half-century ago to watch Hundley, West and Thorn play in what they fondly refer to as Mountaineer basketball's "Golden Era."

From the Golden Eras to the Forgotten Eras, the Mountaineers now have played a full century of basketball, and it's probably high time that someone get it all down for history.

So here's to all of those great coaches, great players and great fans who have made Mountaineer basketball what it is today. This book is for you.

23

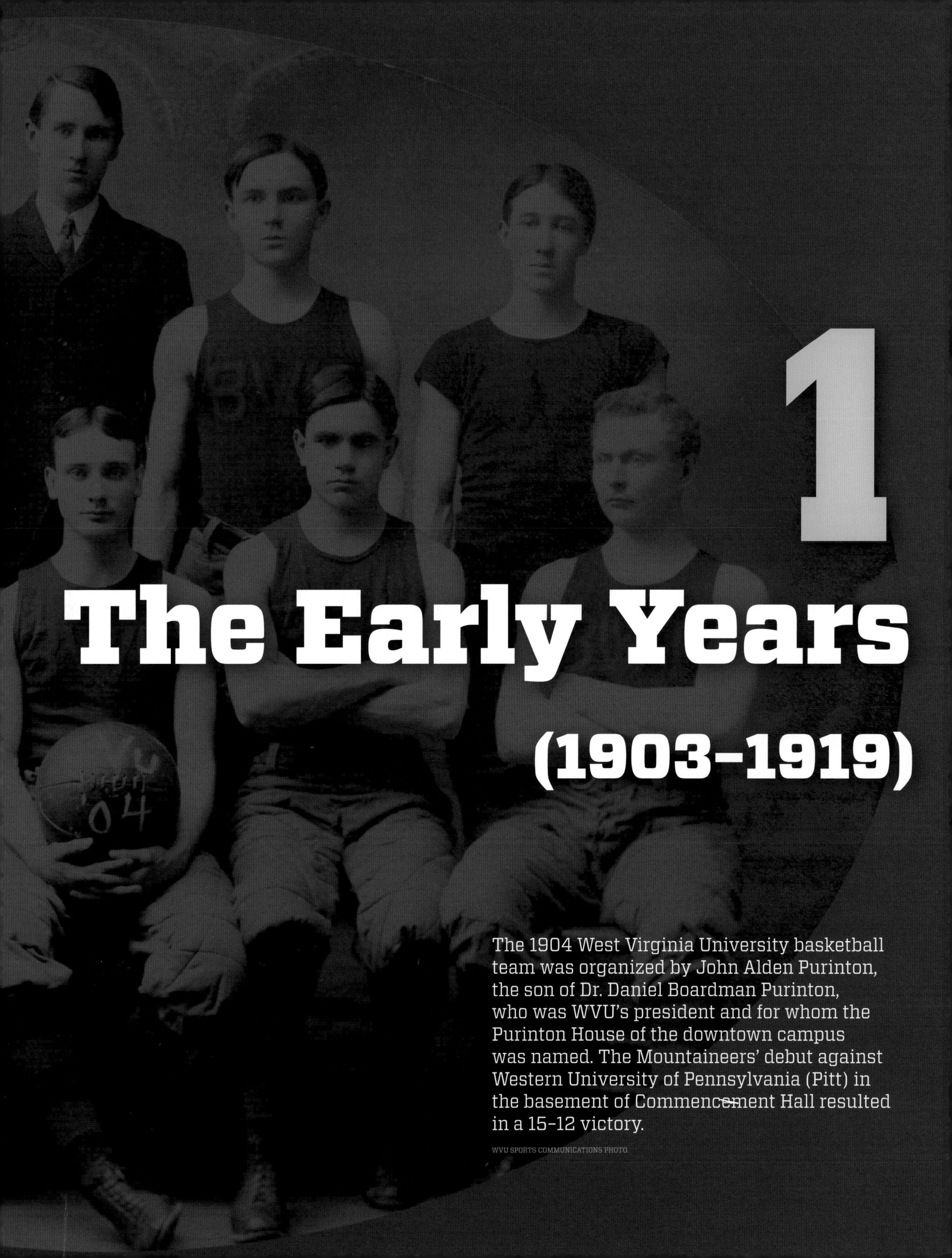

1

The Early Years

(1903–1919)

The 1904 West Virginia University basketball team was organized by John Alden Purinton, the son of Dr. Daniel Boardman Purinton, who was WVU's president and for whom the Purinton House of the downtown campus was named. The Mountaineers' debut against Western University of Pennsylvania (Pitt) in the basement of Commencement Hall resulted in a 15–12 victory.

WVU SPORTS COMMUNICATIONS PHOTO.

John Purinton was credited with introducing basketball to West Virginia University in 1904. As the team's manager, it was his responsibility to greet the opposing team and sell tickets. After that was accomplished, he typically entered games in the second half as a substitute. The first WVU team managed to pay its expenses with Purinton using his own money to help make up the difference.
WVU SPORTS COMMUNICATIONS PHOTO.

Robert P. Strickler was a member of West Virginia University's first basketball team in 1904 and was later awarded a Rhodes Scholarship in 1907. The Philippi native earned his PhD from Johns Hopkins University in 1919 and returned to the Mountain State to teach at Davis & Elkins College.
WVU SPORTS COMMUNICATIONS PHOTO.

Basketball made its official introduction to West Virginia University in 1904 when a roster of nine players, organized by John A. Purinton, faced Western University of Pennsylvania (Pitt) in a game played in Morgantown on Feb. 20, 1904.

The nine guys who suited up that evening for the Mountaineers were Ervin Cathers of Grafton; Otis Cole of Morgantown; James Gronninger of Charleston; Harry Hart of Monroeville, Ohio; DuPont McCormick of Morgantown; Robert Strickler of Philippi; Everett and Shelby Taylor of Morgantown; and Purinton.

Strickler also played on the baseball team, served on the Monticola Board, and was class vice president as a sophomore before earning a Rhodes scholarship in 1907. The Philippi native later received a PhD from Johns Hopkins University in 1919 and eventually returned to the state to teach at Davis & Elkins College.

According to Paul Martin, former editor of the *Martinsburg Journal*, Purinton, the son of West Virginia University president Dr. Daniel Boardman Purinton (whom Purinton House on campus is named after), was familiar with the sport while attending Denison College in Ohio. First introduced to WVU students in 1898, basketball was played on a club or "class" basis until Purinton helped form the school's first official team.

The game of basketball first appeared in 1891, created by Dr. James Naismith in Springfield, Mass., as a means of continuing physical activity during the cold winter months. Naismith's initial creation was composed of two peach baskets and a soccer ball, and he later developed a set of 13 general rules that provided the basis for the game that we enjoy today. Copies of the rules were mailed to YMCAs throughout the country, and the game soon spread to high schools and colleges. The first college basketball game took place on Feb. 9, 1895, when Minnesota State defeated Hamline College 9–3, and the first five-player college game was played on Jan. 16, 1896, when the University of Chicago defeated Iowa 15–12. Only ten years after the first college game, an estimated 88 colleges were playing basketball.

By the time basketball reached West Virginia University in 1904, the free throw line had moved in from 20 feet to 15 feet, the point value for a field goal had changed from three points to two and free throws from three points to one, backboards had become standard, dribblers were not permitted to shoot field goals, and they could only dribble once with both hands.

The evolution of athletics at West Virginia University rapidly accelerated during the 1890s. This was a time when the country's industrial employers were beginning to give their workers a half-day holiday on Saturdays. Vacations (though usually unpaid) were also being offered to employees. Out of this increase in leisure time came the creation of professional baseball leagues and associations, particularly in the big cities of the Northeast and Midwest. While the more cultured and nostalgic were gravitating toward baseball, football was considered a sport for the roughnecks. Football in the late 1890s and early 1900s was brutal, and it was getting a reputation for being a "killer sport."

WVU fielded its first football team in 1891, and baseball, already well on its way to becoming the national pastime, was introduced to WVU students in 1892. The school's sporting teams first came under the control of the university president, the Commandant of the Cadet Corps and the director of athletics, before increased student interest led to the formation of the Athletic Association in 1893. This organization lasted four years until it was abolished because of a lack of adequate funding. It was replaced by a faculty committee that included student representation, and this configuration proved to be much more practical, according to WVU historian J. William Douglas.

What made it possible for West Virginia University to begin playing basketball on a more formal basis was the school's permission for the team to use, first, the basement of Commencement Hall located next to Stewart Hall, and then, when available, the Armory, a brick building located in the southeast corner of campus where the Mountainlair plaza presently sits. The Armory was constructed in 1902 to house the University Cadet Corps following the end of the Spanish-American War. A 40-foot by 70-foot court was marked off, and 15-foot-high netting suspended on portable poles was erected on both ends to protect the spectators from the action taking place below them. A slick floor kept the scoring down and audiences amused.

About 200 spectators, mostly students, crammed into the Armory's basement to watch the first college basketball game at West Virginia University begin at approximately 8:15 p.m. on Saturday, Feb. 20, 1904. The first point was scored by West Virginia's Otis Cole on a free throw. He wound up making 11 of his 13 shots from the foul line, while also tossing in one of the team's two field goals in what turned out to be a 15–12 Mountaineer victory.

At the time, one player was usually selected to shoot all the team's free throws—a practice that lasted until 1924. According to West Virginia's student newspaper, *The Daily Athenaeum* (*DA*), the wide disparity in fouls was attributed to "Pitt being accustomed to playing by national rules instead of AAU [Amateur Athletic Union] rules"—not some home cooking by the referees.

According to the *Encyclopedia of College Basketball* (1995), the YMCA and the AAU had a joint rules committee, but that arrangement soon disintegrated when the AAU forbade Yale from

An encompassing view of West Virginia University's athletic complex at the turn of the century with the Armory in the background. The Armory was constructed to house the University Cadet Corps, but also served as the home venue for WVU basketball games before the completion of the Ark in 1916. The Armory was located where the current Mountainlair Plaza resides.

WVU SPORTS COMMUNICATIONS PHOTO.

competing in 1905 because it was an unregistered team. Yale's rival, Penn, was notified that if it played Yale it would lose its official sanctioning as well.

As a result, colleges wanting to have more of a say in the establishment of rules for amateur sports created the Intercollegiate Athletic Association of the United States (IAAUS) in 1906. The IAAUS, which later became known as the National Collegiate Athletic Association (NCAA), had a big proponent in President Theodore Roosevelt, who was being pressured to address reforms in football to reduce the number of deaths and crippling injuries that resulted from rough play in that sport.

An interior view of Commencement Hall, where the basketball team occasionally played games when the Armory was not available. Commencement Hall was located right next to Stewart Hall on the downtown campus.

WVU SPORTS COMMUNICATIONS PHOTO.

The IAAUS established slightly different rules than the AAU, and schools often chose between the two until they finally merged in 1915.

The *DA*'s account of the game also credited Pitt with being the more organized of the two teams. On two occasions, play had to be stopped because of injuries, though no one was hurt seriously. Near the end of the first half, Pitt demanded that the game's umpire and referee switch places because too many fouls were being called and it was slowing down play. The *Daily Athenaeum*'s account concluded with the prediction that basketball could eventually "be made a paying game here."

That first game against Pitt was the only game West Virginia played that year against another college, with the remaining games played against YMCA and Athletic Club teams. They ended their first season with a 4–3 record.

For the first few years of its existence, the team was essentially left to its own devices, meaning they had to finance their own games, equipment and travel, and the captain usually doubled as the team's coach.

Though primitive by today's standards, basketball games during this period could be quite entertaining. Hiram was awarded a point during a game at Commencement Hall in 1905 on account of spectators hissing at the team. Later, West Virginia got the point back when a Hiram player was whistled for interference.

The Mountaineers, under the direction of Anthony Chez in 1905, expanded their schedule to 15 games, winning six, and West Virginia topped the .500 mark (5–4) under Chez in 1906. Chez, who also coached the football team and served as the school's director of athletics, took WVU teams to neighboring Ohio and Pennsylvania to play games for the first time. His three-year record of 15–21 included victories over Penn State and Bethany. He led the team to an 80–1 bloodbath against Waynesburg College on Feb. 4, 1905, which represented the most points produced by a Mountaineer basketball team until 1942.

West Virginia played a 10-game slate in 1908 under James Jenkins, who was recruited from the student body to coach the team. It was the team's first schedule featuring predominantly college teams, and the stiffer competition caused the Mountaineers' record to dip to 3–7. All three victories came at home, against Davis & Elkins, Marietta and Westminster. The Mountaineers also played a competitive home game against undefeated Allegheny that year, losing by nine points. Richard Nebinger was the team's leading scorer for the season with an 11.8-points-per-game average. In the Davis & Elkins win, Nebinger scored 24 points, a high total for that era. Nebinger was also a shortstop on the baseball team and led the Mountaineers to an 18–8 record as the school's baseball coach in 1909 before moving on to play professional baseball in the Boston Red Sox organization.

Following the 1908 losing season, scant financial resources and untenable conditions inside the Armory led basketball to be reduced to intramural status for the next seven years.

Back From Oblivion

Student pressure forced the school to resume basketball as a varsity sport in 1915. The Athletic Board gave formal approval in October of that year and elected Arlington Fleming as team manager in charge of assembling a schedule. Thirty players came out for the team, and Athletic Director George Pyle was appointed to oversee them. Eventually, the team was pared to 10 members for the varsity team and 10 for a reserve squad.

By this time, more changes had taken place in the game. In 1908, dribblers were permitted to shoot; a year later in 1909, a second official had been added to games to help curb rough play. In 1910, a fourth foul by a player resulted in a disqualification. Coaching was no longer permitted during the course of the game—after a warning was given for the first violation to any offending coach, a second infraction resulted in a free throw for the other team. Four years later, the bottom of the net was left open, and by the time West Virginia was ready to resume play in 1915, college, YMCA and AAU rules had all merged into one set of rules.

The Armory was once again made available for the basketball team, but because of conflicting schedules with the rifle team and damage to the facility by overenthusiastic fans, Commandant of Cadets Richard Weatherill soon canceled that arrangement, forcing the school to consider constructing a facility to use in its place.

The result was the Ark, a barn-like structure constructed (by B. M. Chaplin Company) for $2,500 that doubled as the mess hall for military personnel staying at the Armory. The Ark made it more practical for the school to resume basketball, although conditions were less than ideal with low ceilings and frigid temperatures that hindered play. There were no provisions made for dressing rooms, and players had to run outside in the cold to the adjacent University Heating Plant to get dressed and to use a portable shower installed there. The Ark's existence was marked by constant complaints from players, coaches and spectators forced to use it. The improvised facility, located where Stansbury Hall presently sits, had makeshift bleachers constructed on each side to accommodate approximately 900 spectators with barely enough space in the middle for games.

The Ark was completed on Jan. 4, 1916 (a week before West Virginia opened its season), and served as the home of the Mountaineers for 12 years until the Field House was christened for the 1928–29 season.

Recreational basketball was the only means for WVU students to play the sport from 1909 to 1914 when the school discontinued basketball for financial reasons. Pictured here is the law school basketball team that won the university championship in 1913. Pictured in the front row, farthest right, is Carl Leatherwood, one of West Virginia's great early football players.

WVU SPORTS COMMUNICATIONS PHOTO.

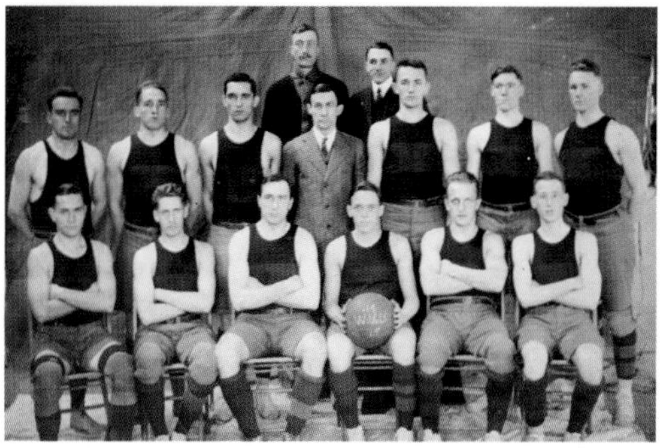

After a seven-year hiatus, student pressure forced the Athletic Board to reconstitute basketball as a varsity sport at West Virginia University for the 1915 season. The 1915 team, coached by George Pyle, compiled a 10–10 record while playing in the new "Ark" basketball tabernacle on Beechurst Avenue.

WEST VIRGINIA AND REGIONAL HISTORY COLLECTION.

The "Ark" was basketball's second permanent home from 1916 to 1928. Constructed at a cost of $2,500, the Ark was an improvement over Commencement Hall but was far from being an ideal venue for basketball games. Opposing players often complained about the facility's frigid temperatures and less-than-ideal playing conditions. In 1928, the team was so anxious to get out of the Ark that it played its home games at Morgantown High while the new Field House was being constructed.

WVU SPORTS COMMUNICATIONS PHOTO.

Harnus P. Mullenex became West Virginia's sixth basketball coach in 1918. Mullenex, a WVU football letterman in 1914 and a basketball letterman in 1915, was coaching at Davis & Elkins College before his WVU appointment.

WVU SPORTS COMMUNICATIONS PHOTO.

Pyle, a Florida graduate, coached the new team for three years from 1915–17, compiling a 29–25 record. His best season came in 1916 when West Virginia produced an 11–7 mark against a schedule that included games against Washington & Lee, Virginia Military Institute, Virginia and Catholic University. The Mountaineers finished the season winning five straight games, including a pair of victories each against West Virginia Wesleyan and Davis & Elkins.

Jack Latterner, a forward from Marietta, Ohio, led the Mountaineers in scoring with an 8.8-points-per-game average. The team also featured football stars Ira Errett Rodgers, Clay Hite and Jaspar Colebank, and was considered one of the most talented teams of that period. Three players—Latterner, Ross Tuckwiller and Rodgers—each scored more than 100 points for the season. All of the players were interchangeable, and there was no noticeable drop in performance when substitutions were made. The group was described by 1918 WVU graduate D. A. Christopher as a "high-scoring, powerful, fast and clever combination."

The presence of football players such as Rodgers, Hite, and Colebank on the basketball team was not unusual at the time. Because basketball did not award athletic scholarships until 1943, rosters were made up primarily of football and baseball players; basketball depended on those sports to supply its best players.

Pyle's 1917 team finished the season winning seven of its remaining nine games after getting off to a rough 1–6 start that included losses to strong Syracuse and Washington & Lee teams. Guard Bill Morrison scored 14 points in a 56–21 victory over Westminster, forward William Steadman and center Frank Ice poured in 18 points each in a 72–26 win over Muskingum, and Latterner scored 20 points in a 36-point victory over Fairmont Normal.

Morrison, a Sutton native, led the team in scoring with an average of 10.2 points per game. It was just the second time in school history that a player appearing in more than 10 games averaged double figures for the season. (Guard Shelby Taylor averaged 11.3 points per game during West Virginia's 12-game slate in 1905.)

Mullenex Takes Over

Harnus P. Mullenex, a member of Pyle's 1915 team, came from Davis & Elkins to coach the Mountaineers in 1918, when Pyle left the university to attend the United States Army Training Camp. The fact that West Virginia was playing basketball in 1918 was a small miracle in itself. A crippling influenza outbreak that claimed an estimated 50 to 100 million people worldwide from 1918–20 was shutting down college campuses throughout the country; West Virginia University suspended operation for a good part of the fall semester, canceling the football season. The Delta Tau fraternity house was transformed into an emergency hospital, and theatres, churches and other public places were immediately closed. Proactive planning by the university and the city had kept deaths to a minimum.

The basketball team had just four wins

against 13 losses in 1918, including a five-game trip through western New York that saw the Mountaineers lose on consecutive days against Syracuse, Niagara, Buffalo, Colgate and Army. Syracuse was considered the strongest team in the country that year with its All-American center Joe Schwarzer. Mullenex tried the same thing the following season in 1919, playing five straight games at Allegheny, Cornell, Syracuse, Colgate and Rutgers. Once again, West Virginia lost all five games.

Despite a .500 record in 1919, Mullenex had an outstanding player in forward Homer "Moose" Martin. The Charleston native averaged 16.8 points per game that year and scored a career-high 31 points in a 20-point victory over Fairmont YMCA. Martin was a fullback on West Virginia's 1922 East-West Bowl team, was the starting catcher and team captain of the baseball team, and he put his impressive physique to good use on the hardwood.

Martin produced 742 points during his 56-game playing career from 1919–22 for an average of 13.3 points per game, and he was posthumously inducted into the West Virginia University Sports Hall of Fame in 1995.

In 1917, West Virginia Wesleyan's Harry Stansbury was brought in to oversee the athletic program, and it was Stansbury who helped pave the way to big-time sports at WVU. He had played on Wesleyan teams that consistently beat West Virginia, and his appointment drew the ire of some boosters of the program who were jealous of Wesleyan's success. But Stansbury quickly placated them with a series of impressive hires that placed WVU athletics on a more prominent level within the region.

Although not yet in a position to adequately fund the basketball program, Stansbury thought it prudent to look outside of the Mountain State for the school's next coach. Basketball at WVU had not experienced much success, posting just three winning campaigns since its inception, and Stansbury wanted to bring in a coach with more of a basketball pedigree. In 1920, he chose Minnesota native Francis Stadsvold to take over the program, and the well-liked Stadsvold wound up coaching the team for 14 years.

Harry Stansbury became West Virginia University's athletic director in 1917 and served in that capacity for 21 years. Stansbury successfully oversaw the construction of Mountaineer Field in 1924, and then, the construction of the Field House in 1928. In both instances, Stansbury had to raise funds during extremely difficult financial times in the state.

WVU SPORTS COMMUNICATIONS PHOTO.

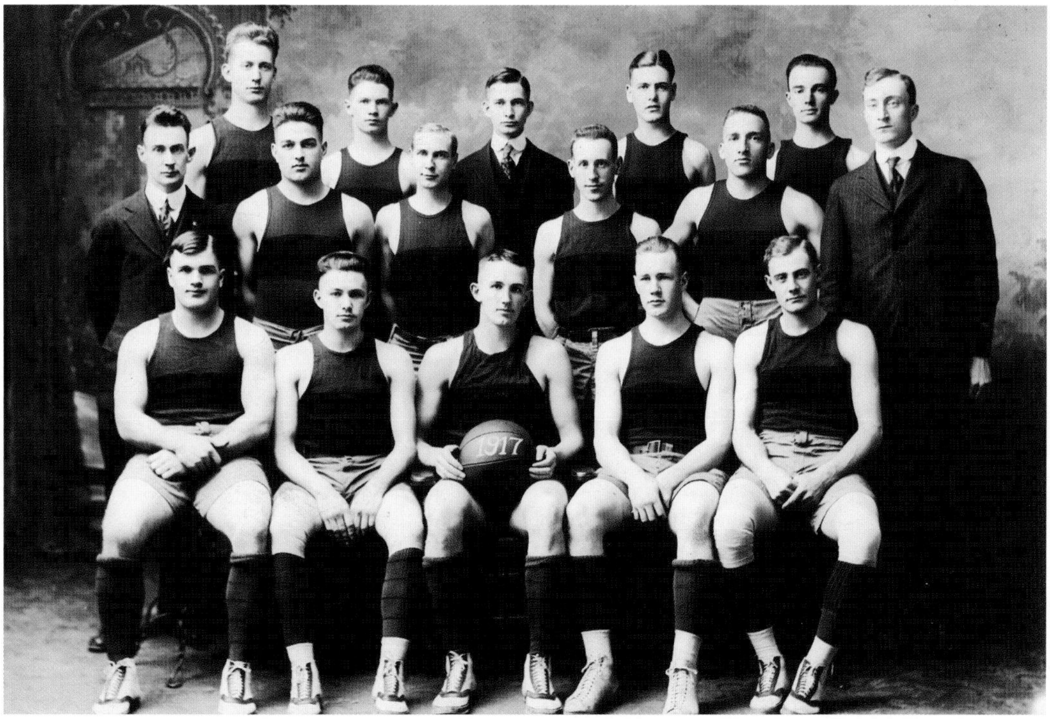

West Virginia's 1917 basketball team finished the season by winning three of its last four games and included consensus football All-American Ira Errett "Rat" Rodgers, seated first on the left in the front row.

WEST VIRGINIA AND REGIONAL HISTORY COLLECTION.

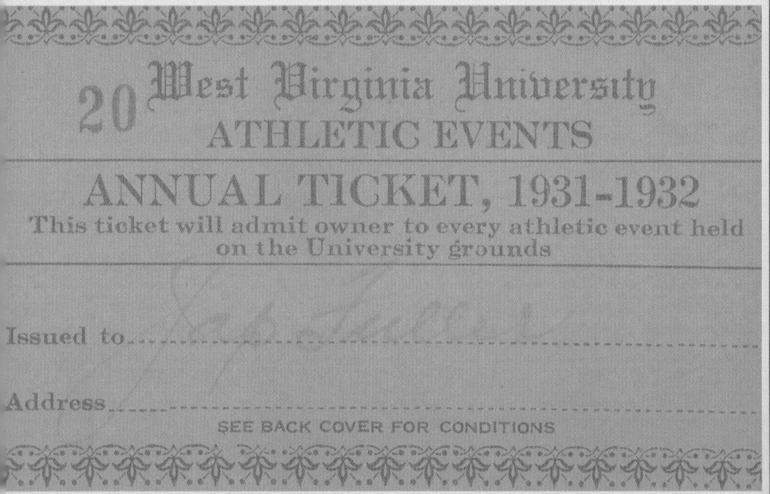

20 West Virginia University
ATHLETIC EVENTS

ANNUAL TICKET, 1931-1932

This ticket will admit owner to every athletic event held on the University grounds

Issued to..................

Address..................

SEE BACK COVER FOR CONDITIONS

2

S-T-A-D-S-V-O-L-D Spells Stability

(1920–1933)

Coach Francis Stadsvold's 1921 team had an 11–9 record and won five straight games to end the regular season, including a 43–24 blowout victory over rival Pitt at the Ark on March 12, 1921.

WEST VIRGINIA AND REGIONAL HISTORY COLLECTION.

Francis Stadsvold was an all-Big Ten center at Minnesota who was hired by Harry Stansbury to coach the Mountaineers in 1920. Stadsvold had a unique arrangement with WVU, leaving for his native Minnesota each summer after the end of the spring term and then returning in the fall. Stadsvold coached 14 seasons from 1920–33 (the second-longest coaching tenure in school history) and compiled a 149–133 record.

WVU SPORTS COMMUNICATIONS PHOTO.

New Martinsville's Clem Kiger appeared in 77 games for the Mountaineers from 1919-22, scoring 414 points, including a career-high 16 in a 49-44 upset victory over Yale on Dec. 31, 1919 at the Ark.

WVU SPORTS COMMUNICATIONS PHOTO.

Francis Stadsvold, an All-American forward at Minnesota in 1917, was serving in an "advisory role" for the Golden Gophers when Stansbury appointed him to lead the West Virginia basketball program for the 1920 season.

Stadsvold arrived two weeks before the start of preseason practice, and he quickly benefited from an influx of new students as World War I veterans began returning to school to complete their degrees. WVU's enrollment nearly doubled, reaching 2,800 in 1920 after dipping to as low as 1,600 during the war.

Great Start

As West Virginia's basketball coach, Stadsvold employed a Midwestern style of play that emphasized aggressive offense and zone defenses. His WVU tenure got off to a great start when his team produced a memorable 49–44 overtime win against Yale in Morgantown to open the season. Paul Cutright scored 17 points, and center Clem Kiger added 16 for the victorious Mountaineers. The game was later deemed one of the school's great victories of that period.

At the time, Yale was considered a powerhouse team in the Ivy League, winning conference titles in 1902, 1903, 1907, 1915 and 1917, and finishing second to Penn in the 1920 league standings with a 16–9 overall record. Two weeks after their victory against Yale, the Mountaineers produced another memorable triumph at Washington & Jefferson on Jan. 14, 1920. The 34–31 win was West Virginia's first against W&J, snapping the Presidents' five-game winning streak over the Mountaineers. Once again, Cutright was West Virginia's top scorer with 14 points.

WVU split decisions with Pitt, losing 38–27 in Pittsburgh and winning 28–26 in Morgantown. West Virginia also won against Carnegie Tech and Union College before wrapping up the season with another triumph over W&J. Stadsvold's 12–10 record was an encouraging start, indeed. When the spring term ended and his teaching duties in the School of Physical Education finished, Stadsvold returned to his native Crookston, Minn., to live during the offseason, a practice he continued through all 14 years he was WVU's coach.

In 1921, Stadsvold produced another winning record behind the outstanding play of "Moose" Martin, who broke the 200-point barrier for his second consecutive season. Martin scored 27 points, and Kiger added 14 in a 30-point blowout victory over Davis & Elkins in the season opener on Jan. 5, 1921—one of four straight wins the Mountaineers claimed to begin the year. Then West Virginia lost five in a row—all on the road—before wrapping up the season with five consecutive victories.

Stadsvold experienced his first losing campaign in 1922 at the same time the football team was reaching its apex under Coach Clarence Spears. In fact, Stadsvold excused forwards Martin, Fred Graham and Pierre Hill, and guards Doug Bowers and Russ Meredith from the start of winter practice to participate in the football team's first-ever postseason appearance in the East-West Bowl game against Gonzaga.

The '22 season began well, with Hill scoring 18 points in a 38–22 victory over Fairmont YMCA. Ten days later, West Virginia snapped Grove City's 34-game winning streak with a 38–29 victory at the Ark. Martin hit three long field goals, Bowers shut down Grove City's top scorer Joe Smith, Hill made 16 free throws, and Kiger consistently won jump balls.

West Virginia's 29–25 victory over Washington & Jefferson was achieved without a single point from Martin. Hill sank 13 free throws—a personal best—and made three field goals to help the Mountaineers overcome a 24–20 deficit with less than five minutes left to play.

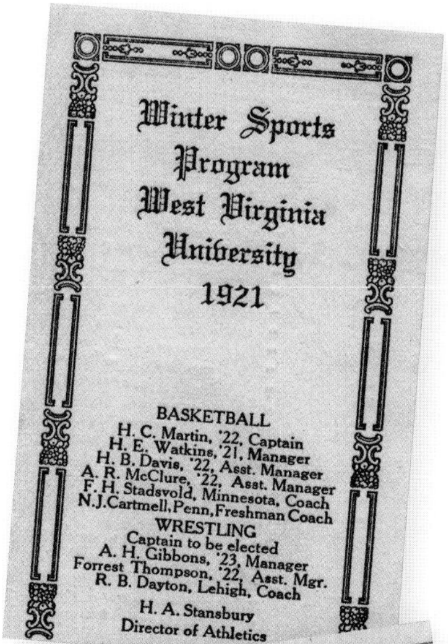
Winter Sports Program West Virginia University 1921

BASKETBALL
H. C. Martin, '22, Captain
H. E. Watkins, '21, Manager
H. B. Davis, '22, Asst. Manager
A. R. McClure, '22, Asst. Manager
F. H. Stadsvold, Minnesota, Coach
N.J.Cartmell,Penn,Freshman Coach

WRESTLING
Captain to be elected
A. H. Gibbons, '23, Manager
Forrest Thompson, '22, Asst. Mgr.
R. B. Dayton, Lehigh, Coach

H. A. Stansbury
Director of Athletics

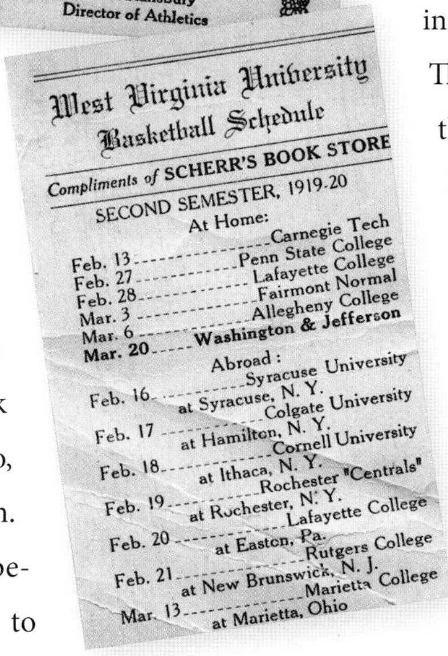
West Virginia University
Basketball Schedule
Compliments of SCHERR'S BOOK STORE
SECOND SEMESTER, 1919-20

At Home:
Feb. 13 — Carnegie Tech
Feb. 27 — Penn State College
Feb. 28 — Lafayette College
Mar. 3 — Fairmont Normal
Mar. 6 — Allegheny College
Mar. 20 — Washington & Jefferson

Abroad:
Feb. 16 — Syracuse University at Syracuse, N. Y.
Feb. 17 — Colgate University at Hamilton, N. Y.
Feb. 18 — Cornell University at Ithaca, N. Y.
Feb. 19 — Rochester "Centrals" at Rochester, N. Y.
Feb. 20 — Lafayette College at Easton, Pa.
Feb. 21 — Rutgers College at New Brunswick, N. J.
Mar. 13 — Marietta College at Marietta, Ohio

An early record of 6–2 was wiped out when West Virginia went on the road to face its toughest stretch of the season. WVU dropped consecutive contests to Georgetown, Penn, Army, CCNY and Princeton by wide margins. It was a trip filled with misadventure. Martin was stricken with a severe case of the flu and remained at the Raleigh Hotel in Washington, D.C. before he was eventually transported back to Morgantown. Meredith, too, was afflicted and had to return.

Hill was the next to become sick before the loss to Penn, and he was eventually sent home. Then center Roy "Legs" Hawley had to be quarantined. West Virginia was left with barely enough players to complete the trip. During the team's eight-point loss to CCNY, the Beavers graciously let Robert Hawkins continue to play after he fouled out. Against Princeton, Stadsvold had only five available players, so he ordered student manager J. B. Davis to put on a uniform when one of the starters was forced to leave the game because of injury. The weakened team only managed to defeat two more opponents in 1922.

Odd Ball

One of the great oddities in Mountaineer basketball history took place during the 1923 season. The date was Jan. 27, 1923, the setting was the Ark, and the opponent was Grove City. Eight days prior, Coach Bob Thorn's Wolverines had produced a 13-point victory over the Mountaineers in Grove City, Pa. In that low-scoring game, West Virginia had managed just five field goals. However, that paled in comparison to West Virginia's shooting woes the second time around. The Mountaineers failed to record a single field goal in a 29-point loss to the Wolverines. The team's only points came from the free throw line—six by Hill on 10 attempts, two by Joe Bartell, and one from Bowers. It remains the only time in school history that a West Virginia team didn't make a single field goal in a basketball game.

Fortunately, the Mountaineers were able to overcome the embarrassment of the Grove City loss by putting together a fine 12–7 record for the season. After falling by 16 points on the road to Navy and its great two-time All-American Ira McKee, West Virginia won seven of its eight remaining games, including victories over Carnegie Tech, Pitt and Washington & Jefferson. An eighth straight triumph was almost achieved in the

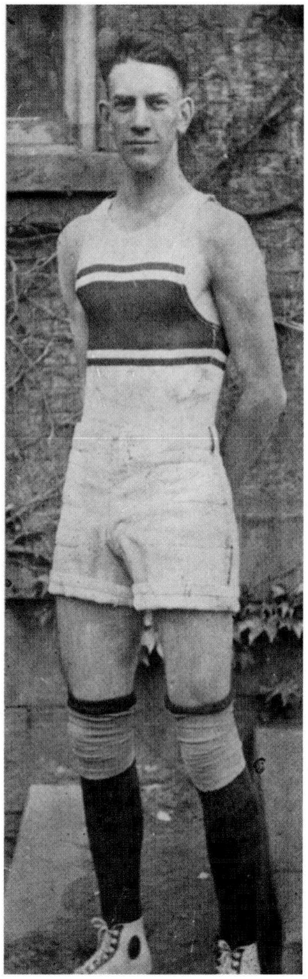

Above Fairmont's Pierre Hill led the team in scoring in 1922 and 1923 and was also a member of West Virginia's Tri-State championship team in 1924. Hill, a forward, scored 617 points and averaged 8.8 points per game for his career.

WEST VIRGINIA AND REGIONAL HISTORY COLLECTION.

Right Homer "Moose" Martin scored 20 or more points in a game nine times during his career and averaged 13.2 points in 56 career games for the Mountaineers from 1919–22. Martin was also a fullback on West Virginia's undefeated football team in 1921 and a catcher on the WVU baseball team, later playing professionally in the Cleveland Indians organization.

WVU SPORTS COMMUNICATIONS PHOTO.

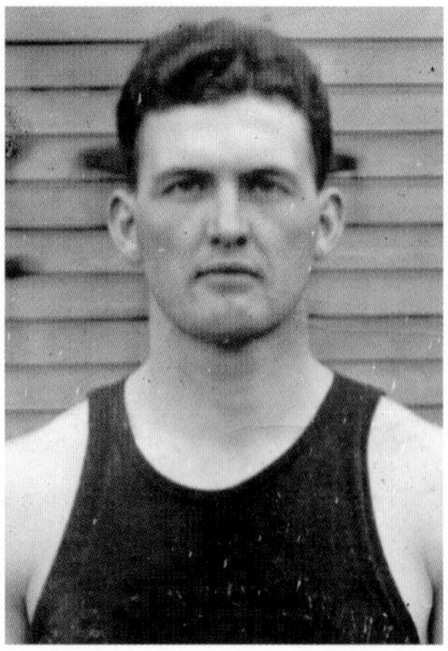

Buckhannon's Nate Rohrbough was a key member of the 1924 team that won 14 of 16 games and captured the Tri-State championship. Rohrbough later became a successful basketball coach at Glenville State, compiling a 304–58 record in 17 seasons for the Pioneers that included two trips to the NAIA tournament.

WVU SPORTS COMMUNICATIONS PHOTO.

season finale against W&J in Morgantown, but the Presidents triumphed 23–22.

All of the key contributors on the 1923 team—Hill, Hawley, Bowers, Fred Funk, Aaron Oliker and Nate Rohrbough—returned for the 1924 season. It was by far the strongest collection of players to suit up for West Virginia on the hardwood to that point. Of the 16 games the Mountaineers played in 1924, the starting five played in 10 of them without ever leaving the floor. For the first time in school history the Mountaineers swept Pitt, claiming an exciting 24–23 overtime decision against Doc Carlson's Panthers in Pittsburgh, and then beating Pitt by a more comfortable 14-point margin in Morgantown. West Virginia's only losses were away games against Kentucky, where they lost by three, 24–21, and W&J, where they fell by two, 23–21. Those five points were all that separated WVU from an undefeated season, and with wins over Grove City and Washington & Jefferson, West Virginia claimed the Intercollegiate Tri-State League title with a 14–2 overall record.

Scoring for West Virginia was equally distributed among five different players that season, the result of a new NCAA rule requiring players to shoot their own free throws instead of having a designated team shooter. Stadsvold's 1924 squad played outstanding defense and possessed tremendous guard play in Bowers and Rohrbough. To recognize the team's outstanding performance during the 1924 campaign, miniature gold basketballs were awarded to the players at the end of the season.

With Hill and Bowers lost to graduation, West Virginia's record slipped to 6–11 in 1925. Nonetheless, Stadsvold served as one of 20 consultants on a book of strategy called *Basketball Hints*. In one chapter, Stadsvold offered his expertise on forward play, a clear sign that

Coach Francis Stadsvold's 1924 team was the strongest of that era, winning 14 of 16 games and claiming the Tri-State championship with victories over Allegheny, Pitt, Grove City and Washington & Jefferson.

WEST VIRGINIA AND REGIONAL HISTORY COLLECTION.

others around the country recognized him as an authority on the sport.

Difficult Times

By the mid-1920s interest in basketball had reached such a high point that the WVU student body had to be divided into two groups to go to the games, with the groups alternating games because the Ark could not seat all of them.

But difficult times were ahead. The Mountaineers' basketball record dropped to 10–11 in 1926, and across campus, the football team's record was also leveling off following the departure of Spears.

The Great Depression, which hit the nation hard in the 1930s, had actually reached the Mountain State several years earlier. The booming coal business during World War I made many West Virginia coal operators millionaires. However, a steep decline in coal prices in the early 1920s bankrupted several companies, which led to a dramatic decline in donations to the athletic department's scholarship fund. Basketball was indirectly affected by the decline because it relied on many football players to make up its roster.

"LEGS" HAWLEY, Captain

Around the same time the West Virginia economy was slumping, Stansbury and university president Frank Butler Trotter had to fight off a movement led by State Superintendent of Schools, George M. Ford, to make West Virginia University a member of the West Virginia Conference. Ford opposed the perceived high salaries being paid to Stansbury and the coaches, as well as the overall exorbitance displayed by WVU to sustain a competitive athletic program. Ford reasoned that moving West Virginia University into a leadership position within the state board of education system was a way of removing the autonomy Stansbury had created for the athletic department, according to WVU historians William Doherty and Festus Summers.

Stansbury argued that the university would lose prestige and the strong position it had attained in eastern athletic and academic circles if the school aligned itself educationally and athletically with prep schools, normal schools and junior colleges.

Predictably, WVU students and alumni reacted negatively to the plan, calling upon the school to no longer schedule any athletic events with West Virginia Conference schools. Nevertheless, West Virginia spent seven months in the West Virginia Conference before the State Council of Administration resolved the issue by ruling that WVU's membership was impractical.

Little Sleepy Leads the Mountaineers

Things improved for Stadsvold in 1927 when the Mountaineers managed a 10–8 record, with memorable victories on the road against Kentucky and Pitt. Football star Rudolph "Swede" Hagberg led the team in scoring with 141 points, while Wease Ashworth contributed 130 points.

The Ark was razed following the 1927 season to make room for the Field House,

Morgantown's Robert Hawkins was a four-year letterman for the Mountaineers, appearing in 68 career games at guard during the 1918, 1920, 1921 and 1922 seasons.

WVU SPORTS COMMUNICATIONS PHOTO.

Inset Roy "Legs" Hawley, who once scored 66 points in a high school basketball game, was a four-year letterman and a three-year starter for the Mountaineers from 1922–25. Hawley later earned distinction as the school's athletic director, a post he held from 1938 until his death in 1954. Hawley was inducted into the National Association of Collegiate Directors of Athletics Hall of Fame in 1974.

WEST VIRGINIA AND REGIONAL HISTORY COLLECTION.

which meant home basketball games in 1928 had to be played at Morgantown High. Considering the Ark's dismal accommodations, it was an inconvenience the team gladly endured.

Three years earlier in 1925, Stansbury had successfully led a fund-raising drive to construct the 33,000-seat Mountaineer Field. The two new facilities were remarkable achievements, considering the hardships many West Virginians had endured during that period. Not only did the Field House give the team a more suitable place to play, it was also built with the hope that the team playing in it could attract better basketball players. In some years, Stadsvold barely had enough players available to scrimmage until football season ended.

The Field House was not the only thing new in the basketball program. At about this time the team also took to wearing much flashier uniforms. The trunks were made of gold silk with blue piping, and the jerseys were a solid blue with "West Virginia" emblazoned on the front in bright gold letters. One reporter described the new uniforms as "looking like part of the wardrobe of chorus girls."

The team's flamboyant new duds didn't seem to hinder the players. In 1928, Truehart Taylor led the Mountaineers with a 13-points-per-game average, but the one player everyone was talking about was forward Marshall "Little Sleepy" Glenn. Marshall's older brother, Albert "Big Sleepy" Glenn, preceded him by two years as a member of the Mountaineer football and basketball teams. It was Big Sleepy who scored both touchdowns in West Virginia's memorable 14–0 victory over Penn State to dedicate the new football stadium in 1925.

According to retired Morgantown *Dominion Post* sports editor Mickey Furfari, the nicknames "Big Sleepy" and "Little Sleepy" emanated from their childhood. When their father was killed in a train accident, Albert was forced to work nights as a "call boy" for the railroad company to help supplement the family income. During school, Albert often dozed off in class and his classmates soon took to calling him Sleepy. When Marshall

Below An early look inside the WVU Field House, constructed in 1928 along Beechurst Avenue. Athletic director Harry Stansbury persuaded the state legislature to appropriate funds for the facility in two equal installments. In addition to providing a venue for basketball, wrestling, boxing and indoor track, it also housed the WVU School of Physical Education.

WEST VIRGINIA AND REGIONAL HISTORY COLLECTION.

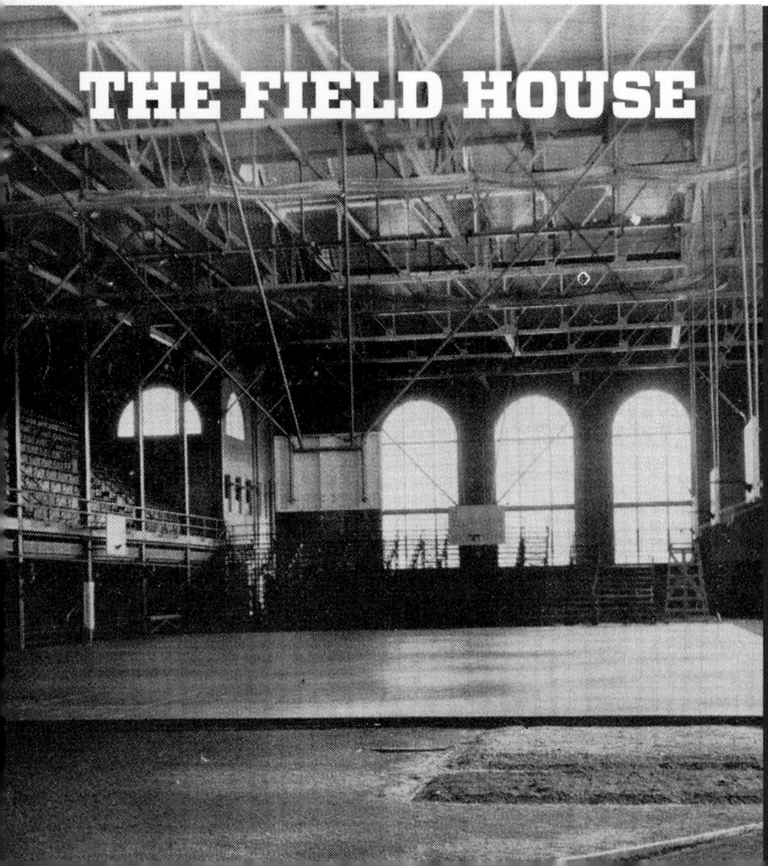

THE FIELD HOUSE

In 1927, the West Virginia Legislature appropriated $85,000 to begin construction of the new facility to be located on Beechurst Avenue. The initial funds were not available until July 1, 1928, so Athletic Director Harry Stansbury arranged a bank loan to expedite construction.

The following year, legislators appropriated another $170,000 available in two installments on July 1, 1929, and July 1, 1930. Once again, Stansbury borrowed money to finish the arena in time for the 1929 season. The outer shell was completed first, and then the inside was finished when the remainder of the funding became available. In the meantime, athletic events were held at Morgantown High.

"Athletic funds were temporarily drawn upon to the extent of $60,000 to equip the Field House, repayment of this amount came along, Albert then became known as "Big Sleepy" while Marshall was called "Little Sleepy." The two were legendary sports figures in Elkins, but in the eyes of most, Little Sleepy was the better athlete of the two. Some even viewed Little Sleepy as the equal to Pitt star forward Charley Hyatt, a three-time All-American and a member of the Panther national championship teams in 1928 and 1930.

"Little Sleepy was such a great competitor," longtime Morgantown sportswriter Tony Constantine recalled in 2001. "If Glenn and [legendary heavyweight boxing champion] Joe Louis were locked in a room and had to fight to get out, I'm not sure Glenn wouldn't be the one to come out standing."

Constantine remembered a story Carnegie Tech coach Max Hannum used to tell about Glenn. Hannum was in the stands scouting a West Virginia game when the referee failed to show up. Hannum had refereed some games in the past and was sought out to be a fill-in. In those days, a center jump was required after each basket, and knowing how aggressively Glenn went after the center tip, Hannum reminded himself to get out of the way once he tossed the ball in the air. Unfortunately, during one of his tosses, he didn't get out of the way quickly enough, and Glenn pounced on the ball like a leopard, crashing down on Hannum's ankle and fracturing it. Another official had to be recruited from the stands to finish the game.

The more laid-back Hyatt, from nearby Uniontown, Pa., had a completely different on-court demeanor than Glenn. Hyatt also played on much better teams, yet the two were equals on several occasions, especially during the 1929 and 1930 seasons. In 1929, Glenn scored 17 points to lead West Virginia to a 40–35 upset victory over the Panthers at the Pitt Pavilion. Two months later in Morgantown, Hyatt gained revenge by holding Glenn to only 4 points in a 41–19 Pan-

Above Right Marshall "Little Sleepy" Glenn is considered the greatest pre-World War II basketball player in school history. Glenn led the team in scoring all three years he played for West Virginia (averaging 11 points per game in 62 career games) and later served the dual role as football and basketball coach for the Mountaineers in the late 1930s.

WVU SPORTS COMMUNICATIONS PHOTO.

being delayed until about 1934," Stansbury later explained to Mickey Furfari, sports editor of the *Morgantown Dominion-News* at the time. "This tremendously crimped us during the intervening years when the banks for miles around were closed." Despite this hardship, all of the notes, bonds and athletic debts were eventually paid without a loss to any individual.

The dedicatory game for the brand new $307,000 facility was played Jan. 3, 1929 with West Virginia defeating Salem, 26–23 before a crowd of 2,500, most seemingly more interested in their new surroundings instead of the game itself. The Field House served as the home for Mountaineer basketball for 41 years from 1929–1970.

The Field House also provided offices for the varsity sports' coaches in addition to serving as a more suitable venue for the School of Physical Education. Commencement exercises, the annual Mother's Day sing, student activities, musical events and large community gatherings were also held in the facility.

Two expansions increased the Field House's capacity from 4,000 when it opened, to nearly 7,000 by the time it was retired in 1970. Today, the Field House is still in use and is known, fittingly,

Stansbury Man Behind Building WVU Stadium and Field House

as Stansbury Hall. As of 2010 the building is home to WVU's Philosophy Department, the Army and Air Force ROTC, the Office of International Programs, the Center for Civic Engagement, and the West Virginia University Press.

ther victory. Hyatt later admitted that Pitt's five-point home loss to West Virginia probably cost the Panthers a chance at a third national title.

The next time the two met in 1930, Hyatt, despite scoring just 3 points, once again got the better of Little Sleepy in a 21–19 Panther victory in Pittsburgh. After Pitt got the lead, Carlson employed his "stall game" tactic, which drew the ire of Stadsvold afterward.

"I will never teach the system of stalling in basketball when our team is in front, for I do not value the victory that highly," said a disgusted Stadsvold. "I intend to give the fans what they want—action."

That's exactly what the fans got when the rematch was played in Morgantown on March 8, 1930 to conclude the season. Glenn bounced back with one of the school's greatest individual performances of that period. He outscored Hyatt 17–9 to lead West Virginia to a memorable 33–25 victory at the Field House in front of a record estimated crowd of 4,500. At the end of the game, Glenn received a standing ovation from appreciative Mountaineer fans witnessing his final home performance.

The first game at the Field House took place on Jan. 3, 1929, a 26–23 Mountaineer victory over Salem College. Forty-one years later, Tigers coach T. Edward Davis was invited to attend a special halftime ceremony during the final game ever played at the Field House on March 3, 1970.
WVU SPORTS COMMUNICATIONS PHOTO.

The Panthers finished the year with a 23–2 record against a strong schedule that included four Big Ten schools, Notre Dame, Nebraska and several other quality teams. Pitt's only other loss that season came against Syracuse.

Forty-one years later when Pitt and West Virginia played the final game at the Field House on March 3, 1970, old-time rivals Glenn and Hyatt were asked to be honored guests at halftime to memorialize the retiring facility.

A gracious Hyatt offered high praise for his West Virginia counterpart. "Sleepy was a better basketball player than I was," Hyatt told Constantine. "I really mean that. I played with a better team. Meaning no disrespect to his teammates, but Sleepy didn't have as good of support as I did." Carlson had this to say about Glenn in 1958: "He could make any team, pro or otherwise, even now."

Back to Minnesota

West Virginia's victory over Pitt to conclude the 1930 season was also the high point of Francis Stadsvold's coaching career. The next three seasons were losing ones, and Stadsvold finally chose to retire in 1933 when he was elected prosecuting attorney in his native Minnesota, where he remained until his death in 1965. Making Stadsvold's decision to depart much easier was the university's decision to reduce salaries by 25 percent to meet the school's worsening budgetary situation.

Stadsvold won 149 career games at West Virginia, including a forfeit victory over Georgetown in 1933 when the team bus broke down as it attempted to travel over the West Virginia mountains to the game. Only Gale Catlett coached longer at WVU than Stadsvold.

Stadsvold's 14-year tenure included many outstanding players: Homer Martin, Bill Mor-

rison, Clem Kiger, Doug Bowers, Pierre Hill, Wease Ashworth, Truehart Taylor, Jim Black, John Doyle, Nate Rohrbough, Wilbur Sortet and Marshall Glenn, all of whom rank among the best players of that period.

Rohrbough became one of the top basketball coaches in the West Virginia Conference at Glenville State, while Bowers served on West Virginia University's Board of Governors, and Legs Hawley eventually became athletic director at WVU.

Stadsvold was later asked to pick an all-time team during his time at West Virginia. The five players he chose were Pierre Hill, Doug Bowers, Nate Rohrbough, Little Sleepy Glenn and Joe Stydahar.

At the time of Stadsvold's resignation, Glenn was coaching in West Virginia, at Martinsburg High School. It seemed only natural that Little Sleepy would be the one to replace his old coach in 1934.

Above Rowlesburg's Glen Ayersman appeared in seven games for the Mountaineers in 1933, scoring a career-high 12 points in a 35–29 victory over Salem College on Jan. 4, 1933.

WVU SPORTS COMMUNICATIONS PHOTO.

Top The 1930 Mountaineers finished the season with four straight victories, including a pair of wins over rival Washington & Jefferson and a memorable 33–25 victory over Pitt at the Field House before a capacity crowd estimated at 4,500.

WVU SPORTS COMMUNICATIONS PHOTO.

Left The 1933 team was the last basketball team Francis Stadsvold coached at West Virginia. Stadsvold, who returned to his native Minnesota every summer during his 14-year coaching career at WVU, returned for good after his team's disappointing 10–14 record that included a pair of four-game losing streaks. Pictured in the front row, second from the right, is Chicago Bears great and NFL hall of famer Joe Stydahar.

WVU SPORTS COMMUNICATIONS PHOTO.

LOTHES
-GUARD-

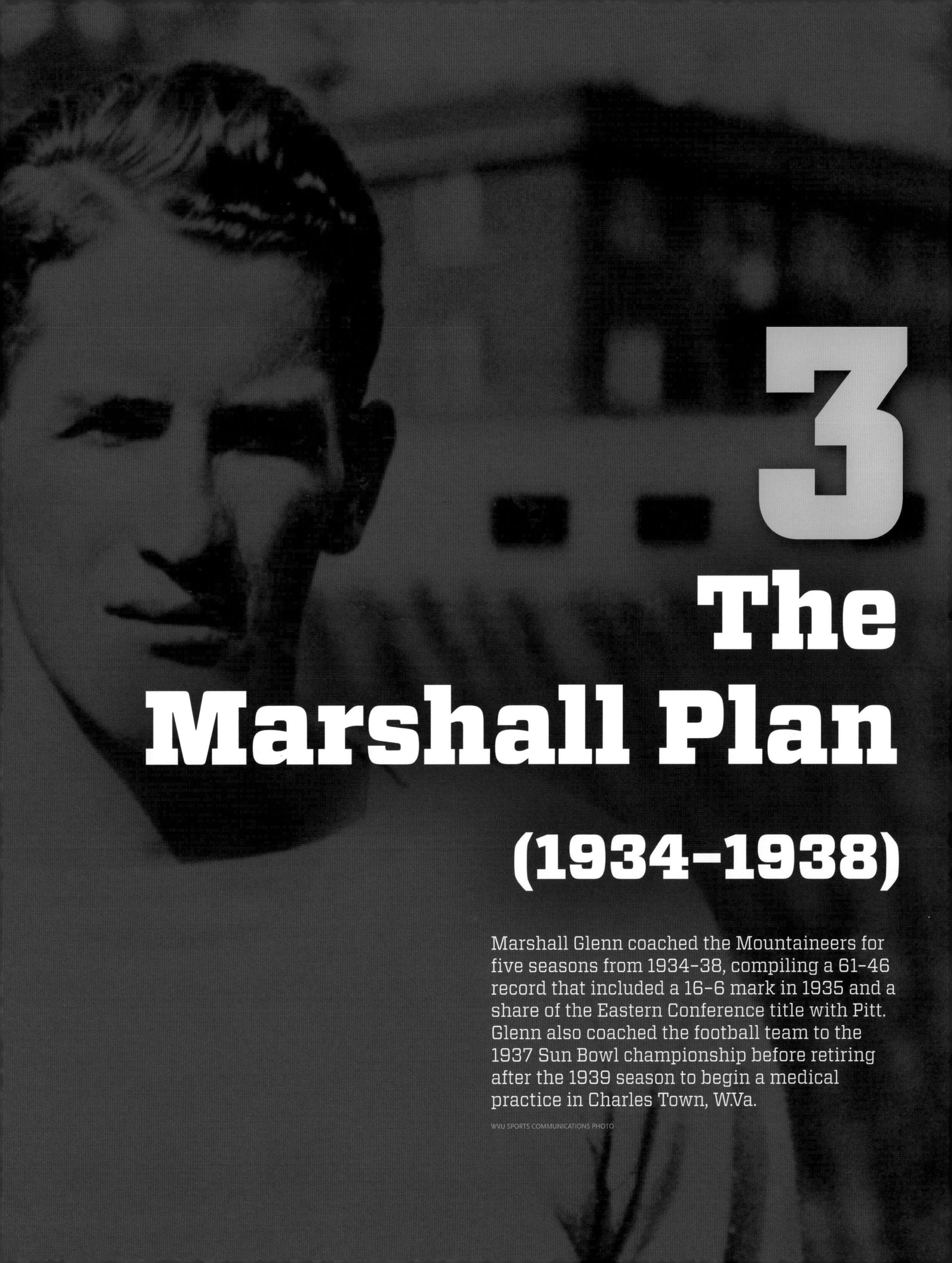

3

The Marshall Plan

(1934–1938)

Marshall Glenn coached the Mountaineers for five seasons from 1934–38, compiling a 61–46 record that included a 16–6 mark in 1935 and a share of the Eastern Conference title with Pitt. Glenn also coached the football team to the 1937 Sun Bowl championship before retiring after the 1939 season to begin a medical practice in Charles Town, W.Va.

WVU SPORTS COMMUNICATIONS PHOTO

Sleepy Glenn's teams played a much faster game featuring great ballhandling, crisp passing and clever play. Glenn was the first coach to introduce preseason practices in October and November and he encouraged his players to focus their attention on basketball year-round to the exclusion of other sports.

WVU SPORTS COMMUNICATIONS PHOTO.

Bellaire, Ohio's Tod Goodwin was better known for his exploits on the gridiron, starring for West Virginia and then playing two years for the New York Giants, but he also appeared in 25 games for the Mountaineer basketball team in 1933–34. Goodwin later enjoyed a decorated military career, reaching the rank of brigadier general in the U.S. Army Reserves.

WVU SPORTS COMMUNICATIONS PHOTO.

Marshall "Little Sleepy" Glenn was the hands-down choice to assume leadership of the West Virginia University basketball program when Francis Stadsvold informed Harry Stansbury in 1933 that he was not returning for a 15th season.

Glenn had been one of the most popular players at WVU as a four-sport star in basketball, baseball, football and track. In football, he was largely responsible for West Virginia's memorable 9–6 upset victory over Pitt, and he was considered one of the school's finest blocking backs. In track, Glenn held the school high jump record. He was also a champion wrestler in the interfraternity league; he won a boxing title at an ROTC camp, played first base on the alumni teams and was proficient in tennis and golf.

Glenn's high school coach, Frank Wimer, recalled in 1962 a story that illustrated what a great all-around athlete Glenn was. "Somebody asked Little Sleepy to come out and help the track team [against Pitt]," Wimer said. "So he went out without practicing and won the high jump, the broad jump, high hurdles, shot put and was second in the discus, and WVU was able to beat Pitt."

Yet, it was on the hardwood where Glenn earned his greatest success. Following graduation in 1931, Glenn served one season as West Virginia's freshman basketball coach before accepting the football and basketball coaching jobs at Martinsburg High. His two years at Martinsburg saw his football teams register a 13–5 record while his basketball teams won 47 of their 54 games.

Upon accepting the WVU basketball coaching position at age 25, Glenn immediately introduced an appealing style of play that incorporated snappy passing and screening to get good shots at the basket. He also kept the zone defense that Stadsvold had used so successfully. When he took the position, Glenn informed Stansbury that he also planned to continue pursuing a medical degree. After each season, Glenn traveled to Chicago where he spent the spring and summer terms at Rush College.

Full Cupboard

Stadsvold's final three years at WVU may have been losing ones, but he didn't leave the cupboard bare. Awaiting Glenn when he arrived in Morgantown was 6-foot-5 center Joe Stydahar, a Greasy Neale discovery in football. As a basketball player, Stydahar was named an Eastern Intercollegiate Conference all-star three times and was considered the school's best center of the pre-modern era. Stydahar's greatest fame came later as a professional football player on George Halas's Chicago Bears in the early 1940s. "Jumbo Joe" was the only guy longtime NFL broadcaster Pat Summerall knew who could drink whiskey, smoke a cigar, and chew tobacco all at the same time. Stydahar was inducted into the Pro Football Hall of Fame in 1967.

Other gridders such as Tod Goodwin, Louis Fidler, William Klug and Patsy Slate joined Albert Colebank and Jess Weiner to form the nucleus of West Virginia's outstanding 14–5 team in 1934.

Two of WVU's five losses that season came to Eastern Conference rival Pitt and its All-American forward Claire Cribbs. The Mountaineers finished second in the conference race to the Panthers in 1934 and again in 1935. The 1935 WVU squad was one of the strongest of that era, with Stydahar and Colebank teaming up with talented sophomores Jack Gocke and John "Squint" Phares.

Gocke, from Victory High in Clarksburg, and Phares, from Elkins High, cracked the starting lineup by the second game of the season. The two combined to score 18 points in leading West Virginia to a 39–29 victory over the Maryland Terrapins. It was one of six straight victories for the Mountaineers to start the season. West Virginia also had two four-game winning streaks against a much stronger schedule. Only two West Virginia Conference schools—West Virginia Wesleyan and Salem—appeared on the Mountaineers' 1935 basketball slate. West Virginia lost twice to a strong Duquesne team that finished 18–1 and lost on the road at Navy.

West Virginia and Pitt split regular-season games to finish the '35 season tied for first place in the Eastern Conference standings with 6–2 records. West Virginia's 17-point victory over the Panthers in Morgantown forced a playoff game five days later that Pitt won, 35–22.

Patrick M. Premo, a professor of accounting at St. Bonaventure, analyzed every basketball season from 1892–1949 (prior to the first Associated Press poll) and determined that Glenn's 1935 WVU squad was one of the 25 best in the country that season.

The Mountaineers' winning record continued in 1936 when the team produced a strong 16–8 record that included outstanding triumphs over 18–6 Temple, 14–6 Maryland, 14–3 Duquesne and 19–10 Pitt. The Pitt game was decided with 10 seconds remaining when Phares sank a free throw to give the Mountaineers an exciting 43–42 victory.

Gocke once again led the Mountaineers in scoring with 267 points and three others—Colebank, Phares and junior Herbert "Babe" Barna—each scored more than 177 points for the season.

Barna, a fullback on the football team and a first baseman on the baseball team, replaced Stydahar at center in 1936. As Stydahar was the first choice of the Chicago Bears in the professional football draft, Barna, too, played professional sports from 1937–43 as a first baseman for the Philadelphia Athletics, New York Giants and Boston Red Sox.

Above Clarksburg's Jack Gocke was a three-sport star at Victory High School whose 770 career points scored was a school record until All-American Leland Byrd eclipsed the mark in 1947. Gocke, a two-time Eastern Conference All-Star, scored a career-high 23 points in West Virginia's 54–31 victory over Penn State on Feb. 22, 1936.

WEST VIRGINIA AND REGIONAL HISTORY COLLECTION.

Above right John "Squint" Phares was a ballhandling whiz for the Mountaineers from 1935–37, helping the Mountaineers to outstanding records of 16–6 in 1935 and 16–8 in 1936. Phares was named to the Eastern Conference All-Star team in 1937.

WEST VIRGINIA AND REGIONAL HISTORY COLLECTION.

Barna continued playing baseball into the early 1950s in the Southern Association, where he once led the league with a .358 batting average at Nashville.

Double Duty

Not yet 30, Glenn had already compiled an impressive 46–19 record in his first three varsity seasons. Sleepy's dual role as the basketball coach and freshman football coach convinced Stansbury that he was also capable of coaching the varsity football team when Charles Tallman resigned to become superintendent of the West Virginia State Police in the summer of 1937. Glenn received unanimous approval from the Board of Governors, becoming the first coach in 25 years to simultaneously lead the WVU football and basketball programs. (He was also the last to coach both.) His double duty paid immediate dividends in football (as well keeping Stansbury's tight athletic budget in line) with Glenn leading the Mountaineers to a Sun Bowl victory over Texas Tech. However, the basketball team's performance began slipping as a result of Glenn having less time to devote to the sport.

West Virginia's basketball record dipped to 9–14 in 1937 even though Gocke and Phares had returned to the Mountaineers. The two were voted to the Eastern Conference all-star team, with Gocke claiming the league scoring title with 273 points. He established the varsity scoring record with 774 points, topping Glenn's school mark by nearly 100 points. Twice, West Virginia played overtime games against Washington & Jefferson, winning 49–47 in double overtime in Washington, and then four days later losing 42–41 in Morgantown. West Virginia also had a fine 10-point victory at the Field House over a strong Temple team that finished the year 17–6. Contributing to the poor record was the loss of Barna for most of the year because of an ankle injury suffered during football season in a game at George Washington. Barna's absence forced 6-foot-3 Gocke to play center.

The losses continued in 1938. West Virginia won just six of 19 games, and during a two-month stretch from Jan. 15 to Mar. 5, the Mountaineers

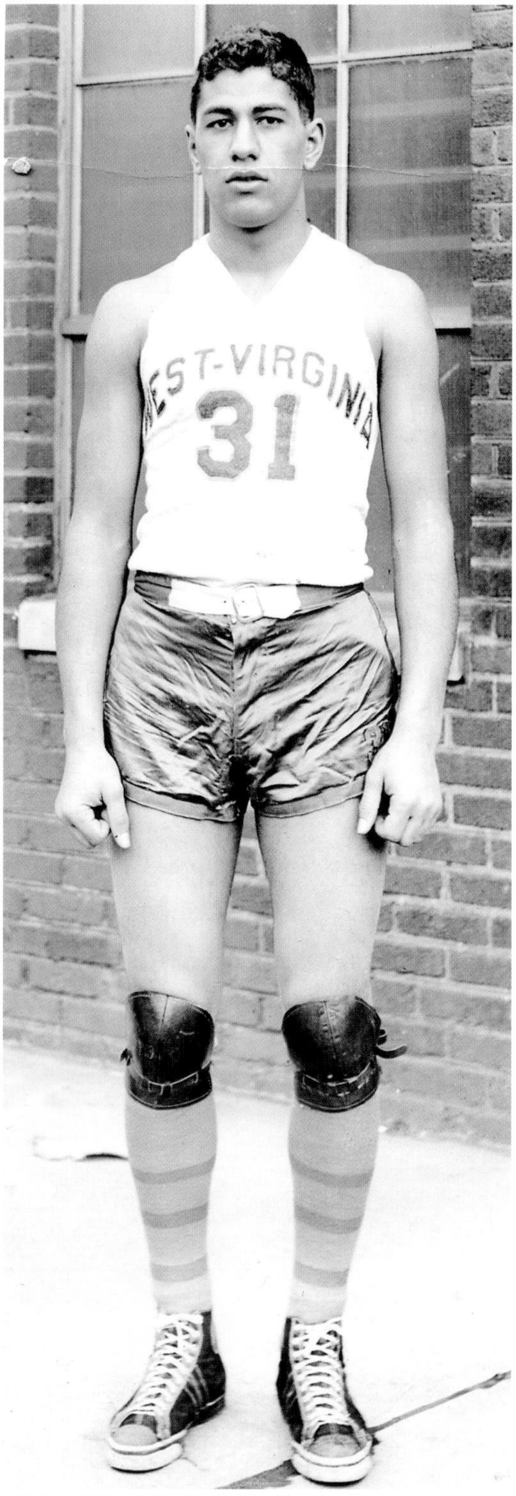

Right Anmoore's Babe Barna replaced Joe Stydahar as West Virginia's starting center for the 1935, 1936 and 1937 basketball seasons. Barna also captained the Mountaineer football team in 1936 and was a star first baseman for the baseball team before later playing parts of five seasons with the Philadelphia Athletics, New York Giants and the Boston Red Sox from 1937–43.

WVU SPORTS COMMUNICATIONS PHOTO.

were victorious just once in 12 tries. Two of those losses, though, came to National Invitation Tournament (NIT) champion Temple and its All-American center Mike Bloom.

WVU center Homer Brooks was the team's top scorer in 1938 with 188 points, while Harry Lothes chipped in with 155 and Steve "Gobby" Chepko added 129. Despite the Mountaineers finishing last in the league standings, Lothes was named to the Eastern Conference all-star team.

Glenn relinquished his basketball coaching duties after the 1938 season, and a year later he gave up coaching altogether after the football team's disappointing 2–6–1 record. By then it was obvious to WVU supporters that Glenn was more interested in his medical pursuits. He tendered his resignation to West Virginia University President Charles E. Lawall on Dec. 3, 1939 to open a practice in Charles Town. Glenn continued to practice medicine there until his death from injuries sustained in an automobile accident on Oct. 12, 1983.

"Glenn was like most of the other coaches at WVU," wrote Shorty Hardman in 1962. "He won when he had talent and lost when he didn't."

More Changes

A year prior to Glenn's resignation, longtime athletic director Harry Stansbury opted to end his 21-year affiliation with West Virginia University to become secretary of the state chamber of commerce.

Stansbury had achieved great things at West Virginia University, most notably the

One of the earliest known action photos of West Virginia University basketball, reproduced from the 1938 Monticola. Action photography was difficult to find during this period because of poor lighting in most gyms.

WEST VIRGINIA AND REGIONAL HISTORY COLLECTION.

Weirton's Patsy Slate was a starting forward on the 1933 team, finishing third in scoring with an average of 6 points per game.

WVU SPORTS COMMUNICATIONS PHOTO.

construction of two first-class playing venues for football and basketball. But he grew tired of presiding over a cash-strapped athletic department struggling to pay its bills. The lack of money was certainly a problem—the yearly football series with Pitt was later discontinued for three years from 1940–42 because of a dispute over money Pitt believed it was owed for a prior game played in Morgantown.

Poor attendance and a weak economy led to a football stadium debt of almost $500,000 that was eventually paid off by state taxpayers in the late 1930s. These and other issues confronted popular Roy "Legs" Hawley when he was named Stansbury's successor on July 24, 1938.

Legs had played basketball and baseball at WVU, and probably would have played football as well if Beaver High School in his native Bluefield had fielded a grid team. Hawley was a center on the WVU basketball team and was the catcher on the baseball team where he batted ninth in the lineup. Hawley struggled so mightily at the plate that it was said that he once tried to lay down a drag bunt on a one-armed pitcher to improve his meager hitting average. Another time against West Virginia Wesleyan, Hawley, a .119 hitter, used some tall grass in right field to leg out his only career home run. Hawley slapped a hit over the first baseman's head and eventually made his way all the way around the bases when the players couldn't find the ball.

"You know," Legs joked, "I had never really been beyond second, and I really didn't know what to do."

It was in basketball where Hawley forged his athletic reputation, once scoring a phenomenal 66 points in a single game against Williamson High School in 1918. After a year of seasoning, Legs became one of the key members of Francis Stadsvold's outstanding teams of the mid-1920s. During his WVU student days, Harry Stansbury took Hawley under his wing and allowed him to sell programs and concessions at football games to make a few extra bucks.

Upon graduating from WVU in 1926, Hawley got a job as the director of athletics at Marshall College, a post he held until returning to Morgantown in 1935 to become secretary of the Alumni Association. The same day Hawley was named athletic director at WVU, there was a small blurb in the paper mentioning that Davis High coach Richard "Dyke" Raese had also been approved by the Board of Governors to coach the university's basketball team.

Not everyone was happy with the hiring of Raese, especially those backing Nate Rohrbough, Albert Colebank, Jack Gocke or Squint Phares—all strong contenders for the job. Some folks in

Clarksburg thought Phares was the best candidate of the bunch, but he was still interested in playing and became a player-coach for a professional team in Clarksburg.

Raese was one of the most successful high school coaches in West Virginia, and he was known for doing more with less, compiling a 110–42 record over six years. Oftentimes Raese would take his Davis teams to play much larger schools in Maryland and win consistently. Raese had just agreed to take the Spencer High job when he found out that Glenn was dropping his basketball duties to concentrate solely on football. Raese and Glenn had been fraternity brothers at West Virginia and had remained good friends.

Glenn told Raese the West Virginia job was his if he wanted it, and Raese thought the opportunity to coach at his alma mater, despite paying less than the Spencer job, was too good to pass up. So he took the WVU basketball job for only $1,400 per year (equivalent to about $21,000 in 2008).

Raese's arrival at WVU came just when college basketball was changing dramatically. The size of the ball had been reduced twice during the 1930s, making it easier for players to dribble and shoot. In 1932, a 10-second line was added at half court to reduce stalling. Players could reenter games by 1934, and a three-second time limit was imposed on players attempting to shoot free throws.

However, the single biggest alteration to the game happened in 1938 when the center jump after each basket was abolished. For years, schools on the West Coast were playing without a center jump to larger and more enthusiastic crowds. The elimination of the center jump nationwide introduced many new fans to a game that was becoming faster-paced and more exciting.

Born out of this more interesting style of play was the NIT in New York City in 1938. The National Collegiate Athletic Association (NCAA) tournament was created a year later by the college coaching association. These numerous developments led many basketball historians to consider 1938 the demarcation point between the pre-modern and modern eras of college basketball.

Dyke Raese was certainly the right man at the right time for Mountaineer basketball.

EASTERN INTERCOLLEGIATE CONFERENCE

Pitt, West Virginia, Temple, Carnegie Tech and Georgetown formed the Eastern Intercollegiate Conference in 1933 for basketball, boxing and wrestling. Bucknell joined the association for one year in 1934, and Penn State participated from 1936–39.

The conference proved profitable for WVU's athletic department, with the triple-header card of wrestling, basketball and boxing drawing large crowds to the Field House.

Pitt captured the basketball conference title in 1933, 1934, 1935 and 1937. Carnegie Tech shared the title with Pitt in 1936 and with Georgetown in 1939, while Temple won the league outright in 1938. West Virginia had a pair of second-place finishes in 1934 and 1935, tying Pitt's 6–2 record during the regular season in 1935 before losing to the Panthers in a playoff.

A lack of cooperation and interest caused the Eastern Conference to disband just prior to World War II.

WVU Eastern Conference All-Stars

1933, Joe Stydahar (first team); Wilbur Sortet (second team)
1934, Joe Stydahar (first team)
1935, Joe Stydahar (first team); Jack Gocke (second team)
1937, Jack Gocke (first team); Squint Phares (first team)
1938, Harry Lothes (first team)
1939, Harry Lothes (first team); Homer Brooks (second team)

The 1942 team was puny, physically and in numbers, by modern standards. But this gutty group of guys was the only Mountaineer basketball team ever to win it all.

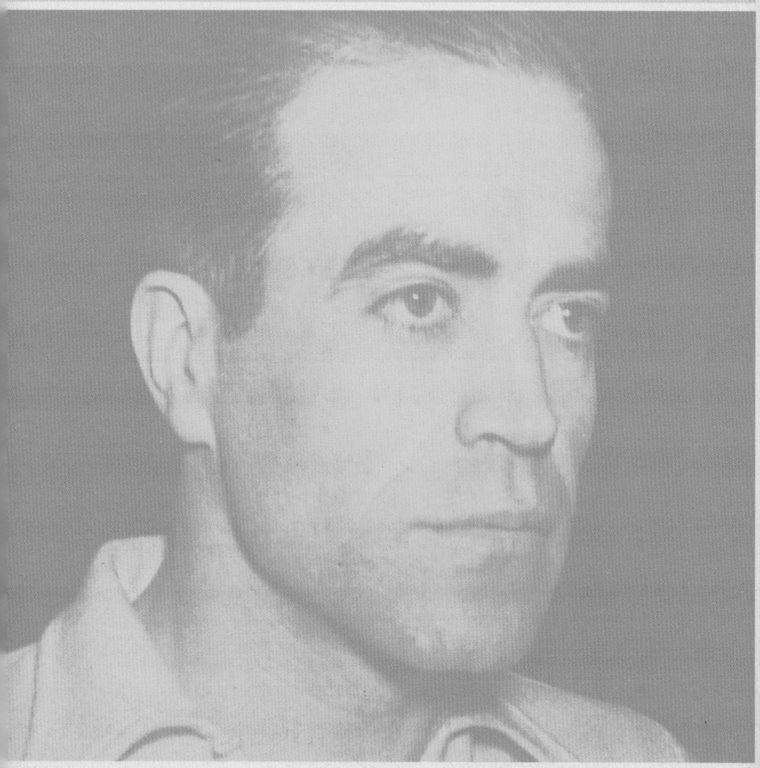

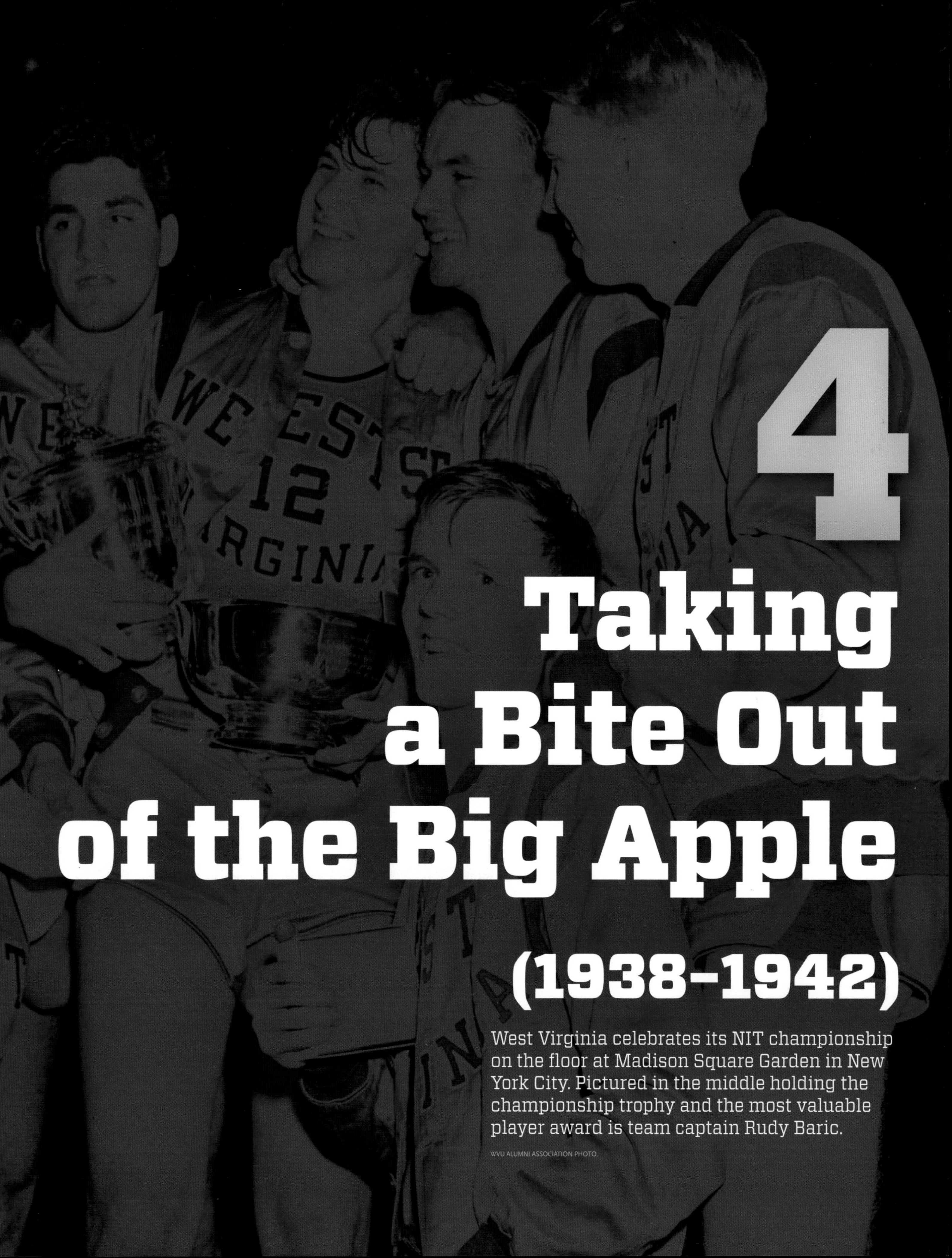

4

Taking a Bite Out of the Big Apple (1938–1942)

West Virginia celebrates its NIT championship on the floor at Madison Square Garden in New York City. Pictured in the middle holding the championship trophy and the most valuable player award is team captain Rudy Baric.

WVU ALUMNI ASSOCIATION PHOTO.

Right Richard "Dyke" Raese was the right man at the right time for WVU, leading the Mountaineers to a 55–29 record and the 1942 NIT championship. One week after West Virginia defeated Western Kentucky in the NIT finals, Raese enlisted in the Navy and served as a coach of several service basketball teams during World War II. Following the war, Raese returned to Morgantown and became a successful businessman.

WVU SPORTS COMMUNICATIONS PHOTO.

Below Elkins guard Harry Lothes averaged 10.8 points per game as a senior in 1939 and was a two-time first-team Eastern Conference honoree in 1938 and 1939.

WVU SPORTS COMMUNICATIONS PHOTO.

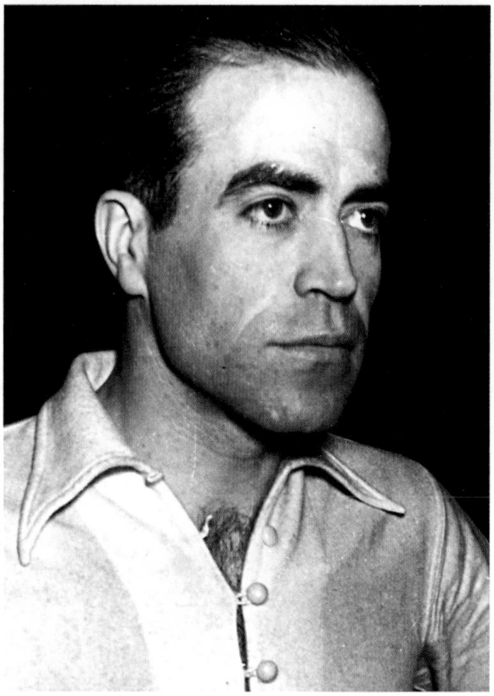

Pitt coach Doc Carlson hated Dyke Raese's zone defense. The game's inventor, Dr. James Naismith, also deplored the zone. A year before his death in 1939, Naismith made his feelings quite clear: "I have no sympathy with it. The defensive team is stalling, which lays back and waits for the offense to come to it. If a soccer team hung back and grouped itself in front of the goal, what could the other team do? The zone is much like that."

The zone was the only defense Raese played at West Virginia, and he had an unusual reason for using it. "If you use the zone," Raese once explained to Morgantown author Norm Julian, "when you get the ball, your players are already in place to run the fast break." The fast break was what Raese's West Virginia teams were known for, along with sharp passing and crisp ballhandling. Those Raese teams were also known for winning.

Raese had an unusual background for a head coach—he never played the game in college. He admitted later that most of what he learned about basketball came from his fraternity brother and predecessor, Marshall Glenn.

However, Raese's mentor didn't leave him with a lot of material to work with when he took over in 1939. Players Melvin Morehead and Thomas Netherland failed to return to school, Clifford Fisher quit the team and Welder Pell left at the end of the first semester. Despite the attrition, Raese managed a winning 10–9 record.

The Mountaineers captured their first two games of the '39 season by comfortable margins over West Virginia Wesleyan and Marietta before beating Salem by three, 46–43. A second victory over Wesleyan was sandwiched between losses to Carnegie Tech and Georgetown.

A pair of back-to-back wins over Temple and a 45–42 upset victory at Pitt were the highlights of the season, along with a 40–39 triumph over Washington & Jefferson at the Field House. Close losses came against George Washington, Penn State and St. John's, who went 18–4 that year and finished fourth in the NIT. West Virginia seemed to have the Penn State game in the bag until Max Corbin sank a three-quarter-court shot at the buzzer to send the game into overtime. The Nittany Lions eventually won 46–43.

Homer Brooks averaged 13.2 points per game, and Harry Lothes also wound up averaging double figures (10.2 ppg). Football players Sam Mandich and Charley Seabright provided effective support, as did baseball crossover Charley Hockenberry.

With the exception of Lothes who graduated, everyone was back for 1940. Two outstanding players from the freshman team, Jimmy Ruch and Rudy Baric, both stood well above six feet to give the coach some much-needed height. Raese managed to parlay that added talent into a fine 13–6 record. The high point of the year came in March when West Virginia defeated Carnegie Tech 66–57 on the road and downed Pitt 42–35 at the Field House. The Mountaineers jumped out to a 22–11 halftime lead against the Panthers and cruised to a seven-point victory behind a team-high 12 points from Steve Chepko. West Virginia also defeated a George Washington team with Red Auerbach, 43–29, in a game played in Cumberland, Md.

West Virginia's 13 wins in 1940 were the most since 1936. Ruch and Baric averaged double figures, and the team set a school record by averaging 46.3 points per game.

Raese's successful two-year record and another strong roster of returning players, enabled the Mountaineers to dramatically upgrade their schedule in 1941. Gone were Marietta, Lafayette and Georgetown. Replacing them were Ohio State, Kentucky, Michigan State, Toledo, Penn State, Army and Duquesne. The previous year's combined record of those seven schools was 112–40.

"I don't see how we're going to get through that kind of opposition with a mark comparable to that of last winter," Raese complained before the season. "We don't have the height and neither do we have the experienced reserve material. We got several promising replacements, but nearly all of them are sophomores."

The Mountaineers were able to beat three of those teams: Michigan State, Penn State and Kentucky. The Kentucky victory on Jan. 11, 1941, just a month after Japan's attack on Pearl Harbor, rates as one of the great victories of that period. West Virginia used a strong second half to pull away with a 56–43 victory over the Wildcats behind Rudy Baric's game-high 18 points. West Virginia's defense was so impressive that Kentucky All-American guard Lee Huber failed to score.

Another memorable victory came a month later when WVU downed Penn State 35–29 in the Field House, while three of WVU's losses were against strong Pitt, Duquesne and Toledo teams. Pitt qualified for the NCAA tournament, where it lost in the second round to Wisconsin. Duquesne went 17–3 and lost to Ohio University in the first round of the NIT after placing second in 1940, and Toledo went 21–3 behind the exceptional play of high-scoring Bob Gerber.

Considering the difficulty of their schedule, the Mountaineers' 13–10 record was quite impressive. Ruch and Baric once again led the team in scoring, with sophomores Scotty Hamilton and Roger "Shorty" Hicks providing solid depth. Hamilton

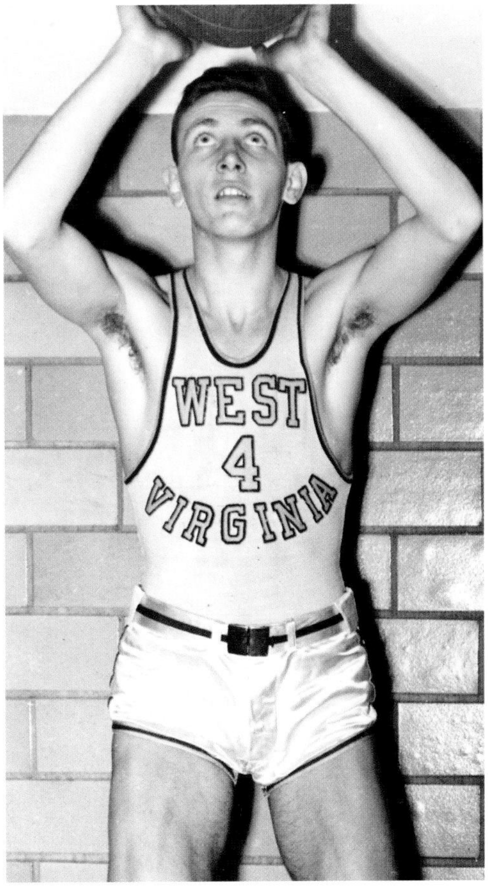

Wheeling's Jim Ruch was a two-year letterman in 1940–41, averaging a team-best 12.5 points per game in 1941. Ruch had a streak of nine straight double-digit scoring games that season, including a career-high 25 points in a 63–43 victory over West Virginia Wesleyan on Jan. 24, 1941.

WVU SPORTS COMMUNICATIONS PHOTO.

Keyser's Homer Brooks scored a career-high 20 points in West Virginia's 51–50 loss to St. John's on Feb. 4, 1939.

WVU SPORTS COMMUNICATIONS PHOTO.

Guard Steve "Gobby" Chepko, from Mona, W.Va., was a three-year letterman who played a key role for the Mountaineers in their 42–35 victory over Pitt on March 9, 1940 by scoring a game-high 12 points.

WVU SPORTS COMMUNICATIONS PHOTO.

quickly became a fan favorite with his dribbling, passing and showmanship. Many West Virginians could identify with Hamilton, who easily exceeded 200 pounds while standing just 5'10".

New York Bound

With the exception of Ruch, who chose not to return for his senior year, and Mandich, who graduated, most of the key contributors were back for 1942. As a bonus, Morgantown's Lou

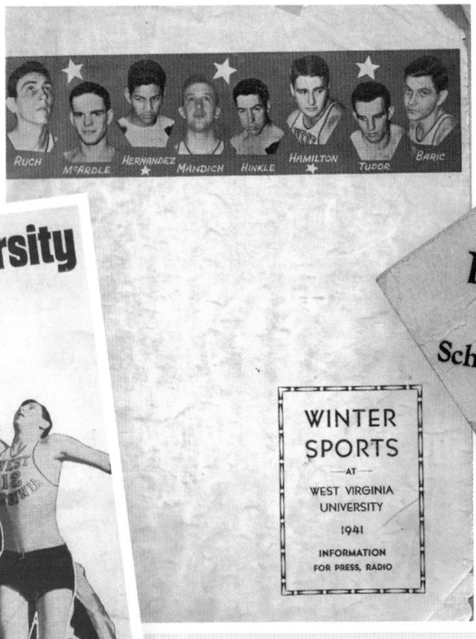

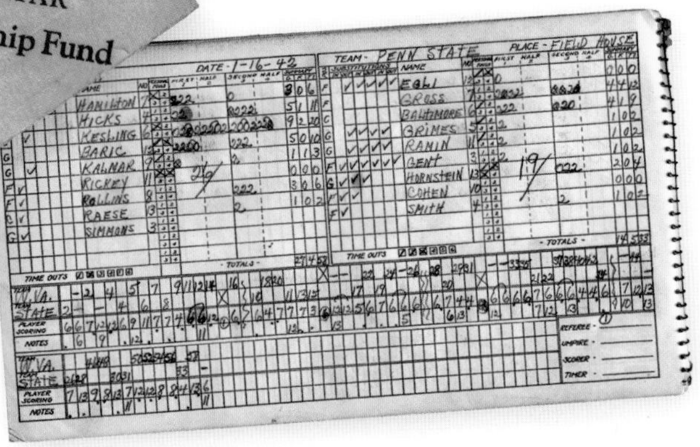

Kalmar, who had lettered in 1940, decided to rejoin the team after taking the 1941 season off. What concerned Raese most about his '42 squad heading into the season was its size—or lack thereof. Among the regulars, only the 6-foot-3 Baric stood taller than six feet. Raese was also working with a much smaller roster because several promising players on the freshman team had failed to return to school.

A pair of blowout victories to begin the 1942 season was offset by a 30–22 loss to Duquesne—WVU's fourth consecutive defeat at the hands of the powerful Dukes. But 10 straight wins, including a 25-point victory over a strong Penn State team, put West Virginia's record at 12–1 heading into a Feb. 20 game at Temple. The Owls, however, snapped the team's winning streak by using some hot shooting from Bob Dorn to down the Mountaineers 46–39. The most disappointing stretch of the season came a week later when West Virginia ended the season with back-to-back losses at Penn State and Washington & Jefferson.

The Washington & Jefferson defeat was especially irritating to Raese because the Mountaineers had things well in hand. Raese's teams were well drilled in the fundamentals of the game, and West Virginia rarely lost leads because it could hold onto the basketball for long periods of time. In this instance, Raese wanted his team to run out the clock. Unfortunately one of his players didn't get the message, firing up a missed shot that eventually led to the Presidents' game-winning basket. Raese was so mad that he could have strangled the offending player, who just happened to be his nephew, Don.

The players believed that a charity game at Salem College would wrap up the finest season in school history. None of them were aware that Everett Morris, a New York sportswriter and a member of the NIT selection committee, had watched West Virginia's 57–40 dismantling of

Army in West Point. He had left the game very impressed with the Mountaineers.

"We never worked the fast break better than we did at Army," Raese recalled years later. "Hamilton was great. When he left the game near the end, the crowd gave him an ovation. We moved the ball downcourt so fast on some plays that we had the ball in the basket before Army knew what happened."

At the time, access to the NCAA tournament was next to impossible for schools such as West Virginia. The eight-team tournament field was selected by district committees designated in eight different areas of the country. Because Morgantown was such a difficult place to reach in the 1940s, the best chance the Mountaineers had of getting into postseason play was by playing well on the road where they could be noticed by tournament scouts.

Making the NIT was a little easier. The pathway to the NIT ran through Ned Irish, a New York City basketball promoter who eventually took the game from smaller venues in the boroughs to Madison Square Garden. Once that proved successful, Irish then arranged games in Buffalo and other cities throughout the state where his scouts could locate teams for his postseason tournament. In the 1940s and early 1950s, before the NCAA began pressuring the nation's best teams to play in the NCAA tournament, many schools, including West Virginia, actually preferred playing in the NIT.

West Virginia Athletic Director Roy Hawley may have been known by everyone as Legs, but it was his right hand that advanced his career. Before anyone could get out a "Hi Legs," Hawley's arm was already extended for a disarming handshake. No one was better at cultivating friendships and allies than Hawley. He enjoyed being around the press, having once run WVU's Bureau of Information before assuming the athletic director's job, and he knew the value of good publicity. Hawley soon began to bombard Irish with phone calls, telegrams and mail about the team in one of the school's first-ever attempts at a coordinated promotional campaign. Irish took a liking to Hawley and rewarded his persistence with a promise that he would consider the Mountaineers for the final spot in the eight-team tournament field. There was a catch, however. West Virginia had to defeat Salem in the pre-arranged charity game to be played in Clarksburg on March 11. Years later, Tony Constantine remembered driving down to Clarksburg with a nervous Hawley, "If we beat Salem I think we're in," Hawley told Constantine.

Athletic Director Roy "Legs" Hawley played a key role in the development of basketball at West Virginia University during his tenure from 1938–54.

WVU SPORTS COMMUNICATIONS PHOTO.

Hawley sat through an agonizing two hours of basketball until West Virginia finally put the Tigers away 77–63. The NIT bid came shortly afterward.

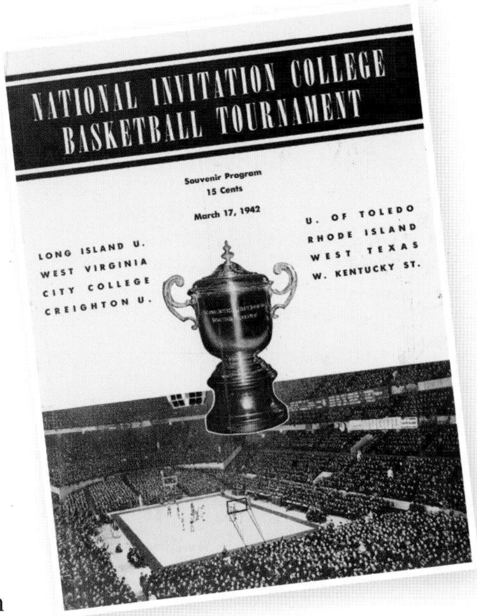

"We had all gone home for vacation. Bud Lawall, our manager, had to call around to tell us to come back because we were going to the tournament," said forward Walter Rollins.

Interest in the basketball team exploded. A network of radio stations was hastily arranged in Charleston, Clarksburg, Huntington, Parkersburg and Morgantown with WAJR sportscaster Charley Snowden being recruited to describe the action. It was the beginning of a radio network later to become known as the Mountaineer Sports

Network that grew to rival any in the country. It was Jack Fleming's colorful descriptions on the radio that later turned West Virginia basketball players into celebrities throughout the state.

Cinderella Team

To round out the NIT roster, Raese recruited Neil Montone off the football team, and the Mountaineers left by train two days before their first game against No. 1-seeded Long Island University, coached by the famous Clair Bee (a Grafton, W. Va. native). The remainder of the field consisted of West Texas A&M, Creighton, Western Kentucky, CCNY, Toledo and Rhode Island. Most considered Toledo and LIU the strongest teams in the tournament.

MOUNTAINEER SPORTS NETWORK

With the highway system in West Virginia almost nonexistent, the only thing that bridged the gap between the West Virginia University campus and the rest of the state was West Virginia's radio network, later known as the Mountaineer Sports Network.

West Virginia first began broadcasting football games on WAJR in Morgantown in 1940. Then in 1942 the excitement over West Virginia's invitation to the NIT led to a network of stations being arranged to carry the Mountaineers' run to the national championship. WAJR's Charley Snowden paid his own way to call the games.

The network expanded soon after Jack Fleming made his on-air debut in 1947. Fleming's colorful descriptions and distinctive style eventually drew legions of fans, including many impressionable high school basketball players, who listened to the games curled up underneath a blanket with the radio.

"I used to listen to West Virginia when I was a little boy," Jerry West recalled in 2009. "It was very interesting listening to these games because they would fade in and fade out. I remember a lot of times not knowing the outcome of the game until the next day because you couldn't get it."

All-American Hot Rod Hundley also used to follow the Mountaineer games on the radio in a makeshift room in the home he was living in at the time.

"I had a room underneath the stairway with a curtain and I would go underneath there and listen to West Virginia games," Hundley said. "Fred Schaus, Leland Byrd and all of those guys were playing. I would take a paper, line it off, and keep score off of Fleming's descriptions. If Schaus hit a shot from the corner, I would put down a 2 next to his name."

The legendary Jack Fleming served as the "Voice of the Mountaineers" from 1947–59, 1962–69 and 1974–96. Fleming's descriptions of basketball games were so accurate that it was said George Washington coach Bill Reinhart used to do his West Virginia scouting reports by listening to Fleming's call on the radio.

WVU SPORTS COMMUNICATIONS PHOTO.

In the 1950s, it became popular for Mountaineer fans to drive their cars to the tops of mountains to pick up WWVA's strong signal. In the early 1960s, rabid Mountaineer fan Dr. Lowell Schwab convinced the Richmond radio station WRVA to carry West Virginia basketball games while he was attending medical school. Schwab went as far as securing a sponsorship on his own to pay for the broadcasting rights fees and telephone charges.

Eventually, West Virginia University gained complete control of the radio network prior to the 1965 season, forming what is now known as the Mountaineer Sports Network (MSN).

Television became a part of the network during the 1960s, and today the radio network blankets the region with more than 50 stations. MSN also has the digital age covered on the Internet with the web site MSNsportsNET.com. Sports coverage has come a long way since the 1942 tournament, and West Virginia fans today can count on a multitude of ways to follow their beloved Mountaineers.

New York sportswriters, getting their first glimpse of the West Virginia players, began sharpening their pencils and putting new ribbons in their typewriters. Rarely did they have such an appealing group of players to write about. Only Baric looked like a basketball player. Kalmar more closely resembled a wrestler, while ghostly looking Hicks barely weighed 150 pounds. And of course there was Hamilton, whom the New York writers immediately took to calling "roly-poly."

Wrote sportswriter Tom O'Reilly: "Diogenes colliding with Abe Lincoln in a blackout wouldn't have been happier than I was on discovering Scotty Hamilton, an honest-to-beefsteak fat man, starring in the Garden as a basketball player. Suet avanti! . . . In my opinion, Scotty brought basketball back to the people."

At the game's outset, things weren't going too well for West Virginia. LIU led 25–18 at halftime, and Raese was late getting to the locker room. "The locker room door was locked and Dyke had to pound on it to get in to talk to the team," Tony Constantine later recalled.

West Virginia caught fire in the second half, however, outscoring the Jaspers 27–20. A free throw by Dick Kesling knotted the game at 45.

"LIU held the ball and had a chance to win it in regulation but missed the shot," recalled Constantine.

During the overtime period, West Virginia outscored Long Island 13–4 to pull off a stunning 58–49 victory. Bee graciously congratulated Raese after the game and sent him telegrams of encouragement for the remainder of the tournament. Back in Morgantown, there was pandemonium throughout the campus. Students paraded through downtown, and the celebrations lasted well into the night.

"The whole town was sitting in front of the radio that night," recalled Fleming. "When they won, it was total bedlam in the streets."

The surprising victory had an unintended consequence. The players had already run out of money. *Morgantown Dominion-News* sports editor Con Hardman found out about their predicament and made mention of it in the paper the next morning. Soon fans began wiring money to the players and the coaches.

When track coach Art Smith, doubling as the team trainer, found out that enough money had been sent to include the staff, he wired back to Hardman—collect. "We're down to our own money," Smith cracked. "Take up another collection."

West Virginia Gov. Matthew Mansfield Neely didn't send money, but he did wire the team, calling them "the real General MacArthurs of the basketball world."

"As Steady as the Blue Ridge Mountains"

The Mountaineers wound up having a much easier time of it in

Above Roger "Shorty" Hicks not only distinguished himself as a member of the 1942 NIT championship team, but was also a campus leader as the school's student body president, president of Phi Delta Theta fraternity, a member of the prestigious Mountain, Sphinx and letterman's honoraries, as well as serving membership on the Athletic Board. Hicks tragically lost his life on November 10, 1944, in combat at Metz, France, with the 328th Regiment, 26th Division of General Patton's Third Army during World War II.

WVU SPORTS COMMUNICATIONS PHOTO.

Right All-American guard Scotty Hamilton captured the imagination of West Virginia basketball fans with his deft ballhandling and swashbuckling style of play. According to an account by University of Pittsburgh sports historian Sam Scuillo, the popular Hamilton once slugged Pitt player Eddie Straloski senseless during a game after Straloski inadvertently struck Hamilton in the side of the head with the basketball while trying to return the ball to the official. Fans from both sides stormed the court in anger, and when a photographer attempted to take a picture of Hamilton, his West Virginia teammates chased the aspiring paparazzo up into the stands. Order was eventually restored, and afterward Hamilton apologized for his actions.

WVU SPORTS COMMUNICATIONS PHOTO.

Benwood's Rudy Baric scored 48 points in West Virginia's NIT victories over Long Island, Toledo and Western Kentucky to earn the tournament's most valuable player award.

WVU SPORTS COMMUNICATIONS PHOTO.

Shinnston's Dick Kesling scored 20 points to help West Virginia upset Long Island in the first round of the 1942 NIT in New York City, and added 14 points against Western Kentucky in the championship game. Kesling averaged 13.8 points per game and shot 73.1 percent from the free throw line in 1942.

WVU SPORTS COMMUNICATIONS PHOTO.

the semifinals against Toledo. The Rockets' top scorer, Bob Gerber, had a strong performance against West Virginia in a previous victory in 1941, but this time Baric was more than up to the task, outscoring Gerber 16–14 and holding the All-American center scoreless in the second half.

After West Virginia's 51–39 victory over Toledo, Western Kentucky took care of Creighton 49–36 in the other semifinal game, setting up an unlikely championship pairing two days later. The New York City papers referred to the seven-eight seeds as "the meek who inherited the basketball world."

According to Constantine, the entire time West Virginia stayed in New York City Raese refused to practice his team. He was never a big fan of scrimmaging and he thought many times coaches simply over-coached their teams.

In the NIT finals, before more than 18,000 fans, West Virginia trailed Western Kentucky for most of the game, until tying the score at 40 with eight minutes left to play. Two Kesling baskets gave West Virginia a four-point lead, but Western Kentucky rallied. It was free-throw shooting that wound up winning the game for the Mountaineers.

Hicks coolly stepped to the line and sank one charity to give West Virginia a 46–45 lead. Baric then made the key play in the game when he intercepted a Hilltopper pass and got the ball to the sure-handed Hamilton. Scotty sank another free throw to make the final score West Virginia 47, Western Kentucky 45. *The New York Times* called West Virginia's performance "as steady as the Blue Ridge Mountains."

Baric had scored a total of 48 points in three games and was voted the tournament's most valuable player. Hamilton and Kesling joined Baric on the all-tournament team. Remarkably, all five of West Virginia's starters came from within 70 miles of the university's campus.

"They knew that any time they walked out on the floor, they were superior to any opponent at handling the ball," Raese said later. "They knew they could keep the ball just as long as they wanted. They could have held it for five minutes or more at a time if they wished."

Baric was the team's leading scorer with an average of 14.4 points per game. Hamilton averaged 13.8 points, which, when combined with his playmaking, ballhandling and defense, made him the first player in school history to earn a spot on the coveted Helms Foundation All-America team.

Fifty years later, Walter Rollins remembered

Members of the 1942 NIT championship team, top row, left to right: Coach Dyke Raese, George Rickey, Neil Montone, Don Raese, Walter Rollins and manager Bud Lawall. Pictured in the front row, left to right: Scotty Hamilton, Lou Kalmar, Rudy Baric, Roger Hicks, and Dick Kesling.

WVU SPORTS COMMUNICATIONS PHOTO.

walking past the trophy case when the team first arrived at Madison Square Garden to see what the last place team was getting. "I think it was a belt buckle," Rollins laughed. "Then, we saw that silver trophy cup the first place team was going to receive and it looked pretty good."

The team also got $65 wristwatches, gold-plated basketballs from the student body, $25 in cash and rings from the Morgantown Elks Lodge, which sponsored a banquet for 650 well-wishers, including Gov. Neely. This time the governor did give money, contributing $50 to the gift fund for the team.

Serving as the banquet's master of ceremonies was *Pittsburgh Press* editor Chester Smith, who confided to the audience that his newspaper was besieged by calls during the tournament inquiring about the outcome of the games.

In the meantime, with the war now occupying the minds of Americans and claiming most of the country's college-aged men, Raese had applied for admission to the U.S. Naval Reserve. Soon after his team won the NIT title, Raese received his commission and spent the next four years stationed in Chapel Hill, N.C. He was preparing to head to the Pacific when the war abruptly came to an end.

Sadly, Shorty Hicks was killed during combat in Europe after graduating from WVU. Two other players—Don Raese and George Rickey of North Bergen, N.J.—also died while serving their country.

The school's policy stated that any West Virginia University employee returning from military service would have his old job waiting on him. Despite that assurance, Raese chose to enter private business when he returned to civilian life. Raese's brief four-year tenure at WVU included a 55–29 overall record. But more important than his outstanding mark was what his teams did for basketball in the Mountain State. Kids soon began practicing out in the streets, and makeshift baskets were starting to crop up everywhere. A whole new generation of basketball fans grew out of West Virginia's remarkable eight-day stay in New York City.

Another key factor in the advancement of basketball in West Virginia was Hawley's foresight by prying the state high school basketball tournament away from Buckhannon in 1939. For the next 15 years the high school tournament was played in Morgantown, meaning the state's top high school prospects spent three days on West Virginia University's campus. Players such as Mark Workman, Hot Rod Hundley, Jerry West and Rod Thorn later wound up attending WVU, in part, because of their experiences playing in the basketball tournament at the Field House.

After Hawley's death in 1954, the state tournament alternated between Huntington and Morgantown until many years later when Charleston became its permanent home.

Thanks to the great coaching of Dyke Raese and the forward thinking of Legs Hawley, basketball was no longer a casual sport at the university.

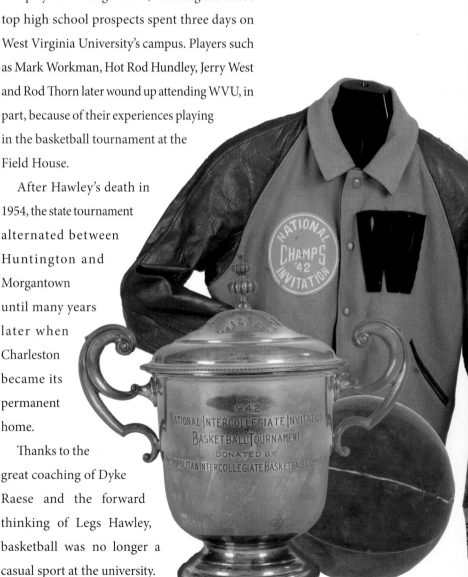

5

The War Years

(1943–1945)

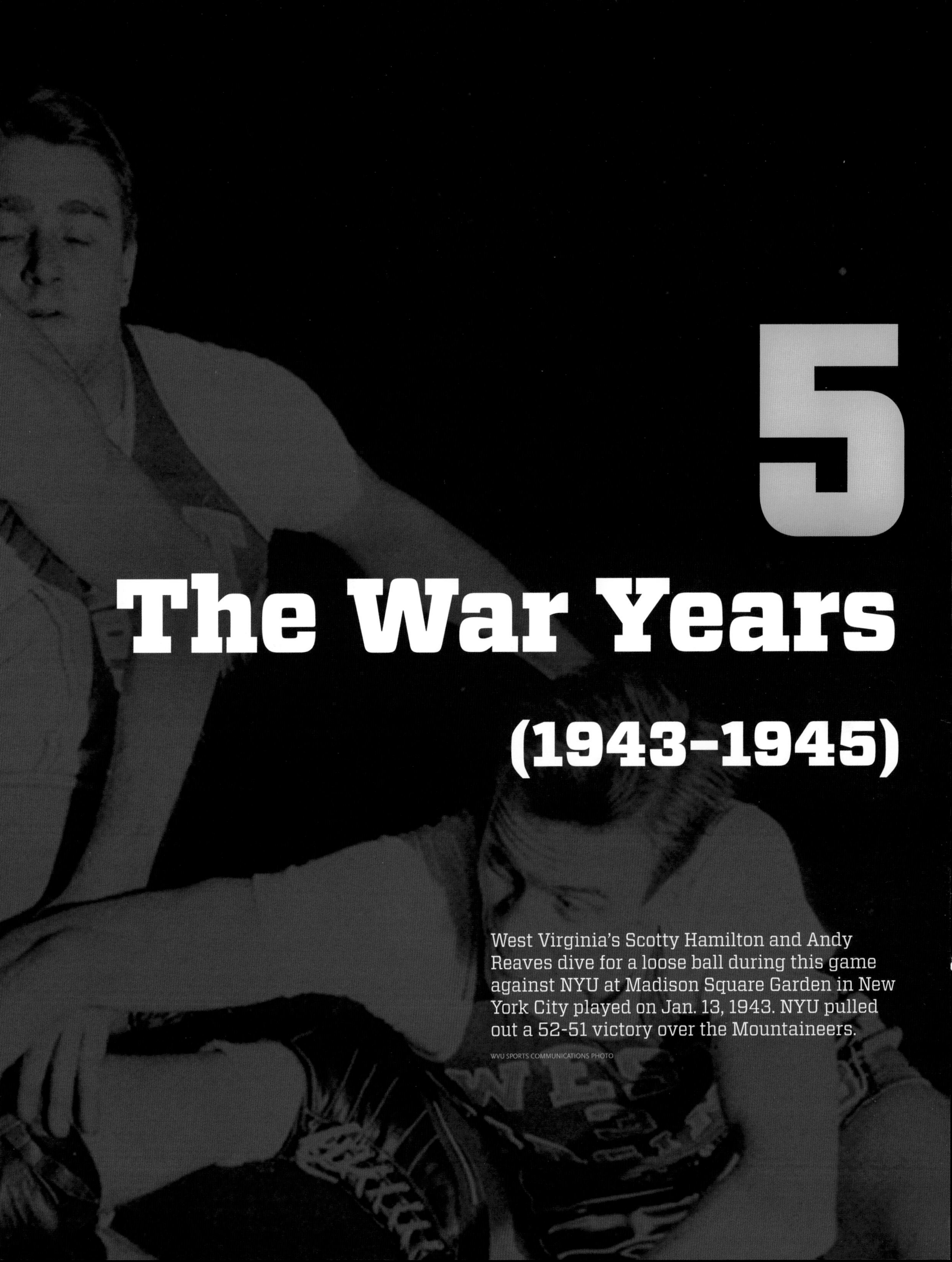

West Virginia's Scotty Hamilton and Andy Reaves dive for a loose ball during this game against NYU at Madison Square Garden in New York City played on Jan. 13, 1943. NYU pulled out a 52-51 victory over the Mountaineers.

WVU SPORTS COMMUNICATIONS PHOTO

1942 NIT MVP Rudy Baric, a native of Benwood, coached the Mountaineers for one season in 1943 when he helped the Mountaineers to a 14–7 record and victories over Penn State, Army, Temple and Pitt. Baric later became a successful coach at Penns Grove High School in Penns Grove, N.J.

WVU SPORTS COMMUNICATIONS PHOTO.

With Dyke Raese in the Navy, Rudy Baric was appointed acting basketball coach for the 1943 season. Only Scotty Hamilton remained from the 1942 team. Dick Kesling, Lou Kalmar and Shorty Hicks graduated, while George Rickey, Don Raese and Walter Rollins enlisted in the service.

Because of the great success enjoyed by the 1942 team, the basketball program now had the opportunity to provide scholarships. Before leaving for the service, WVU had hotly pursued Greenbrier Military Academy stars Floyd Stark and Joe Walthall. In order to get them, WVU had to come up with some type of financial assistance. According to late WVU historian

Pitt coach Harold Clifford "Doc" Carlson, pictured here scooping some ice cream for his Panther players, was one of the most colorful coaches to ever grace the sidelines at the Field House. A WVU fan once got so worked up by Carlson's courtside antics that he poured a cup of water over Carlson's head. Carlson was a good sport about it; the following year, he arrived at the game wearing a raincoat and carrying an umbrella.

PHOTO BY UNIVERSITY OF PITTSBURGH/SAM SCUILLO.

Tony Constantine, football coach Bill Kern was the one who came to the rescue by making the very generous offer of giving the basketball team two of his athletic grants to land Stark and Walthall. As insurance, West Virginia also brought along the remainder of Greenbrier's starting five which included brothers Benny and Bob Lewis from Mullens, and Andy Reaves from Princeton. Eventually, the two donated scholarships morphed into the basketball budget.

For many years, the word around campus was that Hamilton was also receiving some sort of financial assistance. "I believe Scotty Hamilton got some help, too, although I'm not sure where it came from," laughed Leland Byrd.

In the 1940s, schools had varying standards for scholarships in all sports, but especially in football and basketball. Some scholarships consisted of room, board, tuition and fees. Others provided just tuition and fees with athletes required to work campus jobs to cover the room and board portion. A third group of schools, mostly in the south, had wealthy "sponsors" who paid for an athlete's education and provided financial assistance. Other schools did not offer scholarships at all.

By the late 1940s scholarship abuse had become common, and in 1948, a group of university presidents issued the so-called "Sanity Code" which attempted to regulate the practice of awarding scholarships. Still, it wasn't until 1956 that a nationwide standard for scholarships was instituted that eventually became known as the grant-in-aid. The grant-in-aid encompassed room and board, tuition and fees, and a $15 monthly stipend commonly referred to as "laundry money," according to author Keith Dunnavent.

Lighter Schedule

In 1943, Baric's West Virginia team had a relatively easy schedule with games against Bethany, Alderson-Broaddus and West Virginia Wesleyan to begin the season. The Mountaineers also began an annual regular season trip to New York City to play in Madison Square Garden, where West Virginia lost 52–51 to NYU. They would continue to play in New York City well into the 1950s, even after a major gambling scandal that emanated from New York rocked college basketball.

West Virginia's best stretch of the 1943 season came in late January with consecutive wins against Penn State, Army, Fordham and Temple. Unfortunately, wartime restrictions resulted in the cancellation of New Mexico's 11-game tour of the United States that was scheduled to stop at the Field House in early February.

West Virginia's opportunity to make a return trip to the NIT was thwarted after two close losses to Washington & Jefferson, which wound up going to the tournament instead. The Mountaineers finished the season with a pair of victories over Pitt and Duquesne in the Field House, with Pitt and its charismatic coach Doc Carlson making their first appearance in Morgantown since 1940.

Carlson was quite a character who enjoyed playing to the crowd. During a game against Carnegie Tech, he was whistled for a pair of technical fouls when he went on the court to kiss all of his departing senior players. Another time Carlson employed his "freeze game" against Penn State and the Nittany Lion players were so annoyed with the strategy that they camped out underneath their basket with their hands on their hips waiting for Pitt to play. The halftime score was Penn State 5, Pitt 2. While Penn State fans booed, Carlson amused himself by tossing peanuts into the stands.

When his team visited WVU, he usually brought his antics with him. Once during a game at the Field House, a West Virginia fan dumped a cup of water on top of Carlson's head. Upon his return the following year, Carlson showed his sense of humor by walking on the court wearing a raincoat and carrying an umbrella (Red Brown's wife, Mary, also used to bring an umbrella with her to games and once got so upset with an official's call that she walked out on the floor and hit him over the head with it).

Tony Constantine once recalled overhearing a fan asking Carlson what the H. C. stood for on his monogrammed shirts. "High class," Carlson cracked. His name was Harold Clifford.

"He was always on the officials and he played to the crowd," Byrd added. "He liked the spotlight. He always had a red towel and he would wave that red towel around. He really played it up."

Harry Lothes served one year as West Virginia's basketball coach in 1944 when Rudy Baric was called into military service. Lothes led a depleted roster to an 8–11 record, although the Mountaineers did win three of their last four games that season.

WVU SPORTS COMMUNICATIONS PHOTO.

This time Carlson chose to play it straight (no holding the ball), and West Virginia rolled to a record-setting 82–64 victory. Walthall scored 25 points, while Stark and Hamilton added 18 points each. West Virginia's 82 points established a school record, beating the old record of 80 points first set during the 1905 season and duplicated in 1942 against Bethany. The Mountaineers finished the year with a victory over Duquesne and a win against Salem in a charity game benefiting the infantile paralysis fund.

Baric's 14–7 record was impressive considering eight sophomores played alongside Hamilton, the sole senior.

Walthall set the school record for scoring with 377 points, averaging 18 points per game. His best performance was a 32-point effort against West Virginia Wesleyan. Hamilton wrapped up his career with 223 points, while Stark finished third on the team in scoring with 163 points. Stark and Walthall played just one season for the Mountaineers; Walthall opted to enter medical school at Duke, and Stark chose not to return to school.

Baric, too, departed the university to fulfill his ROTC commitment to enlist in the war, where he was seriously wounded in France. Later, a fully recovered Baric became a longtime high school coach in Penns Grove, N.J.

Another former Raese player, Harry Lothes, was assigned the task of leading the Mountaineers in 1944. Lothes was coaching at Shepherdstown High School before joining the West Virginia University physical education staff at the beginning of the fall semester. Hawley officially appointed Lothes to coach the Mountaineers on Nov. 14, 1943, and Lothes took over a basketball team completely gutted by graduation and military service. Nine of the 26 players trying out for the 1944 team were football players, including Triadelphia's Bill Anderson, who had played basketball at West Liberty in 1943, and Eddie Cox, who had played basketball at West Virginia Tech. Sizing up his teams' prospects after two weeks of practice, Lothes proclaimed, "We've got a long, long way to go."

West Virginia won its first three games against inferior competition, but a seven-game midseason losing streak (snapped in a charity game against Bethany) gave the Mountaineers their first losing season in six years.

Earl Allara led the team in scoring with 181 points. An Iaeger, W.Va., native, Allara had decided to come out for the team his junior year, and despite his basketball ability, it was the only season he played for the Mountaineers. Center Bill Johnson finished second to Allara with 177 points.

Above Greenbrier Military Academy star Floyd Stark was one of the first players to earn a basketball scholarship at West Virginia University while playing for Coach Rudy Baric. The 6-foot-4 center lettered one season for the Mountaineers in 1943, averaging 7.8 points in 21 games that year.

WVU SPORTS COMMUNICATIONS PHOTO.

Above Right High-scoring guard Joe Walthall, the brother of WVU star quarterback Jimmy Walthall, played one season for the Mountaineers in 1943 when he scored a school-record 377 points and averaged 18 points per game. Walthall and Floyd Stark were the two key members of the Greenbrier Military Academy basketball team who later wound up becoming the first two players awarded basketball scholarships at West Virginia University. Walthall left WVU after one year to enter Duke's medical school.

WVU SPORTS COMMUNICATIONS PHOTO.

Chop 'Em Down

It was during this time that one of the most unique characters to ever attend WVU basketball games began frequenting the Field House. He was a man in his mid-fifties named Frank Henderson, although anyone who went to the games knew him better as "Chop 'Em Down." Henderson, a lay minister, got his colorful nickname because that was the phrase he always used to heckle opposing players and coaches. Chop 'Em Down liked his nickname so much that he sometimes carried a small hatchet with him when he walked down High Street.

Chop 'Em Down became such a nuisance to opposing players and coaches that schools began requesting that West Virginia put a muzzle on him or, better yet, not let him in the building at all. But WVU students, amused with his antics, would usually help him sneak in through an open window. When Legs Hawley would see—or more likely, hear—Chop 'Em Down, he would turn to his first lieutenant Pat Tork and ask him how he got into the building. Chop 'Em Down saved his best material for Doc Carlson, who sometimes shook a fist at his heckler or asked Hawley to have him removed from the Field House. The AD would have to march across the floor to the student section and tell Chop 'Em Down to cool it or else he would have to leave. Typically, Hawley had to make several trips to warn the man each game.

"He'd get right behind the players' bench—the student section in both football and basketball was right behind the bench," said Byrd. "He had that old wooden ax and he would say, 'Chop 'Em Down! I feel sorry for you!' That was really the rallying cry for the students, and he would get the whole crowd really going."

"Chop 'Em Down used to scare my daughter to death," laughed Al Babcock, who kept the scorebook during home games back then. "My daughter would be in a stroller, and he would be yelling, 'Chop 'Em Down!' She used to cry at that, but he added a lot to the games."

One year, WVU students took up a collection to help Chop 'Em Down travel to New York City to watch West Virginia play in Madison Square Garden. But the sheer size of the arena, plus New Yorkers' ambivalence toward disturbances of this nature, severely limited his effectiveness.

Brickels Takes Over

Stumpy Irishman John Brickels, who led Huntington Central High School to a state title in 1944, took over the WVU coaching duties for the 1945 season. A Wittenberg (Ohio) College graduate, Brickels was a stickler for fundamental play, employing a deliberate offense that required good passing. He also was a funny man who was often the butt of his own jokes. According to Charleston sportswriter Dick Hudson, who got to know Brickels well when he was coaching at Huntington High, Brickels loved to argue almost as much as he loved coaching. His close friends, including professional football coaching great Paul Brown, enjoyed coaxing Brickels into heated

Dave Wilson played for John Brickels at Huntington High and came to WVU with Brickels in 1945. Wilson's best statistical season was his freshman year in '45 when he averaged 9.9 points per game, helping the Mountaineers to a return trip to the NIT.

WVU SPORTS COMMUNICATIONS PHOTO.

disagreements. With Brickels, that proved to be quite easy to do.

"Brickels was a Cam Henderson disciple," said Byrd. "He played zone defense, liked to fast break and come down the middle. Of course he was fiery, too. He would get on the officials—and get on us."

Brickels, also an assistant coach on the WVU football team, brought his two best Huntington

Fiery John Brickels coached one season at WVU in 1945, leading the Mountaineers to the NIT and beginning a string of 20 consecutive winning campaigns. Brickels left Morgantown after one year to join Paul Brown's Cleveland Browns coaching staff, and later became a well-known athletic director at Miami, Ohio, where he was responsible for hiring well-known football coaches Ara Parseghian, John Pont and Bo Schembechler.

WVU SPORTS COMMUNICATIONS PHOTO.

players with him to Morgantown in center Dave Wilson and forward Jack Dial. From Huntington's St. Joseph High School, he added guard Mike Russo. Bobby Carroll, who led Wheeling High to a state title in 1943 and a second-place finish in 1944, also joined the team, as did 6-foot-3 left-hander Leland Byrd from Matoaka High School, located between Princeton and Bluefield near the West Virginia-Virginia border.

During the coaching transition from Lothes to Brickels, it was really Legs Hawley who kept the program going. Hawley was the one who recruited Leland Byrd, Jimmy Walthall and Bobby Carroll to West Virginia. Walthall was also a star quarterback on the football team where he had injured his knee, but he was well enough to come out for the basketball team. Five-foot-eight guard Bob Stakem was the only sophomore on a roster full of freshmen.

"Recruiting wasn't that big back then," Byrd said in 2009. "Legs Hawley came down south to recruit Jimmy Walthall and he had heard about me. Before that he didn't give me much thought, but he came down and offered me a scholarship right on the spot."

Byrd earned the nickname "Hammer" during his freshman season when freshmen were allowed to play because of the war. "We were practicing and I had a really bad fall on my shoulder and my head," Byrd recalled in 2009. "I got up a little groggy. Art Smith was the trainer and he came out and said, 'Are you OK?' Jim [Walthall] hollered out, 'He's OK. You can't hurt the hammerhead!' Well, the hammer stuck."

Years later, Doc Carlson paid Byrd a tall compliment. "You're the blankety-blank who always beat us," Carlson said to Byrd. "I remember one time I looked out there on the floor and your shoulders seemed to be slumping a little. We had a four-point lead and there wasn't a lot of time left. I told my boys that it looked like we would win this one—we had Byrd down.

"But the first thing you know, you stole the ball and scored, then you broke up another play and West Virginia tied us. That finished us."

The team's 18-game schedule in 1945 featured games against Penn State, Army, Temple, Navy, Pitt and Carnegie Tech. A key trip to New York to face LIU at Madison Square Garden

Wheeling's Bobby Carroll served as captain of the 1946 team after leading the team in scoring as a freshman in 1945. Carroll later went on to become a successful high school coach in Bridgeport, Ohio, where one of his pupils was NBA hall of famer John Havlicek.

WVU SPORTS COMMUNICATIONS PHOTO.

and a meeting three days later against NYU in Buffalo led to West Virginia's second postseason invitation to the NIT.

Brickels's Mountaineers managed to beat Clair Bee's Blackbirds behind 20 points from Byrd and 17 from Carroll. "[West Virginia is] a young team and a fast one," wrote *New York Post*'s Arch Murray, "but it's improving and it can score. What was most impressive was the way the Mountaineers tightened their zone defense in the second half."

Against NYU, Carroll was the star, scoring 16 in a 41–40 victory that caught the attention of NIT scouts. Walthall made a key basket with 45 seconds left to put the Mountaineers up by three. West Virginia also finished the season with strong performances against Pitt (50–47) in Morgantown, and against Carnegie Tech (66–35) in Pittsburgh.

A supreme act of sportsmanship led to West Virginia's exciting 52–50 victory over Geneva College at the Field House. In a rough game marred by fouls, Geneva coach Harold Bruce graciously called time-out to allow Byrd have a cut above his eye tended to by trainer Art Smith. Had Bruce not called time-out, Geneva likely would have won the game.

"It's the greatest act of sportsmanship I ever saw," Tony Constantine told Morgantown author Norm Julian.

"We weren't about to call time-out and he did," Byrd remembered. "He came over and said, 'You better get that patched up.' I don't know of any coach that would have done that."

In the NIT, West Virginia's first-round game against DePaul was a big mismatch. The Blue Demons were the top seed in the tournament and boasted 6-foot-9 All-American center George Mikan, who scored 33 points against WVU before fouling out with his team comfortably ahead. DePaul eventually won the tournament behind Mikan's 34 points in the championship game against Bowling Green.

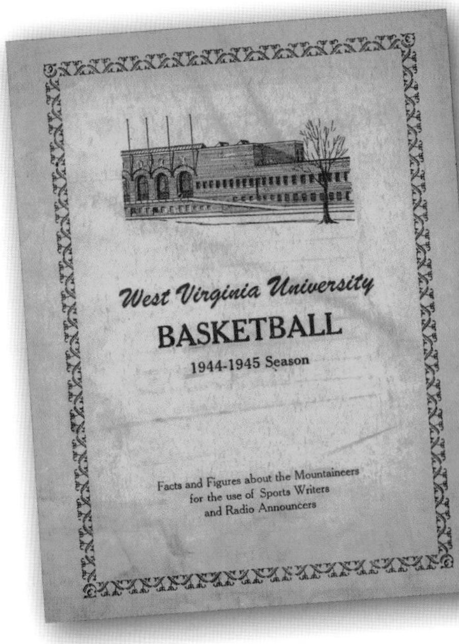

Carroll led the Mountaineers in scoring with an average of 12.2 points per game, while Wilson and Byrd averaged just a shade below 10 points. West Virginia's all-freshman five of Byrd and Dial at forwards, Wilson at center, and Carroll and Walthall at guards is believed to be the first all-freshman lineup to play in the NIT. Walthall was named to the Pic Magazine All-America third team.

Despite having one of the youngest teams in the country and the possibility of adding even more quality players with the war winding down, Brickels instead chose to take an assistant coaching job on Paul Brown's Cleveland Browns staff. Brickels later earned distinction as an athletic director at Miami, Ohio, where he hired football coaches Ara Parseghian and Bo Schembechler, furthering Miami's distinction as college football's "Cradle of Coaches."

Brickels's replacement at West Virginia was former Princeton High coach Lee Patton, whom Hawley had also pegged for the top football post in the event that Bill Kern decided not to return to WVU following the completion of his military service. (Kern did decide to return.)

With players such as Byrd, Carroll, and Wilson just beginning their sophomore year, Patton, like Dyke Raese three years before him, was poised to take New York City by storm.

apel Overflows With Grief-Stricken
As Final Tribute Here Is Paid Patt

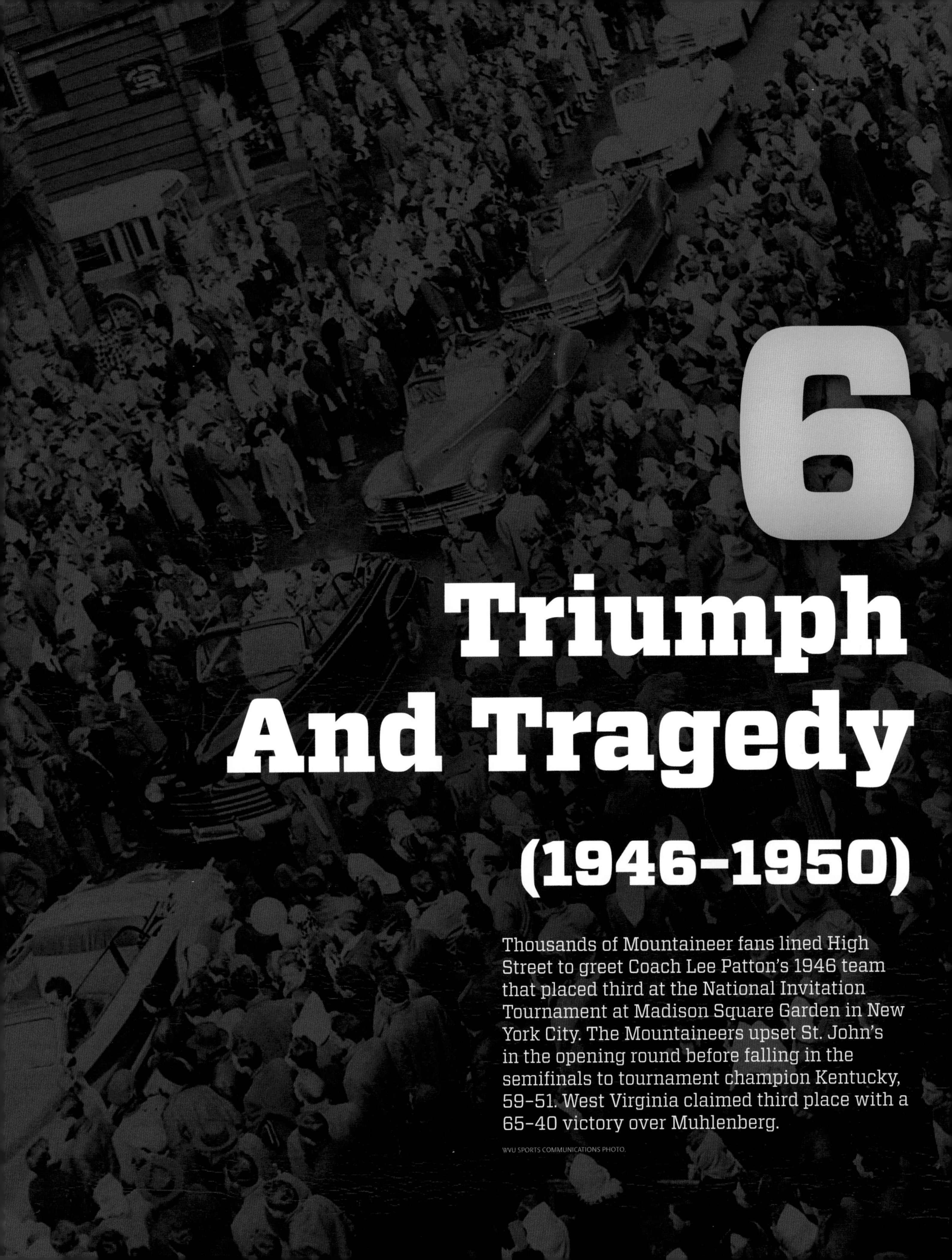

6

Triumph And Tragedy

(1946–1950)

Thousands of Mountaineer fans lined High Street to greet Coach Lee Patton's 1946 team that placed third at the National Invitation Tournament at Madison Square Garden in New York City. The Mountaineers upset St. John's in the opening round before falling in the semifinals to tournament champion Kentucky, 59–51. West Virginia claimed third place with a 65–40 victory over Muhlenberg.

WVU SPORTS COMMUNICATIONS PHOTO.

Lee Patton once told sportswriter Tony Constantine that he preferred the gridiron to the hardwood, but that didn't deter him from producing a dazzling 91–26 record during five successful seasons on the court with the Mountaineers.

WVU SPORTS COMMUNICATIONS PHOTO.

Legs Hawley really had the football job in mind for Lee Patton when he hired the 40-year-old Arizona State graduate to serve as the school's acting basketball coach and assistant football coach for the 1946 season. Patton was well-known throughout the Mountain State for his coaching at Princeton High School, where he had all-state quarterback Jimmy Walthall. Patton led Princeton's football team to an undefeated season in 1943, and that same year, his basketball team finished second at the state championships in Morgantown.

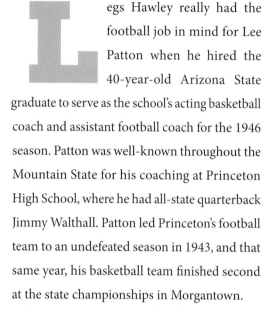

Patton's most recent job had been a one-year stint at Iona Prep in New York City, where he turned out an undefeated football team that beat the Army freshmen and a basketball team that reached the city finals.

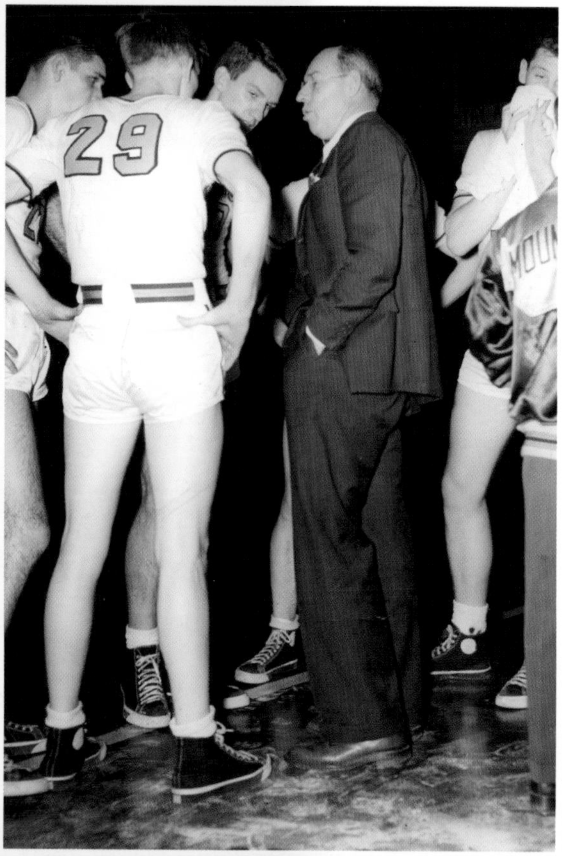

Patton, pictured here giving instruction to his team, became the first coach in school history to win 20 games in a season when his 1946 team won 24 games and finished third in the National Invitation Tournament at Madison Square Garden in New York City.

WVU SPORTS COMMUNICATIONS PHOTO.

Tony Constantine was one of those who got the impression that Patton actually preferred football over basketball. "He used to say football season ended too soon and basketball season seemed to last forever," Constantine recalled.

Patton's basketball philosophy stressed fundamental play and strict man-to-man defense. Practices consisted of a lot of passing drills and frequent movement. Players fondly recalled Patton's high-pitched voice in practice yelling, "Run, run, run!"

"I admired Patton," said Fred Schaus, who played for him. "He had one theory: run, run, run. I liked that way of playing and I liked that way to play when I coached. It kind of fit in for me as well."

"He was a great fundamentalist, too," added Byrd. "Everybody that played for him that went into coaching were fundamental coaches because he stressed that."

Patton read all the literature available on the sport, and he took to heart some sound advice he received from St. John's coach Joe Lapchick. "[Lapchick] said, 'Remember one thing, Lee, it's easy to get five guys who can score 50 points. The whole secret is to get guys who can stop the opposition from getting 50.' I never forgot that sound bit of logic," Patton once said.

Patton supplemented the already strong team Brickels had left him by adding guards Clyde Green from Pratt and Howard Beverly from South Charleston, and bringing in Malverne (N.Y.) High forward Tom Leverte from Long Island, N.Y.

"Tom Leverte was a real peach of a guy," Byrd said. "Everybody loved him and so did the crowd."

Green had the colorful nickname "Hard Times." The nickname was a tribute to his hard-scrabble life growing up along the Kanawha River in Pratt, W.Va. Soon Hard Times became a fan favorite.

The late Jack Fleming fondly described Green's first-ever trip to New York City as a freshman in 1946. "There was Clyde Green standing in the middle of Times Square deep in thought, looking at an animated sign high over a building with something like Bugs Bunny or Felix the Cat acting," Fleming once wrote. "He was totally fascinated and he stood there for what seemed like hours. Then later, as we walked into the Garden, old 'Hard Times' looked over at me and said, 'Jack, this place can sure hold a lot of hay.'"

Green, Beverly and Leverte offset the losses of

Jim Walthall, who chose not to play that year; Jack Dial and Mike Russo, neither of whom returned to school; and Bob Stakem, who developed tuberculosis and was forced to drop out of school.

Patton won his first 13 games (a school record), including a 43–41 overtime triumph over Penn State in Morgantown, along with a pair of wins against Long Island University in New York City and Canisius in Buffalo. A second victory versus Penn State, this time in State College, followed.

Patton's first loss came Feb. 2, 1946 at Temple when the Owls nipped the Mountaineers 48–42, and a five-game winning streak that followed was stopped at Navy, 50–45. West Virginia completed the season with triumphs over Maryland, Washington & Jefferson, Pitt and Carnegie Tech. The Mountaineers' 22-2 regular-season record was the first time West Virginia had ever reached 20 victories in a season. Sixteen times that year WVU won by 20 points or more, including a pair of blowout wins against Pitt. The team also established a Field House record for attendance with more than 125,000 spectators witnessing West Virginia's 11 home games that year, a testament to the program's growing popularity.

NIT Bound, Again

West Virginia once again caught the eye of Ned Irish, and the Mountaineers were invited to an unusually strong NIT field in 1946 that included Kentucky, Arizona, St. John's and, surprisingly, Rhode Island.

Fourth-seeded West Virginia was paired against local favorite St. John's in the first round of the tournament. The Redmen were coached by Joe Lapchick, an original member of the Boston Celtics who steered the Johnnies to NIT titles in 1943 and 1944. During the 1944 NIT finals against DePaul, Lapchick fainted in the second half just after his team took the lead.

"I dealt strategy a helluva blow," he later joked.

Six-foot-nine All-American center Harry Boykoff, back from

Left Clyde "Hard Times" Green, pictured here hounding a Utah player in this 1947 NIT game, was a fan favorite for his defensive prowess and his playmaking abilities. Green played on teams that strung together 43 consecutive victories at the Field House during his four-year playing career from 1946–49. Hard Times later became a high school basketball coach at Romney and Morgantown High Schools.

WVU SPORTS COMMUNICATIONS PHOTO.

Below Tom Leverte, a forward from Long Island, N.Y., was one of the key members of the 1946 team that compiled a 24–3 record and finished third in the NIT. Leverte, pictured here against St. John's in Madison Square Garden, averaged 10.6 points per game in 1946 and scored a career-high 25 points against Geneva on Jan. 30, 1946.

WVU SPORTS COMMUNICATIONS PHOTO.

the service, was St. John's best player. He scored 13 points against Toledo to help the Redmen to the 1943 NIT championship before joining the war effort. West Virginia's three tallest starters—Byrd, Wilson and Leverte—were giving up more than five inches to Boykoff.

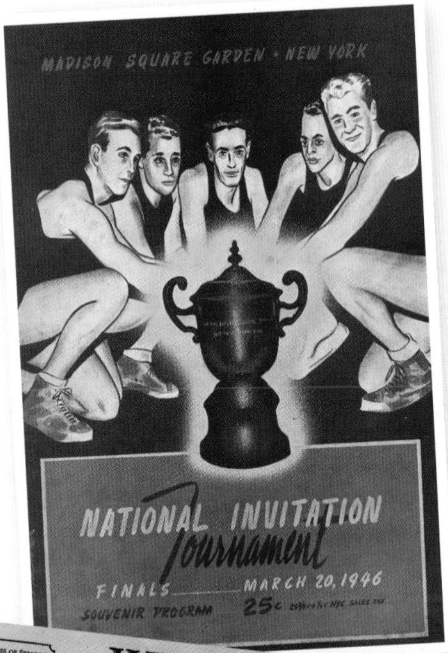

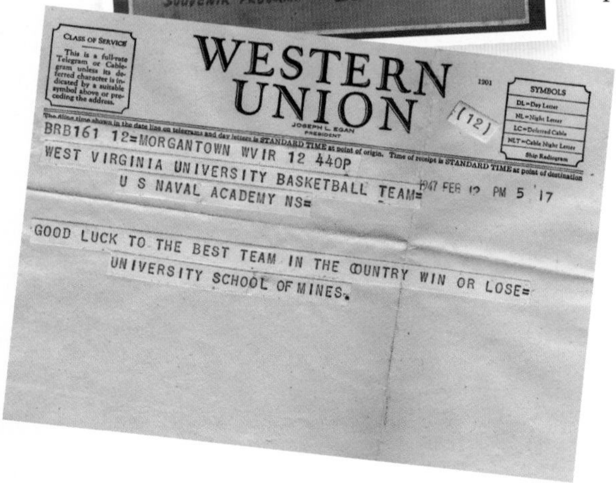
WESTERN UNION

BRB161 12=MORGANTOWN WVIR 12 440P
WEST VIRGINIA UNIVERSITY BASKETBALL TEAM= 1947 FEB 12 PM 5 17
U S NAVAL ACADEMY NS=

GOOD LUCK TO THE BEST TEAM IN THE COUNTRY WIN OR LOSE=
UNIVERSITY SCHOOL OF MINES.

Western Union telegram was the preferred way for schools to communicate quickly in the 1940s.

The West Virginia–St. John's game was the nightcap of Thursday's opening-round doubleheader. The first game pitted 11-point underdog Rhode Island against Bowling Green. The Rams, however, pulled off a stunning 82–79 upset behind the sharp shooting of Ernie Calverley.

Perhaps encouraged by Rhode Island's performance, five-point underdog West Virginia produced another stunning upset. WVU jumped out to a 22-point halftime lead behind hot shooting by Byrd. The Mountaineers got their big lead with eight minutes to go in the first half by scoring 15 straight points.

St. John's eventually warmed up in the second half, scoring nine of 11 points during one stretch, but the closest it could get was 64–56 before two quick baskets by Byrd and Carroll killed the rally. The final score read West Virginia 70, St. John's 58. Byrd scored 28 points to lead all scorers, while Carroll contributed 14 and Wilson added 12. Meanwhile, Boykoff wound up riding the bench at the end of the game, having scored only 7 points.

"Patton coached a year up there before he came here and he had another coach up there that did a lot of scouting for us," Byrd said. "Of course, scouting was something people really didn't do back then.

"Well, he sent a scouting report back that said all we had to do was run Boykoff and he'll tire out. So we ran the heck out of him. After about seven or eight minutes his tongue was hanging out, and he wasn't worth anything."

In the semifinals against a strong Kentucky team with All-American Jack Parkinson, West Virginia had the top-seeded Wildcats on the ropes in the first half before Kentucky caught fire, outscoring the Mountaineers 34–24 in the second half to win 59–51. Howard Beverly was West Virginia's top scorer in the game with 11 points.

West Virginia's performance against a vastly superior Kentucky team drew praise from knowledgable New York City scribes. Wrote Dick Young: "West Virginia, with its flock of rawboned sophs and frosh, can take a deep bow for the scrap it put up. It was a terrifically tough assignment, but they failed to choke up."

Two days later, West Virginia overcame an early 7–0 deficit to defeat Muhlenberg 65–40 to take home the third-place trophy. "This is the greatest gang of kids I have ever coached," Patton said to a group of more than 2,000 fans who greeted the team upon its return from New York.

"We were all West Virginians with one player from Maryland," Byrd noted. "We came to Morgantown from small schools and 4,200 was what the place held the first two years before the balconies were added. That crowd was right on top of you so we were used to the crowd and the noise when we went to the Garden.

"We were also the underdogs and the New York crowd loved the underdog so we usually had more support than teams other than the local teams," he continued. "So many teams were awed by the crowd, but the 17,000 people we played in front of in New York didn't bother us at all."

Rhode Island nearly knocked off Kentucky in the finals, with Calverley earning the tournament MVP honors. Kentucky's win meant that West Virginia's three losses in 1946 had been to teams with a combined record of 52–12. Years later, West Virginia's victory over St. John's was selected as one of the school's finest by the all-time committee. Byrd (11.3 ppg), Carroll (11.1 ppg) and Leverte (10.6 ppg) averaged double figures that season.

An already formidable squad with Byrd, Carroll, Green and Leverte became even stronger in 1947 with Jim Walthall rejoining the team and the additions of Fred Schaus, Bill Zirkel, Eddie Beach and Joe Duff. "When Schaus, Beach and [a year later] Sterling came in we had a lot more talent in those years," Byrd said. Zirkel, Beach and Duff were all from the New York City metropolitan area and came to WVU as a result of Patton's New York contacts. Zirkel averaged 11.9 points per game during his one season with the Mountaineers before skipping out to play pro ball. Beach hailed from Elizabeth, N.J., and became a first-year starter for the Mountaineers as a 17-year-old freshman. Duff, from Cranford, N.J., gave the Mountaineers tough, savvy play in the backcourt. Patton also got some help that year when Red Brown was hired to coach the freshman team.

As for Newark, Ohio's Fred Schaus, he had two "ins" with West Virginia. His junior high school coach was the brother-in-law of John Brickels, and Schaus later met Scotty Hamilton while the two were going through boot camp in the service. Those two influences helped persuade Schaus to enroll at West Virginia when the war was over. He arrived in Morgantown as a mature 20-year-old college freshman and soon earned the nickname "Fireball."

Right off the bat, Schaus displayed an ability to score, producing 21 points in his first game in an easy 40-point victory over Fairmont State. A streak of 12 straight wins to begin the year eventually ended with a 57–55 loss to a powerful Navy team that finished the season with a 16–3 record. Before the Navy loss, West Virginia and Duquesne were the only two remaining undefeated teams in the country. It turned out to be West Virginia's only loss of the regular season.

All-American Leland "The Hammer" Byrd became the first player in school history to score 1,000 points when he hit the mark on the nose during the final home game of his career, a 52–36 victory over Pitt on March 6, 1948.

WEST VIRGINIA AND REGIONAL HISTORY COLLECTION.

FIELD HOUSE WINNING STREAK

Leland Byrd, Bobby Carroll and Dave Wilson can make a boast that very few players can claim during their college careers: they never lost a home game.

West Virginia's impressive 57-game Field House winning streak began after a disappointing 60–57 loss to Pitt on Feb. 26, 1944. Six days later Carnegie Tech was West Virginia's first victim to conclude Harry Lothes's only season guiding the WVU program. In 1945, John Brickels directed West Virginia to a 7–0 home mark with victories coming against Fairmont, Penn State, Salem, Carnegie Tech, Geneva and Bethany. That was also the first year then-sophomores Byrd, Carroll and Wilson began playing for the Mountaineers.

Despite Brickels's success, it was Lee Patton who turned the Field House into a house of horrors for opposing teams before Pitt finally ended the streak on March 5, 1949.

The remarkable winning streak spanned six seasons and three different coaches, remaining to this day one of the most impressive feats in school history.

"Fireball" Fred Schaus, pictured at the bottom wearing jersey number 11, led the team in scoring his freshman and junior campaigns in 1947 and 1949, totaling 1,009 points for his career. Schaus was recognized as a third-team All-American by the Helms Foundation in 1949, and chose to sign a professional contract with the Fort Wayne Pistons instead of returning for his senior season in 1950.

WVU SPORTS COMMUNICATIONS PHOTO.

The Mountaineers whipped St. Francis, N.Y., in New York City, easily downed Maryland and Temple, and managed season sweeps of Penn State and Pitt. At halftime of West Virginia's season-ending blowout win over Carnegie Tech, Patton was first presented a pair of oversized trousers as a replacement for the pair he usually wore out after each game. Then, appreciative Mountaineer fans gave the surprised coach keys to a brand-new car.

West Virginia was the first team invited to the NIT (second overall seed) and the Mountaineers advanced to the tournament semifinals for the second consecutive year. Against Bradley, West Virginia used a 15-point run late in the first half to take an 11-point halftime lead. Bradley fought back to pull within four, 49–45, with 10 minutes to go, but West Virginia managed to hold on for a 69–60 win. Byrd led WVU with 19 points to help the Mountaineers reach the NIT semifinals for the third time in six years.

Utah knocked West Virginia out of the tournament with a 64–62 upset victory. The Utes nearly blew a 10-point lead with a minute to play as West Virginia staged a wild rally. Beach, Duff and Walthall scored late baskets, and Walthall added two more at the free throw line to cut the deficit to two when the clock finally read zero. A disappointed West Virginia team later dropped a 64–52 decision to NC State in the third-place game.

Schaus scored 371 points to average 16.9 points per game. Byrd averaged 12 points and was named to the Helms Foundation All-America first team, becoming the second player in school history to earn that distinction. Beach nearly became the third player to reach double figures, averaging 9.8 points per game. Ed Sterling finished second in the country to St. Bonaventure's Sam Urzetta in free throw shooting, making 88.9 percent of his charity attempts that season.

A cartoon depicting Kentucky coach Adolph Rupp and two West Virginia players that appeared in *Look* magazine.

DONATED BY ELEANOR LAMB.

Once again, the team was treated to a 2,000-person-strong parade down High Street, the throng of well-wishers gathering in front of the Metropolitan Theater to salute their heroes.

An opportunity to land a third straight bid to the NIT in 1948 ended after defeats by Manhattan, Penn State and Washington & Jefferson. Schaus broke his ankle in the W&J loss, which caused him to miss five games. This wasn't the forward's first injury—he had previously fractured his hand and played with a cast for several games.

A 68–64 victory over NC State in Morgantown avenged the loss to the Wolfpack in the previous year's NIT consolation round. Later, the game was included among the school's all-time great victories. A crowd of more than 4,600 was on their feet from start to finish in an exciting game that ended with West Virginia withstanding a late Wolfpack rally. Leading 66–64, Byrd's game-clinching shot put him at 779 points, five points past Jack Gocke as the school's all-time leading scorer. Byrd eventually finished his career with 1,000 points on the nose, becoming the first player in WVU history to reach the four-figure barrier.

Other key wins in 1948 came against Brigham Young, Penn State and Bradley, as well as season sweeps of Pitt and Temple. "Those Mormons are mighty fine people to associate with," were Patton's words after his team's 17-point victory over BYU. The Pitt victory was West Virginia's seventh win in a row over the Panthers in a series that was finally beginning to tilt in the Mountaineers' favor.

"We beat them seven out of eight times," Byrd pointed out. "[Carlson] had Hank Zeller and some other great players, but after Zeller left we probably had more talent so he slowed it down more to stay in games. But it didn't pay off because they couldn't score."

Beach took top scoring honors with 282 points, though Sterling had a slightly better scoring average of 14.2 points per game (injuries kept Sterling out of nine games). Byrd also averaged double digits at 12.9 points per game. Beach was

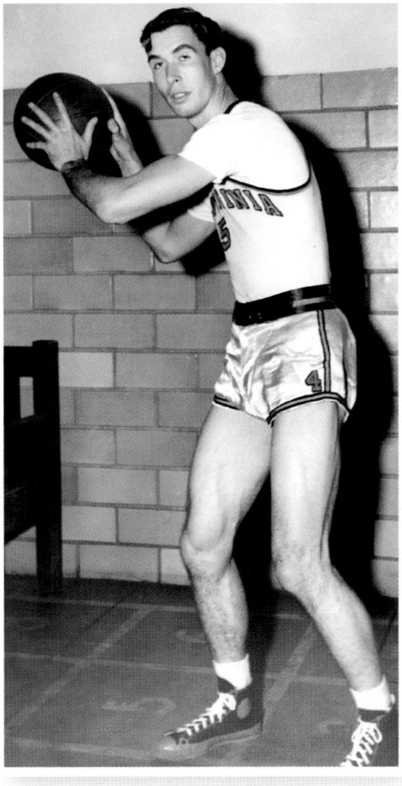

Right Jimmy Walthall lettered two years for West Virginia, helping the Mountaineers to NIT appearances in 1945 for Coach John Brickels and in 1947 for Coach Lee Patton. Walthall was better known for his gridiron exploits as a quarterback where he led West Virginia to a victory over Texas Western in the 1948 Sun Bowl.

WVU SPORTS COMMUNICATIONS PHOTO.

Far right Coach Lee Patton used his New York City connections to land 6-foot-4 center Eddie Beach out of Elizabeth, N.J. Beach started all four years at WVU, compiling a 10.8 scoring average in 90 career games for the Mountaineers. Beach later played professionally in the NBA for the Minneapolis Lakers before being drafted into military service.

WVU SPORTS COMMUNICATIONS PHOTO.

PREMO POWER POLL

In the early 1990s, St. Bonaventure professor Patrick M. Premo conducted an extensive study of college basketball in an attempt to recognize some of the great early teams. Analyzing every season, Premo tried to derive a "strength of schedule" from the results he was able to study. Making his evaluation difficult was the lack of common opponents to more accurately judge each school, as well as the lack of general documentation.

Therefore, some subjectivity was used by Premo to formulate his final yearly rankings leading up to the 1948–49 season when the Associated Press began officially rating teams. The Premo Power Poll was published in Mike Douchant's 1994 *Encyclopedia of College Basketball*.

West Virginia in the Premo Power Poll

- 1941–42, 5th
- 1945–46, 9th
- 1946–47, 13th
- 1947–48, 8th

named to the Helms Foundation All-America third team, and the Mountaineers finished No. 15 in the Helms Foundation final basketball rankings. For the second year in a row, Patton was the beneficiary of some part-time assistance when John Breeden, on leave from his head coaching position at Montana State College, volunteered to help the team. Irvin Howell served in a similar capacity in 1949.

The '49 season was another success with junior Schaus leading the way with a school-record 442 points. He joined Byrd in the 1,000-point club with 1,009 points and in the process, earned third-team All-America honors by the Helms Foundation. It was also the first time a junior college transfer joined the Mountaineer program when 6-foot-3 forward Scotty Perkins came to West Virginia from Williamsburg, Ky. Perkins played one season for West Virginia in 1949, appearing in 12 games and averaging 5.8 points per game. Mountaineer losses that year were to NC State, Bradley, Cincinnati, CCNY, Washington & Jefferson (all away), and to Pitt at home, halting West Virginia's 57-game Field House winning streak.

Pitt's Carlson was once again back to his old tricks in the Panther victory. He let the air out of the basketball, which led to both teams combining to score just 24 points in the first half. Late in the game, West Virginia appeared to have the game won, leading 29–27 with 10 seconds left and the Mountaineers in possession of the ball. But a turnover led to Dodo Canterna's miraculous half-court shot that went in ahead of the buzzer to tie the game at 29. Pitt wound up winning 34–32 in overtime. West Virginia's impressive home winning streak, ironically begun after another close loss to Pitt in 1944, had spanned six seasons and three different coaches.

Transition and Tragedy

The first hint that difficulties were on the horizon in 1950 came before the start of the fall semester when Schaus decided to skip his senior season and give pro ball a try. Schaus had graduated in three years, and the lure of a professional contract was too enticing to turn down.

Graduation also claimed Green, along with key reserves Roy Lester and Bob Miller. Additionally, Beach pulled a tendon in his ankle before the start of the season and missed the opener against D&E. The schedule was much tougher, too. Games against Kansas State, New Mexico, North Carolina, Georgia Tech, CCNY and Cincinnati gave West Virginia its most difficult regular-season slate since 1941. CCNY and Cincinnati were the first WVU opponents ranked by the Associated Press, which began rating teams in 1949. At the time West Virginia played them, CCNY was ranked seventh and Cincinnati, twentieth. The Beavers went on to win both the NCAA and NIT tournaments that season—the only team to accomplish that feat in college basketball history.

Beach, Duff and Sterling had returned, but most of the talk revolved around West Virginia's outstanding sophomore class that included Jim Coalter, Jack Shockey, Dave Steindler, Harry "Moo" Moore and 6-foot-8 center Mark Workman.

Workman had been named the West Virginia amateur athlete of the year in 1948 after breaking the state's scoring record with an average of 32.8 points per game as a senior at Charleston High. His 63 points in the state playoffs against East Bank drew the attention of college recruiters, and the center had more than 30 scholarship offers when he finally made public his choice to attend West Virginia University the summer following his senior season.

Chapel Overflows With Grief-Stricken As Final Tribute Here Is Paid Patton

Funeral Rites Held Today For 'U' Coach Lee Patton

With Workman, 6-foot-5 center Jim Coalter and 6-foot-4 forward Beach, West Virginia was putting its tallest team in school history out on the floor. However, the Mountaineers' height didn't prevent losses to Kansas State, Penn State, Georgia Tech, Niagara, CCNY and Washington & Jefferson that left WVU with a 10–7 record heading into a rematch with Cincinnati in Morgantown. West Virginia lost the game in double overtime to see its record fall to 10–8, but it looked like Patton was finally making some headway. Workman scored 14 points and Coalter added 10 as West Virginia fought its way back in the second half to erase 32–24 halftime deficit.

Patton was expecting additional improvement four days later at Penn State; however, he never made it to the game. While traveling to State College on the Pennsylvania Turnpike, Patton and some players were in publicity director Forrest Crane's car when it was hit head-on by an oncoming vehicle. Riding with Patton and Crane were Steindler, Walt Glenn, and student manager Nicky Cavallaro.

Crane and Patton, sitting in the front seat, were the most seriously injured. Crane suffered fractures to his left leg, left kneecap and left elbow, while Patton had a broken clavicle, seven fractured ribs, a severe laceration over one eye, and an injury to his larynx that impaired his speech.

Both were transported to Timmons Hospital in Bedford, Pa., where Patton remained for two weeks. Following his return to Morgantown and eventual release from the hospital, Patton died unexpectedly at his home from an embolism. His death came as a shock to the entire community.

Junior varsity coach Loren Ward, a graduate student completing his degree in physical education, filled in for the remaining six games. Ward's record of 3–3 included a memorable season-ending victory over Pitt, 59–53, making WVU's final record 13–11.

Lee Patton's five-year mark of 91–26 included back-to-back NIT appearances in 1947 and 1948. Three All-American players came under his guidance, including first-teamer Leland Byrd in 1947. The majority of WVU's 57-game home winning streak also took place during Patton's watch. And because of Patton's outstanding recruiting, a strong junior class awaited Red Brown, named West Virginia's 13th basketball coach in May 1950.

Lee Patton and his wife Agnes outside their home in Morgantown. Patton's death from an embolism, following injuries sustained during an automobile accident while traveling to play a game at Penn State, jolted the Morgantown community.

WVU SPORTS COMMUNICATIONS PHOTO.

NYU

e White 23 75 8 32.4 4
ank Spadafore 10 25 3 33.0 15

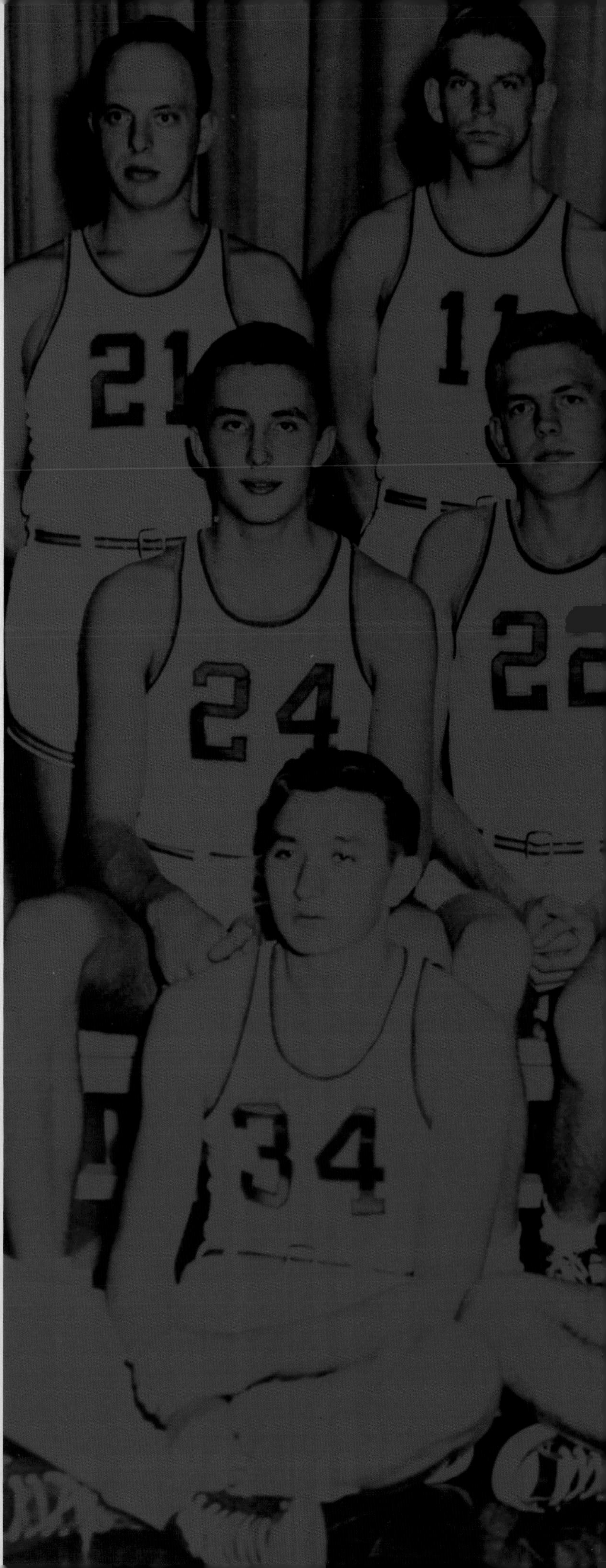
21
11
24
22
34

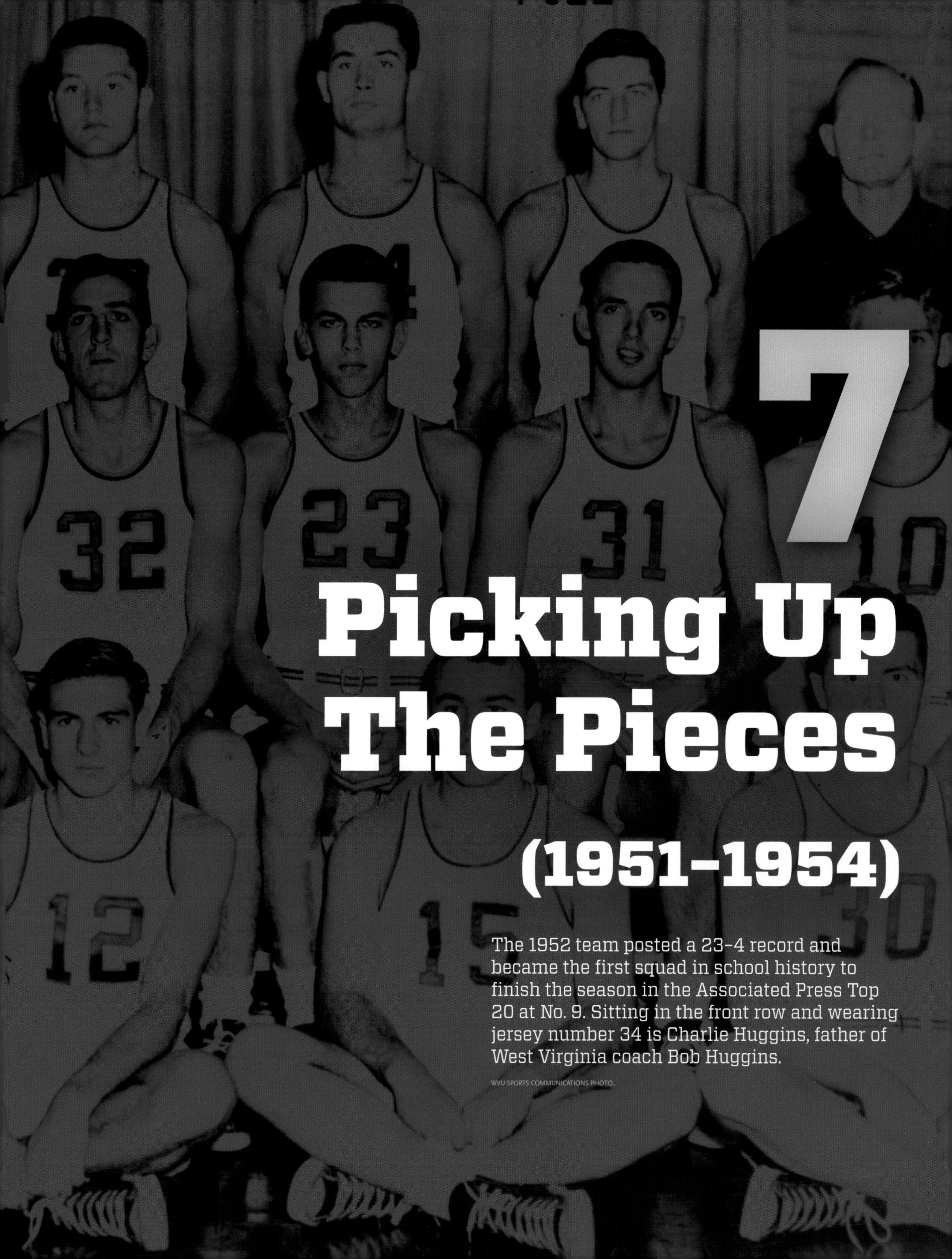

7

Picking Up The Pieces

(1951–1954)

The 1952 team posted a 23–4 record and became the first squad in school history to finish the season in the Associated Press Top 20 at No. 9. Sitting in the front row and wearing jersey number 34 is Charlie Huggins, father of West Virginia coach Bob Huggins.

WVU SPORTS COMMUNICATIONS PHOTO..

Robert "Red" Brown coached the Mountaineers for four seasons from 1951–54, compiling a 72–31 record and earning Southern Conference Coach of the Year in 1952 after leading WVU to a 23–4 record and a No. 9 national rating.

WVU SPORTS COMMUNICATIONS PHOTO.

Throughout the remainder of the 1950 season and on into the spring, the name Red Brown kept popping up whenever the WVU basketball coaching job was discussed. Although Brown hadn't attended West Virginia University, he did have ties to the school. Brown had coached the freshman team at WVU for Lee Patton before assuming the dual role of head basketball coach and athletic director at his alma mater, Davis & Elkins College.

Brown had starred for four years on Scarlet Hurricane basketball teams coached by Cam Henderson, and his high school coaching résumé included stints at Tygarts Valley High School during the 1930s and at Elkins High School in the 1940s. The politically connected and well-liked Brown was officially appointed West Virginia University head basketball coach on April 7, 1950. In addition to his basketball duties, Brown was also hired to coach the tennis team, assist Art Lewis in football, and teach in the School of Physical Education. His official starting date was Sept. 1.

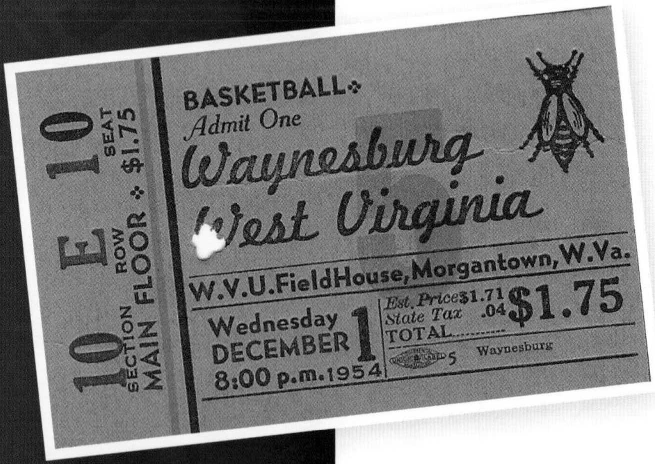

Brown had his own coaching style, different from Patton before him and Fred Schaus afterward. Patton probably emphasized fundamentals a little more than Brown, and Schaus was probably a bit more thorough, but all three were tremendous coaches in their own right.

"Red let us know who we were playing, what their record was and so forth," recalled forward Jim Sottile. "But he didn't go into great detail about officials, players or whatever.

"His practices were tough. We ran hard and we ran long," Sottile said. "Sometimes if we were on a winning streak he wouldn't have real tough practices but if we lost a game, you'd better be prepared for a tough practice. He got the kids in shape and we worked hard and we got the fruits from that."

Brown learned early in his coaching career the value of sportsmanship, honesty and fair play. He rarely said a word to officials during games to the point that his brothers sometimes complained that he was being too easy on the refs and that it was costing his teams on the court. Brown would simply shrug and smile. Personal confrontations were simply not a part of his nature.

When Red arrived in Morgantown, Patton had left him a strong group of players to work with for the 1951 season. As it turned out, Brown would also be leading his new team into a new conference.

Joining the Southern Conference

In the past, West Virginia had failed in its attempts to either join conferences or form new ones. As a consequence, each year scheduling had become increasingly more difficult. Regional rivalries and petty differences shot down a proposed Eastern Collegiate Athletic Conference (ECAC) conglomeration that could have included West Virginia, Penn State, Syracuse, Pitt, Temple, Rutgers, NYU and Fordham in the early 1940s. According to former Sports Information Director Eddie Barrett, WVU and some of its eastern competitors quietly parted ways in the late 1940s when West Virginia counted the football eligibility of five players differently from the others.

Athletic Director Legs Hawley eventually turned to the south and pursued membership in the Southern Conference. An invitation was publicly extended Dec. 9, 1949. The addition of West Virginia, made official on July 1, 1950, gave the Southern Conference 17 schools spanning five states plus the District of Columbia. The opportunity to regularly play schools such as Maryland, South Carolina, Virginia Tech, Duke, North Carolina and Wake Forest was appealing to Hawley—it became much easier for West Virginia to schedule games, and of equal importance for basketball, it gave the Mountaineers a strong conference to compete in. At the time, many believed the new additions made the Southern Conference the strongest basketball league in the country.

Brown's Mountaineers got a taste of Southern Conference action right off the bat with four league games before Christmas. WVU won all four (played at the Field House), topping Virginia Tech (78–67), South Carolina (64–55), Wake Forest (69–63), and George Washington (95–66). The 29-point victory over the Colonials led to West Virginia cracking the AP Top 20 poll for the first time in school history at No. 19.

The team's appearance in the rankings was brief, however. Arizona knocked West Virginia out of the polls a week later with a 68–67 victory at the Field House. Foul trouble doomed the Mountaineers as Mark Workman and Dave Steindler were both disqualified. The game was decided when Workman's backup, Joe Ryan, was called for goaltending on a shot attempted by Arizona's Jack Howell.

Red Brown was the first coach to get West Virginia into the Top 20 when the Mountaineers cracked the Associated Press poll on Dec. 26, 1951.
WVU SPORTS COMMUNICATIONS PHOTO.

Yorkville, Ohio's Ken Alessi was a high school scoring champion who lettered two years for the Mountaineers in 1951 and 1952. Alessi, who stood only 5′7″, had his best season in 1951 when he averaged 10.1 points per game.

WVU SPORTS COMMUNICATIONS PHOTO.

An easy win over Western Reserve was followed by losses in four of WVU's next five games in what turned out to be the toughest stretch of the season. All four losses—Niagara, NYU, Duke and South Carolina—were on the road, and three of the four were by single-digit margins.

Workman broke Fred Schaus's season scoring record against VMI with nine regular season games remaining, and a 94–59 blowout victory over Miami, Ohio was satisfying to WVU fans who had been disappointed that John Brickels had left after coaching the Mountaineers for just one season. Brickels, upset that Brown had kept his starters in the game well after the outcome was decided, afterward expressed to reporters his hope that West Virginia would make a return trip to Oxford, Ohio the following season, much to the amusement of WVU athletic director Legs Hawley.

A strong finish that included back-to-back wins over Pitt gave West Virginia a 17–8 record heading into a Southern Conference tournament first-round game against William & Mary. After a close first half, the Tribe outscored the Mountaineers 54–34 to run away with an 88–67 victory. A makeup game against Penn State four days after the tournament in Morgantown led to the team's 18th victory of the season.

All-Southern Conference center Mark Workman averaged 26.1 points per game to rank third in the country in scoring. It was the first time in school history that a player averaged more than 20 points per game in a season. Five-foot-seven guard Ken Alessi averaged 10.1 points as West Virginia's top outside shooter and Brown's team averaged an entertaining 73.5 points per game.

Controversial Ending

Patton's outstanding freshman class of Coalter, Moore, Shockey, Steindler and Workman were now seniors in 1952. Joining those five was a group of newcomers that included Eddie Becker, Ralph Holmes, Mack Isner, Pete White and Frank Spadafore.

Although it didn't involve West Virginia, a betting scandal nearly brought college basketball to its knees in 1951 when two gamblers were arrested for offering a Manhattan player $1,000 to make sure the Jaspers didn't reach their point spread. Instead of taking the money, the player went to the authorities, and within a few hours, five other gamblers were arrested. The sting eventually uncovered 32 players from seven different colleges who admitted to fixing games from 1947–50. Seven of the 32 players were on the CCNY team that swept the NCAA and NIT championships in 1950. Many of the fixed games took place at Madison Square Garden, and colleges once eager to play in college basketball's most famous arena were now politely turning down invitations. Legs Hawley, though, remained loyal to Ned Irish and the venue that helped launch West Virginia's basketball program, even after Hawley began receiving criticism from the state press for allowing his team to play there.

West Virginia's annual trip to New York City took place Jan. 3, following an impressive 95–74 victory over 19th-ranked Duke that represented the school's first-ever victory against a ranked team. Blue Devil All-American guard Dick Groat scored 26 points, but that was not enough to offset the combined efforts of Workman, Moore, Becker, Sottile and Isner. All five reached double figures.

Center Mark Workman earned All-America honors in 1952 after averaging 23.1 points and 17.5 rebounds per game in leading the Mountaineers to a 23–4 record and a No. 9 national ranking. Workman was the No. 1 overall player selected in the 1952 draft by the Milwaukee Hawks after the Philadelphia Warriors chose Temple's Bill Mlkvy as their territorial pick before the draft. Workman's pro career lasted just 79 games over two seasons.

WVU SPORTS COMMUNICATIONS PHOTO.

With that win, West Virginia took a 6–1 record into New York City where it was facing a very strong NYU team that had won 12 in a row and was ranked sixth in the country.

"There were write ups in the New York City papers wondering whether or not we were going to wear our sneakers—were we going to come up there barefooted?" said Sottile.

Brown threw a new starting five at the Violets—Workman, Sottile, Isner, Holmes and Moore—and WVU jumped out to a quick 13–1 lead. By halftime the lead had swelled to 23 points, and the Mountaineers finished the game with a shocking 100–75 victory. So poorly were the Violets playing that they were left in the ridiculous position of stalling to preserve their Garden scoring record of 103 points. Moore tallied 26 points, Workman scored 24 points and had 19 rebounds, and Sottile finished with 19 points and 10 rebounds. New York writers, cool to the West Virginia players before the game, mobbed them in the dressing room afterward. Their big discovery was Workman, all but forgetting about his two previous subpar performances in the Garden.

Wrote David Eisenberg in the *New York Journal American*: "Workman, the 6′9″ center who flopped in 1950 and 1951 appearances against City College and NYU, more than made up for it last night. Workman played an All-American brand of basketball."

Eddie Barrett said he always played up the small-town persona when he traveled to New York, later often referring to the

Harry "Moo" Moore, the brother of former West Virginia Gov. Arch Moore, scores two of his team-high 26 points in West Virginia's memorable 100–75 victory over sixth-ranked NYU at Madison Square Garden on Jan. 3, 1952. NYU was in the ridiculous position of holding the ball at the end of the game to keep West Virginia from breaking the Madison Square Garden scoring record.

WVU ALUMNI ASSOCIATION PHOTO.

Mountaineers in press releases as "country slickers."

"The New York papers would always make mention of the fact that for several of our players it was the first time that they had ever ridden the subway," Barrett recalled. "We always got some ink out of that."

Two days later in Buffalo, Workman poured in 36 points to help West Virginia defeat Niagara 74–71, and Workman reached celebrity status as the Mountaineers went from unranked to No. 11 in the polls. WVU moved up to ninth following a 30-point victory over Waynesburg and remained near the top 10 for the rest of the season. The only low point was the loss of Sottile for the season after he broke his collarbone in the Bethany win.

"I guess maybe the guy was out to get me," Sottile recalled. "It was a long pass and I was running down court. The pass was coming to me and he ran his shoulder right in my shoulder and he broke my collarbone in four different places. I was in the hospital for six weeks recovering from that."

Despite the loss of Sottile, West Virginia managed a 15–1 record in Southern Conference play and was the top seed heading into the conference championships in Raleigh, N.C.

The West Virginia players, coaches and administrative staff pose for a photo outside their Capital Airlines charter airplane that took the team to the 1952 Southern Conference tournament in Raleigh, N.C.

WVU SPORTS COMMUNICATIONS PHOTO.

The day before the tournament began, the AP All-America team was announced and West Virginia's Mark Workman made the first

Red Holmes drives to the basket to score two of his 11 points during West Virginia's 67–64 loss to 13th-ranked Duke at the Field House on Dec. 19, 1953. Pictured underneath the basket wearing jersey number 33 for the Mountaineers is Eddie Becker.

WVU SPORTS COMMUNICATIONS PHOTO.

five, along with Duke's Dick Groat. Those two were expected to meet again in the Southern Conference tournament semifinals. After WVU got past William & Mary and Duke outlasted Maryland, the marquee match-up was realized.

An overflow crowd of serious basketball fans packed Reynolds Coliseum to watch the two best players in the Southern Conference battle it out to reach the finals. The game turned out to be a classic, with Duke winning on a controversial last-second shot by Dick Johnson, who scored all of 4 points. The Mountaineers were preoccupied with Groat, who burned the nets for 31 points, while WVU's Becker nearly matched Groat's total with 29 points.

Princeton's Jim Coalter was West Virginia's team captain for the 1952 season. Standing 6′5″ and weighing only 170 pounds, Coalter was involved in the controversial ending to the 1952 Southern Conference tournament semifinal game against Duke in Raleigh, N.C., when he was slung to the ground as the Blue Devils scored the winning basket.

WVU SPORTS COMMUNICATIONS PHOTO.

Unfortunately for West Virginia, the outcome was marred by a blown call made by referee Arnold Heft. Late in the game, with the score tied at 88, a scuffle occurred underneath Duke's basket involving West Virginia's Jim Coalter and three Blue Devil players. Coalter was thrown to the floor during the melee, enabling Johnson to get off a shot that appeared to come after the buzzer.

Confusion ensued. Once it was concluded that Duke's goal was going to stand, Brown defused the situation by first shaking the hand of Heft,

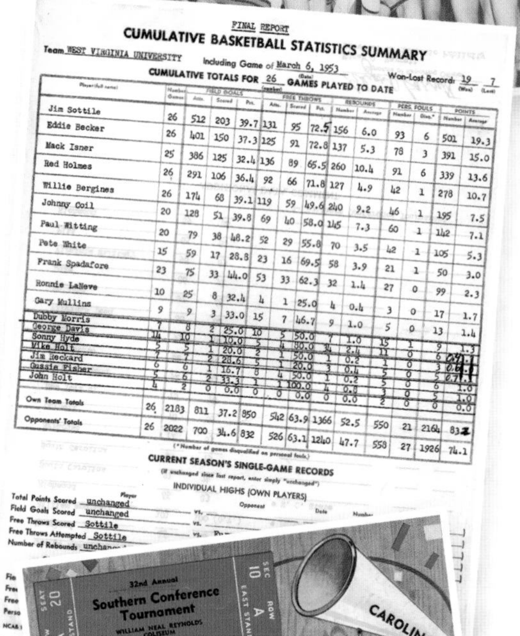
FINAL REPORT
CUMULATIVE BASKETBALL STATISTICS SUMMARY

Team WEST VIRGINIA UNIVERSITY Including Game of March 6, 1953

CUMULATIVE TOTALS FOR 26 GAMES PLAYED TO DATE Won-Lost Record: 19 (Won) 7 (Lost)

Player (full name)	Number Games	Field Goals Atts.	Field Goals Scored	Field Goals Pct.	Free Throws Atts.	Free Throws Scored	Free Throws Pct.	Rebounds Number	Rebounds Average	Pers. Fouls Number	Pers. Fouls Disq.*	Points Number	Points Average
Jim Sottile	26	512	203	39.7	131	95	72.5	156	6.0	93	6	501	19.3
Eddie Becker	26	401	150	37.3	125	91	72.8	137	5.3	78	3	391	15.0
Mack Isner	25	386	125	32.4	136	89	65.5	260	10.4	91	6	339	13.6
Red Holmes	26	291	106	36.4	92	66	71.8	127	4.9	42	1	278	10.7
Willie Bergines	26	174	68	39.1	119	59	49.6	240	9.2	46	1	195	7.5
Johnny Coil	20	128	51	39.8	69	40	58.0	145	7.3	60	1	142	7.1
Paul Witting	20	79	38	48.2	52	29	55.8	70	3.5	42	1	105	5.3
Pete White	15	59	17	28.8	23	16	69.5	58	3.9	21	1	50	3.0
Frank Spadafore	23	75	33	44.0	53	33	62.3	32	1.4	27	0	99	2.3
Ronnie LaNeve	10	25	8	32.4	4	1	25.0	4	0.4	3	0	17	1.7
Gary Mullins	9	9	3	33.0	15	7	46.7	9	1.0	5	0	13	1.4
Dubby Morris	7	8	2	25.0	10	5	50.0	7	1.0	15	1	9	1.3
George Davis	14	10	1	10.0	5	4	80.0	34	2.4	11	0	6	0.4
Sonny Hyde	5	5	1	20.0	2	1	50.0	1	0.2	1	0	3	0.6
Mike Holt	7	7	2	28.6	5	1	20.0	3	0.4	5	0	5	0.7
Jim Heckard	6	6	1	16.7	8	4	50.0	1	0.2	5	0	6	1.0
Gussie Fisher	5	6	2	33.3	1	1	100.0	4	0.8	3	0	5	1.0
John Holt	4	2	0	0.0	0	0	0.0	0	0.0	2	0	0	0.0
Own Team Totals	26	2183	811	37.2	850	542	63.9	1366	52.5	550	21	2164	83.2
Opponents' Totals	26	2022	700	34.6	832	526	63.1	1240	47.7	558	27	1926	74.1

(*Number of games disqualified on personal fouls.)

CURRENT SEASON'S SINGLE-GAME RECORDS
(If unchanged since last report, enter simply "unchanged")
INDIVIDUAL HIGHS (OWN PLAYERS)

Total Points Scored unchanged vs.
Field Goals Scored unchanged vs.
Free Throws Scored Sottile vs.
Free Throws Attempted Sottile vs.
Number of Rebounds unchanged

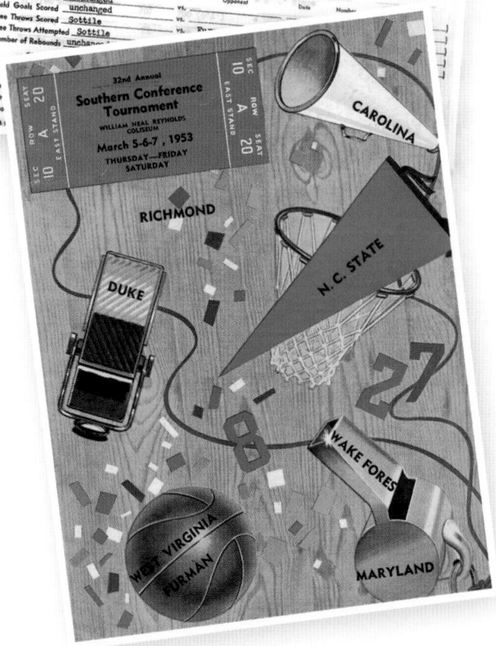

and then congratulating the Blue Devil players. Brown was universally praised by sportswriters attending the tournament for his good sportsmanship.

Duke may have moved on to the championship game, but it was Red Brown and his West Virginia players who gained newfound respect and admiration for the way they handled themselves after such a difficult loss.

"It's too bad that such a game as that had to end on a sour note," Brown said afterward. "It's too bad it couldn't have gone into overtime. But Heft still is the top man on my official's list. He can work any game for me any time."

"I just love that guy," said veteran *Richmond News Leader* sports editor Chauncey Durden of Brown after the game.

Heft was overheard the following morning in the Sir Walter Raleigh Hotel admitting that he had blown the call. "He said I must have blown it because everyone tells me I did," Mickey Furfari said. "To this day, whenever I see Dick Groat I remind him of that call."

One of the school's best-ever teams saw its season end prematurely by someone else's doing. Still, Brown was voted Southern Conference Coach of the Year by the league's sportswriters.

Workman once again led the team in scoring with an average of 23.1 points per game, while also averaging 17.5 rebounds per game. Moore (12.8 ppg) and Becker (11.4 ppg) also averaged double figures.

"I thought we had an outstanding team in the sense that we moved the ball around real well," Sottile said. "We had three guys that could score that year."

Workman was drafted in the first round by the Milwaukee Hawks, but his pro career flamed out after just two seasons. He was the first WVU player to score more than 50 points in a game, and four times during his career he scored more than 40.

Despite standing 6-foot-9, Workman scored many of his points from the outside, especially from the corners where he perfected an accurate set shot. Yet a large number of WVU fans harbored unrealistic expectations of Workman, thinking he should play more like DePaul's George Mikan underneath the basket. That simply wasn't Workman's style.

"In my opinion I didn't think he was aggressive enough," Sottile said. "If he was more aggressive he would have scored even more points and would have gotten more credit."

Workman shot nearly 50 percent for his career and averaged almost 18 rebounds per game during his senior year in 1952. His 1,553 points still rank among the 15-best career scoring performances in school history.

"Our advice was to feed the big boy," Sottile said. "Off of rebounds Moo [Moore] or I were feeding him, but we still got our points."

It was said that later in life Workman often was reluctant to talk about his basketball career—particularly his two-year stint in the pros. That is unfortunate. Mark Workman remains one of the school's all-time basketball greats and was posthumously inducted into the West Virginia University Sports Hall of Fame in 1994.

Without Workman in 1953, Sottile took up the scoring slack, leading the Mountaineers to a fine 19–7 record. Sottile averaged 19.3 points and 6.0 rebounds per game and scored a career-high 33 points in an 82–72 win over Penn State in the Field House, avenging a pair of losses to the Nittany Lions in 1952. For his outstanding play, Sottile was voted to the all-Southern Conference first team.

West Virginia had been lucky to uncover Sottile, who was originally from Bristol, Pa. When he finished high school, Sottile was looking to play basketball at a major school, and he knew about the Mountaineers from their performances at Madison Square Garden in the NIT.

"I was traveling to various schools looking for a scholarship and I happened to stop off at West Virginia," Sottile said. "I went big time. I looked at North Carolina. I stopped off at Kentucky and North Carolina State. Tennessee was interested also. I thought I might be going to Tennessee but I was impressed with the terrain of WVU. I really enjoyed the mountains and the scenery."

Victories were also recorded in 1953 against South Carolina, Syracuse, Virginia Tech and Pitt. A 91–87 triumph over Furman in the opening round of the Southern Conference tournament was followed by an 85–80 loss to No. 12 North Carolina State in the semis. It was the last year for NC State, North Carolina, Duke, Wake Forest, South Carolina and Maryland in the Southern Conference. Those schools broke off to form the Atlantic Coast Conference (ACC), which began play in 1954.

West Virginia badly wanted to be a part of the new conference, but there was little support for a school that was as geographically isolated as WVU was at the time. The interstate highway system in the Mountain State was still two decades away, and teams dreaded navigating the difficult West Virginia mountains to get to Morgantown. Also, air travel in the early 1950s was not yet cost-effective for teams. Not getting into the ACC was a major disappointment for the usually persuasive Legs Hawley.

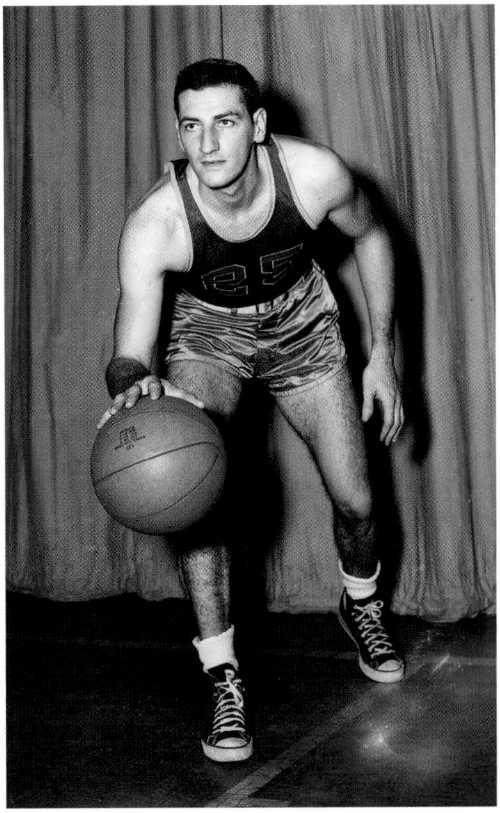

Bristol, Pa. forward Jim Sottile led the Mountaineers in scoring in 1953 with an average of 19.3 points per game to earn first-team all-Southern Conference honors that year. Sottile scored 812 points in 64 games for a career average of 12.7 points per game.

WVU SPORTS COMMUNICATIONS PHOTO.

Babysitting Hot Rod

A large portion of Brown's fourth season in 1954 was spent taking care of hot-shot freshman guard Rod Hundley. Brown rescued Hundley from NC State when the school couldn't admit him and several others after it was discovered that Coach Everett Case had illegally worked them out while they were still in high school.

"The first time I was ever on an airplane was out of Charleston to go down to North Carolina State," Hundley recalled in 2010. "I was in high school and they brought me down there to work as a lifeguard and I couldn't even swim. They gave all of these guys jobs and it was like the United Nations the way they were running guys in and out of there, giving them scholarships."

Hundley was clearly the best high school player in West Virginia, and he was also one of the top recruits in the country. But he had a very unusual background, having been abandoned as a child and growing up with different families in

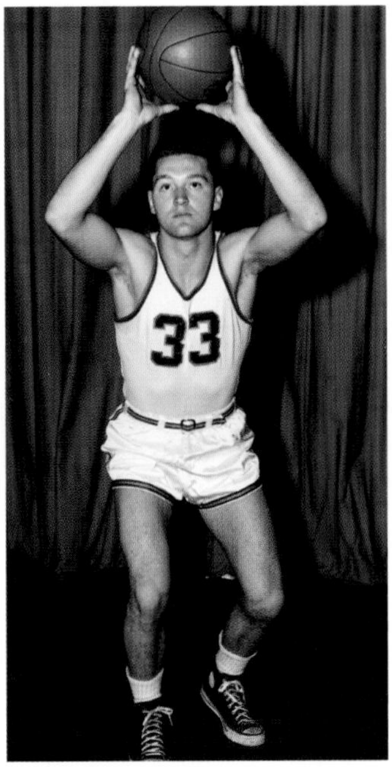

Wheeling's Eddie Becker's two best games came in losing efforts—33 points against St. John's in 1954 and 29 points against Duke in 1952.

WVU SPORTS COMMUNICATIONS PHOTO.

A meeting of three college greats: West Virginia's Hot Rod Hundley and Mark Workman have a conversation with Furman's Frank Selvy, who became the only NCAA Division I player to ever score 100 points in a game when he hit the century mark against Newberry College on Feb. 15, 1954.

WVU SPORTS COMMUNICATIONS PHOTO.

Charleston. Basketball was a means for Hundley to escape his unfortunate circumstances, and his rise in popularity was further accentuated by his amiable nature and his propensity to clown during basketball games.

When Hundley arrived at WVU, he immediately overshadowed the varsity players. The guard scored 50 points in his first freshman game, and he later scored 63 in another. In a matter of a few weeks, Hundley had completely taken over the campus.

Shinnston's Frank Spadafore drives to the hoop for a layup in a game against George Washington at the Field House on March 5, 1954. Spadafore scored 7 points but ninth-ranked GW, behind 40 points from Joe Holup, defeated the Mountaineers 83–74.

WVU SPORTS COMMUNICATIONS PHOTO.

Clayce Kishbaugh, an outstanding player himself and a member of the '54 freshman team with Hundley, recalled how Rod could control games. "When we were freshmen and we were playing West Virginia Wesleyan in Clarksburg—my hometown—the first half I had about 16 points," remembered Kishbaugh. "Rod and I were playing the guard positions and he was handling the ball and setting people up.

"So we come in at halftime and Rod said, 'That's it Clayce, you're done.' I wondered to myself, what does he mean? Well, I scored 2 points in the second half and that's how he controlled a basketball game. He wouldn't pass me the ball."

"Rodney was Rodney," added Sottile. "He was a piece of work. He was a nut. When you come down to it, he relied a lot on his players to do all of the defensive work and give him the ball and shoot it."

There were games when Hundley was scoring so much that he simply quit shooting out of boredom. It was then that Hundley began pulling out the tricks that he had used so successfully during high school games to liven things up. He began to bounce the ball between his legs and whip it around his back. He could fake passes by rolling the ball up his long arms and then stopping it just before it left his fingers. He learned to bounce the ball off his knees. Once an opposing player got his feet tangled up trying to guard Hundley, and he fell to the ground. An amused Hundley put the ball underneath one arm and used his free hand to help the player back to his feet while the fans roared. The more applause Hundley received, the bolder his antics became.

"They would always start stomping their feet and clapping their hands and they would get louder and louder," Hundley said. "They wanted to see the show."

Soon Rod Hundley became "Hot Rod" Hundley (coined by *Fairmont Times* sports editor Bill Evans), and the freshman team was drawing bigger crowds than the varsity. Brown spent as much time making sure his big-shot freshman was making it to class as he did worrying about the varsity team.

The varsity team's record dipped to 12–11 in 1954 and the season ended in the second round

of the Southern Conference tournament with an 83–74 loss to ninth-ranked George Washington. Wheeling's Eddie Becker led the team in scoring with an average of 18.7 points per game.

The same day West Virginia's season ended, Legs Hawley, 53, was rushed to a Pittsburgh hospital with an angina attack. He died fifteen days later. Hawley had been athletic director for 15 years, and his predecessor, Harry Stansbury, ran the department for 21 years prior to that.

Red Brown, having previous athletic director's experience at Davis & Elkins College and knowing the lay of the land, was the obvious choice to replace Hawley.

Brown said he would run a WVU athletic program based on "honesty and integrity." He said winning would not come at all costs. "Our recruiting program has been—and will continue to be—carried out in an ethical and wholesome manner," Brown said, pointing out the solid footing the program had enjoyed under Stansbury and Hawley.

"They eliminated a lot of the problems I would have had to face," Brown said of the two men who had held the position for a combined 36 years.

Most, perhaps, but not all of them. There was still one big problem left to resolve—Brown had to find his replacement.

The Field House became a popular venue for Mountaineer basketball fans. West Virginia averaged at least 5,000 fans per game for five out of six years from 1948–53, including an average of 5,919 fans per game for the 1952 season.

WVU SPORTS COMMUNICATIONS PHOTO.

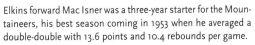

Elkins forward Mac Isner was a three-year starter for the Mountaineers, his best season coming in 1953 when he averaged a double-double with 13.6 points and 10.4 rebounds per game.

WVU SPORTS COMMUNICATIONS PHOTO.

WEST
44
VIRGINIA

WEST
VIRGINIA

TECH
41

WEST
12
VIRGINIA

8

A Golden Era

(1955–1960)

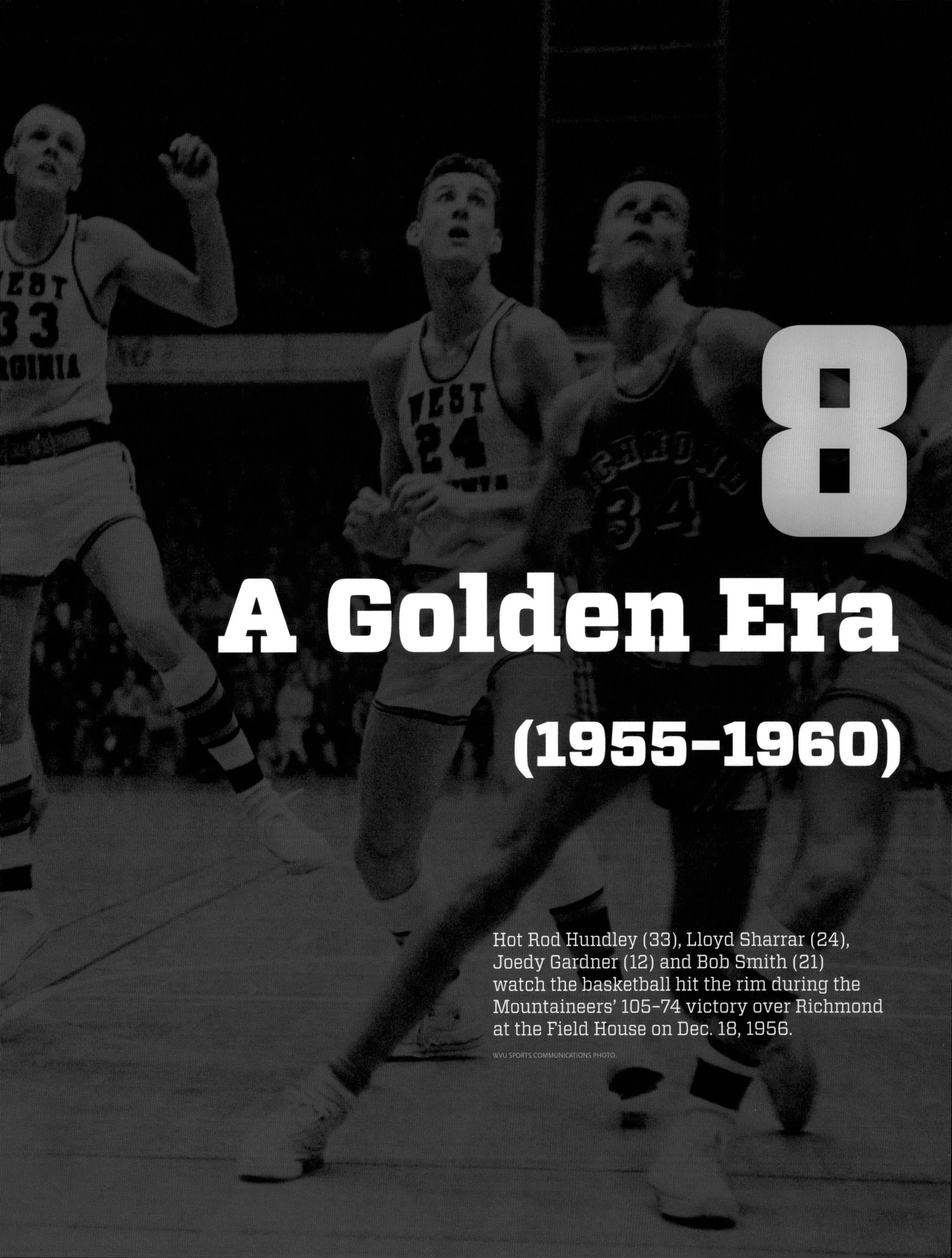

Hot Rod Hundley (33), Lloyd Sharrar (24), Joedy Gardner (12) and Bob Smith (21) watch the basketball hit the rim during the Mountaineers' 105–74 victory over Richmond at the Field House on Dec. 18, 1956.

WVU SPORTS COMMUNICATIONS PHOTO.

Fred Schaus had always wanted to be a basketball coach. As a player at West Virginia University, and later, in the pros, Schaus used to keep a notebook full of plays that he had diagrammed.

Schaus spent five years in the NBA with the Fort Wayne Pistons and the New York Knicks, making the NBA all-star team in 1951 and helping his teams reach the playoffs each year. On occasion, Schaus would return to West Virginia to help Red Brown with summer clinics, and Brown soon grew impressed with his knowledge and maturity. When Legs Hawley died and Brown was elevated to the athletic director's post, Brown zeroed in on Schaus to take his place as coach.

Fred Schaus sitting in his office at the Field House.
WVU SPORTS COMMUNICATIONS PHOTO.

"I had to hire a new basketball coach to coach Rod. It had to be someone special," Brown told author Bill Libby in Hundley's 1970 biography *Clown*. "The fact is Fred Schaus got the job, which led to his getting to become coach and then general manager of the pro Lakers, because I thought he'd be a good coach for Rod. That was the deciding factor."

Asked in 2005 about his hiring, Schaus doesn't remember Hundley's name even coming up during his conversations with Brown when the two met in Pittsburgh to talk about the West Virginia job. "I don't recall having specific discussions about Rod and I'm honest when I say that," Schaus said. "I had been traded to the Knicks and I finished that season with them [1954]. I had plans to go ahead and continue to play another year or two and then Legs Hawley died very suddenly and they hired Red Brown as athletic director. Then, Red turned around and hired me."

Brown first offered Schaus $5,500 and wound up getting him for $6,500. Schaus said he would have taken the WVU job for nothing, and he joked that had Brown known that, he would have gladly arranged it.

The hiring of Schaus did not come without some concern; some thought he was too young and inexperienced for the job. Brown addressed that during a meeting with the Charleston Rotary Club right after he hired Schaus.

"I have heard some criticism about hiring a man who has never had any coaching experience," Brown said. "But I feel that six years of pro basketball is experience enough. Also, I know we have picked an excellent man in Schaus, who was a great player, a great competitor, and above all, a fine gentleman."

More than anything, Schaus, a large, impressive-looking man with hands the size of a first-baseman's mitt, made a great first impression.

"I was one of the first guys to meet Fred when he came on campus," remembered Al Babcock. "I was in the ticket office and this guy was walking up and he asked, 'Where is the athletic director's office?' I walked him across the [stadium] bridge to the director's office.

Hot Rod Hundley was the first nationally known player in school history and the No. 1 player selected in the 1957 NBA draft by the Minneapolis Lakers.

WVU SPORTS COMMUNICATIONS PHOTO.

"He was such an imposing person," Babcock added. "When you shook hands with that guy, you knew you shook hands with somebody. When he had something to say, everybody listened."

"We all had incredible respect for him having been a pro player and a former West Virginia player," recalled Pete White. "He was a very genuine and sincere person. You played hard and you gave it the best that you had for him."

A Major Crisis

The 29-year-old rookie coach had a major crisis to deal with right off the bat: Hundley didn't show up to school for the fall term. Instead of returning to campus for his sophomore season, Rod had decided to turn pro. Hundley had left school before, once to enroll at Morris Harvey College before changing his mind and another time to see a girl he was dating in Ohio, but this time it appeared he was gone for good.

"We talked for five hours about the situation but I could not persuade him to remain at West Virginia," said a heartbroken Red Brown. "He passed 14 hours of C work in summer school to restore his eligibility and then suddenly decided to withdraw. He said he simply did not care to go to school."

When Hundley found out that it wasn't possible to play for an NBA team because he was still an underclassman, former Mountaineer All-American Mark Workman helped arrange Hundley a tryout with the Philadelphia Spas, a team that toured the country with the Harlem Globetrotters. During practice, Hundley badly injured his knee and needed surgery. Team owner Eddie Gottlieb called Fred Schaus and explained Hundley's situation and told him Hot Rod wanted to return to school. West Virginia University paid for the operation, and Hundley worked hard to get his knee ready for the season opener against Waynesburg.

Hundley had previously injured his other knee when he had—of all things—chased a girl around a swimming pool. His knees proved to be a constant problem for him throughout his college and professional careers.

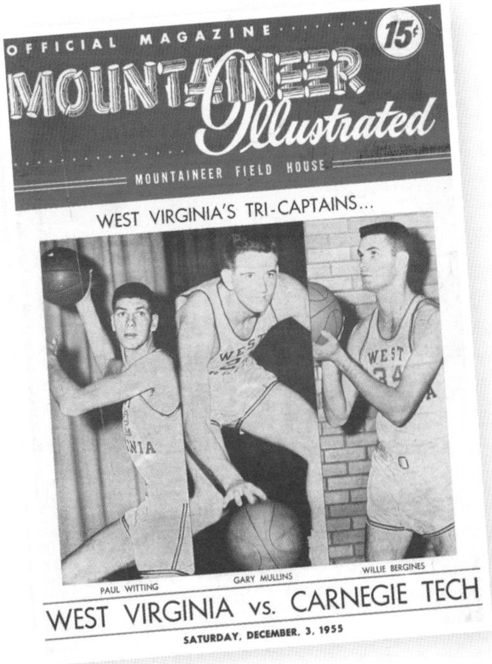

With the Hundley situation being so fluid, Schaus had his hands full before he even coached his first game. "It was a helluva way to start my coaching career," Schaus laughed.

Schaus brought a pro system with him to Morgantown, utilizing a free-wheeling, freelance style that gave his players a lot of individual freedom. He wanted his teams to fast break at every opportunity.

Schaus didn't plan to play Hundley against Waynesburg in the opener, intending instead to have him rest an extra two weeks before starting Southern Conference play. However, the fans began chanting for Hundley, and Schaus relented. Hot Rod wound up scoring only 4 points in his abbreviated season debut, but Frank Spadafore and Paul Witting took care of things, scoring 24 and 19 points respectively.

Above Coach Fred Schaus watches the action from the bench. Sitting to the right of Schaus is freshman coach Quentin Barnette and next to Barnette is popular WVU trainer A. C. "Whitey" Gwynne.

WVU SPORTS COMMUNICATIONS PHOTO.

Right Beckley's Willie Bergines was the team's top rebounder in 1955, pulling down an average of 11.9 boards per game. Bergines grabbed 1,205 rebounds during his three-year playing career.

WVU SPORTS COMMUNICATIONS PHOTO.

Hundley again came off the bench against Carnegie Tech and scored 17 points in the Mountaineers' 68–60 victory.

Having already heard a lot about Hundley, a handful of Pittsburgh sportswriters made their way over to Tech's Skibo gym to get a firsthand look at this basketball curiosity. One of them happened to be an aspiring young *Pittsburgh Post-Gazette* reporter named Myron Cope. "Hot Rod came up from Morgantown Saturday night with the West Virginia basketball team to show the hicks here why he is the nearest thing to Slim Summerville to hit show biz," wrote Cope. Near the end of his story, the reporter admitted that it was the first time he could ever recall a player acknowledging applause—but that was Hot Rod!

By the third game of the year against Washington & Lee, Hundley was in the lineup for good, scoring 31 points in a 96–86 West Virginia victory. Hundley contributed 20 points in a tough, 72–66 upset win against Richmond at the Field House and then dribbled the remaining time off the clock. As the clock ran down, he threw the ball high into the air, timing it perfectly so that when the ball landed on the floor the remaining seconds had ticked off the clock.

"Rod used excellent judgment not to overdo any antic and everything seemed to work out for him when he was doing something like that," Schaus said. "It worked out and I always felt that he was good for college basketball at that point in time."

Even though he usually had to explain away something Hundley had done, Schaus really enjoyed his antics because he had always enjoyed showmanship. It was Schaus who introduced the gold and blue carpet the team runs out on during introductions, thus beginning a long-standing tradition at WVU.

It was also Schaus who had the team warm up with a special gold and blue basketball, and it was Schaus who copied the knee-high socks popularized by North Carolina. Not only did those high socks look good, but they also helped the players identify each other when they were running down on the floor. "You didn't have to look up when you were running the fast break because you could see those socks," recalled Ronnie Retton.

Schaus paid attention to appearances, as well. West Virginia players wore jerseys with buttons in the crotch so they always remained neatly tucked into their pants. Schaus also made his players shave their armpit hair. Some of them mistakenly thought it was for hygienic purposes but the real reason was because Schaus wanted his players to look neat and clean for everyone—he realized that young ladies bought basketball tickets, too.

Sometimes the players got into the act. Hundley got the great idea of dyeing his hair blonde before a game and talked Clayce Kishbaugh into doing the same. "I didn't know they did it until they came out on the floor and those are the kind of days when you wondered why in the hell you were in coaching," Schaus laughed.

With Hundley's clowning, Schaus's impeccable style and the team's exciting brand of basketball, a ticket to the Field House was one of the hardest things to get in the Mountain State.

Right after Christmas, Hundley scored 24 points in the opening round of the Birmingham Classic against No. 17 Wake Forest, but it was Pete White's 27 points, offsetting Wake Forest's Dick Hemric's 43, that really made the difference in a game the Mountaineers won 86–82. Despite losing 96–82 to Alabama in the championship game, West Virginia made it into the national rankings at No. 12. Hundley played poorly in a 13-point loss to Duke in the first game of the

Hot Rod Hundley points to the basket right before he makes a layup against Carnegie Tech in a game at the Field House on Jan. 8, 1955. Hundley scored 35 points against the Tartans, but the Mountaineers lost the game 70–69.

WVU SPORTS COMMUNICATIONS PHOTO.

Coach Fred Schaus and longtime equipment manager Carl Roberts show off the team's flashy new warm-up jackets with the Mountaineer mascot looking on.

WVU SPORTS COMMUNICATIONS PHOTO.

Dixie Classic in Raleigh, but bounced back with a season-high 47 points in a 96–94 loss to Wake Forest.

Putting a Cork in Corky

After back-to-back losses to Carnegie Tech and Westminster put West Virginia's record at 7–6, the Mountaineers won four straight games. Four more losses followed against Richmond, Penn State, Duke, and again to the Penn State team, which was coming off a Final Four appearance in 1954. West Virginia ended the losing streak with an 11-point victory against William & Mary, followed by another tough, seven-point win at Pitt. The key game of the season came at the Field House on Feb. 19, 1955, against No. 5-rated George Washington and its All-American guard Corky Devlin.

Clayce Kishbaugh, inserted into the starting lineup after the Penn State loss, drew the assignment of guarding Devlin. Kishbaugh recalled Schaus calling him into his office earlier in the week to explain exactly how he wanted him to play Devlin.

"He said, 'Clayce I want you to get up in his face and take him out of the game,'" Kishbaugh said. Kishbaugh did exactly what his coach told him to do, but it wound up being Kishbaugh

LET'S ROLL OUT THE CARPET!

Fred Schaus had always enjoyed showmanship. The coach introduced one of college basketball's great traditions in 1955 when the team began running out onto a gold and blue carpet during player introductions. The idea was passed along to Schaus by WVU fan and supporter Alex Mumford who was the director of marketing for the Wunda Weve Carpet Co. in Greenville, S.C.

"I tried to do this and I tried to do that and the carpet was one of those things," Schaus recalled. "We were trying to sell tickets and if something extra could develop with the carpet, that would certainly fit into that mold."

West Virginia University continued this tradition during the George King years before it was discontinued in the late 1960s. Former WVU player Gale Catlett revived the great tradition when he returned to West Virginia in 1978, and it has since become a highlight attraction of pregame introductions at the WVU Coliseum.

Willie Akers leads his teammates out on West Virginia's "magic carpet" for pregame warm-ups.

WEST VIRGINIA AND REGIONAL HISTORY COLLECTION.

who was taken out of the game—on a stretcher.

"Devlin caught Clayce in the throat with an elbow and they had to haul him off the court," Pete White laughed. "He was out."

Like Hundley, Kishbaugh was an interesting character in his own right. He was an all-state player at Clarksburg's Roosevelt-Wilson High and became interested in Indiana when Hoosier coach Branch McCracken discovered him playing in a high school all-star game. However, his mother wouldn't let him go all the way to Bloomington to attend college.

"I told my mother my decision and she said, 'No you're not! You are going to West Virginia!' So I went to West Virginia," Kishbaugh said.

In a moment of excitement, Clayce would sometimes get confused and refer to Penn State as the "Nittany Panthers." He once ordered apple pie a la mode and then asked the waitress if she could also add a little ice cream on top of it. Another time, as the team's charter had finished circling the airport and was in the process of landing, Clayce turned to one of his teammates and asked how long he thought it would be until they arrived.

"Clayce was my man," said Hundley. "I'll tell you what, he was a helluva player."

With Kishbaugh out of commission, Hot Rod was West Virginia's only chance of upsetting George Washington.

Hundley outscored Devlin 39–29, though it took him 42 shots to get those 39 points. Spadafore added 15, and White had a 14-point, 13-rebound double-double to lead the Mountaineers to their first-ever victory against a top 5-ranked team.

A 23-point victory over Rutgers ended the regular season and gave the Mountaineers momentum heading into the Southern Conference tournament. "I remember we played Rutgers at home and Schaus pulled me out and asked, 'What's going on? What's happening?' Hundley was going for the Field House record and he took the first 12 shots of the game," White said. "[Schaus] said, 'What is this, a damned shooting gallery?' It had to be tough for Fred because Rod was almost uncontrollable."

Clayce Kishbaugh attempts a hook shot during West Virginia's 107–93 victory over Pitt on Feb. 23, 1957, at the Field House. Kishbaugh scored 21 points and grabbed six rebounds for the Mountaineers in the game.

WVU SPORTS COMMUNICATIONS PHOTO.

In the first round of the Southern Conference tournament, West Virginia used 27 points from Hundley to get by William & Mary, and Hundley matched that total in a 15-point victory over Washington & Lee one night later in the semifinals.

In the finals, West Virginia met GW for the second time that season, and once again, Devlin was wearing out West Virginia. Out of ideas, Schaus asked Hundley if he could try guarding Devlin, although Hundley wasn't exactly known for his defense, focusing more on his scoring and clowning. In fact, Hundley's defensive shortcomings were the part of his game most often pointed out by his critics.

But Hot Rod rose to the challenge and put a cork in Corky, holding Devlin to one second-half field goal while scoring 30 himself. Hundley also hit a couple of late clutch baskets, and West Virginia upset the Colonials, 58–48, in overtime.

"Schaus had different guys on him and I said, 'Let me have him.' I didn't even let him touch the ball," Hundley recalled. "I face-guarded him wherever he went. I really frustrated him and he couldn't do anything.

"For many years Fred always brought that game up. He said, 'You stopped Corky Devlin.' I never played a lot of defense in college, but I played it when I had to."

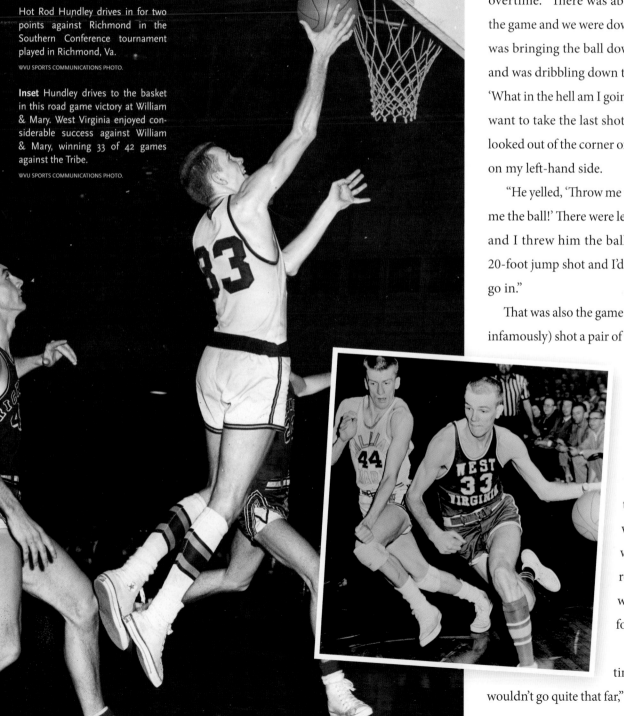

Hot Rod Hundley drives in for two points against Richmond in the Southern Conference tournament played in Richmond, Va.

WVU SPORTS COMMUNICATIONS PHOTO.

Inset Hundley drives to the basket in this road game victory at William & Mary. West Virginia enjoyed considerable success against William & Mary, winning 33 of 42 games against the Tribe.

WVU SPORTS COMMUNICATIONS PHOTO.

Kishbaugh remembered setting up Hundley for the tying shot to send the GW game into overtime. "There was about 20 seconds left in the game and we were down two points and GW was bringing the ball down and I stole the ball and was dribbling down the floor. I'm thinking, 'What in the hell am I going to do because I don't want to take the last shot?'" Kishbaugh said. "I looked out of the corner of my eye and I saw Rod on my left-hand side.

"He yelled, 'Throw me the ball, Clayce. Throw me the ball!' There were less than 10 seconds left and I threw him the ball and he shot about a 20-foot jump shot and I'd be damned if it didn't go in."

That was also the game Hundley famously (or infamously) shot a pair of free throws behind his back when he needed just one point to set the tournament scoring record. Asked by reporters afterward why he shot the free throws the way he did with the scoring record within reach, Hundley replied: "If I make 'em, what do I have to shoot for next year?"

"Oh sure there were times when I wished he wouldn't go quite that far," Schaus laughed. "One time he was leading the cheers after I had taken him out of the ballgame . . . 'We want Hundley! We want Hundley!' But it was fun and Rod was fun to be with and I enjoyed coaching him here."

"What [Schaus] always said was, 'I don't care what you do when we're 20 points ahead. You can kick the ball up into the stands if you want. Just make sure we're 20 points ahead when you do it," Hundley said. "I said, 'No problem, Coach.'"

With the victory over George Washington, West Virginia had claimed its first Southern Conference championship. Hundley drew laughter afterward during the post-game awards ceremony when he went up to receive his MVP award and kissed a very surprised Ethel Smith, a local beauty queen asked to present the awards.

"She didn't know what to think," Hundley chuckled.

An all-night car ride home from Richmond through a snowstorm left just one day for the Mountaineers to prepare for third-ranked and defending national champion LaSalle in the

Hot Rod Hundley became just the fourth player in college basketball history to score more than 2,000 points for his career. Hundley held the school scoring record for only two years before Jerry West came along to break it.

WVU SPORTS COMMUNICATIONS PHOTO.

NCAA East Regional in New York City.

LaSalle coach Ken Loeffler had been in the stands scouting the WVU-GW game and he wasn't the least bit amused with Hundley's antics. "Hundley handles the ball like a magician but he kids around too much to suit me," remarked Loeffler to a reporter after the game. "That doesn't mean he isn't an excellent player. He is. I just don't like guys who shoot fouls from behind their back in a final playoff game."

Right Hot Rod Hundley kisses a very surprised Ethel Smith as he accepts the most valuable player award at the 1955 Southern Conference tournament.

WVU SPORTS COMMUNICATIONS PHOTO.

Below Hundley goes into his act at the Field House against Pitt. Hundley and Coach Fred Schaus worked out an agreement that Hundley could only do his clowning when the Mountaineers had a 20-point lead.

WVU SPORTS COMMUNICATIONS PHOTO.

West Virginia's lack of preparation may have mattered. Then again, it probably didn't. LaSalle, behind All-American Tom Gola, ran West Virginia right out of the gym. The Explorers outscored West Virginia 55–28 in the second half to win easily 95–61.

White wrapped up a fine college career by scoring 19 points going head-to-head against Gola. "I had one of my better games against LaSalle and that may have been one of the reasons I was drafted by the St. Louis Hawks," White recalled.

LaSalle held Hundley to one point in the second half when Loeffler decided to take him out of the game. "I had 15 points in the first half and we were right there with them," Hundley recalled. "I got one point in the second half. They switched to a box and one. I couldn't even get the ball."

LaSalle returned to the NCAA finals before falling to San Francisco and Bill Russell in the championship game.

West Virginia finished the season ranked 19th in the country (the Associated Press did not poll its voters after the NCAA tournament). The Mountaineers won 19 games and lost 10. Hundley averaged 23.7 points, scoring more than 30 points 10 times. It was a great start for first-year coach Schaus and his star sophomore Hundley, and there was a lot more to come.

The Mayor of the Mountainlair

By 1956, Hot Rod Hundley was a bona fide star. The school publicity department put a color photograph of him on the cover of its press guide, and two full pages were devoted to his sophomore season's accomplishments.

Above 1955 Southern Conference Champs.
WVU SPORTS COMMUNICATIONS PHOTO.

Right Clendenin's Pete White averaged 15.8 points and 12 rebounds per game as a senior to lead West Virginia to its first-ever Southern Conference championship and NCAA tournament appearance in 1955.
WVU SPORTS COMMUNICATIONS PHOTO.

Hundley added a few more paragraphs to his biography during his junior year when he led West Virginia to victories over Florida State, Columbia and Miami in the Orange Bowl Classic. Hot Rod didn't play particularly well in the first game against Florida State, scoring only 7 points, but he did recover to score 23 against Columbia and 17 against Miami in the championship game.

Hundley went on to have another outstanding season, leading West Virginia to a 21–9 overall record, including a 10–2 mark in Southern Conference play. A home victory over Virginia Tech on Feb. 11, 1956, set in motion West Virginia's Southern Conference record-setting winning streak that spanned 56 games over five seasons.

Hundley was also performing a little better in the classroom . . . or at least he was going more frequently.

"We had been down to William & Mary and I missed class," Hundley recalled. "Our instructor called out roll and you had to stand up, and there were about 200 kids in the lecture hall.

"So I stood up and he said, 'I see you guys played down at William & Mary last night. How many points did you score?' I said 28. He looked into the newspaper and he said, 'You're right.' Then he called the next person's name and I just sat down quietly."

The Mountaineers swept the Southern Conference tournament with victories over David-

Above The Ashland Oil Company issued trading cards for colleges in Kentucky and West Virginia in 1955, including the Mountaineer team pictured here..
FROM THE DAVID TUCKWILLER COLLECTION.

son, Furman and Richmond to claim its second consecutive league title.

Hundley sank the winning basket with 43 seconds left to defeat the Spiders. He managed to score 26 points despite Richmond coach Les Hooker's desire to play a slow-down game.

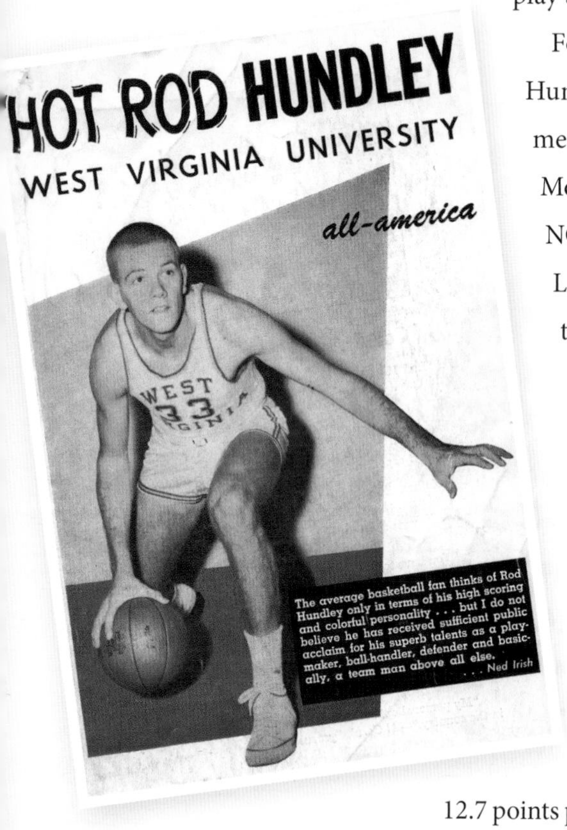

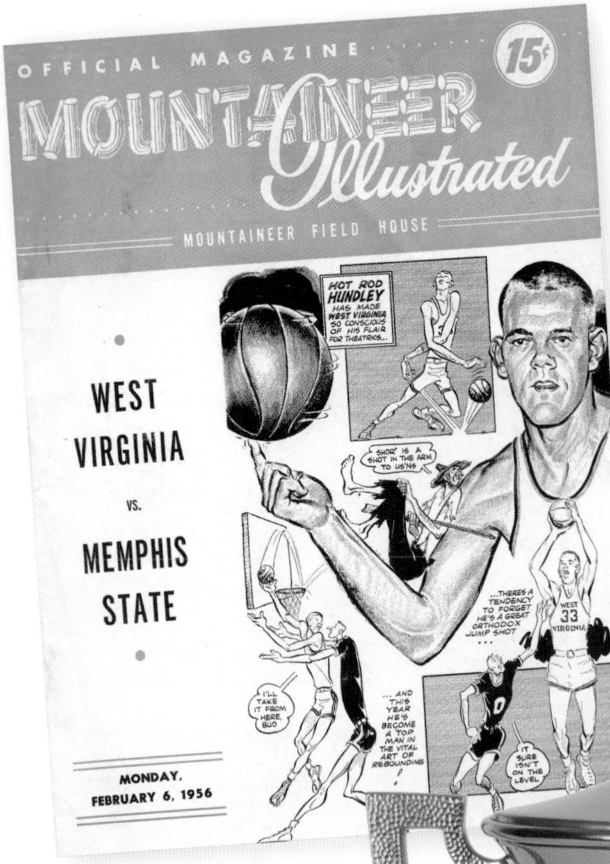

For the second straight year, Hundley was named the tournament's Most Valuable Player. The Mountaineers made it back to the NCAA tournament, but unlike the LaSalle loss the previous year, this time West Virginia fell to an inferior team, losing by two points to Dartmouth in overtime.

Hundley averaged 26.7 points per game for the year to rank seventh in the nation. In only two seasons, Hot Rod had already surpassed Mark Workman's career scoring record. Kishbaugh also had a solid year, averaging 12.7 points per game, and 6-foot-6 senior Willie Bergines wrapped up his fine career by averaging 9.6 points and 11.6 rebounds per game. For the second straight year, WVU finished the season in the national rankings at No. 20 in the AP poll.

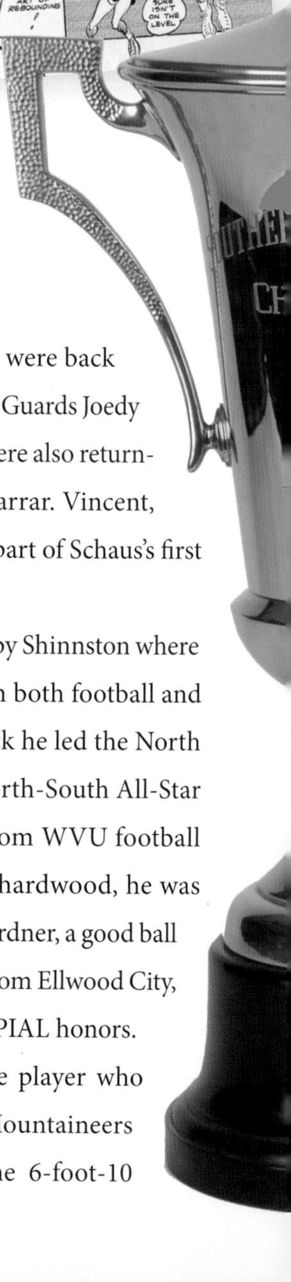

Hundley and Kishbaugh were back for their senior years in 1957. Guards Joedy Gardner and Don Vincent were also returning, as was center Lloyd Sharrar. Vincent, Gardner and Sharrar were part of Schaus's first recruiting class in 1954.

This time Hot Rod Hundley plays it straight. Hundley was known to try hook shots and behind-the-back free throw attempts from time to time when the games were already in the bag.

WVU SPORTS COMMUNICATIONS PHOTO.

Vincent came from nearby Shinnston where he was an all-state player in both football and basketball. As a quarterback he led the North team to a victory in the North-South All-Star Game (drawing interest from WVU football coach Art Lewis). On the hardwood, he was known as a clutch player. Gardner, a good ball handler and defender, was from Ellwood City, Pa., where he earned all-WPIAL honors.

Sharrar was a self-made player who provided something the Mountaineers sorely needed—height. The 6-foot-10

Sharrar was discovered by Schaus while he was playing at Meadville High School in northwestern Pennsylvania. Although gangly and raw, Sharrar had many suitors, including a couple of Big Ten schools.

"I had narrowed my choice down to two Big Ten schools, when Fred came by my home one day," Sharrar was quoted in a 1958 *Sports Illustrated* interview. "We sat around the living room and talked with my folks. I liked him right off and changed my mind about West Virginia."

Schaus took Sharrar under his wing and began to work with him on a right-handed hook shot. Schaus also taught Sharrar an assortment of fakes and moves that he had learned while playing in the pros. Sharrar showed gradual, steady improvement, averaging 9.6 points and 11.6 rebounds as a sophomore in 1956 and 16.1 points and 14.8 rebounds during his junior season in '57.

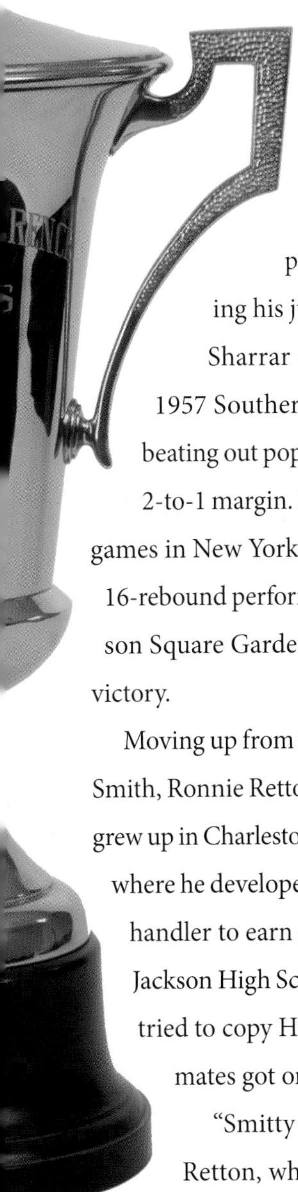

Sharrar was voted the MVP of the 1957 Southern Conference tournament, beating out popular teammate Hundley by a 2-to-1 margin. He also played well in the big games in New York City, producing a 26-point, 16-rebound performance against NYU at Madison Square Garden in an 83–77 Mountaineer victory.

Moving up from the freshman team were Bob Smith, Ronnie Retton and Bucky Bolyard. Smith grew up in Charleston idolizing Hot Rod Hundley, where he developed into a fine shooter and ball handler to earn all-state honors at Stonewall Jackson High School. For a while, Smith even tried to copy Hundley's act before his teammates got on him about it.

"Smitty was a little wild," laughed Retton, who later became the father of famous Olympic gold medalist Mary Lou Retton. "The rest of us pretty much stayed under control."

Retton was discovered by Schaus while playing baseball at tiny Fairview High School, about a 45-minute drive south of Morgantown. "I was really recruited by baseball coach Steve Harrick, but Coach Schaus came to Fairview and watched me play," Retton recalled. "He knew I had a baseball scholarship and he asked me to come out for the basketball team, so I guess I was considered a walk-on."

Bolyard was a tremendous all-around athlete from tiny Aurora, W.Va., located up in the mountains of Preston County. A childhood accident claimed the vision in his left eye, but that didn't stop him from averaging more than 30 points per game as a senior. Like Retton, Bolyard was also an outstanding baseball player.

"Bucky Bolyard was probably the greatest athlete that played on our team," recalled Smith. "Nobody could beat him in anything."

Don Vincent, pictured here making a layup against Pitt at the Field House in 1957, suffered a broken leg in the semifinals of the 1958 Southern Conference tournament against Richmond that proved damaging to West Virginia's NCAA tournament aspirations.

WVU SPORTS COMMUNICATIONS PHOTO.

The starting five for West Virginia's No. 1-ranked team in the country in 1958 from left to right: Don Vincent, Joedy Gardner, Lloyd Sharrar, Jerry West and Bob Smith.

WVU SPORTS COMMUNICATIONS PHOTO.

"That guy was the most remarkable person I ever saw with one eye," said Ronnie Retton. "He could do anything. He could shoot pool, play ping-pong; [Coach] Art Lewis wanted him to come out for the football team his senior year and he could have made a helluva a halfback, but Schaus wouldn't let him do it."

Bolyard lived on Fifth Avenue candy bars and Pepsi. When he wanted a nutritious meal he would buy a bag of peanuts and push them down into the neck of his soda pop bottle. "They once gave Bucky a test for sugar and he passed it with flying colors," former WVU sports information director Eddie Barrett joked.

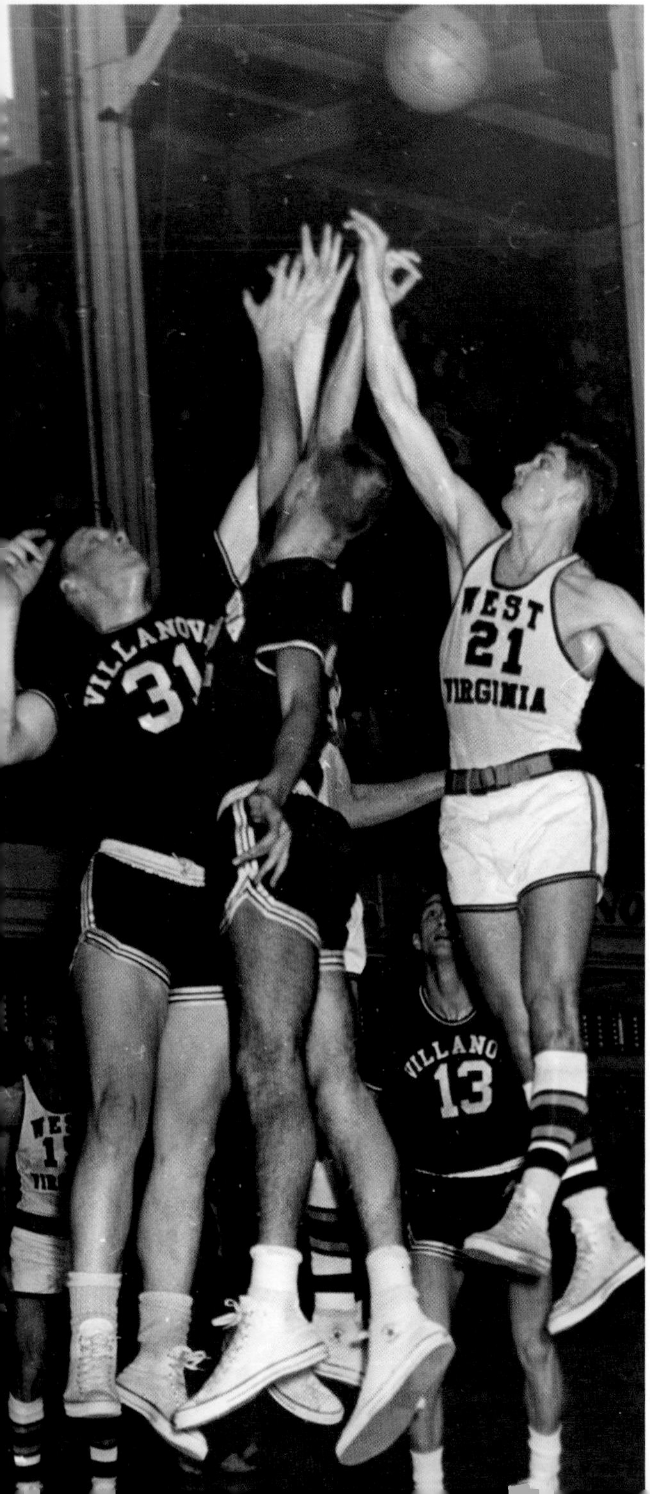

Meanwhile, playing for the freshmen that year were the two top prospects in the state—6-foot-5 forward Willie Akers and a skinny, unsure 6-foot-3 forward named Jerry West.

Akers and West were both hotly pursued by other schools, and some even considered Akers a better college prospect than West. "Willie Akers was very high on anybody's recruiting list," said Schaus.

"We all went to Boys State—all of the players that were first-team all-state as juniors," Akers remembered. "We were all there in camp and my buddy from Mullens told me that there was a good player here named West. I read in the papers that he had scored some points but he did not make all-state. He was just honorable mention.

"Well, we go out and start playing and he is the best player there by far. I recognized how good he was right off the bat and we became friends there."

West, who grew up along Cabin Creek just south of Charleston, used to practice on a court next to a steep slope and whenever he missed a shot the ball would roll all the way down the hill. Tired of chasing the ball, West came up with a simple solution to his predicament: he decided to quit missing. "There was a lot of improvising and I guess it was the love of the game," West said.

Right West Virginia's tallest player, 6-foot-10 Lloyd Sharrar, and West Virginia's smallest player, 5-foot-7 Ronnie Retton, ham it up.

WVU SPORTS COMMUNICATIONS PHOTO.

Left Bob Smith battles for one of his 11 rebounds in this 1957 game against Villanova at the Field House, which the Mountaineers won 92–70. Smith was one of five Mountaineer players to score double figures in the game.

WVU SPORTS COMMUNICATIONS PHOTO.

"When you are in little towns there was a lot more of a chance that you were going to be by yourself a lot and basketball is one of the few games other

than golf that you can practice almost every skill that is important [to the game]."

Despite growing up a Mountaineer basketball fan playing at East Bank High School, West had also developed a fondness for the University of Maryland. However, the Terrapins' style of play ultimately eliminated them from consideration.

"In that point in time when I was being recruited for college Maryland played a very slow-down game and I kind of liked that school a little bit. But I couldn't go there and play that way. It just didn't look like it would have been fun for me to play like that," West said.

Schaus's professional experience also proved very appealing to West. "The fact that he had a professional background . . . I just felt it was a better learning experience for me even though I had no aspirations that I would be a professional player," West said.

"I think the fact that I played in the NBA always helped," added Schaus. "I know it helped me at Purdue. They knew I coached the Lakers and had been vice president and general manager of the Lakers. It at least got the attention of some pretty good athletes, and I was able to recruit quite well because of that."

When West came to school he was extremely introverted and the players tried hard to make him feel welcomed. Sometimes their efforts to engage him backfired. As a freshman Jerry had already reached celebrity status, his exploits well known in the newspapers and on the radio throughout the state. However, he wasn't comfortable with the adulation and would sometimes try and disappear to avoid the embarrassment of having to sign autographs. After one freshman game Bucky Bolyard and Bob Smith decided to put a sign on Jerry's back that read "I'm Jerry West." Once the kids saw the sign they mobbed him.

"When Jerry found out what we did, he tore that sign off the back of his shirt and went back into the locker room mad," recalled Bob Smith. "Well, Fred finds out what we did and he takes us back into his office and he starts yelling at us, 'What are you guys doing? Why are you getting him so mad like that?'"

"I remember Fred talking to us, minus Jerry, and he would say, 'Listen guys, you've been riding Jerry pretty hard and maybe you should ease up a little bit because you're starting to get to him,'" Bob Clousson recalled.

"Jerry was real timid when he first came here," added Ronnie Retton. "You could hardly get a

Above West Virginia players considered Marvin "Bucky" Bolyard to be the best all-around athlete on the team. A childhood accident left him blind in one eye, but that didn't keep him from averaging 10.1 points per game as a senior on the 1959 team that advanced to the national championship game against Cal.

WVU SPORTS COMMUNICATIONS PHOTO.

Above left Mullens forward Willie Akers started 66 games for West Virginia, scoring 669 points and pulling down 573 rebounds for his career. Akers, a top high school prospect, sacrificed his scoring for the betterment of the team. He later became a successful high school coach in West Virginia.

WVU SPORTS COMMUNICATIONS PHOTO.

word out of him. It took a while but he came around. We were all so ornery and did a lot of things together and finally he snapped out of it and wasn't as quiet as he used to be."

Helping with Jerry's adjustment to WVU were the Dinardi sisters Ann and Erlinda, who lived in a small white house along Beechurst Avenue near the Field House. Ann was a West Virginia University graduate and a prominent pharmacist in Morgantown for nearly five decades and Erlinda worked at Chico's Dairy. The Dinardis first opened their home to Hundley for his senior year in 1957 before taking in West, Willie Akers and Joe Posch in the summer of 1958. In addition to cooking them fabulous Italian meals, Ann was particularly good at dragging the players out of bed and making sure they made their morning classes. Dinardi continued to house WVU athletes well into the 1960s. (Decades later, after Ann's death in 2003, West made a $100,000 contribution to West Virginia University to endow a basketball scholarship in Ann Dinardi's name.)

A lot of people on campus thought the freshmen with West and Akers were better than the varsity, which began the season ranked 13th in the country.

That was the year the Soviet Union launched Sputnik, causing near hysteria in the United States, but in the Southern Conference, it was still Hot Rod Hundley doing most of the long-distance bombing. Hundley scored a school-record 54 points against Furman on Jan. 5, 1957, breaking Mark Workman's school standard of 50 points scored against Salem College on Jan. 27,

All-American Jerry West pictured here with Coach Fred Schaus and assistant George King. West said many years later that playing for two ex-professionals was very appealing to him as a young player.

WVU SPORTS COMMUNICATIONS PHOTO.

1951. Hundley made 22 of 48 field goals and had enough energy left to pull down 18 rebounds. Many times during his career he attempted more shots than he scored points, and Hundley is actually the only player among the school's all-time top 10 scorers to finish his career with more shots (2,218) than points (2,180). Who knows how many of those shots were attempted behind his back or off the top of his head?

"Rod really couldn't shoot that well," teammate Jim Ritchie said. "He just shot a lot. If he took 25 shots and made 10, he had 20 points."

Rod poured in 32 points in a win against Pitt, and scored 34 to help WVU defeat Villanova 92–70. West Virginia's 11-game winning streak finally ended at Penn State (80–65), so the Mountaineers started another one by beating Pitt 107–93 at the Field House. Hundley scored 39 against the Panthers and added 27 more in his final home game on Feb. 25, 1957 against William & Mary. Nearly 7,000 spectators packed the gym to see him perform for the last time at the Field House.

The first time Hundley faced William & Mary his sophomore year in 1955, he missed a layup, and instead of running down to play defense, he sat down on William & Mary's bench to take a rest. William & Mary coach Bodyson Baird was beside himself.

"He said, 'Get off the bench!' I said, 'I'm tired, let me rest.' He yelled for the ref to get me off the bench," Hundley quipped. "I said, 'Show me in the rule book where it says I can't sit here.' There was no such rule because nobody would have thought to do anything like that.

"Then, about that time we got the rebound and I said, 'OK I'm gone.' They passed me the ball and I wound up getting a layup."

Late in the game, Hundley had an opportunity to recreate the T-formation they had first tried during a freshman game four years prior. Kishbaugh was the center, Bill King was the motion man, Sharrar was the end, running down the field to catch the pass and, of course, Hundley was the quarterback.

"I centered the ball to Rod, he bounced the ball back like a quarterback, and threw the ball to Lloyd Sharrar going down the court," Kishbaugh recalled. "He caught it and went up and made the basket!"

At the end of the game, when Hundley was taken out, he walked over to Baird to shake his hand. Hundley also shook hands with Schaus and the rest of his teammates before walking toward the locker room. Not a single person in the Field House was sitting down.

Jerry West averaged 24.8 points and 13.3 rebounds per game in 93 career games for West Virginia from 1958–60. The Mountaineers posted an 81–12 record during West's three varsity seasons.

WVU SPORTS COMMUNICATIONS PHOTO.

But there was still work to be done. Now ranked 11th in the country, WVU breezed through the Southern Conference tournament, easily winning all three games. Hundley scored 24 points in the championship game against Washington & Lee, and Sharrar added 16 points and 23 rebounds.

West Virginia was off to New York City to play in the NCAA East Regional against 20–5 Canisius. The Golden Griffins beat No. 17 Alabama that year, and also claimed victories over Villanova, Louisville, Minnesota, Notre Dame and Manhattan. Canisius was a good team, but as was the case with Dartmouth in 1956, it was not the caliber of West Virginia.

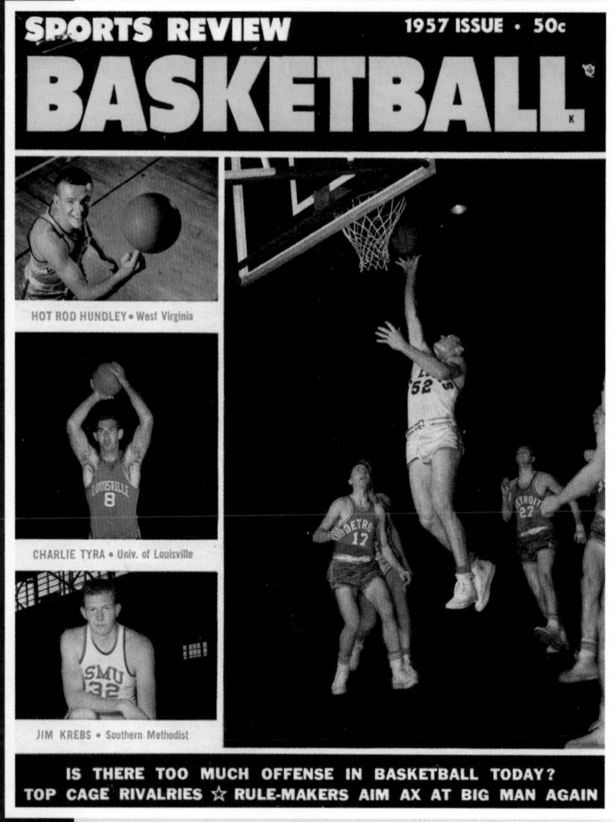

Hundley, pictured here spinning a basketball for the college basketball magazine, *Sports Review*. It was the first time a WVU athlete had ever appeared on the cover of a national magazine.

WVU SPORTS COMMUNICATIONS PHOTO.

Hundley made just 4 of 20 shots, and the Mountaineers converted only 29.4 percent of their field goal attempts for the game. West Virginia was out of it by halftime, eventually losing 64–56.

Just like that, Hot Rod Hundley's brilliant college career was over.

He finished as the school's single-season (798 points) and career (2,180 points) scoring leader, becoming only the fourth player in NCAA history to score 2,000 career points. Six times Hundley scored more than 40 points in a game, including the school-record 54 he scored against Furman. His scoring average of 24.5 points per game was also a school best at the time. Hundley was a consensus All-American selection in 1957, nearly sweeping All-America teams presented that year by the Helms Foundation, Converse, Associated Press, United Press International and *Look* magazine. Only the NEA service made Hundley a second-team pick. West Virginia won the Southern Conference tournament all three years Hundley played on the varsity team, but the Mountaineers could never get past the first round of the NCAA tournament. Naturally, that was one of Hundley's biggest disappointments. However, Hot Rod packed the Field House like no player before him or since. WVU averaged 6,427 fans for its 11 home dates in 1957— the first time in school history the Mountaineers had ever averaged more than 6,000 per game.

"Jerry West was the best basketball player that ever came out of West Virginia, but even today Rod Hundley is still the most popular player in West Virginia," said Kishbaugh.

"When Hundley was there, he was the whole kit and caboodle," said player Bob Clousson. "Everyone else was in the shadows. Clayce Kishbaugh was a great player, but he was there at the wrong time."

"The best thing that ever happened to me was when I came back to West Virginia instead of staying at NC State," said Hundley. "At North Carolina State, we were all about the same players and at West Virginia I was above everybody. It worked out great for me. The things that have happened to me have been wonderful."

The Mountaineers finished seventh in the AP poll and eleventh in the UPI poll in 1957. Meanwhile, the pros were very interested in Hundley. New Minneapolis Lakers owner Bob Short was desperate for a gate attraction and he was talked into trading center Clyde Lovellette for the rights to the No. 1 draft pick for 1957. The Lakers used their newly acquired selection to draft the one college player who they felt was certain to bring fans to the turnstiles: Hot Rod Hundley.

Hundley's pro career never matched the great success he had in college. Hundley once said of his six seasons with the Lakers that he slept all day, partied all night and fit basketball games in between. He was once fined a league record

$1,000 for missing a team flight back to Minneapolis. Years later when he became a successful broadcaster, Hundley was once asked to comment on No. 1 pick Ralph Sampson. His answer? "He's the most overrated player since me."

That's Hot Rod!

To the Top of the Polls

While No. 1 draft pick Hundley was busy barnstorming the state with a group of college "all-star" players he recruited in an effort to make a few extra bucks before reporting to the Lakers, Jerry West was preparing for his first varsity season at West Virginia. Normally when a program loses two players of Hundley and Kishbaugh's caliber, optimism is somewhat tempered. But that was hardly the case at West Virginia with guys like West and Akers moving up from the freshman team. Schaus had once arranged a varsity-freshman game pitting West against Hundley, and Akers is adamant that the freshmen would have won the game if not for some poor calls made by the officials.

"We had them beat and the officials took it from us because they didn't want the varsity to get beat," Akers recalled, his disappointment still evident. "We had a three- or four-point lead and they called a couple of fouls. They thought it through— there was no doubt about that. They didn't want the freshmen beating the varsity."

Mountaineer Sports Network basketball radio analyst Jay Jacobs also vividly remembered playing in that freshman-varsity game. "There were close to 5,000 people in there. We had them beat and they wound up beating us by two," Jacobs said. "You could see the new era just starting to come and the people were very, very excited."

Players know players, and Hundley knew what he was going up against in practice everyday with the freshman West.

"When he was a freshman I could see him coming," Hundley said. "I would have to hurry and hustle to beat him. I could score on him but he was quick. He'd make you rush things or he'd knock down a pass and he had such quick hands."

Hot Rod with all of his press clippings.

WVU SPORTS COMMUNICATIONS PHOTO.

Kishbaugh observed West playing at the 1956 state high school tournament in Morgantown and he saw a very good player, but not the player whose likeness would eventually be made into the NBA logo as one of the game's all-time great players.

"You could tell he was going to be a pretty good ballplayer but I never figured he would be one of the greats of all-time," Kishbaugh said. "Nobody thought that at the time."

"It's like your sister being a beauty queen, but

Lloyd Sharrar averaged 16.1 points and 14.8 rebounds per game to earn first team all-Southern Conference honors in 1957.

WVU SPORTS COMMUNICATIONS PHOTO.

you not recognizing her because she's your sister," Ritchie said. "A lot of Jerry's strengths in college were overlooked. He was the entire package."

Ritchie also thought Schaus helped bring out the best in West. "[Schaus] got your attention," Ritchie said. "Afraid? No. Compliant? Yes. He was intimidating. He was a big man and he had somewhat of a temper. You did what he said and things turned out well when you did what he said."

"I remember the pre-game discussions after our team meal," added Bob Clousson. "Fred would go into such great detail about the referees. He would tell us how they were going to call games."

Jim Sottile worked for Schaus as a graduate assistant coach in charge of scouting, and he thought Schaus's teams were extremely well prepared. "He sent me to different places to scout teams and he was very gracious when I got back so I could explain it to the team," Sottile said. "From those scouting reports he made adjustments. If you were talking about guarding assignments, he would always have the right defensive man on the other team's best offensive man."

This is a rare color photograph of Willie Akers, Coach Fred Schaus and Jerry West. Akers and West developed a friendship while attending Boys State at Jackson's Mill and afterward decided to choose the same college.
WVU SPORTS COMMUNICATIONS PHOTO.

West had time to grow as a player because Schaus had assembled a pretty good supporting cast around him. After two years on the varsity, Vincent and Gardner had become reliable guards. Sharrar was a two-year starter at center, and Bob Smith was developing into a flashy player at forward who was at his best in the open court on the fast break.

"Your great baseball players, your great football players and your great basketball players . . . everybody can recognize great talent," Schaus explained. "The ones that were difficult were the ones that you have to kind of take and you hope that they develop. You are looking at them as 17-, 18-year-old kids and you are thinking when he gets to college, he is going to get a lot stronger and that makes a heck of a difference. The role players are the ones that are difficult to judge and recruit—or even try to recruit."

Schaus knew how to build good basketball teams and he knew how to get the most out of the players that he persuaded to come to West Virginia University. He logged mile after mile in his 1957 Chevrolet driving the winding West Virginia roads searching for talent. Most of the players he recruited to WVU came from West Virginia, with an occasional foray into Ohio and Pennsylvania. Bolyard was a typical Schaus discovery.

Tucked deep in the mountains in the northeast corner of the state, Aurora had a population of 150 when Bolyard starred in high school. The closest train station was 10 miles away.

"The gym in Aurora is so small," Schaus once explained to *Richmond Times-Dispatch* writer Shelley Rolfe. "Six inches. That's all the distance there is from the court's out-of-bounds line to the wall of the gym. Why, a player can't even take the ball out of bounds."

Schaus had similar experiences recruiting West, Akers and WVU's other key players of the late 1950s, most of them growing up in small towns and villages of fewer than 1,000.

"The kids in the small towns, they begin playing when they're this high," Schaus said, his hand hovering right around his waist. "Sometimes it looks as if they've cut a piece out of a mountain to get a spot level enough to put up a basket. They may only have one basket, but that's enough to get a game going."

Virginia Tech coach Chuck Noe used to covet West Virginia players, and he was one of the few coaches able to come into the state and steal some of the good ones away from Schaus.

"He used to look at the box scores of the high school games in Virginia and see the scores in the '40s and '50s," recalled Eddie Barrett. "Then he would look at the scores of the games in West Virginia and see the scores in the '70s and '80s. He said, 'I'm going to West Virginia and get me some of those players.'"

"We played the Kentucky all-star team and they were supposed to have the best players in America," West said. "As it turned out we had the better players. We played them twice and beat them twice. It was a very high caliber group of guys that we had in West Virginia at the time."

It wasn't until after Schaus had been at West Virginia for a few years that he began to journey outside the immediate area to land players such as Jim Ritchie from Drexel Hill, Pa., and Joe Posch from Riverside, N.J.

"Fred's brother lived in a community next to mine in Springfield," Ritchie said. "I guess he read the papers and that was the connection. I had scholarships to all the city schools, plus NC State, Michigan State—a whole bunch of them. But for some reason Hot Rod Hundley was my attraction here."

Schaus's brother also discovered Posch. "I didn't know a thing about the school—nothing," Posch explained. "To tell you the truth, I wasn't going to go. I was going to go to the service. I told Schaus I wasn't coming and then at the last minute I changed my mind and went down there."

As Schaus began to prepare for the 1958 season, he was coy about who he planned to start in the fifth spot in the lineup for the season opener against VMI—West or Akers—and he didn't announce that it would be West until a few days before the game. West's college debut was an effective if not spectacular 9 points and 13 rebounds, but West Virginia won easily with Gardner scoring 22 and Vincent adding 15.

West scored a combined 24 points in West Virginia's next two wins against Furman and Penn State. He added 29 more in victories against William & Mary and Washington & Lee—good, steady efforts. Yet Schaus was looking for more from his sophomore and he considered sitting him down in an effort to develop his bench.

That notion didn't last very long. Schaus quick-

Coach Fred Schaus diagrams a play as All-American Jerry West looks on.

WVU SPORTS COMMUNICATIONS PHOTO.

ly changed his mind after West's game-high 28 points led West Virginia to a 76–74 overtime victory over 19th-ranked Richmond on Dec. 17, 1957. West tied the game with 12 seconds left and he scored seven of the Mountaineers' nine points in overtime, including the game winner.

The Richmond victory gave the No. 8-rated Mountaineers a 6–0 record heading to Lexington, Ky., for the Kentucky Invitational. The Mountaineers were pitted against the fifth-rated Wildcats, with Minnesota facing No. 1 North Carolina in the other game. Naturally, the pairings were made to have a Kentucky-North Carolina final.

But West Virginia wasn't willing to cooperate. The Mountaineers ran off 12 straight points late in the first half to take a 47–32 lead into the locker room. In the second half, West Virginia's lead swelled to 19 before Kentucky rallied. The Wildcats cut it to four on a pair of baskets by Johnny Cox before West and Sharrar answered with big scores.

Cartoon drawings were popular in the 1950s. Pictured here is a clip of West Virginia coach Fred Schaus.

The Mountaineers' 77–70 upset victory left everyone in the arena stunned, including Kentucky coach Adolph Rupp, who had seen his UK teams lose at home just four times during the previous 14 years.

As it did against Kentucky the night before, West Virginia led North Carolina from wire to wire in the championship game. Vincent and Gardner controlled the backcourt and Sharrar played well in the middle. When North Carolina cut the lead to three points, Akers came off the bench to score seven straight during a two-minute span. Another Tar Heel run reduced West Virginia's lead to four. This time Clousson came off the bench and immediately produced a three-point play. Ronnie Retton added another clutch basket. At the end, the scoreboard read West Virginia 75, North Carolina 64. The victory snapped the defending national champions' 37-game winning streak and North Carolina coach Frank McGuire remarked afterward that West Virginia was as good as Kansas, "with the exception of Wilt Chamberlain." Observers called it the best 80 minutes of basketball in WVU history. Sharrar was named tournament MVP.

"I'll never forget these University of North Carolina players talking a little trash," West said years later. "I said to myself, 'We'll see how good they are.' We kicked their fannies big time. Those are the fun things about being competitive."

Schaus had made a bet with his team before the KIT: If they beat Kentucky and North Carolina, he would let them cut his hair. "All of the guys then were wearing crew cuts and sure enough we won and I let Don Vincent cut my hair," laughed Schaus. "The other 10 guys were egging him on to cut it shorter."

The two wins elevated West Virginia into the top spot in the national rankings for the first time in school history. The Mountaineers went from No. 8 to No. 1, believed to be the biggest jump ever to No. 1 in AP poll history. WVU remained No. 1 for seven consecutive weeks from Dec. 24 through Feb. 4.

A miraculous victory at Villanova enhanced West Virginia's standing. West was fantastic, scoring 37 points and grabbing 13 rebounds to help the Mountaineers overcome a 14-point deficit with eight minutes left in the game. West scored 17 of his team's final 23 points and fed Sharrar for the winning basket with two seconds remaining. A mix-up by the officials underneath the Villanova basket resulted in WVU being awarded the basketball that led to Sharrar's game-winning goal.

"I had these Villanova people—you worked in the crowd at the Palestra—and they had been on my back, ON MY BACK," recalled the late Jack Fleming, "Voice of the Mountaineers." "We came back and won the game and I screamed the final score over the air. When we went to commercial, I turned around and said, 'Take it and shove it!'"

By then Fleming was almost as well known as the players. His distinctive style and his willingness to ride the refs on the air sometimes caused problems for the athletic director, Red Brown, and the school's publicist, Eddie Barrett, but the fans loved it and Schaus didn't mind it either. If West Virginia lost, Fleming usually gave the impression that some sinister force (the refs) beyond the Mountaineers' control was the reason. In that respect, radio lent an imaginary façade to the game that television could never duplicate. George Washington coach Bill Reinhart once said Fleming's game descriptions were so detailed that he could get a complete scouting report from the radio broadcast.

The only loss during the regular season came on Jan. 27 at Duke, 72–68. A nine-game winning streak followed with victories over Florida State, St. John's, Penn State and Pitt at home, and against George Washington on the road in double overtime to complete the regular season.

Amongst those games was a win over Detroit that held special meaning to Schaus. His wife Barbara had been seriously hurt in a sled riding accident earlier that week, and the team rallied behind its distracted coach to win easily 98–66.

The George Washington victory displayed another improbable comeback by the Mountaineers, who fell behind by 13 in the second half. Bob Smith's follow-up basket with 10 seconds left tied the game at 89, and Joedy Gardner scored 14 of West Virginia's 17 points in overtime to lead the Mountaineers to a 113-107 victory.

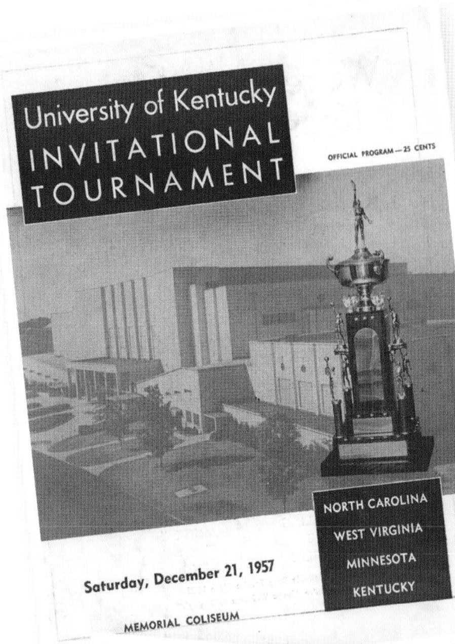

West Virginia claimed its fourth consecutive Southern Conference title with victories over Davidson, Richmond and William & Mary, but its postseason aspirations were dealt a severe blow when Vincent broke his left ankle with five minutes to go in the Richmond win.

"We were winning handily and Fred was taking out players one at a time," said Smith. "Well, Vincent was left in the game for whatever reason and a guy from Richmond took him out and broke his ankle."

After the long drive back from Richmond, West Virginia had to turn around and fly to New York City to play Manhattan two days later in the opening round of the NCAA tournament.

"We didn't even have time to practice," Akers recalled.

Joedy Gardner and Don Vincent hold up the front page of the two local newspapers proclaiming the Mountaineers No. 1 in the country. Also pictured are Ken Ward, Ann Dinardi, Josephine Angotti and sitting in the front, Jim Ritchie.

WVU SPORTS COMMUNICATIONS PHOTO.

Mickey Furfari traveled with the team and recalled a chance encounter he had with St. John's coach Joe Lapchick during the team's workout at Madison Square Garden the morning of the game. Lapchick told Furfari that he thought Manhattan might upset West Virginia.

"I made the mistake of telling that to Fred," said Furfari. "Boy was he mad. He said, 'He has no business saying that!'"

Less than 24 hours after being named regular-season national champions by both wire services, West Virginia was eliminated from the NCAA tournament in stunning fashion. Manhattan played a physical game that resulted in 61 fouls being called on both teams. West, Sharrar, Akers and Gardner all fouled out in the 89–84 loss.

"If I remember correctly they might have shot 50-some free throws, maybe even 60, and we had everybody on the team foul out," said West. "It was a terrible loss and each and every one of us who participated felt that we could play that game 10 times and we were going to win nine of them."

Furfari was on the team charter and he distinctly remembered the cold, dark plane ride back to Morgantown. Furfari could make out the silhouette of Schaus staring straight ahead, and the steam from his breath coming out of his mouth in rhythmic fashion. The Manhattan loss was simply too difficult for Schaus to stomach.

Mountaineers Get Lead in AP Poll

Schaus was a fierce competitor who hated to lose in anything. Jack Fleming once recalled being recruited to play a friendly game of lunchtime tennis with Schaus, Red Brown and Physical Education dean Ray Duncan. Fleming was the worst player of the group, so he was paired with the much younger and more athletic Schaus. Each time Fleming missed a volley or made a bad shot he could sense Schaus's growing irritation. Eventually his frustration got the best of him.

"Damn it, Jack, concentrate. Concentrate!" That was the only time Fleming ever played tennis with Schaus.

Tony Constantine remembered Schaus once commenting that if he ever lost to VMI he would quit the coaching profession. Reminded of that statement a few years later after a particularly

This was a rare sight—a smiling Adolph Rupp presenting the KIT championship trophy to West Virginia's Willie Akers, Coach Fred Schaus and Jerry West. West Virginia's 77–70 victory over the Wildcats on the opening night of the tournament was only the fifth time in 15 years Kentucky was defeated on its home court.

WVU SPORTS COMMUNICATIONS PHOTO.

tough game against the Keydets in 1960, Schaus replied, "Oh yes, but that was before they were giving scholarships."

West Virginia had the nation's second-ranked scoring offense in 1958, averaging 86.9 points per game. West was the team's leading scorer with a 17.9 average, with Vincent, Smith, Gardner and Sharrar also averaging double figures. West and Sharrar earned second-team All-America honors. The players from that era all agree that the 1958 team was the best in school history.

Reaching the NCAA Finals

Sharrar, Vincent and Gardner were gone in 1959, and Schaus had ready-made replacements for them in Bolyard and Retton. Schaus also had the flexibility of moving Smith from forward to guard, and putting Akers in Smith's place at forward. The one position Schaus didn't have a ready solution for was Sharrar's spot at center. The coach ended up choosing Bob Clousson, a player he had discovered walking down High Street one day.

"This blue car pulls up along the curb and it was Fred," Clousson recalled. "He introduced himself and he asked me to come down to the Field House to play with the guys. That's how I got started."

Schaus had no choice but to play a small line-up, so he decided to borrow a trapping zone press defense that Neal Baisi

Jerry West goes high in the air to block a shot against Kentucky in the Kentucky Invitational Tournament in Lexington, Kentucky.

WVU SPORTS COMMUNICATIONS PHOTO.

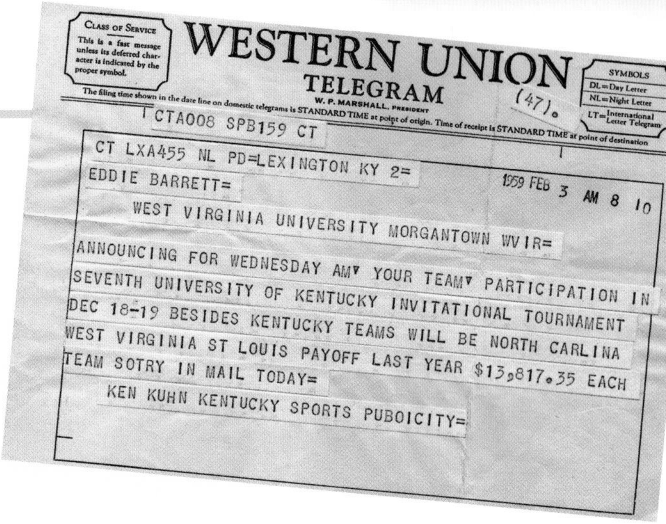

CLASS OF SERVICE
This is a fast message unless its deferred character is indicated by the proper symbol.

WESTERN UNION
TELEGRAM
W. P. MARSHALL, PRESIDENT

SYMBOLS
DL=Day Letter
NL=Night Letter
LT=International Letter Telegram

The filing time shown in the date line on domestic telegrams is STANDARD TIME at point of origin. Time of receipt is STANDARD TIME at point of destination

(47).

CTA008 SPB159 CT

CT LXA455 NL PD=LEXINGTON KY 2=

1959 FEB 3 AM 8 10

EDDIE BARRETT=
WEST VIRGINIA UNIVERSITY MORGANTOWN WVIR=
ANNOUNCING FOR WEDNESDAY AM YOUR TEAM PARTICIPATION IN SEVENTH UNIVERSITY OF KENTUCKY INVITATIONAL TOURNAMENT DEC 18-19 BESIDES KENTUCKY TEAMS WILL BE NORTH CARLINA WEST VIRGINIA ST LOUIS PAYOFF LAST YEAR $13,817.35 EACH TEAM SOTRY IN MAIL TODAY=
KEN KUHN KENTUCKY SPORTS PUBOICITY=

THE KENTUCKY INVITATIONAL TOURNAMENT

It has been called the best 80 minutes of basketball in WVU history. On back-to-back nights West Virginia knocked off No. 5-rated Kentucky and No. 1-ranked North Carolina to win the Kentucky Invitational Tournament.

In both games, West Virginia never trailed. The first night the Mountaineers faced the Wildcats on their home court, and West Virginia made half its shots in the first half and built a 15-point halftime lead over the Wildcats. At one point the Mountaineers scored 12 straight points. In the second half, Kentucky came back and reduced West Virginia's margin to four, but baskets by Jerry West and Lloyd Sharrar increased the lead.

West Virginia was the 77–70 victor, and stunned Kentucky coach Adolph Rupp had to endure only the fifth loss on his home court in 15 years. A band of West Virginia followers celebrated during the final minutes of the game.

The team relaxed the following morning by touring a Kentucky horse farm before facing No. 1-ranked North Carolina, winners of 37 straight games and defending national champions. Once again West Virginia jumped out to an early lead. Guards Don Vincent and Joedy Gardner controlled the backcourt and sophomore Willie Akers came off the bench to score seven consecutive points when the game became tight in the second half. West Virginia held on for a 75–64 victory.

The following week West Virginia was elevated to No. 1 in the national polls—the first time in school history it reached the top of the basketball rankings. The only regular season loss in 1958 was a 72–68 decision at Duke.

West Virginia, without Vincent, who broke his leg during the Southern Conference tournament, finished the year ranked No. 1 in the country but was upset in the first round of the NCAA tournament by Manhattan.

had used so successfully in the West Virginia Conference at West Virginia Tech.

Fourteen times in 1959 West Virginia used second-half comebacks to win games. There were some paybacks, too, like the 101–63 victory over Duke at the Field House to avenge a four-point loss in Durham in 1958.

"It was a really bad situation down there," Akers said. "Those people were brutal so we were really hopped up the next year."

Duke coach Hal Bradley chose to travel on the day of the game and poor weather forced the contest to be postponed for one day. Duke wanted to reschedule at a later date, allowing Bradley's young team an opportunity to get a little more seasoning before facing the No. 4-rated Mountaineers. Schaus would have none of it, demanding they play the next day—a Friday.

Above Guard Joedy Gardner averaged 12 points per game as a senior on the 1958 team that finished 26–2, ranked No. 1 in the country by both wire service polls.

WVU SPORTS COMMUNICATIONS PHOTO.

"He wanted them bad," said Smith. "He said, 'If you get the chance to put one on them, do it.' He never said that before a game."

Schaus's beef with Duke went all the way back to his rookie season in 1955, when he felt the Blue Devils ran up the score in Durham in a game the Mountaineers lost 115–75. The day before, Schaus and publicist Rene Henry went to Duke Indoor Stadium to see Bradley about some court time for practice. According to Henry, Bradley was smug and arrogant and when Schaus extended his hand to shake Bradley's, Bradley sort of brushed him off. Later, during the game, some Duke fans threw debris on the court after a questionable call, compelling the public address announcer to cry that any debris thrown on the court could potentially hurt a Duke player, with no mention of the other team.

Schaus didn't follow through with the threat of running up the score because he didn't have to, pulling all of his starters with nine minutes remaining. The next night the Mountaineers were scheduled to play Virginia at the brand new $3 million Charleston Civic Center. The game was being televised in the Charleston area on WCHS—the first known televised basketball game originating in the Mountain State. The Cavaliers arrived in Charleston having won just once in five tries. Their second victory of the season came that day in stunning fashion.

Paul Adkins, from Branchland, W.Va., burned the Mountaineers for 25 points and another West Virginian, Jay McKenzie from Richwood, added 12 in a 75–72 upset victory. It was an embarrassing loss for the Mountaineers. Bob Smith, a fierce competitor just like Schaus, became unhinged when he overheard one of his teammates laughing on the way back to the locker room.

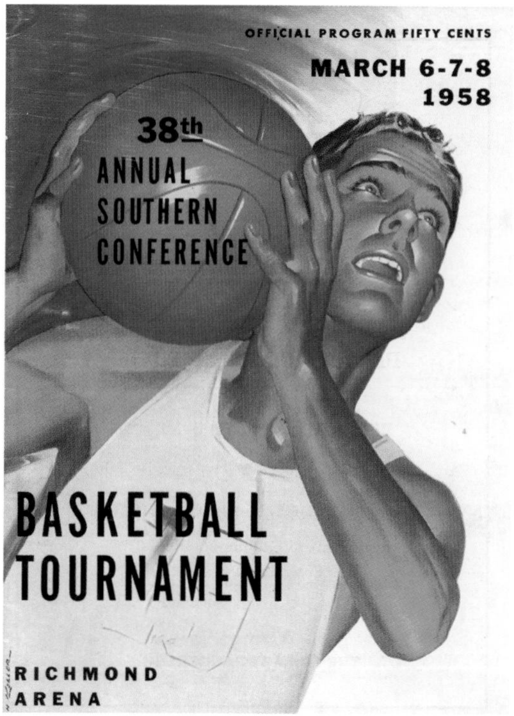

"I said, 'What the hell are you laughing at?' All of the sudden a big hand came down on my shoulder and I turned around and it was Coach Schaus," Smith said.

"I said [to Schaus], 'If you don't want to win I don't ever want to play for you!' He said. 'Don't you say that!' I said it once more and he looked like he wanted to punch me. The guys all jumped into the showers with their uniforms on and [assistant coach] George King came over and grabbed him and pulled him off of me. We were so frightened of Fred."

"We knew the personalities before that happened," added Jim Ritchie. "That was just an explosion. It was done and over."

Two more losses at No. 2 Kentucky and at No. 12 Northwestern in overtime put the season at a crossroads. Another tough road game followed at No. 11 Tennessee.

West, as was usually the case when West Virginia needed him most, came up with a career-high 44 points to lead the Mountaineers to a 76–72 victory over the Volunteers.

Trailing 43–37 at the beginning of the second half, West, Bolyard and Smith scored consecutive baskets to tie the game. The Mountaineers eventually built an 11-point bulge which proved to be enough to withstand a late Tennessee flurry.

'U' Keeps Top Spot In UP Poll

"Schaus was such a great coach because he would say, 'Give Jerry the ball and get the hell out of the way,'" Ritchie laughed. "Not to make a joke out of it, but we understood our roles."

"In the games when we played VMI I got 20 or 21 and Jerry got 15," said Akers. "Then when we really needed him against Tennessee he goes for 44. That's how it was. We laughed about it and made jokes about it."

However, basketball publicist Eddie Barrett was not so amused. It was his job to get West and his teammates national recognition, and in a place as difficult to get to as West Virginia was in the late 1950s, creating publicity for the Mountaineers was not always the easiest thing to do. Several times Barrett tried to talk *Sports Illustrated* college basketball writer Jeremiah Tax into coming to Morgantown to do a feature story on West. Tax never came, despite writing several puff pieces on Cincinnati's Oscar Robertson. Bar-

Far left Bob Smith (21), Lloyd Sharrar (24) and Jerry West (44) get into position for a rebound against Manhattan during this 1958 NCAA tournament East Regional game at Madison Square Garden.

MANHATTAN COLLEGE PHOTO.

Left A difficult scene for West Virginia fans to watch. Manhattan's Ken Norton is carried off the court after his Jaspers upset No. 1-ranked West Virginia 89–84 in the first round of the NCAA tournament East Regional at Madison Square Garden in New York City.

MANHATTAN COLLEGE PHOTO.

rett would often complain to Schaus that he was taking West out of games too early when he could be racking up much larger scoring totals such as Robertson, Marshall's Leo Byrd and Mississippi State's Bailey Howell were doing.

The Tennessee triumph began a 10-game winning streak that lasted through the month of January. A home game against Holy Cross on Feb. 7, 1959 was televised by NBC as the network's game of the week. Special arrangements had to be made because trucks delivering TV equipment for the broadcast could not get over the mountains coming from Washington, D.C. The logistics were eventually worked out, and the Mountaineers won the game 96–90 in front of an East Coast TV audience.

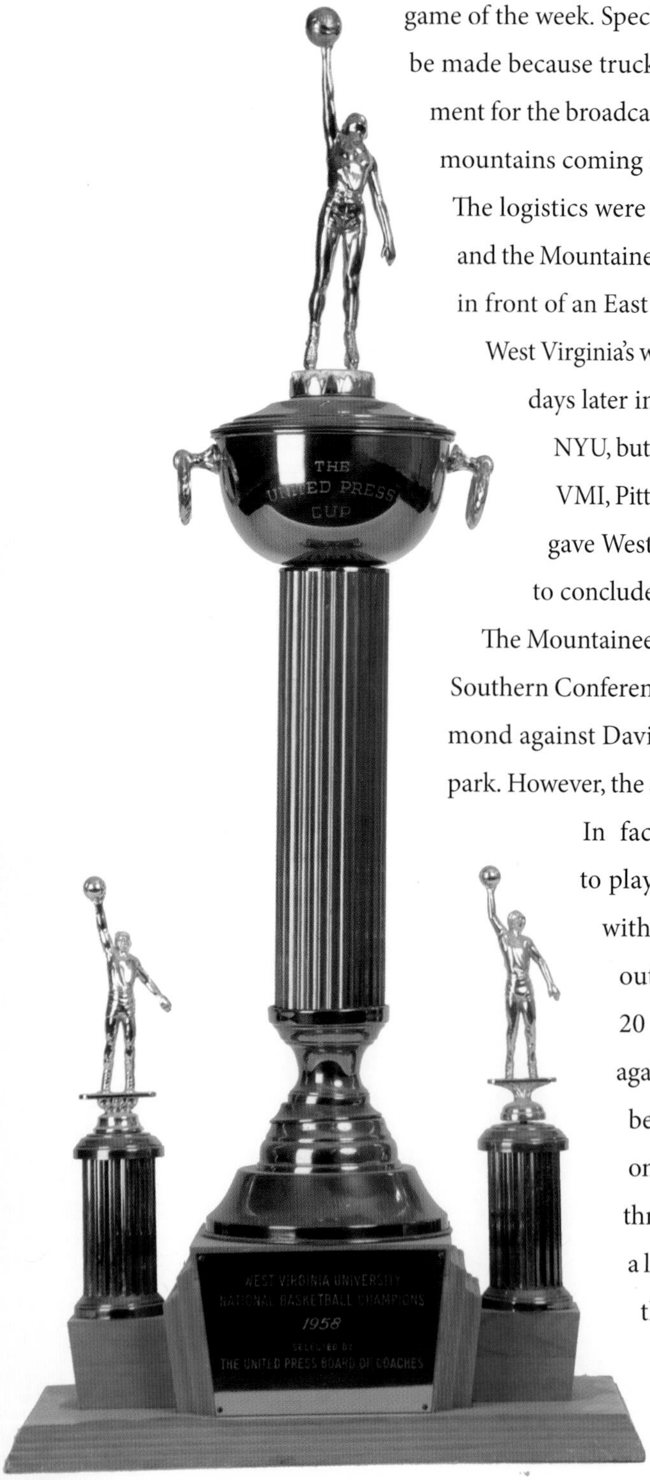

West Virginia's winning streak ended five days later in New York City against NYU, but wins against Richmond, VMI, Pitt and George Washington gave West Virginia a 22–4 record to conclude the regular season.

The Mountaineers' opening game of the Southern Conference tournament in Richmond against Davidson was a walk in the park. However, the semifinal game was not. In fact, West Virginia had to play the final five minutes without West, who fouled out. Lee Patrone, scoring 20 points off the bench against Davidson the night before, came to the rescue once again. Patrone made three field goals, including a long jumper well beyond the top of the key with 2:30 left, to put the Mountaineers into the lead 83–82.

With less than a minute remaining, West Virginia had two tries at the foul line to sew up the game. Both front ends of a one-and-one were missed and a tie-up with 11 seconds left forced a jump ball. Clousson won the tap and the ball quickly moved from Smith to Patrone for the game's deciding basket with two seconds on the clock.

Super-sub Patrone scored 20 points, and West Virginia had a much easier time of it in the championship game, winning 85–66 against The Citadel.

Tenth-ranked West Virginia finally exorcised its NCAA tournament hex by defeating Dartmouth in the opening round, but again faced a premature exit in the second round against St. Joseph's. Early in the second half the Hawks built an 18-point lead before Schaus went exclusively to the zone press. He put West in the pivot and the junior responded by scoring 14 points during a four-minute stretch. With 1:39 remaining, Akers hit a pair of free throws to pull West Virginia to within one, 90–89. West's tip-in basket then gave the Mountaineers their first lead.

St. Joseph's coach Jack Ramsay called time-out with 23 seconds left to design a last-second play. He called a second time-out after seeing what Schaus was going to do on defense. When play resumed, Ronnie Retton gambled and stole the inbound pass and went in for the game-clinching basket. "I don't even know what happened," Retton said. "When I think today how that happened . . . I just don't know. Somehow I anticipated the pass coming in from midcourt and stole the ball and went in and laid it up."

"Somehow they did it again," an elated Schaus remarked after the game. "How they do it I just can't say, but they keep pulling off miracles."

West Virginia's win over Boston University to reach the national semifinals wasn't nearly as miraculous, but the Mountaineers once more had to overcome a second-half deficit. Trailing by four, 67–63, West Virginia got eight straight points from West to pull away with an 86–82 victory. West scored 33 points and grabbed 17 rebounds to extend West Virginia's season to the national semifinals in Louisville, Ky.

West Virginia fans, elated to be going to the national semifinals for the first time in school history, began calling the ticket office after the Boston game. Assistant athletic director Lowry Stoops was in charge of finances for the department and was considered by his peers to be the epitome of integrity when it came to money, according to Eddie Barrett. Stoops's introduction to the world of high finance actually came during World War I when he was serving in France. He began lending money to soldiers and as the war continued, Stoops was forced to raise the interest rates on his loans because, in his words, "the poor [guys] were dying on me."

After West Virginia won the regional final, Stoops wanted to personally make sure tickets would be sold to Mountaineer supporters so he went on the radio and announced that fans could drive to his South Park home on Sunday morning to purchase the 250 tickets that were made available to West Virginia University.

"The cars were backed up way past Westover almost to Clarksburg," laughed Barrett. "He finally had to escape through the back door."

Barrett also recalled another humorous story concerning tickets for the finals. Because Louisville was in the national semifinals, the manager of Freedom Hall caved in to local political pressure and sold some of the tickets that were reserved for members of the National Association of Basketball Coaches. When the NABC and the NCAA discovered what had happened, they threatened not to have the event unless there was some sort of compromise. "As a result, they put the coaches in the aisles," said Barrett. "Guys

The 1959 team made 14 comeback victories to reach the national finals in Louisville, Ky., where the Mountaineers fell to Cal, 71–70. The Mountaineers finished second to Miami in scoring offense, averaging 84.8 points per game.
WVU SPORTS COMMUNICATIONS PHOTO.

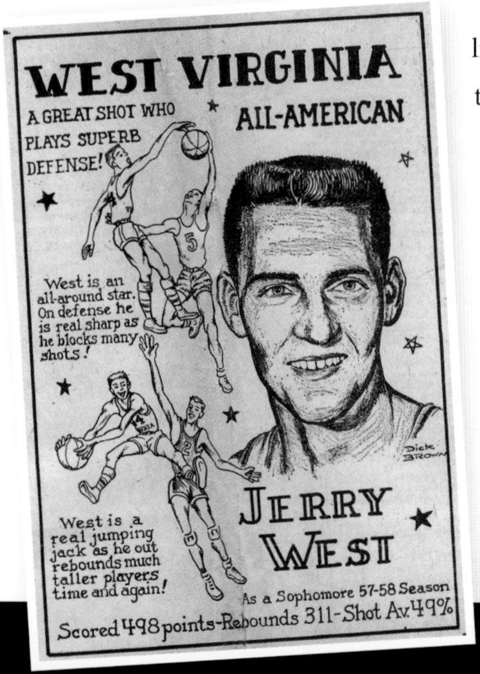

like John Wooden were sitting in the aisles."

WEST VIRGINIA
A GREAT SHOT WHO PLAYS SUPERB DEFENSE!
ALL-AMERICAN
West is an all-around star. On defense he is real sharp as he blocks many shots!
West is a real jumping jack as he out rebounds much taller players time and again!
JERRY WEST
As a Sophomore 57-58 Season
Scored 498 points-Rebounds 311-Shot Av.49%

The Final Four pitted West Virginia against Louisville in one bracket, and California and Cincinnati in the other. The games were being played on Louisville's home floor in Freedom Hall.

Cincinnati and West Virginia had the two best offenses in the Final Four while Cal had the best defense. Louisville was playing over its head, upsetting Michigan State and Kentucky to get to the semifinals, but their luck ran out against West Virginia.

The Mountaineers played perhaps their best game of the season against the Cardinals. West Virginia shot 53 percent from the field while building a 23-point lead early in the second half. West scored 38 points and secured 15 rebounds; Bolyard added 13.

Said Louisville coach Peck Hickman after the game, "My boys pick somebody they think they can lick and then tie into him. The poor guy who gets to pick fifth gets stuck with West."

In the other semifinal game, Cal upset Cincinnati 64–58, ruining the opportunity for a West-Oscar Robertson meeting in the finals.

"We were pulling for Cincinnati to beat Cal because we wanted Jerry to go against Oscar," Smith said. "Now, it didn't have any bearing on the game. We jumped out to an early lead and then all of the sudden things went bad for us."

West Virginia's bad spell came when West went to the bench with four fouls. Referee Red Mihalik, a native of Ford City, Pa., was one of the best in the business and because he had called so many of West Vir-

Jerry West often had to endure to rough play, as was the case in this game against Holy Cross at the Field House on Feb. 7, 1959.

WVU SPORTS COMMUNICATIONS PHOTO.

ginia's games during the regular season, Schaus thought Mihalik sometimes anticipated calls against the Mountaineers.

As it had done many times before during the course of the season, West Virginia fell behind Cal and trailed by as many as 13 points in the second half. Schaus went to the zone press and the Mountaineers gradually clawed back into the game. With 52 seconds remaining, Cal's lead had been shaved to one. The precision and poise Pete Newell's team had used to build its big lead was gone. Then Cal's 6-foot-10 center Darrall Imhoff attempted a wild 20-foot hook shot that rolled off the rim. He quickly went after his miss and tipped in what turned out to be the winning basket with 15 seconds left. Cal conceded a field goal to make the final score 71–70. A mere basket stood in the way of West Virginia claiming the

NBC GAME OF THE WEEK: HOLY CROSS

During the 1958 NCAA meetings in Chicago, West Virginia University athletic director Red Brown had discovered that NBC had some open dates in its weekly basketball coverage for the 1959 season. Brown suggested that West Virginia, coming off a 26–2 season in 1958, would be an attractive team. NBC agreed. A date was worked out with Holy Cross for Feb. 7, 1959, to take part in NBC's weekly afternoon college basketball "Game of the Week."

NBC officials traveled to Morgantown a month before the telecast to get a lay of the land. The logistics proved to be staggering. Mobile units normally used for games could not negotiate the drive through West Virginia so alternate plans had to be made. Equipment was shipped in advance and a portable control room was established in the north end of the Field House.

Because the video and audio signals were transmitted separately, there had to be a coordinated effort with C&P Telephone, American Telephone & Telegraph, NBC-TV and Capital Airlines.

Parabolic reflectors were installed on the top of the Field House to transmit the television signal to a telephone tower on top of Wiles Hill, where it was converted into a microwave signal. From there the signal was first relayed to another tower in Uniontown, Pa., then to Washington, Pa., where it was then transmitted to NBC's regular East-West transmission line to New York.

The audio portion of the telecast was transmitted via C&P Telephone, first to Uniontown, and then to Pittsburgh. It was then sent to Washington, D.C., and then on to New York. NBC's production facility in New York then coordinated the two transmissions into one synchronized broadcast. Because there were only two mobile telephone units available in the area, another unit had to be located in Cleveland to assist with the audio portion of the broadcast.

Six private telephone lines were installed at the Field House to monitor the signal to New York. An 11-person engineering crew from NBC coordinated the event on site, setting up three cameras inside the arena. Two were flanked on the west side of the court (nearest the Monongahela River) and another portable camera was stationed on the southwest corner of the floor near the two team benches. Lindsay Nelson was flown in to announce the game.

With the exception of a few closed-circuit telecasts from The Greenbrier, and a Dave Garroway Show sent from Huntington via AT&T, the West Virginia–Holy Cross basketball game was considered the first televised event carried live and direct from West Virginia to C&P Telephone's national network.

West Virginia University took advantage of the television exposure by presenting a modern dance recital at halftime. The campus dance organization Orchesis produced a nine-minute performance to the music from Broadway shows "Oklahoma!" and "Rodeo" as well as the composition "Legend of the Glass Mountain." The 17 females were outfitted in costumes of pink organdy with pink parasols, then white blouses and straw hats with full skirts, and finally, aqua and white flowing costumes. Of course, no one could appreciate the colorful costumes watching the game on black and white TV sets.

Members from the West Virginia legislature were also invited to help celebrate WVU's 92nd anniversary. As for the game, West Virginia defeated Holy Cross 96–90 in an all-around entertaining afternoon.

national championship in 1959. "We just ran out of time," Schaus said.

West was everybody's All-American, averaging 26.6 points and 12.3 rebounds per game. Smith and Bolyard averaged double figures—Smith at 12.6 points per game and Bolyard at 10.1. The Mountaineers finished the regular season 10th in the AP poll and 11th in the UPI poll and had the nation's second-ranked scoring offense, averaging 84.8 points per game. Afterward, West and Schaus were invited to participate in the Pan-American Games—West as a player and Schaus as a coach.

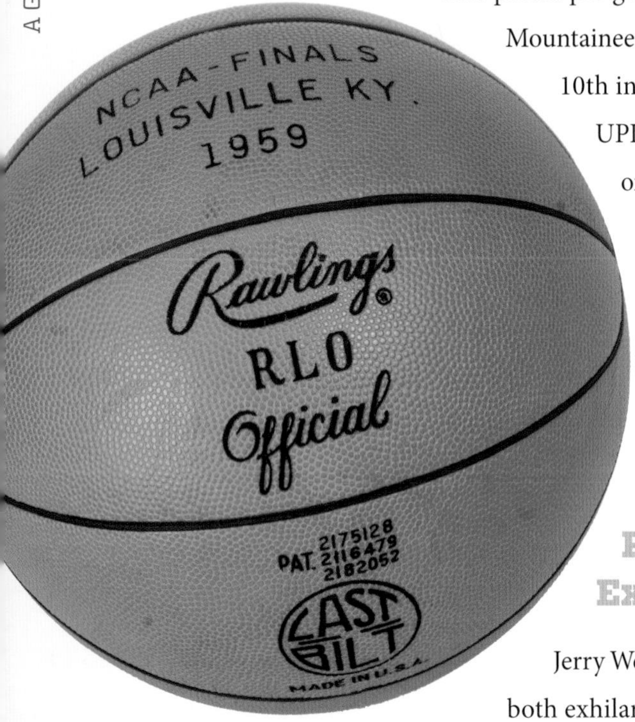

Pain and Exhilaration

Jerry West's senior season in 1960 was both exhilarating and painful. He established a school record by scoring 908 points and averaging 29.3 points per game. He led WVU to 26 victories and a year-long stay in the top 10, finishing fifth in the AP poll and sixth in the UPI poll. West also became the shortest player (6′3″) in NCAA history to score more than 2,000 points and grab more than 1,200 rebounds for his career. But there were also difficult and painful moments, too.

West Virginia's 56-game Southern Conference winning streak ended in Norfolk, Va., Jan. 30, 1960, when William & Mary defeated the Mountaineers 94–86. West scored 42 and pulled down 17 rebounds, but it was William & Mary's bruising 6-foot-7, 225-pound center Jeff Cohen who came out on top with 34 points and 20 rebounds.

It was also a season in which West experienced two broken noses as opposing teams began to look for other ways to try to stop him. The first broken nose came at Kentucky when a flying elbow connected as he was trying to pull down a rebound late in the first half. There was blood everywhere and trainer Whitey Gwynne was not sure he could get the bleeding to stop.

West refused to come out of the game and he scored 33 points and grabbed 18 rebounds to lead West Virginia to a 79–70 win over the Wildcats, giving the school its second KIT title in a span of three years. After the game, West had to be taken to a local hospital to have his nose reset.

West broke his nose a second time in the first half of a rough, 97–93 loss at George Washington on Feb. 17, 1960. Once again he remained in the game to score 40 points and grab 15 rebounds. Eschewing a protective face mask, West came back three days later to score 29 points and grab 13 rebounds in his final home appearance against Pitt. As the remaining seconds ticked off the clock toward an 89–75 victory, West received a standing ovation similar to the one Hot Rod Hundley had enjoyed three years earlier.

The following weekend, a third consecutive Southern Conference championship was out of West's hands. The No. 2-seeded Mountaineers reached the championship game to face top-seeded Virginia Tech by knocking off VMI and William & Mary. With West and Cohen effectively neutralizing each other, the difference in the William & Mary game was Patrone and Jim Warren, who scored 17 points each for West Virginia.

In the championship game, West Virginia showed that it was not just a one-man team. With 12 minutes remaining and the Mountaineers

Lee Patrone earned third-team All-America honors by the Helms Foundation in 1961 and was a three-time member of the Southern Conference all-tournament team.

WVU SPORTS COMMUNICATIONS PHOTO.

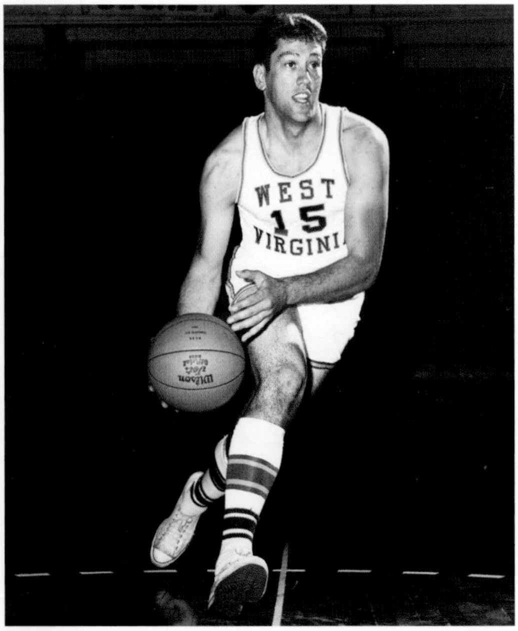

leading by one, West drew his fifth personal foul.

Schaus looked down toward the end of his bench where Warren was sitting.

"Schaus grabbed Warren by the jersey and he said, 'I want you to play the best damned game you have ever played!'" Eddie Barrett chuckled. "Well, Warren goes in and hits three long field goals and we wind up winning the game by 10."

Warren and Patrone combined to score 35 points, and Warren's clutch shooting gave WVU a 60–55 lead with 7:07 remaining. Back-to-back baskets by Patrone and Paul Miller pushed the lead to eight with less than five minutes to play, and West Virginia wound up winning 82–72.

Charleston's Chris Smith—the player many believed was the missing link to at least two national championships for West Virginia—never beat the Mountaineers while playing at Virginia Tech. "He could have fit in there nicely," admitted Schaus. "Of course you could also say Chuck Noe could have won a national championship at Virginia Tech with Jerry West."

The Mountaineers' goal of winning it all was shattered in the second round of the NCAA tournament in Charlotte against NYU. West Virginia was unable to hold onto a 76–72 lead with 1:42 left in the game. A missed opportunity at the free throw line paved the way for the Violets' Russ Cunningham to tie the game with five seconds left.

NYU outscored the Mountaineers 5–4 in the extra session to knock WVU out of the tournament 82–81. West Virginia then beat St. Joseph's 106–100 in a meaningless consolation game. West scored 37 points and grabbed 16 rebounds in his final collegiate performance.

West completed his career ranked first in school history in career scoring (2,309), first in career rebounding (1,240), first in career field goals made (843), first in career free throws made (623), first in career double-doubles (70), first in career 20-point games (64) and first in career 30-point games (29).

"Go look up the box scores," remarked Akers, "Jerry didn't score a whole lot of points in the games that we won easily. It was in the games when we really needed him that he got all of his points."

"Even after I thought it was impossible for Jerry to get any better, he still continued to improve his skills," wrote Smith in his 2005 book, *It's More Than Just Winning*. "Somehow, when I would see him after not seeing him for a while, he would have some new move or better way to execute his maneuvers on the basketball court. In many ways, he was often performing in ways

THE LOGO

There have been hints but never an official confirmation from professional basketball that the likeness of Jerry West is depicted in the official logo of the NBA.

The logo, created in 1969, shows the white silhouette of a player dribbling a basketball against a blue and red background. In 2008 David Davis, writing for FOXSports.com, decided to find out once and for all if it was, indeed, West who was depicted on the logo.

The NBA office refused to acknowledge publically that it is West. A high-ranking NBA official told Davis that the identification of West as the player in the logo was an "urban myth."

Not convinced, Davis tracked down the man hired to design the logo in 1969: Alan Siegel. With the help of college buddy and later famed author and television personality Dick Schaap, Siegel found a picture of a player dribbling a basketball toward the basket he liked and he began designing the logo around the image of the player. And that player? Jerry West.

"It was an action shot of Jerry West dribbling down the court from one of the Lakers' games. I sketched it, cleaned it up a bit and stylized it," Siegel told Davis.

West said the depiction of the person dribbling the basketball in the logo is very similar to a photograph of him dribbling against Joe Caldwell in a game against the Atlanta Hawks. West believed the picture may have been taken by longtime Los Angeles Lakers team photographer Wen Roberts.

Thus, the answer to one of the NBA's worst-kept secrets.

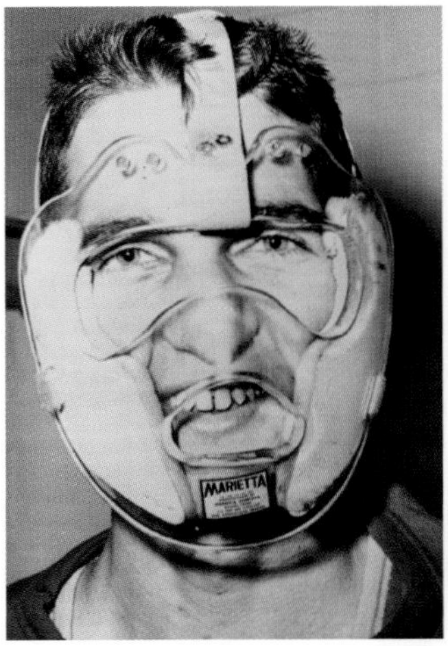

Jerry West models the new protective mask he wore for part of the season after breaking his nose in the Kentucky Invitational Tournament.

WVU SPORTS COMMUNICATIONS PHOTO.

Below left Jerry West goes high in the air for two points against Louisville in this famous photo of West during the Mountaineers' 94–79 victory over the Cardinals in the 1959 Final Four at Freedom Hall in Louisville, Ky. West scored 38 points and grabbed 15 rebounds for victorious West Virginia.

WVU SPORTS COMMUNICATIONS PHOTO.

Inset Jerry West, pictured in the second row second from the right, was a member of the gold-medal winning 1960 U.S. Olympic basketball team.

WVU SPORTS COMMUNICATIONS PHOTO.

that the rest of us had not seen, and he was actually plowing new ground or inventing basketball as we watched."

For the second straight year West was a consensus All-America choice and he was selected to participate in the 1960 Olympic Games in Rome. He was also the No. 2 overall selection (behind Cincinnati's Robertson) in the NBA draft by the Los Angeles Lakers.

That West had been selected so high in the pro draft was not surprising. What was surprising to Mountaineer basketball fans everywhere was his coach following him to the pros. Even though Schaus had turned down an offer to coach the Washington Huskies the year before, no one saw this one coming.

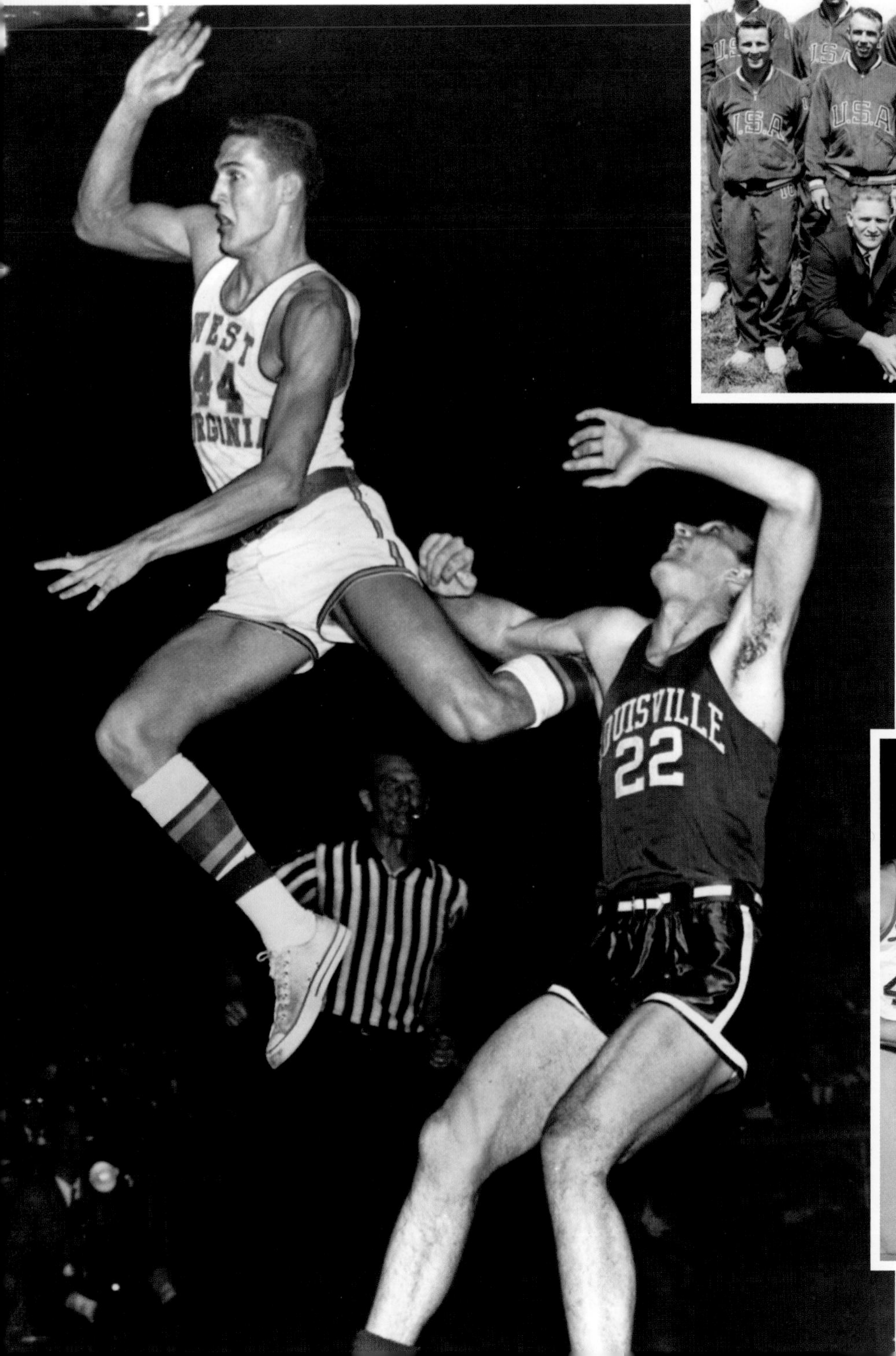

West Virginia takes over Tinseltown! Los Angeles Lakers coach Fred Schaus with his two former Mountaineer players, Jerry West and Hot Rod Hundley.

WVU SPORTS COMMUNICATIONS PHOTO.

1959 NCAA CHAMPIONSHIP GAME

Darrall Imhoff is probably best known as the guy who tried to guard Wilt Chamberlain when he scored an NBA record 100 points on March 2, 1962.

But to old-time West Virginia basketball fans, Imhoff is the player who stood in the way of the school's best chance at a national championship. It was Imhoff's tip-in basket (some called it a fluke) with 15 seconds left that derailed another Mountaineer comeback in a 71–70 NCAA championship game loss to California at Freedom Hall in Louisville, Ky.

Cal's Darrall Imhoff battles West Virginia's Joe Posch and Willie Akers for the basketball in the championship game of the 1959 Los Angeles Classic in the L.A. Memorial Sports Arena. The Bears won the game 65–45.

UNIVERSITY OF CALIFORNIA PHOTO.

The distance of Imhoff's tip away from the basket has increased, as most tales usually do through the passage of time.

"Imhoff tipped it in from the foul line," recalled Willie Akers in 1999.

"It's often said there is a tremendous amount of good fortune in sport," Jerry West added. "We didn't have a lot in that game. The basket that counted to win the game, the guy slapped at the ball and it went in."

Of course Imhoff doesn't quite remember it that way. Interviewed by the *Charleston Daily Mail's* Mike Cherry in 1999, Imhoff said the winning basket was the result of hustle and a fear of disobeying his coach Pete Newell.

"We come down and Pete said, 'Do not take any shot until a lay-in.' I take a left hook. I missed it. I was so scared, I cut across and tipped it in for 71–68 . . . (Fred) Schaus said it bounced off my shoulders once. But I took the shot from one side and it was an obviously controlled tip from the other."

Imhoff didn't have a great statistical game against West Virginia, scoring 10 points and grabbing nine rebounds—he was far better against Cincinnati in the semifinals scoring 22 points—but his size (four inches taller than West Virginia's tallest player) and Newell's composure were enough to withstand another frantic Mountaineer comeback.

The Mountaineers were the original "Cardiac Kids." Fourteen times in 1959 West Virginia overcame second-half deficits to win basketball games. None was more dramatic than an NCAA tournament second-round victory in Charlotte when West Virginia zone-pressed its way back from 18 points down to beat St. Joseph's 95–92.

In the title game, West Virginia's early 10-point lead vanished when Jerry West got into foul trouble. Cal led by six at halftime and had built a 13-point bulge midway through the second half. No problem. It was simply time for Schaus to put on the press.

Soon the poise Cal showed earlier in the game had deteriorated into panic. West Virginia's frenetic pace had gotten it back into the game.

"The key to our pressing zone defense was the guards," Schaus remarked in 1988. "They had to be everywhere to put pressure and the fact that we had three of them was a great asset."

West Virginia had finally got to within striking distance when Imhoff tried his wild 20-foot hook shot that he wound up chasing down for the deciding goal.

"Jerry and I used to give Darrall quite a bit of ribbing about that shot," Schaus said. "He was with us on the Lakers squad so we had plenty of chances to reminisce about the play.

"Of course he remembered things a little differently than we did. He always was claiming that he went way above everyone to snatch the ball out of the air high above the rim and toss in the winning basket. Who knows? He may be right. Time has a way of dimming the memory."

OSU
31
24
WEST
25
VIRGINIA

WEST
14

WEST
44
VIRGINIA

9

King And His Court

(1961–1965)

Coach George King calls out instructions during a game at the Field House.

WEST VIRGINIA AND REGIONAL HISTORY COLLECTION.

Below A small college scoring champion at Morris Harvey in Charleston, George King replaced Fred Schaus as West Virginia's basketball coach for the 1961 season and led the Mountaineers to a 102–43 record for five seasons before taking the Purdue job in 1965.

WVU SPORTS COMMUNICATIONS PHOTO.

Inset A portrait of the King family in 1961. Pictured are George and Jeanne King and their five children: George, Kristy Jeanne, Kathy Jan, Kerry Jo and Gordon Scott.

WVU SPORTS COMMUNICATIONS PHOTO.

Fred Schaus and George King were attending Jim Ritchie's summer wedding in Morgantown when the two began talking about the 1961 basketball season and Schaus asked King what he would do if he were head coach.

King talked about recruiting and the normal things he did as an assistant coach. Schaus asked again, re-phrasing his question to ask what would GEORGE KING do if he were head coach.

King did a double-take. "What are you trying to say?"

It was then that Schaus told King that he had accepted an offer to coach the Los Angeles Lakers. He had recommended that King take over as his replacement.

"As the years went by with some pretty good wins I knew we had something special going here," Schaus said. "That's why it was difficult to leave, but I just had to take that opportunity because that was another idea that I had—to play in the NBA and to one day coach in the NBA."

Schaus's .798 winning percentage remains the best in school history. In 1997, college basketball historian Mike Douchant listed West Virginia's three consecutive unbeaten seasons in Southern Conference play as the 16th greatest achievement in major college basketball history. Schaus later became one of only four coaches to take a college team to the Final Four and a pro team to the NBA finals. Nearly 50 years later, almost 40 school

records are still held by Schaus's teams, including highest scoring average (89.5 ppg), and highest winning percentage in a season (.929). He also became the first coach in NCAA history to take a team to the national tournament six consecutive years to begin his coaching career.

Schaus knew George King was more than qualified to be his successor. King was a small-college scoring champion at Morris Harvey who later earned fame in the pros by leading the Syracuse Nationals to the 1955 NBA title. It was King's last-minute free throw and steal that preserved the victory for the Nats.

"George was one of the very outstanding point guards in the NBA that could handle the ball and make the fast break a success," said Bob Lochmueller, who played with King in the pros and eventually followed him to West Virginia as his assistant coach.

After his pro career, King returned to college to get a master's degree and was operating a sporting goods store in Charleston when Schaus called to offer him a job as the school's first full-time assistant basketball coach. King accepted, and West Virginia was the beneficiary of having two young ex-pros leading the program.

Years later, Jerry West said the King-Schaus duo proved very appealing to young basketball players. "Both of them were younger and both of them had just retired," West said. "It was a great environment for any of us who wanted to learn, and more importantly, to engage two people that had played basketball at a different level than any of us had played."

The two often jumped in and participated in drills, and would sometimes play two-on-two games with some of the players after practice.

"[Schaus] was dirty," Joe Posch recalled. "He would step on your feet. He would pull your pants down or hold your shirt. He got all of that stuff from the pros."

"Fred's arms were like logs and when he stuck them out you couldn't get around him," Clousson added. "You learned things from him."

West believed some of those sessions with King really helped him develop the confidence he needed to become one of the game's great players. "He was very experienced and very smart and I found out that I could play against him OK and it wasn't going to be embarrassing for me," West said.

A Natural Resource

George King and Fred Schaus had completely different personalities. Schaus was a fiery, demonstrative man and a stern disciplinarian. King was much more laid-back and easygoing. He rarely ever yelled at his players, and if he did have a problem with someone, he usually chose to handle things privately.

"In the three years that I played for him I don't think he yelled at me once," recalled guard Jim McCormick.

"Even in practice he wouldn't show you up," remembered another player, Buddy Quertinmont.

King, pictured here with All-American guard Rod Thorn, led West Virginia to Southern Conference tournament titles in 1962, 1963 and 1965.

WVU SPORTS COMMUNICATIONS PHOTO.

All-American Rod Thorn pictured here with his father Joe Thorn, a police chief in Rod's native Princeton and a former pitcher in the St. Louis Cardinals system. Joe invaded Iwo Jima with the Marines during World War II, was severely wounded and, for a time, reported missing in action.

WVU SPORTS COMMUNICATIONS PHOTO.

"He would wait and get you off to the side and then talk to you and tell you what you were doing wrong and what was expected of you."

"George was a gentleman and he tried to be fair and relate to his players," added Rod Thorn. "He wasn't a screamer where Fred was much more fiery and passionate from the standpoint of getting on players. If George raised his voice you knew he was really upset."

Lochmueller said their roles were the reverse of most head coach/assistant coach pairings. He took on the role of disciplinarian while King was usually the consoler. "That was the kind of role we played," Lochmueller said.

"George was a very handsome guy," Thorn said. "He always looked like a million dollars. Lochmueller was a nice guy also. They were good men and I thought they did a very good job."

King was also a capable recruiter who was around when Schaus signed Thorn, although Thorn said he dealt primarily with Schaus. "I really didn't know George at that time," Thorn recalled. "Fred was the guy that really recruited me."

By the time Thorn had reached high school, there were very few basketball fans in the state who didn't know who he was. Hot Rod Hundley recalled first meeting Thorn after a WVU basketball game when Thorn was just a freshman in high school. His father, Joe Thorn, an iconic figure in Princeton, was a former minor league pitcher who first began working with Rod when he was just four years old. As a youngster, before Rod's hands were big enough to hold a basketball, his father had him use a volleyball instead. When he was six, Thorn started playing organized basketball with kids nearly twice his age on a touring team called the "Rinky Dinks."

In the summertime, Thorn's father would take him down to the ballfield and work with him all afternoon on his hitting.

"I could hit curve balls when I was six or seven years old because he threw them to me all of the time," Thorn recalled. "He wanted me to be a baseball player because he never quite made it to the majors and that was his goal. That's where I was headed until I got hurt my senior year in college." (Thorn was hit in the back of the head by a baseball that rendered him unconscious during a WVU game.)

By Rod's senior year of high school in 1959, the Thorns had received letters from just about every major basketball school in the country. Rod narrowed his choices to Duke and West Virginia, with the opportunity of attending Duke Medical School a very enticing proposition. The West Virginia Legislature complicated things for Schaus by declaring Thorn a "natural resource," imploring him to remain in the state.

"I think it probably put a little added pressure on me to be thought of that way," said Thorn. "At the time I remember thinking, 'What in the world is this [legislator] thinking about because West Virginia has problems other than that?' But once I analyzed it, it was certainly a nice thing for somebody to do."

Eventually, Thorn picked West Virginia, in part because he thought he could be more successful later in life practicing medicine in the state. Thorn and West wore the same uniform number, 44, and bore a close physical resemblance, lending credence to the belief by many that Thorn was the second coming of Jerry West. But as Pittsburgh writer Roy McHugh later wrote, "The Jerry Wests of the world do not come in pairs." For Thorn, the comparison to West was a tremendous burden to bear.

"There was great affection for all of us," West said. "I think the expectations for Rod there . . . I didn't think they were fair. Everyone should have let Rod Thorn seek the depth of his own water so to speak, and let him find a place for himself in terms of what he was able to accomplish as a player.

"People put a lot of pressure on him and expected so much of him," West added. "Sometimes that's a very difficult thing. I think Rod would probably echo that."

"Had I known then what I know now I would have requested a different number," said Thorn. "Not only because it was Jerry, but also because you need to make your own way. A number should not have anything to do with it but in this case, because Jerry was such a great, great player . . . unless you are Kobe Bryant, Michael Jordan or LeBron James, you're going to come off not looking as good."

"Rod's mother was a teacher and his father was police chief," former WVU sports information director, Eddie Barrett, said. "When the other kids were going out for ice cream after the game, Rod had to go home and study. He rebelled against that and also against being compared to Jerry West."

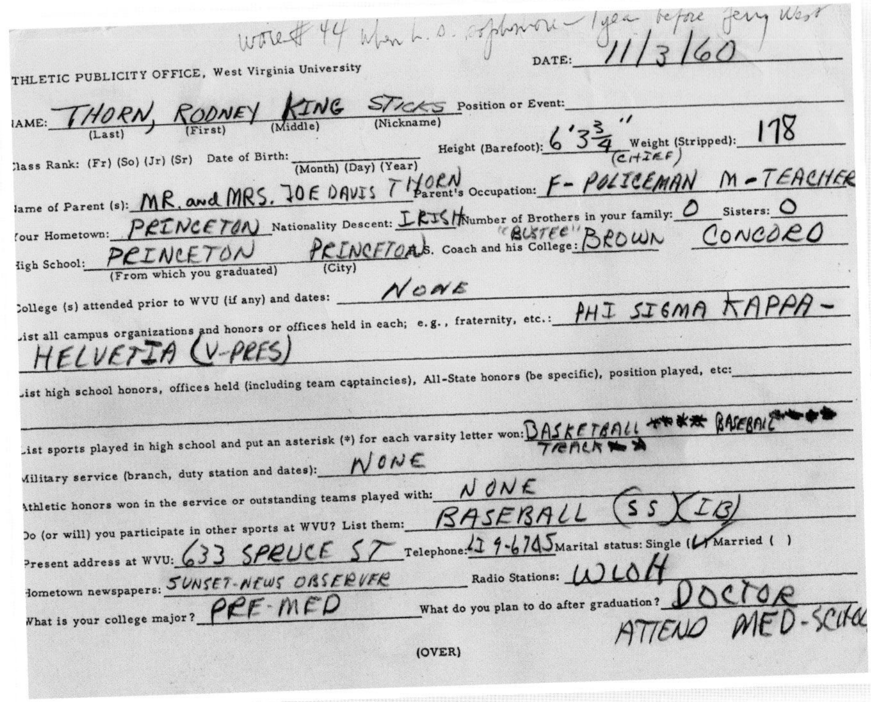
DATE: 11/3/60

THLETIC PUBLICITY OFFICE, West Virginia University

IAME: THORN, RODNEY KING STICKS Position or Event:
(Last) (First) (Middle) (Nickname)

Height (Barefoot): 6'3 3/4" Weight (Stripped): 178

Class Rank: (Fr) (So) (Jr) (Sr) Date of Birth:
(Month) (Day) (Year)

Name of Parent (s): MR. and MRS. JOE DAVIS THORN Parent's Occupation: F-POLICEMAN (CHIEF) M-TEACHER

Your Hometown: PRINCETON Nationality Descent: IRISH Number of Brothers in your family: 0 Sisters: 0

High School: PRINCETON PRINCETON H.S. Coach and his College: "BUSTEE" BROWN CONCORD
(From which you graduated) (City)

College (s) attended prior to WVU (if any) and dates: NONE

List all campus organizations and honors or offices held in each; e.g., fraternity, etc.: PHI SIGMA KAPPA - HELVETIA (V-PRES)

List high school honors, offices held (including team captaincies), All-State honors (be specific), position played, etc:

List sports played in high school and put an asterisk (*) for each varsity letter won: BASKETBALL *** BASEBALL *** TRACK **

Military service (branch, duty station and dates): NONE

Athletic honors won in the service or outstanding teams played with: NONE

Do (or will) you participate in other sports at WVU? List them: BASEBALL (SS) (1B)

Present address at WVU: 633 SPRUCE ST Telephone: 29-6745 Marital status: Single (✓) Married ( )

Hometown newspapers: SUNSET-NEWS OBSERVER Radio Stations: WLOH

What is your college major? PRE-MED What do you plan to do after graduation? DOCTOR ATTEND MED-SCHOOL

(OVER)

Mountaineer players are required to fill out information cards like this one submitted by Rod Thorn in 1960.

WVU SPORTS COMMUNICATIONS IMAGE.

Thorn's sophomore season at West Virginia in 1961 was exceptional by most standards—18.5 points per game and a solid 46.2 shooting percentage (despite using an unorthodox two-handed jump shot)—but it didn't meet Thorn's personal standards or the enormous standards West had established before him.

West Virginia lost just four times in 1961, and all four losses were by single-digit margins. A

Forward Jim Ritchie was one of the few out-of-staters who played for the Mountaineers in the early 1960s. A native of Drexel Hill, Pa., Ritchie averaged 11.6 points and 7.4 rebounds per game as a senior in 1961.

WVU SPORTS COMMUNICATIONS PHOTO.

shaky 2–2 beginning to the '61 season preceded an eight-game winning streak that included an outstanding 86–82 victory over 18th-rated Memphis State in the championship game of the Sugar Bowl tournament in New Orleans.

Lee Patrone was fantastic, leading the Mountaineers with 33 points. Thorn scored 17 and grabbed 13 rebounds, while Jim Ritchie added 13 points.

While growing up in Bellaire, Ohio, Patrone once dove into the Ohio River to save a drowning woman. After high school he signed with Ohio State and spent a week in Columbus before deciding the school was too big for him. He wound up coming to West Virginia where he led the freshman team in scoring.

Patrone had a reputation for being supremely self-confident. "Good enough to be cocky and cocky enough to be good," is how one sportswriter described him.

Despite standing 6-foot-1 and only weighing about 185 pounds, Patrone preferred playing inside against much bigger players. And no matter where he was on the floor, he almost always tried bank shots. "'Benny Banker' is what we called him," Ronnie Retton laughed.

"He was the best bank shooter I ever saw," added Jay Jacobs.

West Virginia's eight-game winning streak ended with a five-point loss at Villanova. Twelve more wins followed, allowing West Virginia to complete the regular season with a 23–3 record. WVU returned to the top 10 following victories over NC State in Charleston, NYU in New York, and Richmond at Richmond Arena.

The Mountaineers completed the regular season with a No. 8 ranking, but their season came to a premature conclusion in the semifinals of the Southern Conference tournament against William & Mary.

Jeff Cohen was once again unstoppable, scoring 38 points and grabbing 19 rebounds to lead the Tribe to an 88–76 upset victory. Patrone scored 34 points and Paul Miller added 14 for WVU. However, Thorn failed to score a single point in the semifinals, going 0 for 6 from the floor and 0 for 5 from the free throw line.

"Rod had a bad game in the Southern Conference tournament and he just disappeared—he went away. The coaches had to go get him and bring him back," Barrett said.

What came out of Thorn's dismal performance in the Southern Conference tournament was a lengthy 1962 *Sport* magazine article entitled "The Destruction (And Rebuilding) of Rod Thorn." The story detailed Thorn's struggles trying to maintain a B average to get into medical school and the intense pressure many major college players endured trying to succeed both academically and athletically. *Sport* magazine's editorial board even commented on Thorn's "unsolvable dilemma."

"I was feeling sorry for myself at that time and when I got back to school [after the tournament] I wasn't going to school everyday and I got behind, so I decided to drop out for the remainder of the semester," Thorn explained. "I always planned to come back."

For all of his troubles (real and imagined), Thorn actually led the team in scoring and rebounding, and was second on the team in shooting percentage and assists that season.

Patrone finished the season averaging 14.6

points per game. Ritchie also had a fine season with averages of 11.6 points and 7.6 rebounds, and sophomore Jim McCormick proved that he could handle the other guard position by averaging 12.7 points per game. The Mountaineers were No. 9 in the AP poll and No. 12 in the UPI poll—West Virginia's seventh consecutive season-ending finish in the top 20.

A reinvigorated Thorn got off to a good start in the '62 opener against William & Mary, scoring 23 points, and then in subsequent games produced 24 versus The Citadel, 30 against Furman and 21 against Richmond.

However, when Thorn struggled shooting the ball against VMI and Penn State, McCormick was there to pick up the slack. The New Martinsville native scored 25 in the VMI victory, and hit for 16 on the road at Penn State to boost West Virginia's record to 6–0.

Despite WVU's strong start, the No. 7 Blue Devils were able to come into the Field House before Christmas to snap West Virginia's winning streak, 69–65. Jack Mullen and Art Heyman combined to score 45 points, while West Virginia native Buzzy Hairston added 14. Forty-two of West Virginia's 65 points came from Thorn and McCormick.

McCormick's route to West Virginia University had more twists and turns than a country road. Despite averaging nearly 30 points per game at Magnolia High School, he first spent a year at Greenbrier Military Academy before coming to WVU. Schaus didn't offer him a scholarship right away and McCormick had to pay his own way to school his first year in Morgantown. Eventually, his outstanding play warranted a full scholarship when King took over.

"Jim McCormick was later drafted in the third round by Cincinnati and that was when the draft had seven or eight picks in the first round," said Thorn. "He was one of the top 25 players in the country his senior year."

A pair of losses to Utah and No. 9 Purdue followed in the Los Angeles Classic. Then, a victory against Army during the final night in Los Angeles started an eight-game winning streak that included a 52-point win at George Washington. The Mountaineers produced a record 120 points—

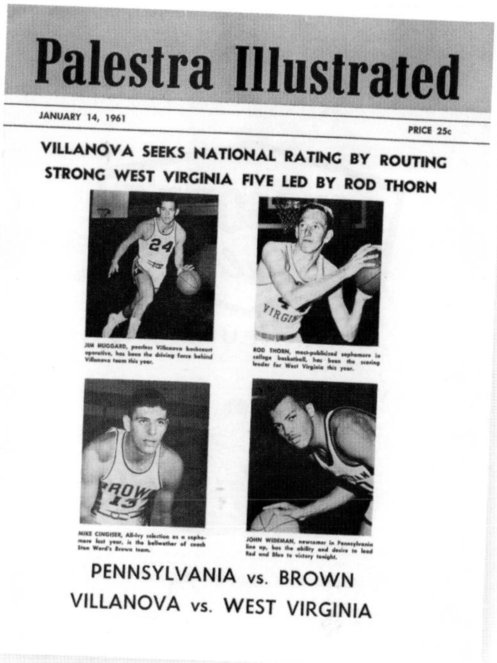

Palestra Illustrated

JANUARY 14, 1961 PRICE 25c

VILLANOVA SEEKS NATIONAL RATING BY ROUTING STRONG WEST VIRGINIA FIVE LED BY ROD THORN

JIM HUGGARD, peerless Villanova backcourt operative, has been the driving force behind Villanova team this year.

ROD THORN, most-publicized sophomore in college basketball, has been the scoring leader for West Virginia this year.

MIKE CINGISER, All-Ivy selection as a sophomore last year, is the bellwether of coach Stan Ward's Brown team.

JOHN WIDEMAN, newcomer in Pennsylvania line up, has the ability and desire to lead Red and Blue to victory tonight.

PENNSYLVANIA vs. BROWN
VILLANOVA vs. WEST VIRGINIA

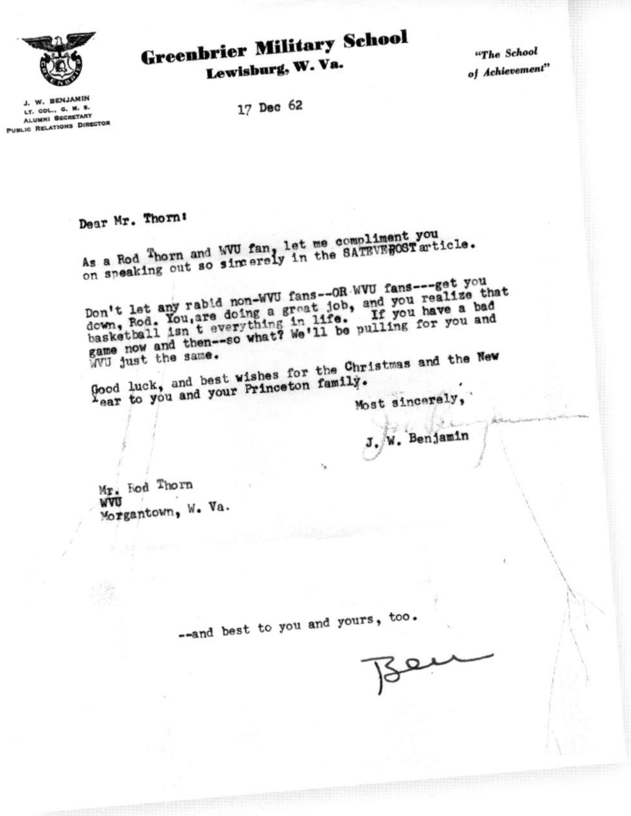

Greenbrier Military School
Lewisburg, W. Va.

"The School of Achievement"

J. W. BENJAMIN
LT. COL., G. M. S.
ALUMNI SECRETARY
PUBLIC RELATIONS DIRECTOR

17 Dec 62

Dear Mr. Thorn:

As a Rod Thorn and WVU fan, let me compliment you on speaking out so sincerely in the SATEVEPOST article.

Don't let any rabid non-WVU fans--OR WVU fans---get you down, Rod. You,are doing a great job, and you realize that basketball isn t everything in life. If you have a bad game now and then--so what? We'll be pulling for you and WVU just the same.

Good luck, and best wishes for the Christmas and the New Year to you and your Princeton family.

Most sincerely,

J. W. Benjamin

Mr. Rod Thorn
WVU
Morgantown, W. Va.

--and best to you and yours, too.

Ben

Thorn scored 32, McCormick had 20, and Paul Miller added 18—as West Virginia shot nearly 60 percent for the game.

The streak eventually ended in Blacksburg

with an 85–82 loss to the Hokies. Tech's win was the 30th in a row at Cassell Coliseum, and it snapped West Virginia's 10-game Southern Conference winning streak.

West Virginia pulled off another big victory in Charleston against Wake Forest two days after the Virginia Tech loss. McCormick scored a career-high 35 points, and Thorn added 26 in a foul-plagued game that saw 59 personals called. Wake's 6-foot-8 forward Len Chappell, who, along with guard Billy Packer, would lead the Demon Deacons to the Final Four that year, scored a game-high 37 points and grabbed 17 rebounds. February began with a controversial finish to West Virginia's 82–81 win over NC State in Greensboro. Both teams were hovering over the scorer's table at the end of regulation when referee George Gasser waved off McCormick's 25-foot shot from the left side of the court that he banked in as he fell flat on his face.

"Later, somebody sent me a picture which showed my shot in the air and the red light atop the basket still hadn't come on," McCormick said. "So it really should have counted." With McCormick's basket voided, the game went into overtime.

More discussion took place at the end of the game after West Virginia, clinging to an 82–79 lead, saw Ken Rohloff score a basket with 10 seconds left to reduce WVU's lead to one. Right after Rohloff's basket, Tom Lowry's inbound pass was batted into the air and State's Russ Marvel came down with it, misfiring on a quick shot just ahead of the buzzer. NC State coach Everett Case argued that he had called time-out with two seconds remaining. The referee and official scorer could not verify Case's claim and ruled the game over. Making the victory even more remarkable was the fact that Thorn did not play because he was nursing a sprained ankle that he aggravated against Tech. Six different WVU players scored double figures, with Miller and Lowry each contributing 14 points.

The Mountaineers finished the season winning five of their remaining six games and took a 20–3 record into Richmond for the beginning of

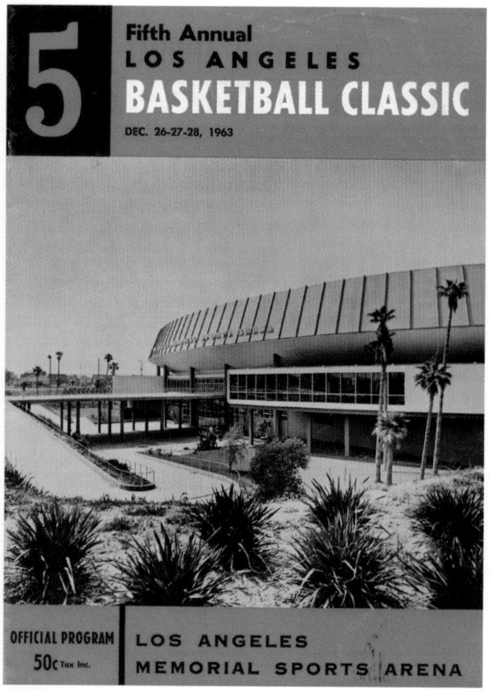

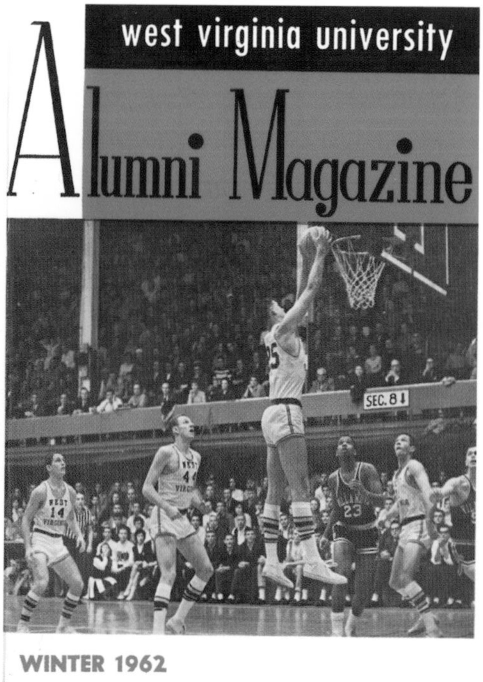

the Southern Conference tournament. Twenty-two-point and 13-point wins over Richmond and George Washington set up a title-game rematch against Virginia Tech.

Jim McCormick sails high to hit a 20-foot jump shot over Oregon State's Steve Pauly and Terry Baker in the first game of the 1962 Kentucky Invitational which West Virginia won 70–65. Just a few days before that game Baker won the Heisman Trophy as a quarterback for the Beavers.

WVU SPORTS COMMUNICATIONS PHOTO.

West Virginia held off the Hokies, 88–72, with sophomore guards Donnie Weir and Kenny Ward as the game's heroes by scoring 17 points each. Weir was playing in place of starting guard Dick Dubois, who had been injured two nights earlier against Richmond. Thorn played a fine all-around game by scoring 15 points and grabbing 16 rebounds, while Gale Catlett contributed 12 points and grabbed 6 rebounds despite playing with an assortment of ailments. It was West Virginia's seventh Southern Conference tournament title in eight years.

Weir's rescue effort earned him a spot on the all-tournament team. "Being named to the all-tournament team probably was the highlight of my career," Weir admitted later.

West Virginia's season ended nine days later when Villanova defeated the Mountaineers, 90–75, in an NCAA tournament first-round game at The Palestra in Philadelphia. Thorn's 23 points were not enough to overcome Hubie White's 28 in front of the partisan Villanova crowd. A key moment in the game came late in the first half when Lowry crashed down on his hip, which rendered West Virginia's center ineffective for the remainder of the game. Additionally, Catlett was nursing a leg injury and suffering from the flu.

"We had played Villanova during the season in Morgantown and we beat them in a really close game [88–82]," Thorn recalled. "They were good, number one. Number two, Wali Jones was terrific [he scored 27 against the Mountaineers]. I scored a bunch of points, but I thought I just played OK in the game."

West Virginia's 24–6 record was the school's seventh straight 20-win season—a remarkable achievement considering that all but one player on the '62 team missed at least one game because of injury. Thorn averaged 23.7 points to earn second-team All-America honors by Converse, AP and UPI. McCormick, Ward, Lowry and Miller also averaged double figures, with Thorn and Lowry both pulling down more than 10 rebounds per contest. West Virginia finished 15th in the AP poll and 16th in the UPI poll.

With Thorn, McCormick, Lowry, Catlett, Weir and Dave Shuck returning, West Virginia was the favorite to claim the Southern Conference title once again in 1963. The Mountaineers began the season ranked fifth in the country and moved up to third after a pair of easy victories over The Citadel and VMI. West Virginia's first loss came at Ohio State on Dec. 8, 1962, when the Mountaineers committed 22 turnovers in a 76–69 defeat.

Charleston reporter Bill Smith recalled a humorous incident involving Mickey Furfari at the Ohio State game. Furfari was upset with the way some of the Buckeye players were roughing up Thorn, and during one particular drive to the basket, Thorn was knocked right into the crowd without a foul being called. Furfari leapt out of his chair and yelled, "No blood, no foul, huh?" The guy sitting next to him was a former Ohio State player and the two started to argue.

"When the guy stood up and Mickey saw how big he was, Mickey had other thoughts," laughed Smith.

Fourteen days later, West Virginia lost 79–75 to Kentucky in the championship game of the Kentucky Invitational Tournament (KIT) in a meeting of top 10 teams. Kentucky's Cotton Nash scored 30 points to overcome an early Wildcat 8–0 deficit.

A pair of victories followed against Boston College and St. Bonaventure before West Virginia lost to No. 4-ranked Illinois in the championship game of the Holiday Festival in New York City. The Mountaineers won seven of their next nine to take a 13–5 record into Pittsburgh to face the Panthers at Fitzgerald Field House.

Despite leading by 16 points early in the second half, the Mountaineers had to hold on for dear life in a game that ended in controversy. Pitt's triangle-and-two defense held Thorn to 14 points and McCormick to 7, while Lowry led the Mountaineers with 19 points. Pitt thought it had pulled out a victory when Dave Roman nailed a 40-foot shot with three seconds left that would have made the score 69–68.

However, an official correctly ruled that Pitt players Tim Grgurich and Ben Jinks had called

Rod Thorn attempts a shot over Ohio State All-American center Gary Bradds in this game at St. John's Arena in Columbus, Ohio on Dec. 8, 1962. The Buckeyes defeated the Mountaineers 76–69.
WVU SPORTS COMMUNICATIONS PHOTO.

WEST
44
VIRGINIA

Below Center Tom Lowry tries a jump shot over NYU's Happy Hairston in this 1963 NCAA tournament East Regional consolation game in College Park, Md. Lowry scored 12 points to help West Virginia to an 83–73 victory over the Violets.

WVU SPORTS COMMUNICATIONS PHOTO.

time-out before Roman got the shot off, and the basket was waved off. Panther fans protested furiously. Pitt's second try at a winning basket by Jinks was unsuccessful. Afterward, Pitt coach Ben Timmons said he called a time-out in order to set his team up for a better shot opportunity. In the end, it was Lowry's basket with six seconds left that provided the winning margin for West Virginia.

"We wanted anyone to take that last shot as quickly as possible—anyone with a good, open shot," King explained after the game. "Lowry got it near the key and he made a beauty."

Pitt got revenge 11 days later in the Field House in a rough game that saw Pitt's Brian Generalovich and West Virginia's Gale Catlett ejected in the second half for fighting. West Virginia was also playing without Thorn, who was resting in the university infirmary with the flu. As was the case in Pittsburgh, the game came down to the wire with the losing team having a chance to win it. After King called time-out with nine seconds remaining, the Mountaineers had two tries to pull ahead, but shots by Bill Maphis and Shuck missed. Pitt's victory snapped West Virginia's 13-game winning streak over the Panthers.

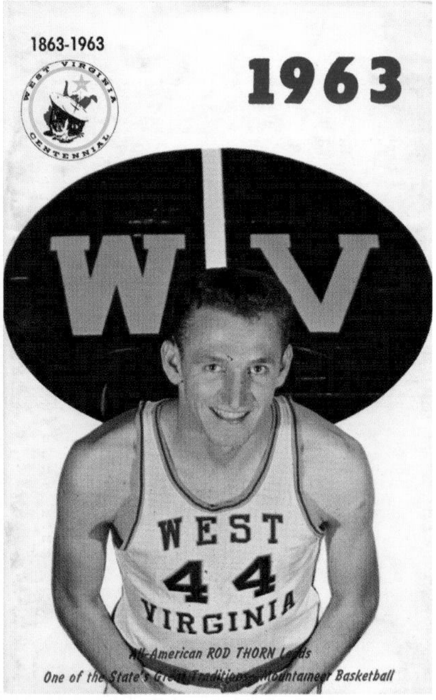

"We had never lost to Pitt," Thorn recalled. "If I had to do it over, I would have played that game even though I had a 102 degree fever with the flu. I thought we could beat those guys even if I didn't play."

Another physical game took place at University Park, resulting in Catlett getting tossed out of the game again, this time for breaking the nose of Nittany Lion reserve forward Terry Hoover. West Virginia had built a 13-point lead when the Lions staged a furious rally with 3:30 remaining. Penn State's Earl Hoffman, who scored a game-high 35 points, had a chance to win it for the Lions, but he missed in the closing seconds. A day later, a remorseful Catlett issued a public apology in the local newspaper.

"Gale was like my policeman," laughed Thorn. "He really took care of them."

The Mountaineers wrapped up the regular season in Morgantown with a 104–86 victory over George Washington to make their record 18–7.

A pair of easy wins over Richmond and Furman set up a meeting with up-and-coming Davidson in the Southern Conference tournament championship. The Wildcats were undergoing a revival under its young coach Lefty Driesell, who

Right Rugged Gale Catlett was West Virginia's defensive enforcer during a three-year varsity career that saw trips to the NCAA tournament during his junior and senior seasons in 1962 and 1963.

WVU SPORTS COMMUNICATIONS PHOTO.

had one of the country's best big men in 6-foot-9 center Fred Hetzel.

West Virginia had to play a long stretch of the second half with Thorn on the bench after his knee buckled trying to block a shot taken by Davidson's Terry Holland. Thorn managed to return with the Mountaineers trailing 61–57, and he keyed the comeback. His pair of free throws with 35 seconds remaining iced the 79–74 victory.

"I thought the show was over," remarked King when Thorn went down. "His return gave us a big boost. You could see it."

The deciding play came with 1:22 left when Mike Wolfe put the Mountaineers ahead 75–72. It was Wolfe's first field goal since the tournament's opening game against Richmond.

Thorn finished the game with 22 points and was named most valuable player for the second straight year. He wound up scoring a total of 75 points in the three tournament games.

"We were really fired up and we got off to a great start with about a 20-point lead early and then I hurt my knee," Thorn recalled. "I remember sitting over there and they kept coming back and coming back. We had to make free throws to win the game."

In the first round of the NCAA tournament in Philadelphia, sophomore Ricky Ray made seven of eight free throws during the remaining 2:26 to lead West Virginia to a 77–71 victory over Connecticut, making it just the third time in eight NCAA appearances that the Mountaineers advanced past the first round.

Thorn managed to lead WVU with 17 points despite playing on a knee that was heavily bandaged, requiring him to play under the basket for most of the game.

Thorn had the best game of his career against St. Joseph's in the second round at College Park, Md., but that was not enough to stop the Hawks, who pulled out a 97–88 triumph. Thorn scored a career-high 44 points, making 16 of 28 from the field and adding 12 of 15 from the free throw line. Jim McCormick scored 23, but St. Joseph's was much more balanced with its four top players all scoring between 17 and 23 points.

"We lost to St. Joe and we should have beaten them," said Thorn. "Duke was the better team [at the regional], and I don't think we would have beaten Duke because Duke handled St. Joe in the finals."

A day later Thorn wrapped up his WVU career with 33 points in a consolation-round victory against NYU. Thorn's two-game total of 77 points broke Jerry West's Eastern Regional scoring record set in 1959. "The consolation game

A bad knee prevented Romney's Bill Maphis from attaining star status accorded to West Virginia's other homegrown high school All-Americans Hot Rod Hundley, Jerry West and Rod Thorn. Still Maphis managed to average 9.5 points per game for his career, including a 13.5-points-per-game average as a senior in 1965.

WVU SPORTS COMMUNICATIONS PHOTO.

we played NYU with Happy Hairston and Barry Kramer, who was the second-leading scorer in the nation that year and ended up getting drafted in the first round of the NBA, so they had a good team," Thorn said.

"I'll never forget it, I had 33 points with 10 minutes left in the game and we went into a stall. I kept thinking, 'This is a third-place game and we're going into a stall?' We ended up winning but I never scored again. I would have had at least 44 in that game if we would have kept playing."

Thorn averaged 22.5 points per game his senior season and finished his career third on the school's all-time scoring list behind West and Hundley. *Look* magazine, Helms Foundation, *Coach & Athlete* magazine and Converse all named Thorn to their All-America teams.

Thorn was the third overall pick in the 1963 NBA draft by the Baltimore Bullets, behind Cincinnati's Tom Thacker and Duke's Art Heyman, and ahead of such players as Nate Thurmond, Gus Johnson and Larry Brown. He played eight seasons with four different teams, averaging 10.8 points per game during an injury-plagued pro career.

McCormick also wrapped up a fine college career by scoring more than 1,000 points, giving West Virginia one of the best one-two backcourt scoring combinations in school history. The

Right Rod Thorn attempts a shot over St. Joseph's John Tiller during the 1963 NCAA tournament East Regional semifinals in College Park, Md. Thorn scored a career-high 44 points against the Hawks, but that was not enough to keep St. Joseph's from winning 97–88.
WVU SPORTS COMMUNICATIONS PHOTO.

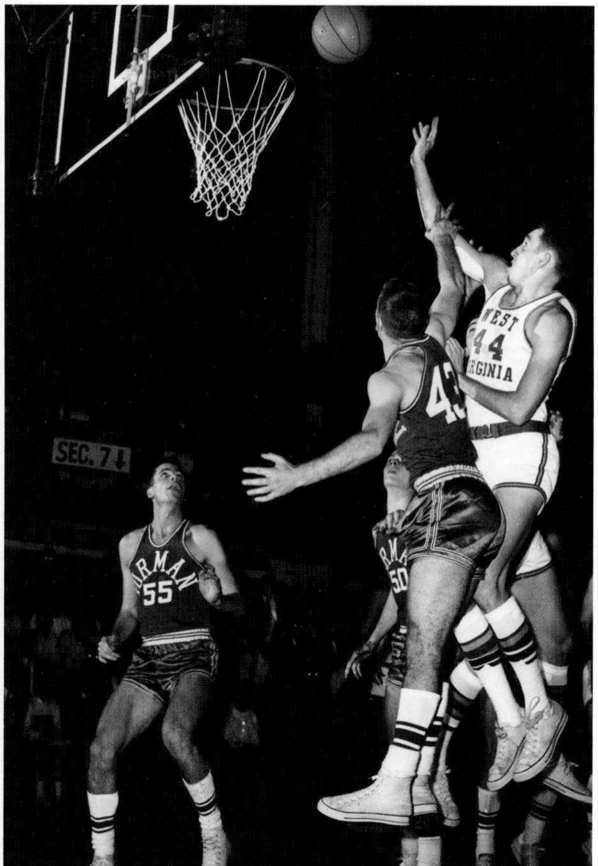

Below Rod Thorn scores two of his team-high 38 points in West Virginia's 101–86 victory over Furman on Feb. 24, 1962.
WVU SPORTS COMMUNICATIONS PHOTO.

Mountaineers finished 16th in the final UPI poll, making it the ninth straight year West Virginia completed a basketball season in the rankings.

Trouble on the Horizon

With Thorn, McCormick, Catlett and Shuck gone to graduation, West Virginia was confronted with a rebuilding season for the first time in 10 years. It was something Mountaineer fans were not totally prepared for.

West Virginia's 18–10 record in 1964 would have been acceptable by most standards, but not those dyed-in-the-wool WVU fans spoiled by the great string of All-America players and Southern Conference championships the school had regularly produced since 1955. West Virginia had a good, solid team with Lowry (15.6 ppg), junior Buddy Quertinmont (10.3 ppg) and Ray (10.2 ppg) leading the way, but it did not possess quite the star power it had in the past with Hundley, West or Thorn.

"My sophomore year I sat because I played behind Thorn, McCormick and Weir. Back then you had to wait your turn because there were just too many damned good players," Quertinmont said.

WVU also faced a difficult regular-season schedule with St. John's and Duke coming to Morgantown to play in the Centennial Classic, games against Illinois and USC in the Los Angeles Clas-

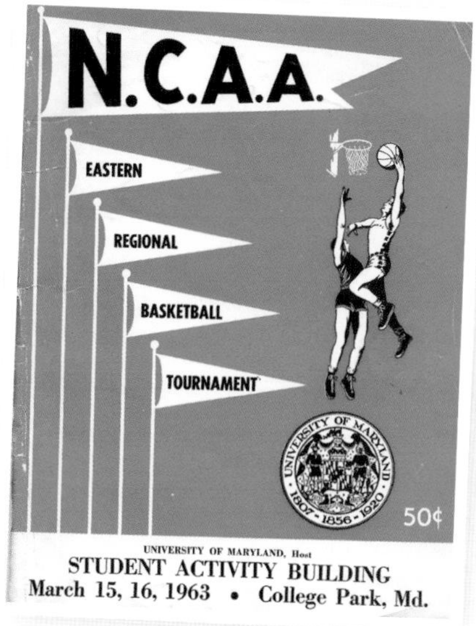

Below Huntington's Rick Ray, pictured here in this 1964 game at the Field House against Pitt, averaged 10.2 points per game that season including scoring a career-high 22 points in a 75–73 victory over VMI.

WEST VIRGINIA AND REGIONAL HISTORY COLLECTION.

sic, and non-conference match-ups against Maryland, Syracuse and Penn State.

A bizarre finish to the West Virginia-Davidson game played in Charleston led to one of the biggest upset victories in school history. The Wildcats brought a 15-game unbeaten streak and a No. 3 national rating into the capital city for a Jan. 29, 1964 meeting with the Mountaineers.

A tight game throughout, the contest was decided with two seconds left when Marty Lentz heaved a one-handed, half-court shot that Fred Hetzel tipped away from the basket just as the horn sounded. Official Red Mihalik called goaltending and awarded the two points to the Mountaineers for a 75–73 victory. Davidson coach Lefty Driesell ran after the game's other referee Otis Almond—either to argue his case or to strangle him.

"It's a heck of a way to lose," remarked Driesell after the game. "If I'm going to get beat on a shot from 50 feet, I would accept it more easily than I do on goaltending."

"I couldn't tell if the shot was going in from where I was," King added. "It looked like the shot was going to be close, but I couldn't see if it was high enough.

"That shot was definitely not something we worked on in practice. But I think I will have Lentz start working on it tomorrow," King joked.

Lost in all the commotion was Lowry's fantastic performance against Hetzel. West Virginia's center finished with 19 points and 19 rebounds, and was WVU's only reliable shooter in a game in which the Mountaineers made just 34.9 percent of their field goal tries.

The Davidson victory set in motion a seven-game winning streak that boosted West Virginia's record to 16–8. One of those seven victories came against Pitt in Morgantown when Maphis scored 22 points and grabbed 16 rebounds in what was becoming a typical "Backyard Brawl" that was marred by 68 fouls and six disqualifications.

West Virginia's season ended in the semifinals of the Southern Conference tournament when George Washington upset the Mountaineers 88–80. It was only the second time in 10 years

A STREAK OF ALL-AMERICANS

They used to say that WVU publicist Eddie Barrett had the easiest job in the country. He just waited to see who arrived on campus during the fall semester to begin promoting another basketball All-American.

West Virginia's All-America tradition began in 1942 when guard Scotty Hamilton was named to the Helms Foundation All-America team. Five years later Leland Byrd was honored in 1947.

Then the streak of West Virginia All-Americans continued with center Mark Workman in 1952 and spanned 11 years until 1963.

In succession, West Virginia had Workman, Hot Rod Hundley, Jerry West and Rod Thorn. Hundley earned All-America honors in 1956 and 1957, West was a two-time All-American in 1959 and 1960, and Thorn twice captured the award in 1962 and 1963.

There were other All-America players sandwiched in during that period as well. Center Lloyd Sharrar made the Associated Press All-America second team in 1958 and guard Lee Patrone was named to the Helms Foundation All-America third team in 1961.

that West Virginia failed to make the Southern Conference tournament championship game.

Perhaps King's biggest accomplishment in 1964 was convincing high school All-America guard Ron "Fritz" Williams from Weirton to attend West Virginia University. Williams, like Thorn, West and Hundley before him, had a long list of schools pursuing him. What made him reluctant to commit to West Virginia was his concern that the basketball program at WVU was not yet integrated—he would be the first African American to play at West Virginia. Other schools he was considering, such as Michigan and Ohio State, were already integrated.

"Ron didn't want to be the first one," recalled former Sports Information Director Eddie Barrett.

King's solution was to recruit three African American players to go along with Williams. King pursued Williams' Weir High teammate Ed Harvard; Washington, D.C. forward Jimmy Lewis (on a tip from former professional teammate Earl Lloyd); and ex-Marine Norman Holmes.

"Norman was the one who kind of looked after Ron," recalled Buddy Quertinmont.

In 2004, four years before his death, King said he had no idea those four players were the first African American players to play in the Southern Conference. "I'm surprised they were the first," King said. "I never sat in on any plan to integrate our program. I don't remember there being any expressed idea from anyone that we were integrating the Southern Conference. It was a situation where we were simply looking for the best players we could recruit."

In 1962, Williams played in one of the most talked about high school tournament games in state history in Morgantown when his Weirton team lost a buzzer beater to Beckley.

"My mom [Blanche] was unsure about me going to WVU," the late Williams once recalled for Morgantown author Norm Julian. "We lost the state high school finals in Morgantown. I got 35 points and could have got 50, but I fouled out and we lost the game. Most of the fouls were offensive, and mom thought they were singling me out."

King assured the Williams family that there would be no problems for their son either in Morgantown or when the team traveled to other schools in the Southern Conference. He also brought along Athletic Director Red Brown for reassurance. King, Brown and some gentle pressure exerted on Williams' father, Raymond, by Weirton Steel executives led Williams to sign with West Virginia.

For the most part, Williams encountered few problems during his college career and when he did, it usually came on the road at some of the southern schools. One time Williams remembered being heckled by some

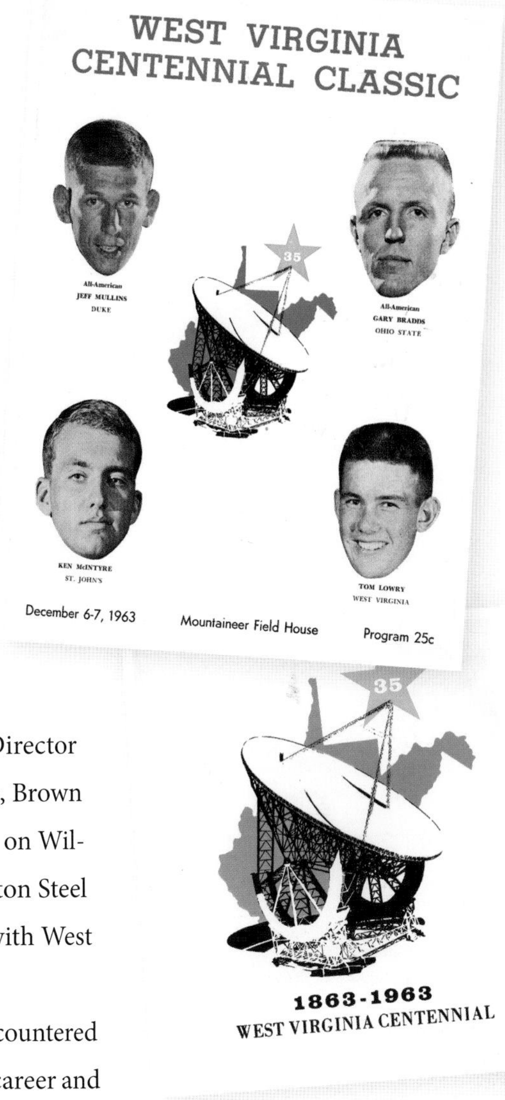

Buddy Quertinmont grew up nine miles from campus in Point Marion, Pa., starring at Albert Gallatin High School. Quertinmont averaged 10.1 points in 68 career games for the Mountaineers from 1963–65.

WVU SPORTS COMMUNICATIONS PHOTO.

In 1965 Bob Camp led the Mountaineers in scoring (15.9 ppg), rebounding (9.8 rpg) and assists (2.5 apg) to join Rod Hundley (1956), Jerry West (1960) and Rod Thorn (1962) as the only players in school history to lead the team in all three statistical categories in one season.

WVU SPORTS COMMUNICATIONS PHOTO.

fans sitting behind the bench until longtime trainer Whitey Gwynne stood up with a water bottle and squirted them right in the face. "They quit heckling us," Williams laughed.

Unfortunately for George King, Williams was not available for the 1965 season, having to spend it instead on the freshman team.

The 1964 season was viewed as a huge disappointment by the fans, but the discord with King actually dated further back than that. Midway through the 1963 season, following a lackluster performance against VMI, WVU students hanged King in effigy.

Thorn was somewhat surprised King's teams struggled after he left because he thought there were good players waiting in the wings. "Bill Maphis I thought was going to be a top player but he ended up getting hurt and never reached his potential," Thorn said. "When he was a freshman, I said, 'Boy, this kid is going to be good.'"

The rope and pillows were out once again for King at the start of the '65 season when the Mountaineers dropped a 75–73 decision to The Citadel (King did not coach that game because he was in the hospital with back spasms). At one point, West Virginia lost six in a row for the school's longest losing streak in 11 years. Attention soon turned to Williams and the undefeated freshman team as the losses began to pile up. King quit talking to popular Morgantown reporter Tony Constantine over a column Constantine had written criticizing King's game strategy. Constantine had enjoyed unfettered access to WVU football and basketball coaches for nearly four decades, and King's decision to cut him out turned out to be an ominous sign. Rock bottom came at St. John's on Feb. 15, when the Mountaineers lost by 19, scoring a season-low 61 points.

A players-only meeting after the St. John's loss led to a school-record 127 points in the season finale against Virginia Tech. The 54-point victory was West Virginia's biggest margin ever against the Hokies. Lentz led the scoring barrage with 27 points as the Mountaineers shot a sizzling 59 percent in the first half.

The team's torrid shooting continued in the Southern Conference tournament. West Virginia beat George Washington 94–83 before going into overtime to upset No. 6 Davidson 74–72 in the semifinals. The Mountaineers were able to survive a near-fatal, second-half collapse that saw the Wildcats come back from 13 points down to tie it in regulation. West Virginia scored the first basket of overtime and never trailed. John Lesher's follow-up basket with 3:33 remaining gave the Mountaineers a more comfortable cushion. Lesher finished with a team-high 26 points.

The Mountaineers needed more overtime magic to defeat William & Mary 70–67 in the finals to claim their most unlikely tournament championship since joining the Southern Conference in 1950. This time it took two overtimes.

Maphis got West Virginia into the second overtime with a driving layup at the buzzer to tie the game at 63. In second extra session, Bob Camp scored five of West Virginia's seven points to lead the team with 18 points.

A few days after the game, Mickey Furfari made good on a bet he had made in a column declaring that he would dance a jig on the courthouse square if West Virginia won the Southern Conference tournament. "We made sure he did it," laughed Quertinmont.

West Virginia's season may have been extended

by one game, but it ended abruptly at The Palestra on March 8, 1965 when fourth-ranked Providence forced 30 Mountaineer turnovers in a 91–67 Friar victory. West Virginia had reached the NCAA tournament with a .500 record, but the loss gave the school its first losing season in 21 years.

The team's losses that year only added to the criticism of King. Near the end of his final season at West Virginia in 1965, King was heavily criticized for not playing Marty Lentz and John Lesher much earlier in their careers. Lentz scored 27 in West Virginia's 127–73 win against Virginia Tech and averaged 17.4 points over the remaining five games of the season. Lesher, too, got hot at the end of the year by scoring 26 in the Mountaineers' big 74–72 upset victory over sixth-rated Davidson in the Southern Conference tournament semifinals and averaging 15.4 points during the final five games of the '65 season.

Also, despite having a reputation for being an outstanding recruiter, King suffered some stinging losses on the recruiting trail that contributed to fan discord in 1964 and 1965. Forward Ron Sepic, considered one of the five best high school players in the country in 1963 from nearby Uniontown, Pa., considered the Mountaineers before picking Ohio State, where he was a three-year starter for the Buckeyes and a 1,000-point scorer. That same year, King also lost South Charleston's Gary Gregor to Chuck Noe at South Carolina. Gregor later played six years of professional basketball with five different teams.

King Takes Purdue Job

A month after the Providence loss, King chose to accept Red Mackey's offer to replace Ray Eddy at Purdue. King's five-year record at West Virginia of 102–43 was second only to Schaus's 146–37 mark.

"The people in West Virginia indicated that they expected me to do a real good job next year with a bunch of sophomores," King said shortly after his resignation. "The pressure is considerable. There is a lot more pressure than there should be."

"I think there was some relief on his part to leave West Virginia because he knew that no matter what he did he couldn't fill the large shoes that Fred Schaus left," Barrett said.

King's West Virginia teams relied on full-court pressing, turnovers and fast break baskets, but he wasn't the type of coach to get down on his knees and draw up winning plays. In that respect, his approach was very similar to the way John Beilein coached at West Virginia four decades later.

"There wasn't a great deal of offense," Lochmueller recalled. "I know when I went there they really didn't have much in the way of an offense against the zone. One that I had used in high school we incorporated and it worked real well for us because we had the people that could shoot outside in Thorn and McCormick."

"We used to practice fast breaking off of everything you could think of including taking the ball out of bounds and foul shots," said Buddy Quertinmont. "George loved to fast break."

Lochmueller said King's WVU teams were typically guard-oriented because the guards were better than the inside players they had at the time. "For example, during Rod Thorn's last year he led our team in rebounding," Lochmueller said. "We tried to block out with inside people and let him release from the outside so he could get the break started by either getting it out to McCormick or taking it himself."

Lochmueller got the impression that they had

Alexandria, Virginia's Marty Lentz had a solid three-year career for the Mountaineers, earning second-team all-Southern Conference honors in 1965, but he never matched the great fanfare he achieved in high school after breaking Elgin Baylor's area scoring record with 74 points in one game against J. E. B. Stuart in 1961.

WVU SPORTS COMMUNICATIONS PHOTO.

BREAKING DOWN BARRIERS

George King was looking for some good basketball players. After eight straight 20-win seasons West Virginia had slipped to 18–10 in 1964 and King was starting to hear it from the fans.

One of the best high school basketball players in the country that year just happened to be located in Weirton, W.Va., named Ron Williams. He also happened to be black. The West Virginia basketball program was not yet integrated, and despite a lot of pressure to remain in-state, Williams was reluctant to become a racial pioneer at West Virginia University.

1965 WEST VIRGINIA UNIVERSITY FRESHMAN BASKETBALL SQUAD
Front: Jim Lewis, Letcher Humphries, Dick Penrod, David Reaser, Ron Williams.

"He was as difficult a recruiting project as there was," recalled King in 2004, two years before his death.

Williams could very easily have gone to Michigan where Cazzie Russell was starring, or to Ohio State where Woody Hayes had integrated the Buckeye football program in the 1950s. West Virginia played in the Southern Conference and was just beginning to integrate its athletic program with Phil Edwards joining the track team in 1961, and Dick Leftridge and Roger Alford arriving to play on the freshman football team in 1962.

King had seen firsthand what overt racism was like playing professional basketball in the 1950s because, at that time, there were places his black teammates could not go. "Pro ball in those days a black man was accepted like anyone else," King recalled. "There were no differences made. In fact, we got upset during the few occasions when they were treated differently like when we went to Baltimore. Earl Lloyd couldn't stay in our hotel and that made us all mad."

King's friendship with Lloyd grew over the years. In fact, it was Lloyd who steered Virginia's Jim Lewis to West Virginia. King also began recruiting Norman Holmes, a more mature player fresh out of the Marine Corps, in hopes of convincing Williams to choose WVU." He was almost supposed to be like Ron's big brother to watch after him and teach him a little bit," teammate Buddy Quertinmont recalled.

King also recruited Williams's Weirton teammate Ed "Possum" Harvard. "We didn't do any cheating, but to get Ron we also had to take the Possum," said assistant coach Bob Lochmueller.

Finally, King took Athletic Director Red Brown to Weirton for a visit with the Williams family to alleviate any concerns they might have had about their son going to West Virginia.

"There were a lot of people that wanted him to go to West Virginia because at that time he was like a Jerry West coming out of high school," said Harvard. "He was a legend and everyone in the country wanted him. George King kept coming and kept coming and he finally committed to WVU. Everybody in the state of West Virginia was very happy."

"I recruited Fritzy basically to kind of fit a pattern that the university had fallen into maybe accidentally of having a great player kind of lead you and spark the rest of the people," King recalled. "It started with Hot Rod Hundley and Jerry West and then Rod Thorn. All of these guys were in the 6´2˝, 6´3˝ range; great players, great ball handlers, great shooters and great scorers. I really

Ron Williams (top) and fellow freshmen Jim Lewis, Ed "Possum" Harvard and Norman Holmes successfully integrated Southern Conference basketball as members of the 1965 West Virginia freshman team, pictured above.

WVU SPORTS COMMUNICATIONS PHOTOS.

recruited Fritzy to fall into that same category . . . . That was where I was going with him."

King said the fact that Williams, Lewis, Harvard and Holmes would be the first African American basketball players in the Southern Conference had never even entered his mind.

"I'm surprised they were the first," he said. "I never sat in on any plan to actively recruit and integrate our program. If it happened, I didn't know about it. I don't remember anyone mentioning any of that to me."

King never got an opportunity to coach Williams and the rest of his freshman players. He took the Purdue job after the 1965 season before Williams moved up to the varsity.

"I just was there the one year with Fritz and the rest of them. Freshmen weren't eligible then so I didn't have the chance to travel with them," King explained. "To a degree, I thought he did do the things that I thought he could do. My style of coaching was a little more freelance than Bucky [Waters] would have been involved with. I was more of an individualist.

"In fact, I remembered reading an article about my '69 Purdue team and they quoted the kid that made me a hell of a coach for three years—Rick Mount. Rick said Coach King let us play the game the way we wanted to play the game—or something to that effect. That was really the thought I had in mind with Fritz, too."

Not only did Williams have a fabulous career at West Virginia, but he also served as a direct link to the Mountaineers' next great player—Uniontown, Pa.'s Wil Robinson. "I was recruited by all of the Pittsburgh schools and colleges all over the place," Robinson said. "Ron Williams was really the reason I went down there. When Fritz was a senior he spent a lot of time at my house and we became good friends. He used to talk to me about how great the basketball tradition was at West Virginia, and I just had a lot of respect for him."

worn out their welcome by 1965. "[Purdue] contacted George and he came out here in Indiana and talked to them," Lochmueller said. "He came back and he was pretty positive. His wife was a little reluctant."

"When George King got the Purdue job he said to me, 'Sit down, you won't believe this,'" Barrett recalled. "'I got the job at Purdue and I'm not going to make some of the same mistakes I made here.'"

"It turned out great for him," Thorn said. "He ended up going to the Final Four there with Rick Mount."

With King gone, Red Brown was now faced with the prospect of hiring his third basketball coach in 11 years. With no compelling candidate available with WVU ties, Brown decided to step outside the Mountaineer basketball family to hire his next coach. The man he eventually found was only 29 years old. That formula—hiring a young, unproven coach—had worked remarkably well once before for Brown when he hired Fred Schaus in 1954.

West Virginia got on a roll at the end of the year in 1965 when John Lesher finally got an opportunity to play. It was Lesher's 26 points that led to WVU's 74–72 upset victory over sixth-rated Davidson in the Southern Conference tournament semifinals.

WVU SPORTS COMMUNICATIONS PHOTO.

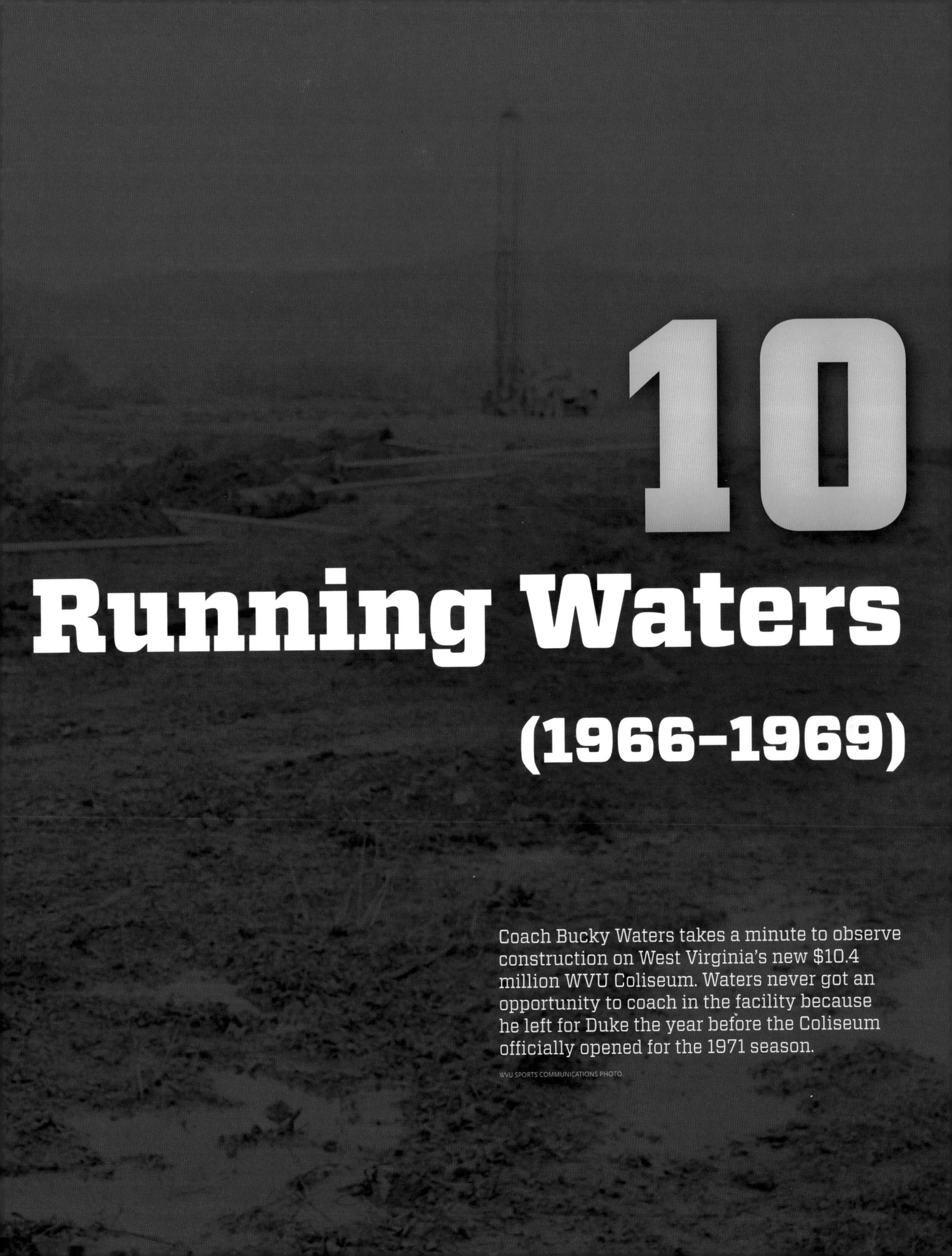

10

Running Waters

(1966–1969)

Coach Bucky Waters takes a minute to observe construction on West Virginia's new $10.4 million WVU Coliseum. Waters never got an opportunity to coach in the facility because he left for Duke the year before the Coliseum officially opened for the 1971 season.

WVU SPORTS COMMUNICATIONS PHOTO.

Red Brown was holed up in his office at Mountaineer Field working the phones trying to find a new basketball coach. Outside, factions were starting to form. The players took a vote and overwhelmingly supported freshman coach Quentin Barnette. WVU backers in the Clarksburg-Fairmont area were in favor of hiring highly successful Fairmont State coach Joe Retton. In the southern part of the state, folks were split on West Virginia Tech's Neal Baisi and former WVU star player Willie Akers, then coaching at Logan High School. Akers had been under the impression that he was going to be George King's assistant coach for the 1966 season.

Bucky Waters was the No. 1 assistant coach at Duke before taking the West Virginia job in the spring of 1965.
WVU SPORTS COMMUNICATIONS PHOTO.

"I was already hired to go with George King because Lochmueller was leaving," recalled Akers. "I was locked in. Then all of the sudden Red Brown calls and says George is leaving and going to Purdue, but that everything was OK and that I would be there."

But circumstances changed when Brown turned his attention to up-and-coming Duke assistant coach Raymond "Bucky" Waters. Waters grew up near Philadelphia in New Jersey before going to NC State to play basketball for Everett Case. Following graduation in 1958, Waters briefly coached high school basketball in North Carolina before taking a job on Duke's staff as freshman coach. Eventually, he rose to Vic Bubas's No. 1 assistant after Fred Shabel went to Connecticut.

When the WVU job came open Red Brown wasn't the only athletic director pursuing Waters. "I had an offer from LSU and it came down to LSU and West Virginia," Waters said. "At that time basketball was really, really important at West Virginia with its great tradition. If I had gone to LSU, I would have been the redheaded stepchild."

Waters Takes Over

Waters was young, handsome and well-spoken. He made a great first impression, but there were many Mountaineer supporters concerned about his youth and inexperience. Others thought that he was simply using West Virginia as a stepping stone to Duke when Bubas retired.

"We're going to my press conference to announce I'm being hired and Eddie Barrett was with Red Brown and Jack Fleming, and they were just grilling me," Waters recalled. "I'm 29, I've got my sleeves rolled up and I'm ready to attack the world and Eddie says, 'What would you say if the press asks you if you want to play Marshall?' I said, 'Sure.' The three of them jumped on me and said, 'You can't say that!'

"'Why, are they that good?' They said no and then they went into this whole political thing that I had no idea about. I got a real education there."

Waters was dramatically different from George King. King coached a freelance style with very few set plays and a lot of individual freedom while Waters employed a much more disciplined system. Waters worked his players like a Marine drill sergeant. They were not allowed to talk during practice, they were required to sprint to their next drill, and when there were short water breaks, the players were ordered to sit in chairs spaced far enough apart to discourage small talk. Bucky had pre-recorded music piped into the gym to simulate crowd noise and he issued a pair of lace practice pants to any player whose performance was deemed "ladylike." Once, forward Dave Reaser split the backside of his shorts during practice and the only replacements available were Waters's lace practice shorts. Reaser opted to continue practicing in his ripped pants. Waters had one drill where he rolled the ball out on the floor and two players were required to dive after it, often skinning their knees and bruising their arms in the process.

Bucky also had a flair for the dramatic. He introduced spotlights and hoops for the team to run through during pre-game introductions and he had special cheering sections created for the fans. He even came up with catchy names for personnel groupings to make his reserve players feel more important such as the "Blockbusters," the "Gangbusters" and the "Trouble Shooters."

When he wanted to hold the ball and run out the clock, he yelled "mongoose!" On road trips it was a rule for his players to wear sport coats and hats. And when being addressed, the players were required to answer "yes, sir" and "no, sir."

When Waters arrived at WVU as the nation's youngest major college basketball coach, he made it known right away that he wasn't all that impressed with what King had left him, especially the freshman team that was rated one of the five best in the nation by *The Sporting News*. He downplayed the freshmen, saying they were no better than most of the freshman teams he had seen in the ACC. Waters had scouted West Virginia's frosh in person at Pitt, and in his words, he "wasn't awed by them." Of course, Waters was hedging his bets.

Lochmueller thought differently, saying they set Waters up with a good nucleus of young players. "Reaser was a good player right outside of Charleston, and I recruited a player out of Elkhart, Ind., named Dick Penrod. And of course there was Fritz Williams. We felt that group had a lot of potential," he said. "When we left we didn't feel like the cupboard was bare."

There remained openings on the roster and

Bucky Waters ended the West Virginia tradition of the players running out on the carpet during the pregame introductions. Under Waters, the West Virginia players ran through a hoop from the other side of the floor directly to the team's bench.

WEST VIRGINIA AND REGIONAL HISTORY COLLECTION.

the first thing Waters did was steal junior college All-American forward Carl Head away from Wake Forest. Head was the first of several junior college players Waters recruited to West Virginia.

"They had a losing season the year before and I'm sure that brought some heat on George," Waters said. "We had to infuse some talent with Carl Head and kids like that."

Carl Head was one of the great forgotten players in WVU history, averaging 17.1 points per game and shooting 53 percent from the floor for his Mountaineer career.

WEST VIRGINIA AND REGIONAL HISTORY COLLECTION.

Waters soon began competing with football's Jim Carlen (another young head coach hired at about the same time) for Red Brown's attention. The two could be very persuasive.

WEST VIRGINIA
The Tradition Goes On:
New Coach Bucky Waters, Athletic Director Red Brown
1966

"First of all, Red was a basketball guy and that helped," Waters said. "He said to me one time, 'Bucky, you and Carlen are going to be the death of me.' He's got these two young bulldogs on a leash and he says, 'You are pulling me one way and he's pulling me the other, and I can't stand up straight.'"

Waters's starting lineup for the '66 season opener against VMI in Charleston included two newcomers—sophomore Williams and junior Head. Charleston's Bob Benfield, John Lesher and Dave Palmer—part-time starters in 1965—were also in the lineup. All eyes were on Williams, who was fighting a bad case of the nerves in his varsity debut. Williams made just 5 of his 22 field goal attempts for 12 points in an 11-point Mountaineer victory. A sportswriter standing next to Williams's locker made mention in the paper the following morning of Williams's trembling hands while he was being interviewed.

Fritz loosened up three nights later against George Washington, scoring a game-high 30 points to lead West Virginia to a 105–80 victory. He then scored 68 points in two games at the Milwaukee Classic to earn MVP honors.

Later that year, Williams would set a Southern Conference tournament record with 23 assists in three games. He averaged 19.7 points per game and handed out a team-best 153 assists during his first varsity campaign. Right away pro scouts were impressed. "Williams is the kind we can use right now," said St. Louis Hawks scout Marty Blake. "He's tough, smart and he knows what to do with the ball."

West Virginia's first big victory under Waters came in Raleigh, N.C., against North Carolina on Dec. 31, 1965—one day after losing by 17 to NC State. Still smarting from the loss to Wolfpack, Waters informed Palmer just two hours before the game that he was going to guard North Carolina's top scorer, Bob Lewis, who was averaging 34 points per game.

Palmer and John Cavacini tag-teamed Lewis all game, holding Lewis 22 points below his season's average. Williams, playing with a sore wrist, scored 18 points in the first half to give the Mountaineers a six-point halftime lead. WVU built its lead to 10 in the second half but had to hang on for a 102–97 victory. Williams and Head scored 25 points each, with Head also grabbing 12 rebounds.

"We are fairly green, but we are real pleased at the way we held our poise when Carolina came back," Waters remarked after the game. "It was a great mental problem to come back against a team like this after looking bad much of the game the night before."

Two months later, Waters pulled off one of the most stunning victories of the year when West Virginia knocked off top-rated Duke in Charleston. Duke was No. 1 at the time it faced West Virginia, but Kentucky was poised to jump ahead of the Blue Devils in the AP poll the next morning. Duke had lost just once in 16 games when it arrived in Charleston, and the Blue Devils boasted two terrific players in Jack Marin and Mike Lewis.

Despite playing just once in a span of 23 days, Duke showed little rust in jumping out to an early 19-point lead. Then Waters put in the "Gangbusters"—Cavacini, Gary Shaffer and Norman Holmes—and they helped close West Virginia's deficit to three by halftime. In the second half there were 11 lead changes until the Mountaineers took the lead for good on a Lesher basket. Two Lesher free throws extended the margin to a more comfortable five points with 2:12 remaining

Waters was mobbed on the floor by happy West Virginia fans when the game was over and afterward he showed genuine remorse for beating the man who had given him his first college job. Some saw it as a touching tribute to Vic Bubas. Others were rubbed the wrong way, believing it was proof that Waters's heart wasn't completely with West Virginia.

After a loss to Richmond, West Virginia ended the regular season with a memorable 99–95 overtime victory over a Syracuse team featuring All-American guard Dave Bing and his bespectacled backcourt mate, Jim Boeheim. The Mountaineers came back from an eight-point second-half deficit when Syracuse coach Fred Lewis's decision to hold the ball backfired.

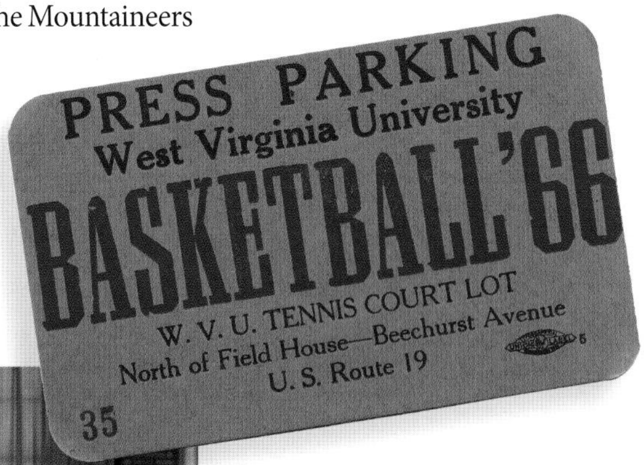

Bucky Waters's 1966 club was the first integrated varsity basketball team in school history.

WVU SPORTS COMMUNICATIONS PHOTO.

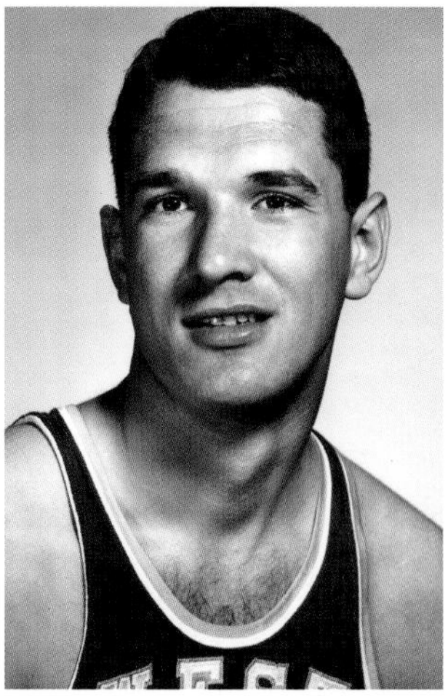

Bill Ryczaj scored a season-high 19 points off the bench to help West Virginia upset No. 1-ranked Duke in Charleston on Feb. 7, 1966.

WVU SPORTS COMMUNICATIONS PHOTO.

In overtime, Head pulled West Virginia ahead, 91–88 with a pair of baskets, and Bill Ryczaj sealed it with a jumper and a pair of free throws. Head was magnificent, scoring 28 points and grabbing nine rebounds. Ryczaj scored 19 and Cavacini contributed 18. Bing made 22 points for Syracuse, but was just 11 of 29 shooting.

West Virginia eventually reached the Southern Conference tournament championship game where it lost 80–69 to Davidson. It was an outstanding first season for Waters, although some complained that Waters kept Williams on too tight a leash. Years later, Bucky said it was actually the opposite.

"If anything, I wish there were times when he would have been more assertive," Waters explained. "If I had a fault with Fritz it was that there were nights when he didn't have that much talent around him, and there were nights when I'd get right up in his face and I'd say, 'Fritz, take over. Here's the steering wheel.'"

A Shaft of Light

In the meantime, Red Brown finally saw a shaft of light shine on his decade-long dream of building a new basketball arena. Preliminary plans for a basketball facility were developed in the early 1960s after Fred Schaus left for the Lakers. The initial plan called for a $6 million facility with bleacher seating. As the years went by and the plans were modified several times—one far-flung idea included a retractable roof constructed over the bowl end of the football stadium—the school finally began to focus its attention on a project that was practical and functional. Gradually, it was also decided to remove the $6 million ceiling on the price tag.

With designs and drawings sitting in his desk drawer, Brown watched the university undergo the largest campus expansion in its history. A school of 5,000 in the mid-1950s, it had more than doubled in size in less than 10 years. Finally, Brown's long awaited basketball arena was coming closer to becoming a reality. There remained competing interests, however.

"From my standpoint, our responsibility to the university, as I told Red, was if we don't get

Carl Head goes high in the air for a rebound against Syracuse in this 1966 game played at the Field House. Head scored 28 points to lead the Mountaineers to a 99–95 overtime victory over the Orangemen.

WVU SPORTS COMMUNICATIONS PHOTO.

WEST VIRGINIA 94, DUKE 90

Coach Bucky Waters gets a victory ride from his jubilant players following West Virginia's 94–90 upset of Duke in Charleston.

WVU SPORTS COMMUNICATIONS PHOTO.

Bucky Waters liked to think up nicknames for his West Virginia basketball players, which is something 30-year-old coaches sometimes do. He had a group of players he called the "Gangbusters." There was another group he called the "Blockbusters." He also began calling others the "Trouble Shooters."

The idea behind it was to make everyone feel important. It gave each player a specific job and an identity. "Instead of just being sixth, seventh, eighth and ninth men, they all have specific roles," Waters once explained. "It's good for morale. More boys are playing, but not with mass confusion."

Waters came up with an additional nickname after his team's stunning 94–90 upset victory over No. 1-ranked Duke on Feb. 7, 1966 in Charleston—the "Firemen."

His team was trailing the Blue Devils 31–12 after the first eight minutes of the game so he put in reserves John Cavacini, Gary Shaffer and Norman Holmes with one set of instructions: create havoc.

By halftime, a 19-point Duke lead had been whittled down to three.

"I thought they were going to run us clear out of town," Waters said after the game. "Right then I was the oldest 30-year-old coach in the country."

In the second half, Duke built its lead back to eight, but West Virginia answered with a pair of John Lesher baskets and a rainbow from the corner by Bill Ryczaj to take a 61–60 lead with 10:28 remaining. The lead changed hands 11 more times until Lesher's long jumper with 2:54 left put the Mountaineers up for good, 83–82.

A pair of Lesher's free throws expanded West Virginia's advantage to five with 2:02 to go, and four free throws by Lesher and Cavacini to answer another Duke run secured the four-point victory for West Virginia.

When the horn sounded, fans stormed the court and hoisted Waters on their shoulders for a ride off the Civic Center floor. Waters greeted Duke coach Vic Bubas at midcourt to shake the hand of the man who recruited him to North Carolina State, gave him his first major college basketball job at Duke, and then recommended him for the West Virginia job.

"Nice game, Buck," Bubas said.

Waters couldn't manage a word.

"What could I say to him," said Waters when asked to describe his emotions after the game. "He picked me up by the ears and made me a basketball coach."

Duke's two big guns, Mike Lewis and Jack Marin, had fouled out of the game. The Blue Devils had previously been idle for 23 straight days leading into the game. "Who can tell how much it hurt? We hated to be idle, but we got a tremendous start against West Virginia, probably our best since an early win over UCLA," said Bubas.

Lesher was the game's leading scorer with 28 points, but it was Ryczaj's 19 off the bench that provided the difference in the game. Ryczaj was the only WVU player scoring in the first half when Duke built its big lead.

"I thought the two areas that hurt us were West Virginia's pressure defense and the tip-ins they got," said Bubas.

"It was very trying," Waters said. "I've never been in a game as a player or coach that took so much out of me. Not only was the game exciting and hard-fought, but there I was on the floor looking at the man and the players who were actually responsible for my being at West Virginia."

The euphoria of the Duke conquest lasted exactly four days. West Virginia's next game at Richmond was an 84–82 loss to the Spiders at the Richmond Coliseum.

this coliseum now, you can kiss the Mountaineer basketball tradition good-bye," Waters said.

"I'm calling every week trying to explain to [the Board of Governors], 'I know this sounds selfish, but I'm telling you in the world of recruiting, facilities mean everything and we're getting passed by,' " Waters explained. "We just couldn't continue to do it in the building we are in."

Waters understood well the political ramifications should the Board of Governors choose to fund a basketball arena over sorely needed academic projects. "For all the right reasons, they talked about the need for a new law school and an addition to the hospital—all of them first-rate, unquestionable university needs," Waters said. "We were just caught out there."

Soon other academic departments began lobbying state legislators.

"The guys in Charleston said, 'That's it. You've got to figure out how you're going to divide up the pie.' *The Daily Athenaeum* called it 'Bucky's Palace' and why do we need 'Bucky's Palace?'" Waters said.

While Waters performed the public relations, Brown worked the back channels, shrewdly bringing the School of Physical Education into the equation. He also listed all of the non-athletic events that a new coliseum could provide to the community. Brown's well-reasoned arguments proved compelling.

Workers look over design plans with the framework of the new WVU Coliseum taking shape in the background.
WVU SPORTS COMMUNICATIONS PHOTO.

In the fall of 1967, Waters recalled getting a telephone call from an excited Brown asking him to quickly prepare a presentation for the Board of Governors the next morning. A decision was going to be made on what capital projects were going to be funded.

Waters was sitting in Brown's office at the football stadium when the announcement came over the radio that the Board of Governors had approved construction of a new basketball arena, which later would be named the WVU Coliseum. The decision was made Sept. 23, 1967, and bulldozers were on-site within a week to begin clearing ground for a new 14,000-seat arena located a mile north of campus on Monongahela Boulevard.

By then, Waters had reached the peak of his popularity at West Virginia. His team had another fine record in 1967, getting off on the right foot with an early season victory against Illinois to crack the UPI Top 20.

Shots West Virginia didn't convert in close wins against East Carolina and William & Mary, the Mountaineers made against the Illini. Dave Reaser's buzzer-beating basket—the result of a full-court inbound pass from Williams—led the students to storm the court. Head finished with 24 points, Reaser had 23 and Williams, with new contact lenses to help him see more clearly, scored 18. Before wearing contacts, Williams used to have to rely on his teammates to read the scoreboard for him.

West Virginia's first loss of the season came against Washington State in the Far West Classic. Three straight losses to St. Louis, Davidson and Maryland—two of those in overtime—left West Virginia's record at 6–4.

The Mountaineers gained revenge against Davidson and Maryland in Morgantown, winning back-to-back games. Wins also followed against Pitt and Penn State before WVU wound up the season with back-to-back victories against George Washington. Williams, Head and Greg Ludwig scored more than 20 apiece in a 30-point victory over the Colonials in Morgantown.

West Virginia zipped through the Southern Conference tournament, beating East Carolina by 29, upending Richmond by 12, and defeating Davidson in the championship game by 16. Head, Reaser and Williams combined to score 63 of West Virginia's 81 points, but it was the play in the paint of Benfield that was the difference in the game against the Wildcats. The 6-foot-8 center grabbed 16 rebounds and played a strong defensive game.

Raymond "Bucky" Waters coached West Virginia four seasons from 1966–69, leading the Mountaineers to postseason trips in 1967 and 1968.

WVU SPORTS COMMUNICATIONS PHOTO.

"Bob blocked a couple of shots in a quick flurry and things started to go our way," remarked Waters after the game. "He intimidated their shooters near the basket."

Head had strong second halves in all three games and was named the tournament's most valuable player, while Williams set the school and conference record for assists in the finals with 15.

The Mountaineers met Ivy League champion Princeton in the NCAA tournament first round in Blacksburg, Va. Head got into early foul trouble, and Princeton was able to keep West Virginia's fast break in check to eliminate the Mountaineers 68–57. It was WVU's poorest shooting performance of the season, the team hitting only 39 percent of its field goal attempts while making a disappointing 11 of 25 from the free throw line. Head and Williams scored 41 of West Virginia's 57 points.

In two seasons, Head tallied 943 points to

THE WVU COLISEUM

Red Brown waited a long time to get his basketball arena. The topic of a new basketball facility first came up in 1958 when Fred Schaus was being pursued by the University of Washington for its basketball job. Schaus turned down the Huskies when West Virginia agreed to begin exploring the possibility of building a new arena to replace the Field House.

The process took 12 long years to complete. At the end of each year, Brown was required to file a report to Central Administration summing up the athletic season. In each report he sent downtown, he always stuck in a few paragraphs about the need for a new basketball arena.

In the early 1960s, there was finally some interest on the part of university president Paul Miller once Schaus left to take the Los Angeles Lakers job. The preliminary plans for a new arena called for a $6 million facility with bleacher seating. Eventually the $6 million cap was eliminated.

"They reasoned that if we were going to do this, then we better do it right," said former Sports Information Director Eddie Barrett.

The inside of the Coliseum as workers continue to pour concrete for the Coliseum dome.

By the mid-1960s West Virginia was undergoing its biggest expansion in school history. In roughly a 10-year period from the late 1950s to the late 1960s, the school had more than doubled in size, forcing the campus to expand out into Evansdale.

Brown finally saw a crack of light in 1967. The state legislature was willing to consider a bond for the construction of a basketball arena, a new law school and a much-needed addition to the Medical Center.

What eventually transpired was a turf war of competing interests, and WVU basketball coach Bucky Waters said he wound up getting stuck right in the middle of it. "They allocated $20 million for the Law School, the hospital, the new field house and about two other things," Waters recalled. "Everything else was academic or medical and when all of the bids came back it was over $40 million.

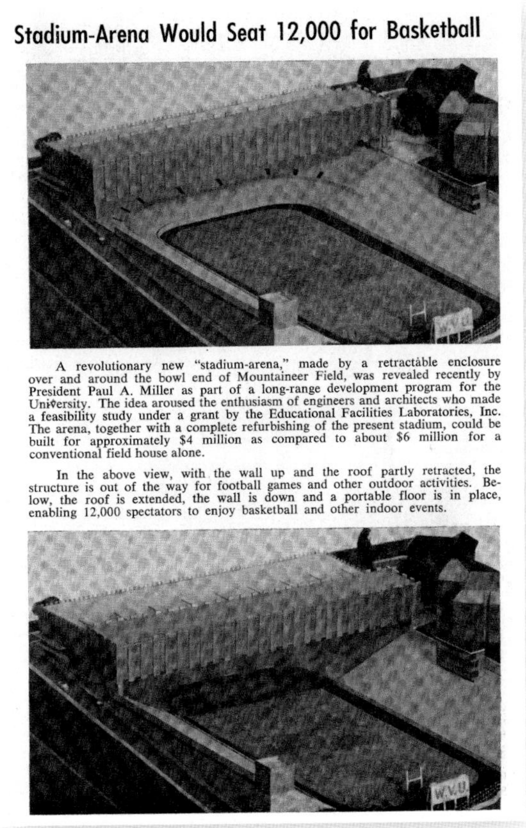

Stadium-Arena Would Seat 12,000 for Basketball

A revolutionary new "stadium-arena," made by a retractable enclosure over and around the bowl end of Mountaineer Field, was revealed recently by President Paul A. Miller as part of a long-range development program for the University. The idea aroused the enthusiasm of engineers and architects who made a feasibility study under a grant by the Educational Facilities Laboratories, Inc. The arena, together with a complete refurbishing of the present stadium, could be built for approximately $4 million as compared to about $6 million for a conventional field house alone.

In the above view, with the wall up and the roof partly retracted, the structure is out of the way for football games and other outdoor activities. Below, the roof is extended, the wall is down and a portable floor is in place, enabling 12,000 spectators to enjoy basketball and other indoor events.

"The Coliseum was over $10 million. So the guys in Charleston said, 'Boys we gave you $20 million—you figure it out.' So there was this huge dogfight. The dean of the law school called it 'Bucky's Castle.' Why do we need this thing? We need a law school and we need classrooms.' It was a great argument.

"I said, 'If we don't get this now—you've got Cole Field House to the East, Ohio U. has a better arena than we've got, never mind St. John's Arena at Ohio State. We're surrounded by good facilities and the Mountaineer basketball tradition cannot survive unless we have an incredible run of kids from West Virginia,' which at the time we didn't."

Brown knew a stand-alone athletic venue would never fly, so he ingeniously got the School of Physical Education involved. He also talked about the value a new basketball arena could mean to the community.

It worked.

"Red calls me the day before the board meets on a Saturday morning," Waters said. "He said, 'Okay, you've got an audience with the board.' I said, 'Great Red, how long do I have?' He said I had 10 minutes.

"I said, 'That's 10 minutes for $10 million.' He said, 'I'm sorry that's the best I can do.' I had all these charts and comparisons and I just went in there with my heart and I said, 'It may seem like an extravagance but you have to measure what the Mountaineer tradition means and its continuance. I'm not a miracle worker.'"

Waters was sitting in Brown's office in the football stadium when the announcement came later that afternoon that the Board of Governors had approved the funding for a new basketball arena, soon to become known as the WVU Coliseum.

Examining the new arena are Athletic Director Red Brown and Coach Bucky Waters.

Work crews were on-site the following week and the project was completed before the start of the 1970–71 academic year. A number of concerts and events were held that fall in the new WVU Coliseum before the basketball team officially christened it with a 113–92 victory over Colgate Dec. 1, 1970.

"The first time I came back to the Coliseum to do a [television] game it was a Big East game and I said, 'Red Brown would be just rejoicing right now.' He wanted something like that so much," Waters said. "He thought big in hoops."

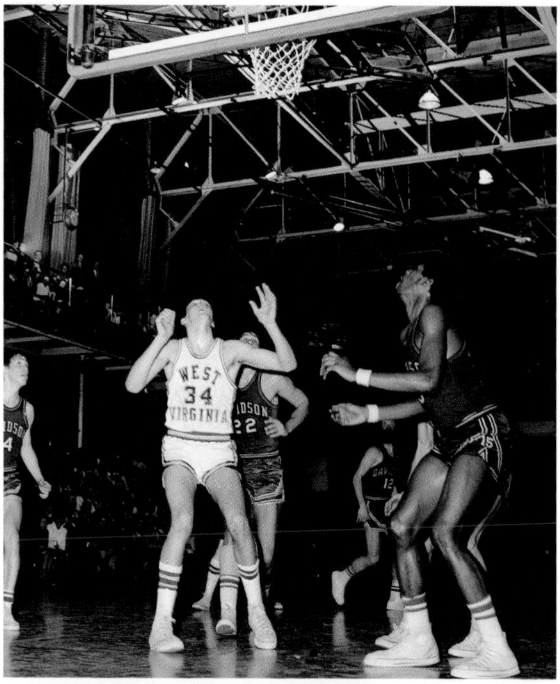

Top Dick Penrod watches a shot go up in this 1967 game against Davidson at the Field House. West Virginia defeated the Wildcats 89–86 in overtime. Penrod majored in journalism and served as the promotion manager of *The Daily Athenaeum*.

WVU SPORTS COMMUNICATIONS PHOTO

Above A rare color action photo of forward Dave Reaser playing against Princeton in the 1967 NCAA East Regional in Blacksburg, Va. Coach Butch van Breda Kolff's Tigers defeated the Mountaineers and shortly after Princeton was ousted in the regional semifinals by North Carolina, van Breda Kolff replaced Fred Schaus as the coach of the Los Angeles Lakers.

WVU SPORTS COMMUNICATIONS PHOTO.

average 17.1 points per game. At the time, the 6-foot-4 forward was the most proficient shooter in school history, converting 53 percent of his career field goal tries. A substandard scoring performance by Reaser against Princeton kept him from becoming the third player that season to average 20 points per game. His average was reduced to 19.9 points after scoring just 3 against the Tigers.

It was another 19–9 record for Waters in 1967, bringing his two-year mark to 38–18. Waters was able to overcome season-ending injuries to Dave Palmer and Jim Lewis to lead the Mountaineers to their ninth NCAA tournament appearance in 12 years. A new arena was under construction, and all signs pointed toward continued success with Williams returning for his senior season in 1968.

Because Waters had done so well with Head at WVU, he continued to scour the junior college ranks for players. Many West Virginians saw this only as a quick fix and Waters eventually felt obligated to defend his practice of recruiting JC players. "Junior college transfers are becoming more and more in favor in college athletics," Waters said in 1968, noting the success UCLA and USC were enjoying in football with juco players.

Another reason Waters was forced to go the junior college route was because he was missing out on big-name high school players such as Pete Maravich and Dana Pagett that he was targeting. Pagett, from Los Angeles, committed to Waters, but his father wouldn't sign the grant-in-aid, so Pagett wound up going to USC. Maravich was also very interested in West Virginia before his father, Press, got the LSU job. Flushing (N.Y.) High School product Eddie Fogler was another player West Virginia couldn't land, Fogler choosing to attend North Carolina instead.

"I was responsible for recruiting in West Virginia but we didn't have that many [prospects in the state]," recalled Sonny Moran, an assistant coach for Waters. "He gave me the responsibility to go out to Hutchinson, Kan., for the junior college tournament. But trying to recruit kids to come into West Virginia at that time was very difficult because the road situation was not good. I had [*Bluefield Daily Telegraph* sports editor] Stubby Currence on my butt for not getting down there often enough. I said, 'Stubby, I can get to Canada quicker than I can get down there.'"

Waters also had great difficulty recruiting big men. West Virginia did not have a player standing taller than 6-foot-7 (Dick Penrod) on its 1968 roster. The Mountaineers' lack of size directly resulted in losses to Florida, LaSalle and Davidson. However, size had no bearing on West Virginia's disappointing 92–90 overtime setback to VMI. The Mountaineers shot just 39.5 percent and Williams, Bob Hummell and Carey Bailey fouled out as West Virginia sent the Keydets to the line 44 times.

A strong finish with victories over Georgia Tech, Maryland, Richmond, Syracuse, Pitt and George Washington gave West Virginia hope of a repeat performance in the Southern Conference tournament. But the Mountaineers barely got by East Carolina in the opening round before knocking off Richmond by 21 in the semifinals. Then West Virginia's lack of size caught up with it in the finals against Davidson. The game was over by halftime, the Wildcats leading 47–24. Davidson had a 49–34 advantage on the glass and its three front-court players, Mike Maloy, Doug Cook and Jerry Kroll, combined to score 49 points and grab 29 rebounds.

West Virginia accepted an invitation to play Dayton in the 16-team National Invitation Tournament in New York City, but there was apathy among the fans and even some of the players.

"The players were at home for spring break at the time the criticism of our NIT acceptance appeared in the state press," said Waters. "Some people said it was a tournament full of losers and wondered why we should go to a tournament we couldn't be favored in.

"We are here because the players wanted to come. After all that we've been through the past three years, and all the boys have done for me, I'd go anywhere and play anybody with them."

Once more, West Virginia got handled in the paint. Dayton's 6-foot-10 center Dan Obrovac scored 30 points and All-American forward Don May added 24 to lead the Flyers to an easy 87–68 opening-round victory. Dayton went on to defeat Fordham, Notre Dame and Kansas to win the NIT. In the meantime, Williams produced 19 points in his final game for West Virginia.

Williams scored 1,687 points and averaged 20.1 points per game, becoming just the fourth player in school history to average more than 20 points per game for his career. He scored double figures in 80 of 84 career games and had nine 30-point games. His 6.0 assists per game average was also a school record. Williams's fellow senior, Reaser, a 6-foot-6 forward from St. Albans, was also an outstanding player who had more than 1,000 points for his career. Twice he scored more than 40 in games against Richmond and Minnesota.

Williams was named to the Converse All-America team and was drafted by the San Francisco Warriors (ninth overall pick) of the NBA and the Dallas Cowboys of the NFL. Additionally, he turned down an invitation to try out for the U.S. Olympic team. Williams played eight NBA seasons with the Warriors, Bucks and Lakers from 1969–1976.

Center Bob Benfield averaged 9 points and 11.5 rebounds per game for West Virginia in 1967, helping the Mountaineers reach the NCAA tournament that year. Bob's father, William, played basketball at Davidson and later became a Presbyterian minister in Charleston.

WVU SPORTS COMMUNICATIONS PHOTO.

Ron Williams carries West Virginia's Southern Conference championship trophy into the team hotel. Williams scored 58 points in three tournament games and handed out a school-record 15 assists against Davidson in the championship game to earn all-tournament honors.

WEST VIRGINIA AND REGIONAL HISTORY COLLECTION.

"Jerry West was the best, hands down," said Williams's teammate Jim Lewis. "From there it's all about personal preference and, as far as I am concerned, Fritz Williams was the next best. We're talking about an elite, world-class athlete."

More than just being a great basketball player, the late Williams was also a tremendous, well-respected human being. "He never had a bad day," said Lewis. "He never met a person that he didn't like. He was just a real gentle man who had an easy laugh about him who loved life. He loved his family, he loved his friends and he loved basketball."

Above Carey Bailey played high school basketball in Beckley before heading west to play at Long Beach (Calif.) Junior College. Bailey's cousin, Bill "The Hill" McGill, was an All-America player at Utah.

WVU SPORTS COMMUNICATIONS PHOTO.

Above right A color photo of guard Ron "Fritz" Williams playing against Princeton in the 1967 NCAA tournament East Regional in Blacksburg, Va. Williams scored 21 points but that wasn't enough to keep the fifth-rated Tigers from winning 68–57.

WVU SPORTS COMMUNICATIONS PHOTO.

Leaving the Southern Conference

Waters posted his third consecutive 19–9 record in 1968, but problems were on the horizon in 1969. Williams, Reaser, Holmes and Lewis had graduated, and Waters again didn't have much size to work with. And the 1969 squad was by far his most inexperienced team. To compound matters, West Virginia, at the urging of football coach Jim Carlen, left the Southern Conference and its very manageable schedule after the '68 season. The basketball staff was not pleased with the decision.

"Very frankly, we were coming back from Huntington one night—George Krajack, Buck, Red and I and Buck asked me how I felt about getting out of the Southern Conference," Sonny Moran recalled. "I said, 'Buck I wouldn't want to do it. We ought to stay in the Southern Conference for another couple of years or so.' We had been able to win the conference championship for several years running and another couple of years would help us with recruiting before we went into the new Coliseum. But Jim Carlen had strongly favored going out as an independent. He felt the so-called "Big Four" [West Virginia, Pitt, Penn State and Syracuse had a loose association mainly for football] was only a handicap to us because it restricted us in scholarships and also took away our redshirting possibilities," Moran added. "He felt like we weren't playing enough games in football or basketball to justify being in an arrangement that hampered us somewhat."

"We had no place to land with the NCAA tournament, and things like that were now out of reach," Waters said. "We didn't have any business being an independent at that point. But that was the hand that was dealt you and you had to play it out."

As a consequence, the basketball schedule experienced an immediate and dramatic upgrade. Gone were VMI, The Citadel, William & Mary and East Carolina and in their places were Kentucky, UCLA, Arizona, St. John's, Notre Dame,

Maryland, Florida, Ohio State and Syracuse. West Virginia's last year in the Southern Conference in 1968 saw the Mountaineers face seven teams during the regular season with winning records. The number of winning teams more than doubled to 15 in 1969. By 1971, Moran's second year as West Virginia's head coach, the Mountaineers faced 18 teams that season with winning records. "Red Brown was the guy who wanted to go to New York every year," Waters said. "He wanted to play UCLA. He thought big and that was OK with me."

The UCLA game was arranged as a stopover on the way to the Rainbow Classic in Honolulu, Hawaii. The trade-off was UCLA agreeing to return to Morgantown to help open the brand-new WVU Coliseum when it was ready for the 1970–71 season.

"I loved Red Brown, but that was the deal," Waters said. "I went out there to be a sacrificial lamb against [Lew] Alcindor and those guys with the idea that we'd showcase them back in the new Coliseum."

Any thoughts West Virginia had of upsetting UCLA went out the window 10 days before the game when the Mountaineers lost at home to Richmond. West Virginia's tallest player was 6-foot-5 going up against the 7-foot-1 Alcindor (later known as Kareem Abdul-Jabbar). Waters had a simple game plan in store for UCLA: Hold the ball and only shoot it when Alcindor wasn't in the paint. The strategy was working beautifully until Carey Bailey upset the UCLA giant.

"Alcindor turns to try a little baby hook and Carey Bailey jumps up and blocks his shot," said Waters. "One of our guys picks up the ball and we've got a three-on-two. Our player sets up to take a shot and here comes Alcindor, nostrils flaring and eyes bulging, chasing him. He's trying to catch the ball out of the air—not block it.

"But he couldn't quite catch the ball and he crashes into the backboard," Waters said. "Everyone had this expression of did I see what I just saw? My guys are looking around at each other thinking 'uh oh,' so I called time-out."

As Waters began explaining to the team that it was just one play and there was still most of the game left to be played, he noticed the eyes of his players slowly rising as he talked. Their eyes continued looking up.

"That's when I knew Alcindor was walking past our bench," laughed Waters. "I turned to Carey and I said, 'Thanks a lot. That block really didn't help us out, pal. You just ticked off the big guy.'" UCLA scored 29 of the next 35 points and the game was over.

"Some people would ask, 'What was it like taking the ball out against them?'" said guard

Above Forward Jim Lewis (33), pictured here going up for a rebound against Pitt at the Field House, played in only 36 career games because of knee injuries. Lewis later became a college and professional basketball coach, most recently serving on Liz Dunn's coaching staff for the WNBA's Indiana Fever.

WVU SPORTS COMMUNICATIONS PHOTO.

Above left Allentown, Pennsylvania's Skip Kintz was the team's number three scorer in 1969, averaging 11.9 points per game.

WVU SPORTS COMMUNICATIONS PHOTO.

West Virginia won a tough recruiting battle for Charleston's Curt Price, fending off former Mountaineer coach George King at Purdue. As was customary at the time, West Virginia coaches Bucky Waters and Sonny Moran join Price's family and high school coach Lou Romano for Price's official signing.
WVU SPORTS COMMUNICATIONS PHOTO.

Bob Hummell. "I tell them, 'Hell, we're still trying to get the ball inbounds.'"

What stuck in Waters's mind more so than the awesome team UCLA coach John Wooden had assembled was the competitive fire the 59-year-old coach displayed, even when the game was well in hand. "One of my kids comes back and says, 'Coach, John Wooden is yelling at us.' I said, 'What?' He said, 'Yeah, every time we get close enough to him he starts talking to us.' I said, 'You've got to be kidding me,'" Waters laughed.

"So I look down and sure enough—he's a wonderful man, a great Christian man and a beautiful person—but he's also a competitor. I look up and every time the ball comes into the corner where he's sitting he's got that program rolled up and he's leaning forward and using it like a megaphone," Waters said.

"If you weren't really looking you'd never know he was doing that. He looked very studious with the program all rolled up and I'd be darn if he wasn't talking to them. He'd yell, 'Watch out! Don't turn the ball over! You're going to walk!' I couldn't believe it, and for many years, I would kid him about it.

"He would just say, 'Well . . .'"

There were more losses to follow, including five straight in the middle of the year, to drop West

MISSED OPPORTUNITIES

Through the years there have been many players who either verbally committed to West Virginia University or gave the Mountaineers serious consideration before deciding to play at other schools.

The two who might have made the biggest difference were John Havlicek and Pete Maravich. Havlicek chose Ohio State and Maravich went to LSU.

One of the first letters Havlicek received during his junior year of high school was from West Virginia's Fred Schaus. "I thought that was quite an honor," Havlicek said. Schaus had found out about Havlicek earlier than other schools because of Bobby Carroll, a teammate of Schaus's at West Virginia and Havlicek's coach at Bridgeport (Ohio) High, located right across the river from Wheeling, W.Va.

"We knew about him because of Coach Carroll and we knew about him early," Schaus said. "That was important many times in recruiting to get in on the ground floor during their sophomore or junior year before everybody knows about them."

Schaus thought he had a pretty good shot of landing Havlicek if not for the Ohio North-South All-Star Game. It was at that game that Havlicek wound up committing to Ohio State.

"I tried to get it set up that Havlicek was going to room with Ed Bode, who we were recruiting that year from a little school in Southeastern Ohio," Schaus recalled. "Apparently Havlicek was later getting there and so they put him in with Jerry Lucas. If I had any chance of getting Havlicek, I sure as hell didn't have any chance when Lucas and Havlicek spent the weekend together."

Schaus saw Havlicek as the perfect bridge between Jerry West and Rod Thorn. "He could have filled in nicely there, huh?" Schaus said.

A few years later Bucky Waters went after Pete Maravich, whose College Board scores were not high enough to get into the ACC where his father Press Maravich was coaching at NC State. Waters hired George Krajack, who played for Press at Clemson and knew the Maravich family well, to be his assistant coach at West Virginia. Maravich knew a lot about West Virginia and he liked Jerry West and the Mountaineers' wide-open style of play.

"He did not want to play for his dad," Waters said. "It looked like a lock."

Then, Press got the LSU job and Pete's college boards were no longer an issue. After some haggling, Pete eventually went with his dad to LSU.

Virginia's record to 7–9. After beating George Washington, two more setbacks to Davidson and Maryland made West Virginia's record 8–11. The season ended with West Virginia losing three of its last four games. "If you look at the schedule, we had just gotten out of the Southern Conference and we were playing a big-time national schedule," Hummell explained. "I know as each year goes by you tend to fabricate things a little bit more, but I think we had like the fourth-toughest schedule that year.

"In hindsight, we may have gotten a little bit ahead of ourselves, and I don't think our recruiting was commensurate to the type of schedule we were playing," Hummell added.

Jerry West, by then starring for the Los Angeles Lakers, was still paying attention to what was going on at his alma mater. "Sometimes things don't work right," said West. "Sometimes they pass on kids that are pretty good players. Who knows what happens? Things do run in cycles. For everyone who has ever played sports, you are hopeful that you can be successful for a longer period of time."

Just weeks before the end of the season, Vic Bubas announced that 1969 was going to be his last year at Duke. Immediately, attention turned to Waters. Instead of returning to Morgantown with the team after the Florida game in Jacksonville, Waters flew straight to Durham to interview for the Duke job.

The Blue Devils took their time naming Bubas's successor, and that left West Virginia in a huge bind. Duke Athletic Director Eddie Cameron couldn't make up his mind because there was a groundswell of support growing for former Duke player Lefty Driesell, who had built a powerful program at Davidson and would later do the same at Maryland. At one point it looked like Waters might remain at WVU for the 1970 season.

Unbeknownst to Brown, who thought President Harlow was going to terminate Waters's contract, Harlow and Waters were actually negotiating a new deal when the telephone in Harlow's office rang. It was Duke's president.

Far left Larry Woods, a junior college forward from Peoria, Ill., was a two-year starter for the Mountaineers in 1969–70, averaging 12.8 points and 8.9 rebounds per game for his career.

WVU SPORTS COMMUNICATIONS PHOTO.

Left Moundsville's Bob Hummell. The guard scored 1,117 career points and led the team in scoring in 1969 with an average of 15.5 points per game.

WVU SPORTS COMMUNICATIONS PHOTO.

"That morning when I was hired at Duke I said, 'Thank you very much, but I'm staying,'" Waters said. "Then, I get a call in Harlow's office and he went ballistic and says, 'This is beyond anything I've ever seen.' So they all leave the room and I'm talking to the Duke president. Here I am spinning around in this chair and I'm a volleyball between these two guys."

Waters consummated the deal with Duke in Harlow's office. Sensing that Waters was eventually going to return to Duke, Harlow had taken a straw poll of Athletic Council members a week earlier to gauge their thoughts on promoting assistant coach Sonny Moran should Waters choose to leave. Because of Duke's prolonged flirtation with Waters, all were in agreement to hire Moran. It was probably less an election and more a coronation for Moran. West Virginia actually

announced Moran as Waters's successor before Duke could reveal Waters as its new coach.

"We knew that Bucky was interested in the Duke job but it was a question of whether or not he was going to get offered the job," Moran recalled. "I knew if he was offered the job he would take it. We were in limbo there for a little while waiting to see what was actually going to occur."

Bucky Waters's four-year record at West Virginia was 69–41. His critics say he killed West Virginia's basketball tradition. However, he did play an important role in the construction of the WVU Coliseum, while also presiding over a basketball program undergoing significant changes. For that matter, the entire youth culture in the late 1960s was changing. Waters got a much more potent dose of it when he went to Duke.

"It was a sensitive time," Waters said. "There was campus unrest, Kent State, the long hair . . . and now they'll say, 'Hey coach, we really screwed up. We appreciate you holding your ground and we realize that it was painful for you.'

"The most poignant statement was, 'There's no reason for us to act that way except we thought that was the way we were supposed to act—just to be adversarial against everything,'" Waters said. "You could understand the kids with Kent State and Vietnam and all of that. But it really got into the culture that if you were a coach or a college president or anything of a traditional authority figure, then immediately, not only did they dismiss you, but it was like, 'Hey how are you doing?' And they were like, 'What, are you manipulating me?' It was bizarre. It was the reason I left coaching."

Of the 111 basketball games Bucky Waters coached at West Virginia University from 1966–69, only 40 of them were played at the Field House; getting good teams to come to Morgantown was next to impossible.

It was Red Brown's hope that the new Coliseum would change that.

The Field House served the Mountaineers well but by the late 1960s it was getting more difficult to get teams to come to Morgantown.

WVU SPORTS COMMUNICATIONS PHOTOS.

VILLANOVA
33
WVU
24

Pitt
Pitt

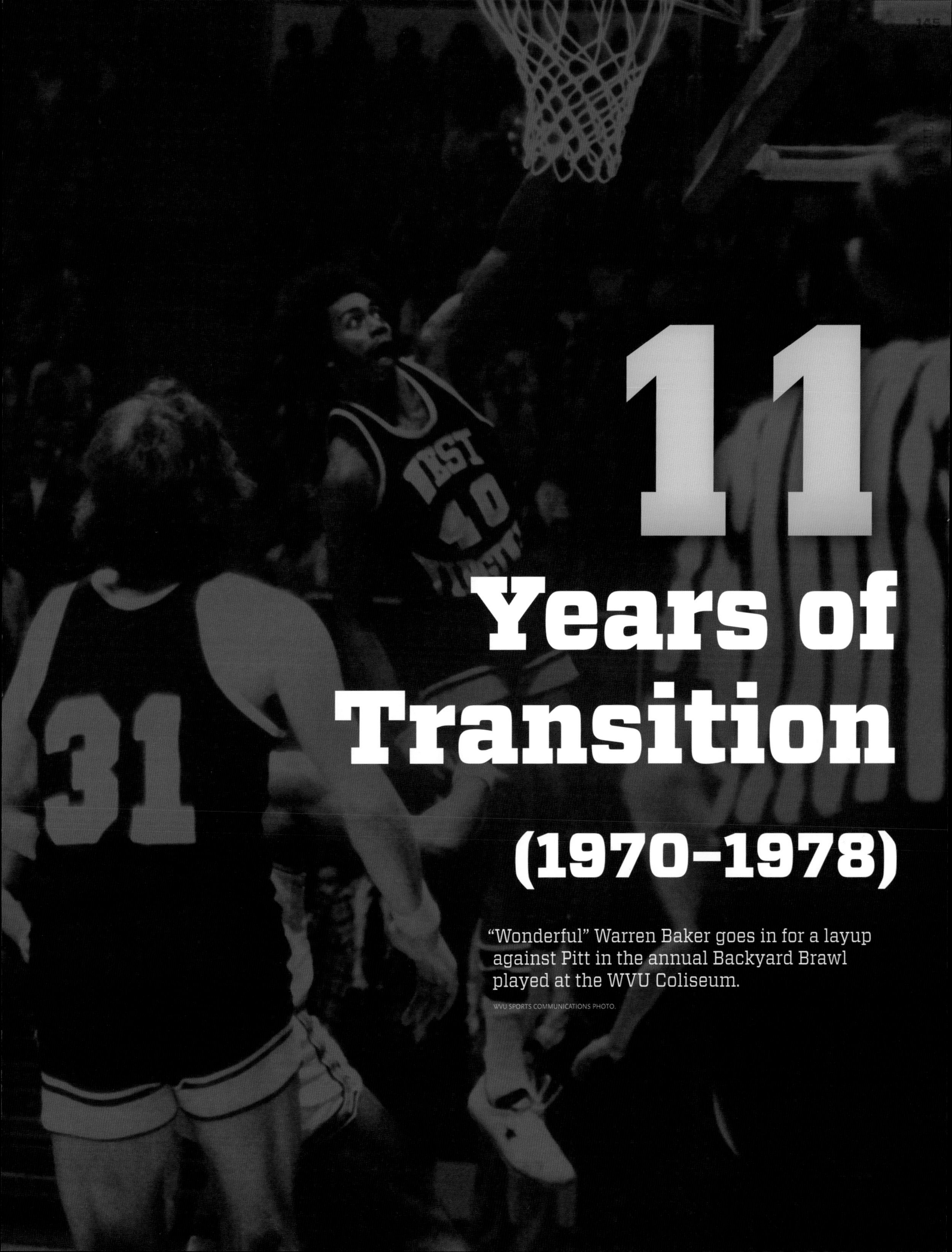

11 Years of Transition (1970–1978)

“Wonderful” Warren Baker goes in for a layup against Pitt in the annual Backyard Brawl played at the WVU Coliseum.

WVU SPORTS COMMUNICATIONS PHOTO.

Garland E. "Sonny" Moran's five-year coaching tenure at West Virginia was marked by disappointment and tragedy. Extenuating circumstances and factors—many beyond his control— led to a 57–68 record and his decision to resign with five games remaining in the 1974 season.

Moran came to West Virginia in 1965 as Bucky Waters's No. 1 assistant coach after compiling an impressive 148–74 record in 12 seasons at Morris Harvey College. Moran's basketball coaching résumé also included stints at Elkview and Stonewall Jackson high schools. After starring at Stonewall Jackson, Moran enrolled at WVU for a brief time before joining the Army. Following his discharge, he returned to his native Charleston where he played basketball at Morris Harvey College. Moran's Morris Harvey teams had a reputation in the West Virginia Conference for playing an exciting, wide-open style.

Coach Sonny Moran poses with his coaching staff in his new office at the WVU Coliseum.

WVU PHOTOGRAPHIC SERVICES.

"I had my own program at Morris Harvey College and Red Brown called me and wanted me to come to West Virginia as an assistant," Moran recalled. "I gave it an awful lot of thought because I had a good program at Morris Harvey and we had success. But the opportunity to go to your state university was very appealing, so I accepted the job."

When Moran took over head coaching duties, freshman coach Chuck Windsor remained with Moran on the WVU staff, while former VMI coach Gary McPherson was added as basketball's No. 1 assistant coach.

A Program in Flux

When Moran assumed control of the WVU program, he was presiding over a team in flux, a school no longer competing in a winnable conference and facing a vastly improved schedule. Also, the Mountain State had experienced its largest population decline in its history, meaning fewer high school prospects for Moran to recruit in West Virginia. In another year, Moran was also going to lose the enormous security blanket that was the old Field House where the Mountaineers were virtually unbeatable.

"The future of WVU basketball at West Virginia can be bright with our new Coliseum," Moran said in 1970, "but it won't be a cure-all. We will lose the home court advantage we had at Mountaineer Field House with the wall-to-wall people."

Right out of the gate, Moran's recruiting suffered. Because it took so long for Duke to hire Waters, any chance West Virginia had of landing outstanding Mullens guard Mike D'Antoni was lost. He wound up signing with Marshall after also considering West Virginia and Duke.

"The very day I received the job I immediately went to Mullens to talk with the D'Antoni family," Moran said. "I was very much interested in getting Mike. I knew we were fighting an uphill battle because of his family contacts with Marshall, but nevertheless, I wanted to take a good shot at him and I spent the night at the D'Antoni home. But he decided to go to Marshall."

The new-look Mountaineers in 1970 played five games against teams ranked in the top 15, while also facing St. John's, Maryland, Pitt, Florida, Ohio State, Penn State, Duke, Syracuse and Virginia Tech. It was a brutal slate considered the fourth toughest in the country by a Wright State University professor who evaluated college basketball schedules.

"I was talking to Shorty Hardman from the [Charleston] *Gazette* one day and I said to him, 'Shorty, I am going to name you some of the teams and you tell me what you think about playing them.' He said, 'Well I don't think those are good teams.' I said, 'No they're not. But those are the teams West Virginia has played through the years in the first round of the NCAA.'

"I said, 'Now we're playing a non-conference schedule where we're immediately jumping into the Big Ten, the ACC and these other conferences.' "

Most of the Southern Conference schools that had helped West Virginia become the nation's fourth winningest basketball program over a 25-year period were no longer on the schedule. "Sonny really had a tough schedule," said Leland Byrd. From that perspective, West Virginia's 11–15 record in 1970 was understandable. But most Mountaineer supporters, spoiled by WVU's remarkable success, didn't see it that way. Five of West Virginia's setbacks that year were by five points or less, with two of them being gut-wrenching defeats against Virginia Tech. A matter of only 27 points could have turned an 11–15 record into a much more successful 16–10 season. Moran's detractors thought he could have averted some of the close losses.

Forward Dick Symons goes up for two of his 16 points during West Virginia's 92–87 loss to Pitt in the final game ever played at the Field House in 1970.
WEST VIRGINIA AND REGIONAL HISTORY COLLECTION.

However, there were some memorable moments in 1970.

For instance, West Virginia snapped a three-game losing streak with a 67–66 overtime victory at Pitt. Forward Larry Woods won the game by following up Bob Hummell's miss with 12 seconds left, and sophomore guard Wil Robinson burned the Panthers with 17 points—much to the dissatisfaction of Pitt rooters, who briefly interrupted the game when one lobbed a dead fish on the floor while Robinson was attempting a free throw.

"I knew [West Virginia-Pitt] was a big rivalry, but I felt it more when I came down to West Virginia," said Robinson. "I grew up in Pittsburgh—I went to grade school and junior high there before going down to Uniontown for high school."

Robinson was considered one of the top guards in the country at Laurel Highlands High, and he was hotly pursued by many colleges. Eventually, he chose West Virginia over Pitt, Duquesne, Michigan State and Illinois.

"Ron Williams was really the reason I went down there," Robinson said. "When Fritz was a

INDEPENDENCE

Sonny Moran was not in favor of leaving the Southern Conference because Mountaineer basketball would no longer have a clear path to the NCAA tournament.

WVU SPORTS COMMUNICATIONS PHOTO.

Football coach Jim Carlen got his way in 1968. From almost the moment Carlen arrived at West Virginia in 1966, he campaigned to get WVU out of the Southern Conference. He believed it harmed his recruiting and handicapped the Mountaineers' ability to schedule more intersectional football games.

He wanted more games against California, Stanford, Indiana, Colorado State and Miami, Fla., and fewer games against William & Mary, VMI and The Citadel.

In the 18 years West Virginia played in the Southern Conference from 1950–68 the football program won 79.3 percent of its games and claimed eight league titles. Basketball had an even better record, capturing 10 Southern Conference titles and posting a 183–34 record that included a 56-game conference winning streak from 1956–60.

"The Southern Conference was a real comfort zone for us," recalled Bucky Waters. "I wasn't sure we had another place to go. I know Jim was interested in the football side of things, and there were two different mentalities there."

The move proved beneficial for football and catastrophic for basketball. West Virginia's six seasons of basketball independence from 1968–74 saw the Mountaineers post four losing seasons and an overall 69–82 record against a dramatically improved slate. It was one of the factors that ultimately cost Sonny Moran his job in 1974.

"George King and I were teammates in college and certainly taking nothing away from Fred Schaus—they enjoyed tremendous success and they deserve all the credit they got—but playing that schedule in the Southern Conference when you could go 11 out of 13 years winning the conference, that's a pretty good indication of their schedule," said Moran.

"You figure you are going to have a winning year, then a couple of games against Pitt, Penn State and Syracuse, you figure if you can win your fair share of those you can have one of those great years. We just didn't have that to go with."

Seventeen times West Virginia faced nationally ranked opponents during the school's six-year period of independence. The Mountaineers lost all 17 times.

Eventually, in 1975, West Virginia became a member of the 39-team Eastern Collegiate Athletic Conference (ECAC) that was divided into four different districts. Teams in each district were selected for four, four-team tournaments; the winners of those tournaments earned berths in the NCAA Tournament.

This setup lasted for two years until West Virginia joined the Eastern Collegiate Basketball League, which later became the Eastern 8 and then the Atlantic 10 Conference in 1983.

"I think West Virginia University was a football school looking to find its basketball program," recalled former assistant coach and top recruiter, Jim Amick. "I don't know that it's true now because I think they've kind of come out of that. At that point [early 1970s] that's what they were. Basketball had been good for so many years and then they hit that dry spell and they weren't. Interest just dropped down a lot."

Bob Huggins breaks the press during West Virginia's 75–73 upset win over Pitt in the 1975 ECAC tournament played at the WVU Coliseum in Morgantown.

WVU SPORTS COMMUNICATIONS PHOTO.

senior he spent a lot of time at my house and we became good friends. He used to talk to me about how great the basketball tradition was at West Virginia, and I just had a lot of respect for him.

"West Virginia wasn't going under the table because at the time I was coming out of high school a lot of colleges were doing a lot of things for a lot of people," Robinson recalled. "I just didn't want to go in that direction. They were straight. All they did was promise me an education."

Robinson, the most well-liked and popular player on the team, had a legion of fans at WVU. But that didn't mean everyone in Morgantown knew who he was. The late Dick Polen, the school's sports information director at the time, once recalled a funny story that circulated around campus for years concerning the first-ever meeting between Robinson and WVU President James Harlow, brother of Richard Nixon advisor Bryce Harlow.

At the outset of his presidency, before becoming more reclusive in his later years, Harlow enjoyed coming down from his ivory tower now and again to keep a pulse on the student body, sometimes picking up student hitchhikers needing a ride to and from campus. One morning on his way to work, Harlow noticed Robinson and some of his teammates thumbing along University Avenue, so he pulled over to give them a lift. When Robinson got into the front seat of the car, Harlow asked him if he was a student.

"No, sir," Robinson answered, "I'm a basketball player. Who are you?"

"I'm the president," Harlow answered.

"Oh."

That is the story (likely embellished) of how the two best-known men on campus met.

Another humorous Robinson story involved a tight game at George Washington midway through his sophomore season in 1970. With the score tied, West Virginia had the basketball and was trying to run down the clock to win the game in regulation. After calling time-out, Moran instructed his players to get the basketball into Robinson's hands to take the last shot. "Let the clock run all the way down before you shoot it," were Moran's specific instructions.

When play resumed, Robinson got the ball and dribbled toward the key, backing his way in to get closer to the basket. Then he heard the George Washington students begin counting down . . . five, four,

Left and Below Wil Robinson scored 40 or more points in a game five times during his senior season in 1972. Robinson averaged a school-record 29.4 points per game that year when academic suspensions, injuries and a tragic automobile accident completely gutted the Mountaineer program.

WVU PHOTOGRAPHIC SERVICES.

three, two, one . . . With about 10 seconds actually left on the clock, a confused Robinson quickly heaved up a desperation shot that missed and the Colonials were able to rebound. GW called timeout with time still left to win the game.

"What were you doing, Wil?" Moran asked as the players began to huddle. "I told you to run the clock down."

"I thought they were telling the truth," Robinson said.

Dick Symons, a husky forward from Toronto, Ohio, chimed in. "Hell, Wil, this is Washington, D.C. Nobody tells the truth around here!"

In overtime, Robinson ignored the GW hecklers and sank a 20-footer with 22 seconds left to give the Mountaineers a hard-earned 92–91 victory.

Coach Sonny Moran offers instruction to his team while assistant coach Gary McPherson watches in the background.
WVU PHOTOGRAPHIC SERVICES.

Ten days after the Pitt win, West Virginia scored 121 points in a 56-point victory over Hawaii at the Field House. Woods, Skip Kintz and Mike Heitz together produced 71 points to help the Mountaineers register their biggest win in 14 years.

The most bizarre game of the year came in Morgantown against Syracuse. The contest was stopped with 1:01 still showing on the clock and the Mountaineers leading 94–84 when a near-riot broke out on the floor. The fracas began when

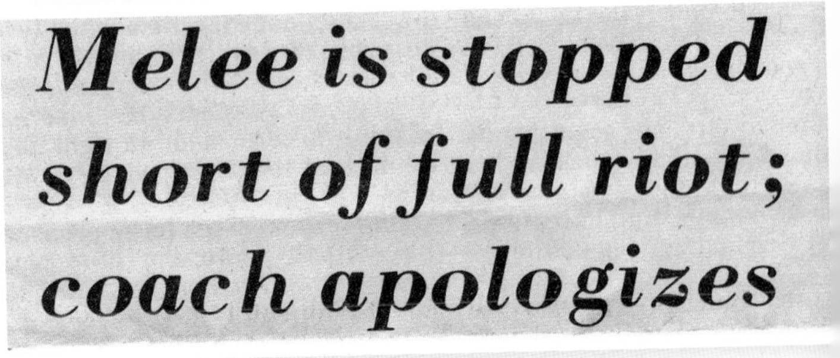

Melee is stopped short of full riot; coach apologizes

Syracuse center Bill Smith took a swing at referee Herb Young after being called for his fifth personal foul. Smith later said that he had thought Young pushed him.

Another Syracuse player, Bob McDaniel, came off the bench and slung his warm-up jersey at the same official. McDaniel was still steaming after his ejection for committing a flagrant foul a few moments earlier.

In the meantime, Smith continued throwing punches as members of the city police force tried to restore order. While both teams were on the floor taking swings, a series of scuffles erupted in the stands before police got control of the situation. When cooler heads prevailed, it was mutually agreed to discontinue the game.

Syracuse's discontent grew from a sequence of calls that went against it with less than two minutes remaining in the game. The first came when two points were erroneously awarded to Robinson while he was fouled attempting to make a pass to Woods. Woods followed through with the play and made the basket, leading to the confusion. After a lengthy protest the basket was finally removed. The second dispute came when McDaniel was thrown out of the game.

Assistant coach Gary McPherson had seen a

similar scene a few nights earlier in Pittsburgh while scouting the Syracuse-Pitt game. "It was a very rough game and I remember going to a pay phone and calling Sonny and telling him that we may have a problem down in Morgantown," McPherson said.

"[Syracuse coach Roy] Danforth apologized over and over again," recalled Moran. "We were good friends and we remained good friends. He was so embarrassed that his kid would do that."

The fight against Syracuse took place a month after the WVU campus was rocked by the disappearance of two university coeds, Karen Ferrell and Mared Malarik, whose decapitated bodies were later found eight miles south of Morgantown. Also, in May, the West Virginia state police had to be called in to put down a disturbance on campus when students marched on Stewart Hall less than a week after four Vietnam War protestors were killed by the Ohio National Guardsmen at Kent State University. More than 100 state troopers were able to peacefully disperse an estimated 2,500 students that had gathered near Woodburn Circle. It was a very unsettling time, even for a school such as West Virginia University, which was geographically removed from a great deal of the turmoil going on in the country at the time.

Moran said he tried his best to deal with the cultural changes going on then. "We had the problems with the Afro haircuts and the facial hair and the whole bit because we were trying our best to present a good image," Moran recalled. "I told the kids when we had a team meeting, 'I have to go out and beg money for your scholarships and all I'm asking for you to do is clean up your act and not let your peer groups get to you.'"

Meanwhile, the 1970 season ended disappointingly in March when West Virginia blew a 19-point first-half lead and lost to Pitt 92–87 in the final game at the Field House. A planned celebration with balloons and the band playing "Auld Lang Syne" was abruptly canceled. Afterward, Moran looked like a man who had just gotten both of his eyes poked out.

"Anyone who hadn't watched us play this year could have seen our season right there in that game," explained a disappointed Moran afterward, pointing out his team's inability to shoot straight, handle the basketball, or stop the other team's top scorers.

The Pitt loss was a distant memory when the WVU Coliseum was finally available for use on Dec. 1, 1970. More than 11,000 came out to watch Grand Funk Railroad christen the arena in September, but not quite as many

(9,378) showed up to see the basketball team defeat Colgate 113–92 in the '71 season opener. Wil Robinson scored 39 points in a game marred by fouls (54) and turnovers (49). West Virginia guard Levi Phillips presented the game ball to Athletic Director Red Brown after he scored the first field goal in the new facility. The only complaints came from those waiting in traffic outside while the game was going on. To this day, a lack of adequate parking has been one of the few design flaws with the Coliseum.

Inset Guard Levi Phillips presents the game ball to Athletic Director Red Brown after scoring the first-ever basket at the WVU Coliseum against Colgate on Dec. 1, 1970. A crowd of 9,378 watched the Mountaineers defeat the Red Raiders 113–92 in an entertaining game.

WVU SPORTS COMMUNICATIONS PHOTO.

Six nights later, West Virginia almost knocked off fifth-ranked Kentucky in an entertaining 106–100 loss to the Wildcats at the Coliseum. A near capacity crowd of 13,323 saw West Virginia nearly erase a 17-point deficit. Robinson was once again West Virginia's top scorer with 29 points.

A 74–71 victory over Bobby Knight's Army team got the inaugural Mountaineer Classic off to a rousing start, but West Virginia fell 94–91 to Virginia in the championship game to begin a six-game losing streak. Another bitter defeat followed at NC State, when State's Rick Holdt tapped in a basket ahead of the horn to give the Wolfpack a 100–98 victory. At the end of the game, West Virginia was playing without Robinson, who was ejected after throwing the basketball at Bob Heuts when Heuts tried to take him out on a driving layup. Heitz and Phillips were also disqualified because of fouls.

"Wil Robinson was having a fantastic game," Moran recalled. "Well, he stole the ball and was

Below The WVU Coliseum lit up at night can be an intimidating sight to opposing teams.

WVU PHOTOGRAPHIC SERVICES.

going in for a layup and this kid from NC State actually just about tackled him. Wil kind of turned around and threw the ball at him and the official threw him out of the ballgame. I just could not believe that."

Moran said his teams also endured bad experiences at Syracuse's Manley Field House.

"I used to get so disgusted with Syracuse," he said. "The football team would sit behind the basket and they would actually rock the basket when you went to the free throw line. I could not believe the gutless officials would not call that. Their athletic director would say that he could not control that football group.

"Plus, every time I came out of there I would have about a week's worth of sinus problems with all of the sawdust in that place."

A small portion of the game film was clipped out of West Virginia's 71–62 victory at Penn State a week before the NC State loss. Red Brown had complained several times that he was sick and tired of hearing about fights that Sam Oglesby was getting into. As far as Brown was concerned, one more slipup from Oglesby and he was gone. Moran decided to put assistant coach Gary McPherson in charge of Oglesby because it was McPherson who had recruited him out of junior college.

"Sonny said, 'Gary, you've got to take care of this,'" McPherson recalled. "Sam wasn't a bad guy—he just didn't like anyone getting too close to his face. Whenever it happened it usually set him off."

McPherson thought he had things settled with Oglesby. Then the team went to Penn State and midway through the first half, there was a scuffle underneath the basket and backup Nittany Lion center Paul Neumayer caught Oglesby with an elbow to the chin. Sure enough, Oglesby spun around and gave Neumayer a quick punch to the jaw that sent him staggering to midcourt. The game's two referees did not see Oglesby's punch because they had already turned to run down to the other end of the floor.

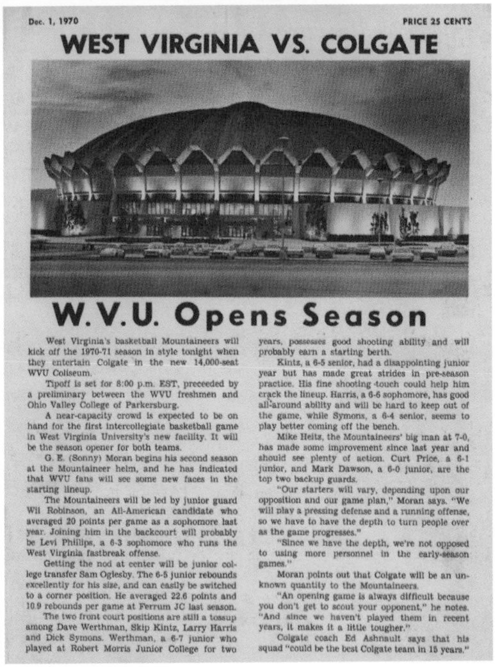

Dec. 1, 1970 PRICE 25 CENTS

WEST VIRGINIA VS. COLGATE

W.V.U. Opens Season

West Virginia's basketball Mountaineers will kick off the 1970-71 season in style tonight when they entertain Colgate in the new 14,000-seat WVU Coliseum.

Tipoff is set for 8:00 p.m. EST, preceeded by a preliminary between the WVU freshmen and Ohio Valley College of Parkersburg.

A near-capacity crowd is expected to be on hand for the first intercollegiate basketball game in West Virginia University's new facility. It will be the season opener for both teams.

G. E. (Sonny) Moran begins his second season at the Mountaineer helm, and he has indicated that WVU fans will see some new faces in the starting lineup.

The Mountaineers will be led by junior guard Wil Robinson, an All-American candidate who averaged 20 points per game as a sophomore last year. Joining him in the backcourt will probably be Levi Phillips, a 6-3 sophomore who runs the West Virginia fastbreak offense.

Getting the nod at center will be junior college transfer Sam Oglesby. The 6-5 junior rebounds excellently for his size, and can easily be switched to a corner position. He averaged 22.6 points and 10.9 rebounds per game at Ferrum JC last season.

The two front court positions are still a tossup among Dave Werthman, Skip Kintz, Larry Harris and Dick Symons. Werthman, a 6-7 junior who played at Robert Morris Junior College for two years, possesses good shooting ability and will probably earn a starting berth.

Kintz, a 6-5 senior, had a disappointing junior year but has made great strides in pre-season practice. His fine shooting touch could help him crack the lineup. Harris, a 6-6 sophomore, has good all-around ability and will be hard to keep out of the game, while Symons, a 6-4 senior, seems to play better coming off the bench.

Mike Heitz, the Mountaineers' big man at 7-0, has made some improvement since last year and should see plenty of action. Curt Price, a 6-1 junior, and Mark Dawson, a 6-0 junior, are the top two backup guards.

"Our starters will vary, depending upon our opposition and our game plan," Moran says. "We will play a pressing defense and a running offense, so we have to have the depth to turn people over as the game progresses."

"Since we have the depth, we're not opposed to using more personnel in the early-season games."

Moran points out that Colgate will be an unknown quantity to the Mountaineers.

"An opening game is always difficult because you don't get to scout your opponent," he notes. "And since we haven't played them in recent years, it makes it a little tougher."

Colgate coach Ed Ashnault says that his squad "could be the best Colgate team in 15 years."

But McPherson saw the entire episode from the bench, and he was afraid it was going to show up on the game film. So he waited at the office until late in the night for the courier to arrive with the film. When he put it into the projector, sure enough, Oglesby's punch was as clear as day. In the meantime, Brown had heard

Guard Levi Phillips looks for an open teammate during West Virginia's 87–75 victory over NC State at the WVU Coliseum on Dec. 6, 1971.

WVU SPORTS COMMUNICATIONS PHOTO.

about the incident, and he asked McPherson to bring the game film down to his office as soon as it was ready.

McPherson quickly stopped the projector, pulled the film out, and took a straight razor out of his desk drawer and cut out the clip of the Oglesby punch. He then spliced the film back together. McPherson's quick film editing rendered West Virginia's official game film about six seconds shorter than Penn State's version, and it preserved Oglesby's spot on the roster.

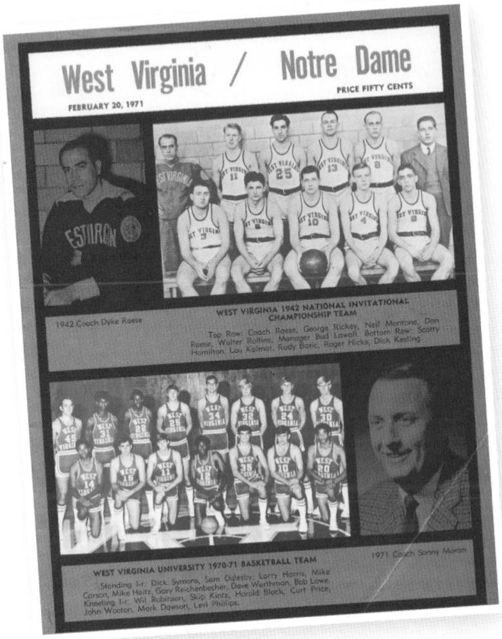

Moran was also glad McPherson spliced the film because Bobby Knight had asked for a copy. His Army team was going to play Penn State a couple of nights later.

"They wound up losing the game and Bob was so mad at them that he threw their lunches off the bus and didn't feed them until they got all the way back to West Point," laughed Moran.

Sam Oglesby signs his scholarship papers at the WVU Coliseum with assistant coach Gary McPherson looking on.
WVU SPORTS COMMUNICATIONS PHOTO.

Following a 17-point win over Rhode Island, WVU was the beneficiary of some more fan misbehavior at Pitt in a 95–91 victory. The Panthers were trailing 92–91 with 14 seconds left when a technical foul was called on the Pitt student section for throwing debris on the court in protest of a foul called on the Panthers. Wil Robinson's three free throws—one for the technical and two for the regular foul—helped provide the game's deciding margin.

It was the second technical whistled against the Pitt students that evening. In the first half, some of them threw garbage on the floor following another disputed call. Pitt coach Buzz Ridl got on the public address system to try and calm them down, warning that a technical would be called. They ignored him.

The same game actually got a late start because someone had heaved a raw egg at the West Virginia players while they were warming up, requiring a brief delay for maintenance workers to clean up the mess.

Robinson finished the season by scoring a career-high 45 points against Penn State, adding 21 in a two-point win against Pitt that was decided on a late Larry Harris basket, and producing 30 more in a 104–95 home victory against Virginia Tech that gave the Mountaineers a winning 13–12 record.

Robinson averaged 25 points per game in '71 while shooting 46.5 percent. Oglesby (14.7 ppg) and Harris (11.1 ppg) also averaged double figures.

Those three, plus Heitz, forward Dave Werthman, and guards Curt Price and Levi Phillips, were returning for the 1972 season. Mike Carson, Mark Catlett and Bob Hornstein were moving up from the freshman team to join them.

Tragedy Strikes

In 1972, Moran and his coaches were finally ready to enjoy the fruits of their labor. Tragically, it all came crashing down during a two-week stretch to begin January.

West Virginia started the season strongly, with six consecutive victories allowing them to make a return to the top 20 for the first time in five years. By the end of December the Mountaineers had defeated NC State (with 7-foot-4 center Tom Burleson), captured the Mountaineer Classic with victories over Columbia and Northwestern, and easily downed a strong Davidson team that won 19 games that year.

Then, in January, the rug was completely pulled out from beneath Moran's feet. First, Moran was informed that starters Larry Harris and Levi Phillips were academically ineligible for the remainder of the season.

"All of a sudden, John Semon, the head of the physical education department, walks into my office and tells me I was going to lose two of my players," Moran said. "I said, 'John, damn it, we didn't have a single failing grade on our ballclub. What are you talking about we're losing two of them?' He said, 'We've got a progressive thing that we have in the department and two of your players didn't meet that at the end of the semester.'

"I said, 'Now wait a minute. Football has the entire spring semester and a whole summer to get eligible for the next year and you're hitting me at midterm with two of my players?' He said, 'Well that's the way that it is.'"

Twelve days later while driving on a stretch of four-lane road on I-79 two miles south of the U.S. 250 interchange, Larry Harris lost control of his 1961 Corvair and struck a bridge abutment. The accident claimed Harris's life and Oglesby's basketball career. Harris was pronounced dead at the scene; Oglesby survived but was rendered a paraplegic.

"Deacon Harris had an aunt that lived over in Fairmont and so he went over there to have dinner with her and Sam went with him," Moran said. "They had already had dinner and they were

Charleston's Larry "Deacon" Harris averaged 11.1 points and 7.1 rebounds per game as a sophomore in 1971. Harris was sitting out the second semester of his junior year in 1972 when he tragically died in an automobile accident while returning to Morgantown from his aunt's house in Fairmont.

WVU SPORTS COMMUNICATIONS PHOTO.

on their way back. The state police called and said, 'Coach we've got terrible news for you. There was an accident and Sam Oglesby is up at your hospital now and we think the other person is Deacon Harris but we're not sure. We want you to come down and identify him.'

"Herb Warden was the chairman of our athletic committee and he worked at the hospital and he told me Sam would survive but would never walk again," Moran added. "I jumped in the car and took Curtis Price with me and we got over to the Fairmont hospital. The state policeman asked me, 'Are you sure you want to do this?' I said, 'Not particularly, but I understand that you can't identify him.' We went in and they took the sheet down and it was Deacon. It was a terrible, terrible situation."

West Virginia's misfortune continued. Replacements Gary Reichenbacher and Bob Hornstein were lost for the season—Reichenbacher to a broken leg and Hornstein to a collapsed lung. Mark Dawson, held out because of a heart murmur, found a doctor willing to clear him and he once again became available to the team midway through the season.

"My leading rebounder was Sam Oglesby, my second leading rebounder was Deacon Harris, and my playmaking guard and second leading scorer, Levi Phillips, were all gone," said Moran. "I lost five of my top seven players and the bad part about it was they were all underclassmen."

Despite the myriad problems, Wil Robinson was having his best season. He scored 39 points in a memorable 97–87 victory at Notre Dame, hit for 37 against Navy, produced 40 against Virginia and had 45 against Furman. Robinson's 41 points in the Manhattan game included the winning basket. Afterward, fans rushed the court and mobbed him; Robinson had to eventually be escorted off the floor away from his well-wishers.

Robinson tallied 32 against Virginia Tech, but it was Price and Dawson who provided the true heroics in that victory. The Mountaineers overcame a three-point Hokie lead in the final seven seconds without the benefit of having a 3-point shot.

After Price nailed a bank shot from the corner ("an im-

Seven-foot-one center Mike Heitz from Garrett, Ind., averaged 13.5 points and 9.0 rebounds per game as a senior in 1972.

WVU SPORTS COMMUNICATIONS PHOTO.

possible shot" said assistant coach Gary McPherson) to make the score 82–81 with five seconds remaining, West Virginia was trying frantically to get the ball back for one more shot.

"After Curt made that shot I remember sitting on the bench near the end line where referee George Conley [the father of Kentucky great Larry Conley] was standing," said McPherson. "We were pressing like crazy. I remember saying, 'They've only got five seconds to get the ball in.' He said, 'I know, I'm counting.'"

With Conley counting away, Tech's Alan Bristow panicked and threw a long inbound pass to midcourt that Dawson intercepted. All Dawson had time to do was fire up a half-court prayer.

It went in.

Stunned Virginia Tech fans watched as West Virginia players danced and celebrated on the court below them. Price even pulled himself up and sat on the rim.

After Dawson made the shot, Virginia Tech coach Don DeVoe walked down to the scorer's table to ask Conley what had happened. Moran was right there to hear Conley's reply. "I'll tell you what happened, Don. You just got your ass beat!" Moran recalls Conley saying.

Robinson's final college game at WVU was a 42-point performance in a 104–90 victory over Pitt. He finished the season with a 29.4 ppg average, eclipsing West's school record by one-tenth of a point. Robinson ranked fourth in the country in scoring and earned first-team All-America honors by *Basketball Weekly*, United Savings and the Helms Foundation. He also made the Converse All-America second team and was named a third-team AP All-American. His 1,850 career points included a school-record six 40-point games, while his 45 points scored against Penn State still remains a record for WVU players at the Coliseum.

Through all of the disappointment and tragedy, West Virginia was able to manage a 13–11 record. But more ominously, the automobile accident, the academic suspensions and Robinson's graduation had completely gutted the basketball program.

Wil Robinson scored a career-high 45 points against Penn State on Feb. 24, 1971 at the WVU Coliseum. Robinson made 17 of 34 field goal attempts and was 11 of 14 from the free throw line. Pictured here in this 1971 game against Columbia, Robinson scored 26 points to lead the Mountaineers to a 106–53 victory.

WVU PHOTOGRAPHIC SERVICES.

"I had the program exactly where I wanted it [before the academic suspensions and the car accident]," Moran explained. "I remember Mickey Furfari asking me, 'Sonny, what do you think West Virginia would have done that year if you wouldn't have lost all of those players?' I said, 'Oh, we probably would have been like 20–4.' He said, 'Who in the hell was going to beat you?'

"The bad part was the Eastern Regionals were going to be on our campus [in 1972] and it was made to order for us," Moran said. "We had the

Mullens guard Jerome Anderson drives to the hoop in this 1974 game against Villanova at the WVU Coliseum. Anderson averaged 12.6 points in 77 career games for the Mountaineers from 1973–75.

WVU SPORTS COMMUNICATIONS PHOTO.

ballclub we wanted. We had the right people in the right places and then to be completely wiped out, it just destroyed us."

The overall health and well-being of Mountaineer basketball was now in the hands of new athletic director Leland Byrd, hired to replace Brown in 1972. Byrd's résumé, like Brown's, was heavily slanted toward basketball. The former All-American was coming to WVU after serving 10 years as director of athletics at Miami Dade Junior College.

"Red has certainly brought the program a long way," Byrd commented in 1972. "Not only are the teams improved and not only has the program been expanded, but also West Virginia's facilities are now as good as any school's in the country."

In 1973, Moran fielded one of the youngest basketball teams in the country—two freshmen and three sophomore starters (it was the first year freshmen were allowed to play with the varsity)—and the Mountaineers suffered through a difficult 10–15 campaign.

Six-foot-seven freshman center Warren Baker led the Mountaineers in scoring with an average of 16.6 points per game to go with sophomore Jerome Anderson's 12.1 average, but both players had been thrown into the fire and were not ready to lead the team.

"When I came in they were in a situation where they really didn't have a lot of guys," Baker remembered. "It was the first year that freshmen were allowed to play. The year before Jerome played on the JV team, but he really didn't have a lot of experience."

West Virginia had won a tough recruiting battle to keep Greenbrier East standout Baker in-state. He took trips to Clemson, Virginia and to Michigan State because he liked the Spartans' colors (they were the same as his high school).

Baker also made a visit to Duke, where Bucky Waters was already under siege. He remembered sitting behind the Blue Devil bench with guard John Lucas during a game and having to duck from debris being thrown at Waters by the Duke students. "We were getting hit with things that they were throwing at Bucky," Baker laughed.

Dissatisfaction with Moran was also growing in Morgantown. When talking about his team, Moran usually did so in a glass-is-half-empty fashion that turned some people off. His analysis was always steeped in reality, which in the 1970s was all too familiar with Vietnam, Watergate, school busing, Stagflation, the energy crisis, environmental concerns and urban decay repeatedly being shown on the nightly news. Times were doubly tough in West Virginia.

Moran was booed by the student section when asked to present the winning trophy to his team after it had claimed its own holiday tournament. Later, the stunned coach refused to leave the bench when the announcement was made for him to present the tournament's MVP trophy.

"It was a very discouraging type of thing," Baker recalled.

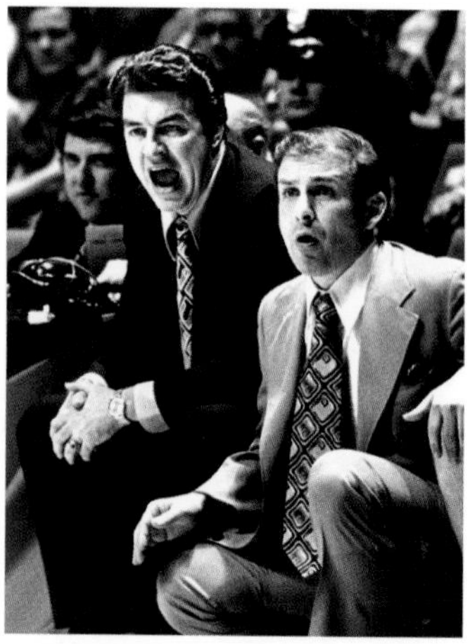

Penn coach Chuck Daly barks out instructions during his team's 78–67 victory over Villanova at the WVU Coliseum in the 1972 NCAA East Regional. Athletic Director Red Brown used his connections to steer the tournament to Morgantown, but he was criticized for the city's lack of accommodations to host an event of this size. One Philadelphia reporter wrote, "The only way to get here is to fly to Pittsburgh and then come by vines." South Carolina coach Frank McGuire, a native of New York City, was also unhappy, particularly that his team was headquartered at Mont Chateau on Cheat Lake. "Every morning I woke up and talked to deer," McGuire quipped.

WVU SPORTS COMMUNICATIONS PHOTO.

Despite a strong 3–1 start to the '74 season that included fine victories over Pitt, Cal and Oregon State, the discord continued. A five-game mid-January losing streak ratcheted the pressure, and Moran, following a meeting with Athletic Director Leland Byrd, decided to announce his resignation with five games remaining. West Virginia won only one of those games, a 101–100 double-overtime victory over Manhattan, to finish the year 10–15.

In his resignation letter to President Harlow made public, Moran cited his desire to give the university ample time to find a replacement as his main reason for quitting before the end of the year.

Eight times during the 1974 season, West Virginia lost games by five points or less. That happened 27 times during Moran's five seasons at WVU. Just 76 additional points (the score of one game) strategically placed could have made Sonny Moran's West Virginia record 84–41. That's how close Moran's WVU teams were. Following his resignation, Moran became athletic director at Morehead State and later served as commissioner of the Gulf Coast Conference before retiring from athletics in 1991.

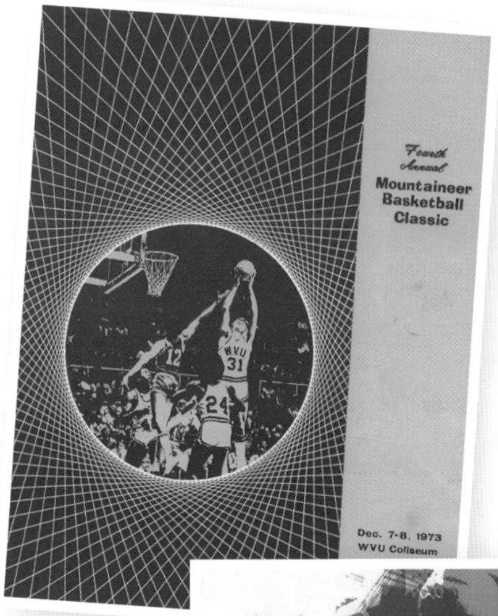

"That car accident really hurt Sonny's program," said Byrd.

One other item of significance that occurred during Moran's tenure came during his final year in the season opener against Pitt when he employed an all-black starting lineup for the first time in school history. Making history on Dec. 1, 1973 in Morgantown were Levi Phillips, Eartha Faust, Jerome Anderson, Larry Carr and Warren Baker. With civil rights and forced school busing in the south still fresh on people's minds in the '70s, there was a lot of attention paid to things like that. Today, thankfully, very few people would even think twice about it.

"I was going to play my five best players and I hoped our people would understand that," Moran said.

They did.

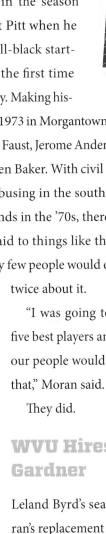

WVU Hires Gardner

Leland Byrd's search for Moran's replacement took him to the NBA to gauge Rod Thorn's and Jerry West's interest. It took him 15 miles south to Fairmont where Joe Retton had one of the

Athletic Director Red Brown presents the Mountaineer Classic championship trophy to Wil Robinson and Dick Symons. Standing in the background is longtime WVU assistant athletic director Ed Shockey.

WVU PHOTOGRAPHIC SERVICES.

Coach Joedy Gardner pictured here with assistant coaches Bill Ryczaj and Jim Amick.
WVU SPORTS COMMUNICATIONS PHOTO.

best small college programs in the country. And it took him out west where he became enamored with former Mountaineer player Joedy Gardner, coaching his second season at Arizona Western Junior College in Yuma, Ariz. Gardner had compiled a 50–12 record there and had Arizona Western in the national junior college playoffs as the nation's No. 6-rated team. When Byrd eventually offered Gardner the job, he accepted right on the spot.

"It was no big decision for me," Gardner said at the time of his hiring. "When I was offered the job, I immediately accepted."

Gardner was flown to Morgantown for a quick news conference at the WVU Coliseum before an NCAA tournament regional game between Pitt and St. Joseph's. He was asked if there was any concern about taking over such a storied basketball program with so little coaching experience. Gardner's answer caught reporters off guard. "Have you ever had a SAM missile launched at you?" Gardner asked, bringing up his military service in Vietnam as an A-4 pilot. "That's scary. I didn't keep count, but I guess I flew over 100 missions."

It was rare at the time for junior college coaches to get Division I jobs because junior colleges were often looked down upon. It was the old adage if a player is in junior college, he's there for a reason and it's usually not a good one. But with Jerry Tarkanian and Cotton Fitzsimmons enjoying great success, the door eventually opened for other junior college coaches to get Division I jobs. The year Gardner went to West Virginia, Oral Roberts also hired Jerry Hale from the College of Southern Idaho.

Plus, in Gardner's case, he felt his coaching experience in the military didn't receive its proper due. "The playing and coaching that I did in the military was quite extensive actually," Gardner said. "There were several college coaches that coached in the military at that time. It was high level and most of us were coaching several years and really studied the game, had clinics and did all of that. But when we got to college none of that was recognized."

After completing his duties at Arizona Western, Gardner asked his junior college assistant coach Jim Amick to come back with him to WVU and the two began scouring the country for players. The third member of Gardner's staff was former Mountaineer player Bill Ryczaj, who was mainly responsible for scouting.

"Joedy talked me into coming," Amick recalled. "When I first went there it was a spring day in early March right after the national juco tournament. I flew there and he picked me up at the airport and it was an ugly, gray, nasty day. We drove a little winding road all the way to Morgantown. I thought to myself, 'What in the world have I just gotten myself into?'"

Gardner was inheriting two fine players in Baker and Anderson, and he had another good one sitting out in Ohio University transfer Bob Huggins, though Gardner told Huggins that he wasn't sure he could play in the up-tempo system that he was planning to use. "Perhaps he was just testing me," Huggins once recalled.

Coach Joedy Gardner posing with Jerome Anderson, Scott MacDonald and Warren Baker in front of the WVU Coliseum for the cover of the 1975 media guide.

WVU PHOTOGRAPHIC SERVICES.

Gardner quickly got Welch High standout Maurice Robinson to switch his commitment from Wake Forest to West Virginia.

"We knew he was the No. 1 player in West Virginia and it would launch us to at least a platform where people might be happy if we could get him to change his mind," Gardner recalled. "We were able to do that. We spent a lot of time

Stan Boskovich, from nearby Masontown, Pa., averaged 17.7 points and shot 82.7 percent from the free throw line during his fine two-year career with the Mountaineers in 1975–76.
WVU SPORTS COMMUNICATIONS PHOTO.

with him and [Gov.] Arch Moore got involved a little there. There was a lot of pressure on him to go to West Virginia because he was a West Virginia kid."

Then Gardner brought in high-scoring forward Stan Boskovich from Yavapai Junior College. Boskovich was from nearby Masontown, Pa., where he had played at Albert Gallatin High School, and he was a distant nephew of Pitt coach Buzz Ridl. West Virginia tried to sign him out of high school, but there were problems with his transcript.

Boskovich had played a couple of good games against Gardner's junior college team so Gardner signed him. "I liked the way he played," Gardner said. "He played with gusto and he could shoot the ball."

Gardner rounded out his first recruiting class by adding forward Sid Bostick and Logan guard Ross Scaggs.

Meanwhile, access to the NCAA tournament had improved dramatically for West Virginia when it became a member of Eastern Collegiate Athletic Conference, where the top four teams in the 39-member monstrosity now qualified for postseason play. Leland Byrd said the conference really came about as a means to help arrange officiating for football and basketball games. Had Penn State and Pitt been able to settle its differences and take on more of a leadership role, Byrd believes an eastern all-sports conference was well within their grasp in the mid-1970s.

The new ECAC conglomeration proved massive, cumbersome and confusing, with the 16 top-rated teams in the New England, New York-Connecticut, and the Metropolitan New York-New Jersey areas, and the southern districts of Maryland, Pennsylvania and West Virginia being divided into four, four-team playoffs.

West Virginia was picked as the host site for the 1975 Southern District playoffs. The district also contained Duquesne, Georgetown, George Washington, Morgan State, Navy, Penn State, Pitt, St. Francis, Pa. and Villanova.

Gardner got off to a good start with three straight wins against Georgia Southern, Pitt and Villanova. Baker poured in 31 points and grabbed 22 rebounds to lead West Virginia to an 82–78 victory over the Panthers in overtime. He scored 24 of his game-high 31 in the second half to help the Mountaineers overcome a 10-point deficit.

Purdue ended West Virginia's modest winning streak, 94–83. Other tough losses came at American and against Virginia Tech in Morgantown. Two weeks later, West Virginia had a chance to knock off 19th-rated Rutgers at the Coliseum. With the score tied at 84, Baker was whistled for traveling with four seconds remaining. After calling time-out, Rutgers got the ball to freshman Steve Hefele in the corner where he sank a 25-footer ahead of the buzzer for an 86–84 victory.

The 84–81 win over Syracuse seemed unlikely when West Virginia fell behind by 21 points in the first half. But the Mountaineers came back when Robinson converted two free throws with 15 seconds remaining. Baker, Huggins and Anderson scored 37 of West Virginia's 59 second-half points.

What Gardner remembers most about the Syracuse victory was Maurice Robinson making one-handed free throws to win the game.

"As talented a player as he was, the first time I saw him play in the Dapper Dan All-Star Game in Pittsburgh I thought to myself, 'Oh my God, he's not a fundamentally sound shooter.' He didn't shoot the ball right, but he had everything else."

So Gardner taught Robinson to shoot free throws by taking one arm and putting it behind his back, taking his shooting hand and placing the ball in the palm of his hand, and making him shoot it that way.

"You have to bring your hand back, keep the ball level, twist your hand, and you've got to keep that L-shape and the proper way to hold the ball and shoot it up there and release it," Gardner explained. "As I recall, [Syracuse] fouled him intentionally figuring he wasn't going to make them, and he made them both."

Despite the Syracuse victory, a respectable 12-7 record totally disintegrated with season-ending losses to Virginia Tech and Illinois State that seemingly put the Mountaineers' postseason hopes in the dumpster. The Illinois State loss was especially disturbing.

"We were just out to have fun in that game," Boskovich said. "I think we even got a technical for dunking in pre-game warm-ups."

Despite losing 8 of its final 11 games, West Virginia still managed to get into the ECAC playoffs as the last team when Duquesne choked twice at the end of the season. In the first round the Mountaineers were pitted against top-seeded Pitt, coming off an NCAA tournament appearance in 1974.

Warren Baker scores two of his 19 points in this 1975 game against Pitt at Fitzgerald Field House. Tom Richards and Kirk Bruce each scored 18 points to lead the Panthers to an 83–77 victory over the Mountaineers.

WVU SPORTS COMMUNICATIONS PHOTO.

The death of Maurice Robinson's father, James, and the failure of Eartha Faust and Bob Sims to return on time from spring break left West Virginia with only nine available players for the tournament. Against the Panthers, the Mountaineers reeled off 10 straight points to take a 46–37 lead after trailing by one at halftime. West Virginia increased its lead to 13 with 11:52 to go. Then Pitt came to life, scoring the next

10 points, reducing its deficit to one, 54–53. A three-point play by Boskovich and a pair of free throws by Baker eventually pulled out a surprising 75–73 victory.

One night later, West Virginia's bid to make the NCAA tournament was denied when Georgetown sank the Mountaineers on a last-second shot, 62–61. After twice trailing by six, West Virginia battled back to tie the game at

Maurice Robinson struggled at the foul line during his first two seasons, shooting below 50 percent, before he changed to a one-handed shooting style that helped him to 71.6 percentage as a junior and a 65.2 percentage as a senior.
WVU PHOTOGRAPHIC SERVICES.

56 on a pair of long jump shots by Huggins. Leading by one with 10 seconds remaining, West Virginia had an opportunity to make it a three-point lead with Earnie Hall at the line for a one-and-one, but Hall missed the front end. Georgetown grabbed the rebound and Hoya freshman guard Derrick Jackson hit a running 20-foot jump shot from the left corner with two seconds left to win the game.

"Earnie Hall, who had long fingernails, tried to steal the ball and it hit his fingernails and broke two of them off," said Huggins, recalling the play. "If he knocked the ball away, we win. But he overran the ball, Jackson caught it, and he threw up a shot at the buzzer to win it."

"That was unbelievable that the ball goes in," said Gardner. "If it doesn't go in, we go to the NCAAs."

Georgetown's win gave Coach John Thompson his first NCAA tournament appearance—the first of 20 in a brilliant 27-year coaching career.

Despite a 14–13 record, there were a lot of positives to build on during Gardner's first season. One such positive was Boskovich's 17.6 average as the team's lead scorer. "I averaged about 18 points in about 18 minutes per game," Boskovich joked. "Every time I tried a behind-the-back pass or something crazy, Joedy would always yank me."

Baker (16.4 ppg), Anderson (14.1 ppg) and Hall (10.0 ppg) also averaged double figures. Boskovich poured in 40 against Davidson, and Baker had 39 against Boston University. Those two were back for 1976, along with Huggins, Bostick, Hall, Robinson and Dave McCardle.

Six-foot-eleven center Junius Lewis arrived from Richmond, Va., guard Dana Perno came from nearby Uniontown, Pa., and Amick used his junior college contacts to locate Russell Chapman and Tony Robertson.

Amick was a very persuasive recruiter, and he got Robertson to sign without him ever visiting Morgantown. "He was at Eastern Arizona Community College and the coach there had gone to school at the University of Arizona, and I think they were kind of thinking that he was going to go there," said Amick. "Well, I got him to sign the papers on the back of the trunk of my rental car outside the dorm. We had a big ceremony—he was standing there, I got the papers out, he signed them, we shook hands, and I said, 'I'll visit your mom and dad when I get to Detroit.' That was the end of that."

"With JC kids, we didn't have any choice when we went in there," Gardner added. "We didn't want to recruit a bunch of JC kids but we were forced to. Then once we got that group in there and they played a few years we weren't recruiting JC kids at all."

The Mountaineers posted another winning season in 1976, with quality victories against Temple, New Mexico, Duquesne, Penn State, Virginia and Pitt. West Virginia qualified for the ECAC tournament once again, but was eliminated in the first round, 99–97, by George Washington, whose Pat Tallent scored 32 points to lead the Colonials.

"[Tallent] used to wear Huggs out," laughed Robertson. "We used to tease him about that later. Don't get me wrong, he scored on the whole team, but we always mess with Huggs about that whenever we get together."

The GW game was interrupted with 11:12 remaining by a fight that led to the ejections of Chapman and GW's Jim Smith. The player who started the fight, Boskovich, somehow managed to stay in the game. The disturbance began when Boskovich grabbed Haviland Harper and wrestled him to the floor as the two players were going after a loose ball. Players from both teams piled on. Eventually officials and policemen had to intervene to restore order.

A victory over Villanova in the ECAC consolation game made West Virginia's final record 15–13. Robertson and Boskovich averaged better than 17 points per game that season, and it had been a battle to see which player was going to get off the most shots.

"My junior year I played point guard and I had a guy on the right wing who shot it every time and a guy on the left wing who shot it every time [Boskovich and Robertson], and it was a matter of which one had a better chance to make a shot because neither one was going to pass it much," said Huggins.

Gardner said Huggins was really a fourth coach on the floor when he played. "He played not only the mental game, he played the psychological game and he's still doing it today the way he coaches," Gardner said in 2010. "People would ask me all the time what he was like as a player, well, just watch him coach. That's the way he played."

Warren Baker is the only player in school history to lead the Mountaineers in rebounding all four years he played. Baker averaged a double-double (14.8 points and 10.2 rebounds) for his 105-game career.

WVU SPORTS COMMUNICATIONS PHOTO.

With the exception of Boskovich and Baker, the rest of the key players were returning for 1977. Robinson, now a junior, moved into Baker's center spot, and Amick worked his magic once again to land star guard Lowes Moore from Mount Vernon, N.Y.

Amick talked his way out onto the tarmac at LaGuardia Airport to sign Moore right in the plane as he was preparing to leave for a high school all-star game. "The stewardess is kind of looking at me like what in the world is going on?" Amick said. "I found Lowes in the back of the plane and I said, 'Lowes, you've got to sign these.'

"After that I immediately headed to Mount Vernon to have his mother sign the papers. I didn't want to take a chance of him going to that tournament and being approached by a bunch of other coaches, which is exactly what happened."

Gardner and Amick were not afraid to go into metropolitan areas to recruit the top players even though they were coaching at a rural school. "We looked at our competition and Rutgers had good

Right A publicity "slick" issued by the Sports Information office of some of the key players for the 1976 season. These would often end up in the storefront windows along High Street.

WVU SPORTS COMMUNICATIONS PHOTO.

Inset Tony Robertson battles for a rebound in this 1975 game against Purdue. Robertson, a junior college transfer, had a terrific two-year career for the Mountaineers, scoring 1,020 points and averaging 18 points in 57 career games.

WVU SPORTS COMMUNICATIONS PHOTO.

teams, Syracuse had good teams, Georgetown had good teams and that was because they all had a certain level of talent playing for them and we had to match that," Gardner said. "We weren't going to take lesser talent and go and out-coach anybody—you're just not going to do that.

"We went to some of our strongholds and when I was a JC coach we recruited Chicago all of the time. We recruited Chicago, Detroit, New York and D.C. heavily," Gardner said. "I always thought any kid there that's a player, why wouldn't he want to go to West Virginia University? The parents of those kids did."

In 1977, Gardner produced his best record (18–11) at WVU. The Mountaineers were not a big team with the 6-foot-7 Robinson playing center, but they were athletic and they could score a lot of points. Excellent wins came against Syracuse in the Hall of Fame Tip-Off Classic in Springfield, Mass., and against Virginia Tech, Duquesne, Pitt, Penn State and Duke.

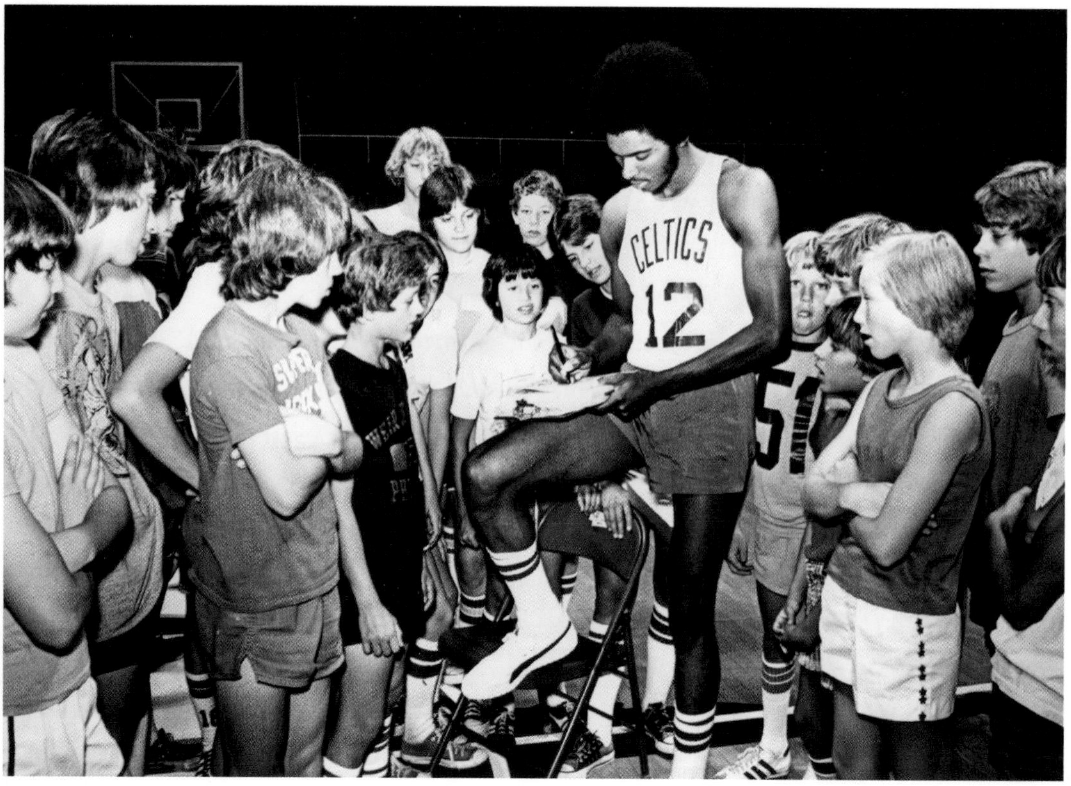

Below Jerome Anderson, a member of the world champion Boston Celtics, returns to campus to sign some autographs at a WVU basketball camp in 1976.

WVU SPORTS COMMUNICATIONS PHOTO.

Huggins, now a senior, was the central figure in the Duquesne and Duke wins. An inadvertent Huggins elbow that caught Duquesne's B. B. Flenory in the head rendered him unconscious during West Virginia's 97–82 victory over the Dukes in Morgantown.

The Duquesne guard wound up being hospitalized from the concussion, and two seasons later, he chose not to make the trip to Morgantown with his Duquesne teammates out of fear of being injured once again.

In the Duke victory a month later in Morgantown, Huggins was the star of the game with 16 second-half points to snap West Virginia's five-game losing streak—all five of those defeats coming on the road.

West Virginia's best victory of the season was against Notre Dame on Feb. 18, 1977. The 17th-ranked Irish had 17 wins and were already in great position to lock up another NCAA tournament berth.

"The thing I remember the most is Maurice and I were walking into the Coliseum and Notre Dame was out on the floor with a big boom box and they were stretching," Huggins recalled. "I was kind of watching them and Digger walked over to me and said, 'We are going to whip you tomorrow, boys.' We didn't say anything. We just went upstairs and went back to Towers."

As West Virginia's lead grew well into double digits late in the game, Robinson made it a point to walk past the Notre Dame bench. "We're up 16 or 17 with a minute to go and I remember Maurice walking over to Digger and Digger was standing up yelling and screaming. Mo looked over and said, 'We beat your ass today, boy.' I thought that was pretty good," said Huggins.

Robinson played one of the best all-around games of his career, scoring 21 points and grabbing 15 rebounds in the 81–68 victory. Gardner called it the "biggest win in our program."

Gardner was particularly miffed with the way Phelps had acted before, during and after the game as if the Boston Celtics had come to town. It was simply Digger being Digger. "After the game he didn't even walk over [to shake hands]," Gardner recalled. "He just took off and went to the dressing room."

West Virginia completed the regular season with easy victories over Cleveland State and Buffalo State. Following a 66–54 win against Pitt at the Spectrum in the first round of the Eastern Collegiate Basketball League tournament (before fewer than 300 people), the Mountaineers were eliminated in the semifinals in overtime by Villanova, 83–75.

A long Huggins jump shot and a free throw by Robertson gave West Virginia a 69–67 lead with 1:40 remaining in the game. Then the Wildcats trapped backup guard Dana Perno in the corner and took the ball away from him, leading to Rory Sparrow's game-tying shot with 30 seconds left. Huggins's shot to try to win the game in regulation rolled off the rim with two seconds left.

Gardner had Perno in the game because he

Guard Bob Huggins averaged 13.2 points, 4.1 rebounds and handed out a team-best 109 assists as a senior in 1977.

WVU SPORTS COMMUNICATIONS PHOTO.

Below The 1977 team won 18 games, finished first in the ECBL West Division and fell to Villanova 83–75 in overtime in the ECBL tournament semifinals. Pictured in the back row, fifth from the right wearing jersey number 35, is Bob Huggins.

WVU SPORTS COMMUNICATIONS PHOTO.

WVU recruiter Jim Amick was able to talk his way onto an Eastern Airlines flight to sign New York City guard Lowes Moore.

WVU SPORTS COMMUNICATIONS PHOTO.

was an excellent foul shooter. He also thought Perno was fouled on the steal. "Dana was pretty shaken up afterward, but it was a tough position to be in," Huggins noted. "He hadn't played the whole game, and Villanova definitely fouled him, but you aren't going to get those calls."

A consolation-round loss to Massachusetts the next day removed any possibility of West Virginia receiving an NIT bid despite its outstanding record.

"We should have made the NIT," Robertson said. "We beat Massachusetts twice during the regular season and they sent them."

Actually, West Virginia could have gone to the NIT but turned the bid down for financial reasons, according to Gardner. "I argued that we couldn't afford not to go," said Gardner.

Robertson passed the 1,000 point mark in just two seasons at WVU, while averaging a team-best 18.1 points per game. Robinson (15.5 ppg), Huggins (13.2 ppg) and Chapman (13.0 ppg) also scored double digits in helping the team average 81.6 points per game.

"That year we played that 1-1-3 hockey defense and Huggins made that thing go," said Gardner. "He was the glue in that thing. I never had a team before or after that could play it like that."

Deteriorating Relationship

Coming off an 18-win season, it appeared things were running smoothly for Gardner. But in reality, his relationship with Athletic Director Leland Byrd was beginning to deteriorate. The two were at odds over almost everything.

"I always told Joedy, 'You've got to be careful who you pick your fights against.' Joedy and Leland were constantly bickering about things, and they weren't big things," Amick recalled. "It was little things like how far can I go to play a game? How far can I recruit? Leland was a good, honest man, but he thought you could get every good player you needed within a 75-mile radius of Morgantown."

"Number one, I really respected Leland," added Gardner. "He was a great player and he was always very polite. Leland and I never had an argument. The problem I had was that every single penny had to be accounted for."

Gardner also wanted to have more of a say in scheduling. "I would make recommendations, but they were never really considered," Gardner said.

Fan apathy and discontent with Gardner's program grew in 1978 as the losses began to pile up. A five-game losing streak in mid-February dropped West Virginia's record to 7–14. West Virginia finished the regular season at 10–15 heading into the Eastern 8 Championships in Pittsburgh. The ECBL had changed its name to the Eastern 8 and the league was now made up of Rutgers, Massachusetts, Duquesne, Pitt, George Washington, Villanova, Penn State and West Virginia. "Each year we played in the league they kept changing the name," Maurice Robinson said.

Gardner actually expected the regular season to play out the way that it did. "We were playing freshmen, they were going to grow and at the end of the year we were going to be good and we were," Gardner said. "Plus, we had a great recruiting class coming in."

The Mountaineers finished last during the regular season and were paired against No. 1-seeded Rutgers in the opening round of the tournament.

The talk in Morgantown heading into the Eastern 8 tournament opener was whether or not Gardner would be around for a fifth season. Newspapers were reporting that Gardner's only chance of returning was if he won the tournament—and he nearly pulled it off.

West Virginia upset Rutgers 81–74 in the quarterfinals, and then held on to beat Duquesne 59–57 in the semifinals. The Dukes had a great chance to win the game, trailing by one point with five seconds left. Bostick missed the front end of a one-and-one, giving Duquesne's John Moore an opportunity to call time-out at midcourt. However, the Dukes were already out of time-outs and a technical foul was assessed. Lowes Moore's free throw accounted for the final margin.

West Virginia lost to Villanova 63–59 in the championship game to complete a 12–16 season. The Wildcats, with outstanding guard Rory Sparrow and forwards Keith Herron and Alex Bradley, later advanced to the NCAA regional finals.

Gardner, his lifeline about to be pulled, recalled Villanova coach Rollie Massamino joking with him before the game. "Rollie comes up to me before the game and he says, 'Coach I've got a big family and I've got a big bill to feed my kids and we can't have you beating me now,'" Gardner chuckled. "He was saying he had to win the game to keep his job."

A day later, Gardner was informed that his contract was not going to be renewed for the following season. Byrd also left shortly afterward to take the commissioner's job at the Eastern 8, and was replaced by Big Eight Conference assistant commissioner Dick Martin.

Amick said he never had a sense of job security the four years he was at West Virginia because the state prohibited multi-year contracts. "Other coaches would tell a player, 'How do you know they're going to be there next year?' That was one of the points of contention Joedy had with the administration at that time."

Gardner's tough, military background sometimes rubbed players the wrong way. Baker remembered once being asked by Gardner to tell the team to quit complaining on a charter flight that they were taking to Philadelphia. Baker said the plane looked old and rickety and most of the players were afraid to get on it.

"The heating line froze and there was absolutely no heat on the plane at all. Guys were huddled up and shaking and Joedy jumped me and Earnie Hall because we were the captains and we were with the guys sitting there all bundled up," Baker recalled. "He thought that since we were the captains, we should be the ones walking down the aisle telling the guys that it wasn't all that bad."

"I had a military background but I was really a fighter pilot," Gardner explained. "I wasn't impressed with the way the Marine Corps treated

Above Maurice Robinson (45) tips in a basket against Massachusetts in this 1977 game at the WVU Coliseum. Robinson scored 16 points and grabbed 17 rebounds to lead the Mountaineers to 91–70 victory.

WVU SPORTS COMMUNICATIONS PHOTO.

Left Jeannette, Pa.'s Sid Bostick started all 29 games as a junior in 1977, averaging 9.2 points and 6.3 rebounds per game.

WVU PHOTOGRAPHIC SERVICES PHOTO.

WOMEN'S BASKETBALL

It began with an act of Congress. That's how women's basketball became an official sport at West Virginia University. In 1972, Congress enacted Title IX, which mandated that all schools receiving federal assistance must provide the same athletic opportunities to women as to their male counterparts.

In 1973, West Virginia University Director of Athletics Leland Byrd hired Kittie Blakemore from the School of Physical Education to coach the women's team. He gave her keys to a university van and together they established a 10-game schedule made up mostly of West Virginia Conference schools.

Blakemore recalled what a struggle it was getting the women's program established. "In the beginning we weren't sure if we were going to be with the physical education department or the athletic department," Blakemore said. "We wanted to be with athletics because, financially, they were more stable."

That problem was solved, but Blakemore encountered several others. Just a handful of the 37 girls who tried out for the team actually knew how to play the game. One player was told by her high school coach that a good shot should not hit the backboard, so she thought she had blown every bank shot that went into the basket.

"Basketball had just started in West Virginia so the girls really didn't know that much about the game," said Blakemore, now retired and living in her native Manassas, Va. "I remember going to the first high school state tournament and thinking to myself, 'Oh my, I've got to recruit these girls!'"

Blakemore eventually selected 15 girls for the school's first team and after one quit, Blakemore, her assistant coach Barbara Walker, and trainer Diane Nolan took 14 girls over to West Liberty to play West Virginia University's first women's basketball game on Wednesday, Jan. 16, 1974. Because uniforms had yet to arrive, the players had to use "pinnies"— a vest-like jersey that tied at the waist. West Virginia defeated the Hilltoppers 59–55.

West Virginia continued to play local schedules consisting primarily of schools such as Concord, Davis & Elkins, Fairmont State, Marshall, Shepherd and West Liberty until 1980, when schools such as North Carolina, James Madison, Penn State, Dayton, Cincinnati and Rutgers began appearing on the schedule.

WVU center Georgeann Wells made history when she became the first female player in NCAA history to dunk a basketball in a game on Dec. 21, 1984 against Charleston at the Randolph County Armory in Elkins, W.Va.

WVU SPORTS COMMUNICATIONS PHOTO.

It was right around the same time that the women's program began offering scholarships. Guard Cathy Parson was the first women's basketball player at West Virginia to earn an athletic grant in 1980. It was bumped up to a full scholarship when Blakemore was able to offer J. D. Drummonds and Patricia Ryan full rides in 1981.

By 1989, West Virginia had a team good enough to qualify for the NCAA tournament and three years later, in 1992, led by All-American guard Rosemary Kosiorek, West Virginia cracked the national rankings and advanced to the NCAA tournament "Sweet 16" for the first time in school history.

More recently, interest in the Mountaineers has exploded since Coach Mike Carey has taken over. Carey has guided WVU to more NCAA tournament appearances (four) than all previous coaches combined, his teams have spent more weeks in the Associated Press Top 25 poll and have defeated more ranked teams than all previous years combined, and his most recent team in 2010 posted the best record in school history (29–5). The program has experienced a 232 percent increase in yearly average attendance since Carey's first season in 2002, a great indication of the overall growth women's basketball has experienced at West Virginia University.

the enlisted people so I had compassion for that. I liked the discipline of life, you get up early, you have your day planned and you don't waste time.

"And I had empathy and sympathy for the kids," Gardner added. "The kids that I had at West Virginia I really enjoyed them. Some of them thought I was a hard-ass at times, but it was sort of like tough love."

Robinson also had his disagreements with Gardner. "He had that Marine-type mentality," Robinson said. "It was like we were soldiers to him, 'Do this and do that.'"

Gardner's four-year record of 59–53 included memorable victories over Syracuse, Notre Dame and Rutgers—the win over the Scarlet Knights coming just two years after they appeared in the Final Four in 1976.

Gardner was also responsible for recruiting future pro players Tony Robertson and Lowes Moore. Robertson was one of the best two-year performers in school history, scoring 1,026 points and averaging 18 points per game. He was a first-team all-Eastern 8 pick and was also named to the 1977 all-tournament team.

Gardner's first recruit, Maurice Robinson, wound up leading the league in rebounding as a senior in 1978 while also scoring 1,307 career points. Stan Boskovich averaged 17.7 points for his career and nearly reached the 1,000-point mark in just two seasons. Russell Chapman was another fine two-year player who averaged 13 points and 6.9 rebounds per game as a senior.

Some of Gardner's best players at West Virginia were those he was familiar with while coaching in the junior college ranks. "In those days most schools recruited within a 100-mile radius," Amick said. "And very rarely did you ever hear of a West Coast kid going to the East Coast. In football there were a lot of good players within a 100-mile radius. Basketball-wise that wasn't necessarily true.

"I heard it many, many times—there is a player down at blank, blank high school and he's another Jerry West," Amick said. "If I heard he's another Jerry West once, I heard it a thousand times while I was there. . . . Obviously, there wasn't another Jerry West."

After his dismissal, Gardner immediately landed a job at Northern Arizona. "It wasn't like I was losing a job and was going to be out on the street," Gardner said. "I already had a job with twice the money. I kept telling everybody, 'Thanks for the time here.' I had four great years as a player and four great years as a coach and to this day I thank West Virginia University for everything that I have, including my wife. If it wasn't for West Virginia I wouldn't have the life that I have, which is pretty darn nice right now."

Huggins, who has since earned wide acclaim as one of college basketball's top coaches, was Gardner's best-known player. Huggins would eventually bring West Virginia's '70s era—and his coaching career—full circle in 2007.

Super-fan Junior Taylor gets the crowd fired up during a home game at the WVU Coliseum. Many fans still consider Taylor the best Mountaineer mascot in school history.

WVU PHOTOGRAPHIC SERVICES.

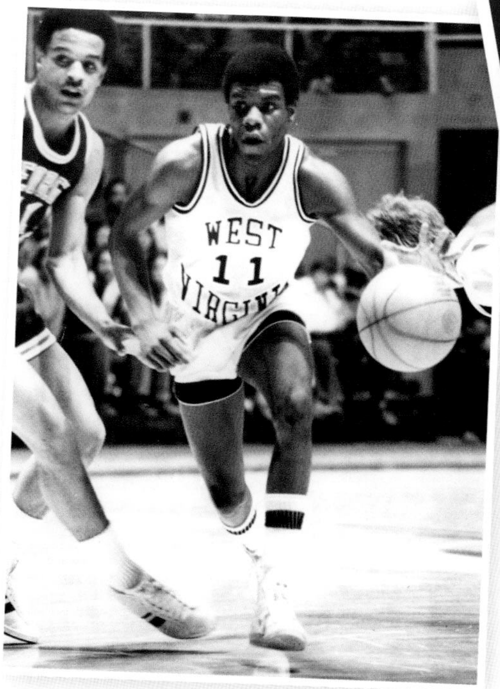

Guard Lowes Moore scored 1,696 points during his four-year Mountaineer career from 1977–80. Moore was named the 1980 Eastern 8 tournament most valuable player despite the Mountaineers losing the championship game to Villanova.

WVU SPORTS COMMUNICATIONS PHOTO.

CINCINNATI
23

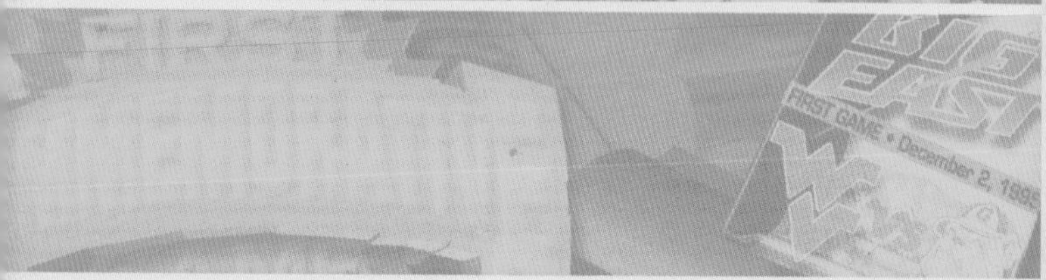
BIG EAST
FIRST GAME

WEST
24
Pitt
15
WEST
11

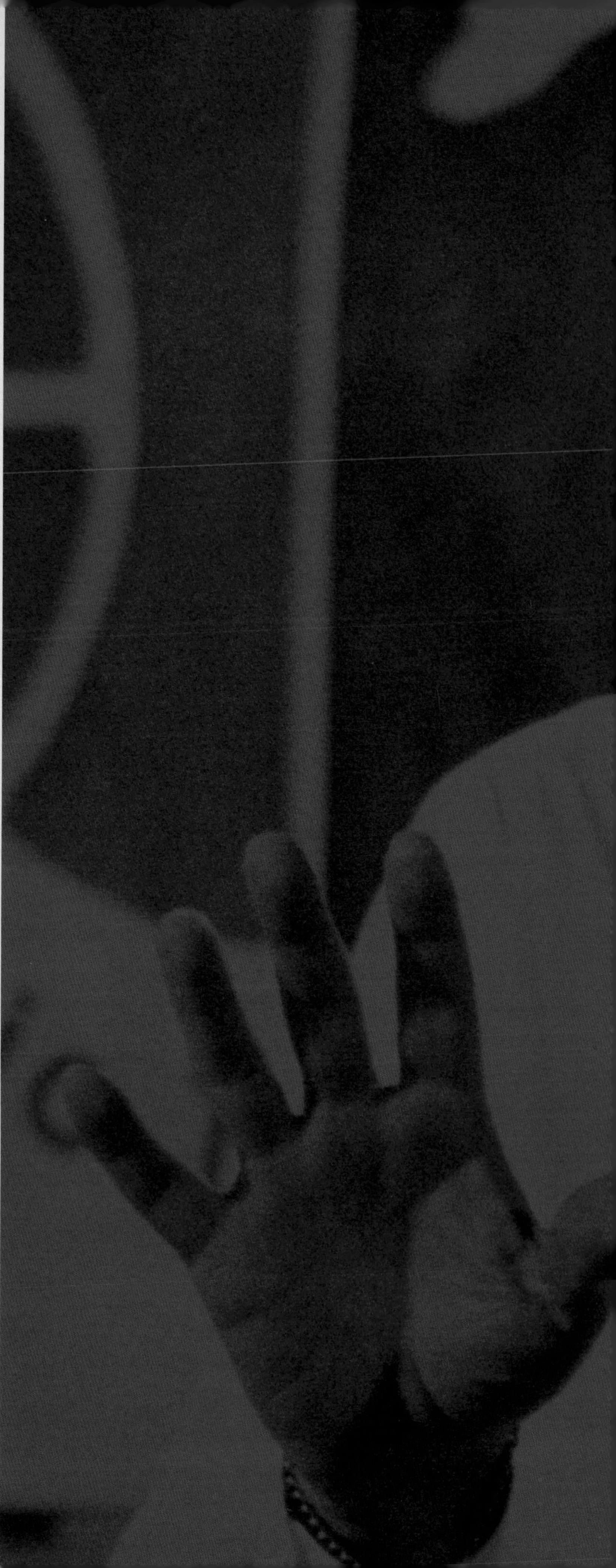

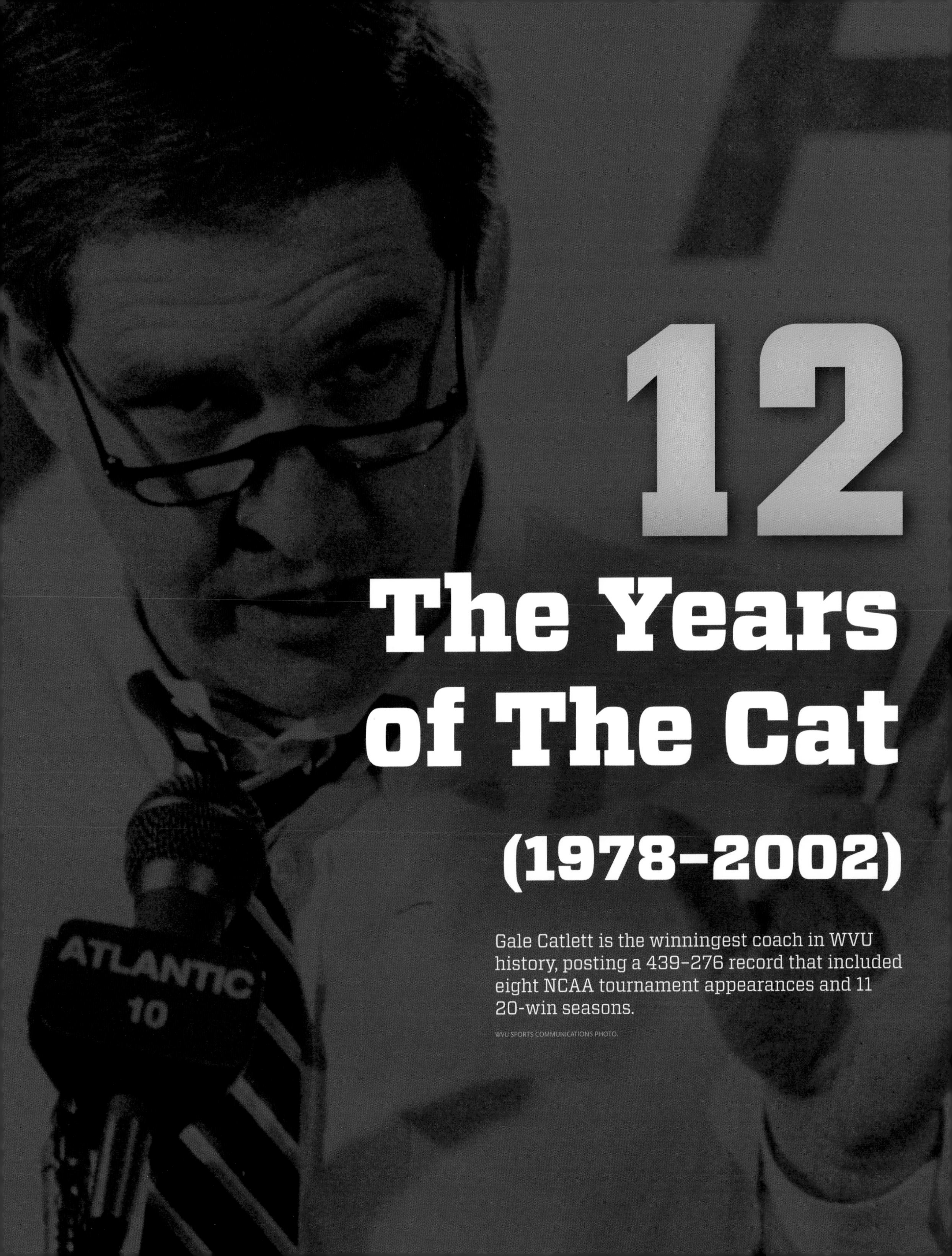

12
The Years of The Cat (1978–2002)

Gale Catlett is the winningest coach in WVU history, posting a 439–276 record that included eight NCAA tournament appearances and 11 20-win seasons.

WVU SPORTS COMMUNICATIONS PHOTO.

Leland Byrd first gauged Gale Catlett's interest in the West Virginia job in 1974 while searching for Sonny Moran's replacement. More than 35 years later, Catlett recalled a dinner conversation he had with Byrd and Red Brown early in his coaching career at Cincinnati. Byrd and Brown had traveled to the Queen City to try and persuade Catlett to take the West Virginia job.

"We had dinner together and we were into our conversation an hour or so and they said that they wanted me to come back and coach," Catlett said. "I always respected Red Brown tremendously, and Leland was such a great guy, and I said, 'Look, how long is your contract for?' [Leland] said, 'What do you mean by that?' I said, 'Well what is the length of the contract you can guarantee?' They said, 'We only give year-to-year contracts.'"

Gale Catlett addresses reporters at a press conference introducing him as the school's 19th men's basketball coach on March 29, 1978.
WVU SPORTS COMMUNICATIONS PHOTO.

At that point, Catlett politely told them it was pointless for them to continue their conversation because he had a five-year rollover contract with the Bearcats.

Catlett had risen rapidly in the coaching profession after his solid three-year playing career at West Virginia University ended in 1963. In a span of eight years from 1964–72, Catlett served as assistant coach at Richmond, Davidson, Kansas and Kentucky. Each stop was a progression in his coaching career.

"He didn't just start out at a small school like a lot of coaches did back then, he started out at Richmond and then worked for some of the best basketball coaches in the business," remarked WVU teammate Jim McCormick. "He knew what he was doing."

Even as a player, Catlett showed a deep understanding of the game. Virginia Tech forward Chris Smith recalled how Catlett used to deliberately delay games when the Mountaineers were in their zone press defense and Catlett sensed that his teammates needed a break to refresh their legs. "He would just lie on the ground and their trainer would come out and stretch him out," Smith laughed. "All he was doing was catching his breath. When the trainer was finished, he would jump up and they'd get back into that press and get a few more steals."

Catlett was the fiercest competitor on a team full of fierce competitors. "It didn't matter whether we were shooting pool, playing cards, running a race or whatever, Gale didn't like losing," said McCormick.

Willie Akers added, "If he thought he had to knock somebody in the head, he knocked somebody in the head. That's how he played."

One of Catlett's biggest contributions to the team was keeping Rod Thorn upright. Whenever teams tried to take out West Virginia's star player, Catlett was usually the person there to clean things up.

"I would have to help him a little bit," Catlett laughed. "He was the star player and some teams tried to beat him up and thug on him, so I had to protect him."

The son of a railroader, Gale grew up on a farm in Hedgesville, W.Va., in the state's eastern panhandle, the youngest of 13 children. His father died when he was 13, which left some of his older brothers and sisters to help raise him. He was the first person in his family to attend college.

"I was a pretty good high school player, but my mother never came to a game," Catlett recalled. "She didn't care about sports. I remember one time when I was a senior, she said, 'You better get rid of that ball and make something out of yourself.'"

He wound up taking half of her advice. Catlett kept the ball and made something of himself anyway.

The most important year in Catlett's career advancement came in 1972 when he spent a season on Adolph Rupp's staff at Kentucky. It was there that he put himself into a position to land his first head coaching job at Cincinnati. It was only after a glowing recommendation from Rupp that Catlett moved to the top of Cincinnati's wish list.

Rupp told those heading the UC search committee that Catlett was responsible for Kentucky winning the Southeastern Conference that year, and a zone defense Catlett had developed helped the Wildcats beat Marquette in the NCAA tournament. Rupp's endorsement was almost like an edict from God.

Catlett won right away at Cincinnati, and by the time Byrd was shopping for a coach a second time in 1978, Catlett had guided the Bearcats to NCAA tournament trips in 1975, 1976 and 1977.

When Byrd pursued Catlett in 1978, he found a creative way around the state law for one-year contracts by having the WVU Foundation underwrite a four-year deal for roughly the same salary Catlett was receiving at Cincinnati. Byrd said the opportunity to offer a multi-year contract came about when it was discovered that the hospitals were using the WVU Foundation to underwrite contracts to attract surgeons and doctors. "We realized that the Foundation was a way we could fund coaches' contracts," Byrd said.

The financial package Byrd and his staff prepared for Catlett was extremely creative for that time. In fact, many years afterward Catlett would often get quizzed by his coaching buddies about the structure of his contract, the fringe benefits the school had assembled, and the corporation that was established in his name within the WVU Foundation that enabled the athletic department to get around the state's archaic law.

Former West Virginia University president Gene Budig also served as president of professional baseball's American League from 1994–99.
WVU SPORTS COMMUNICATIONS PHOTO.

Catlett took two telephone calls from assistant athletic director Bob Goin before agreeing to meet Goin and Byrd in Zanesville, Ohio. Then later, he met with the selection committee at the Daniel Boone Hotel in Charleston during the West Virginia high school state tournament before leaving Charleston for a family vacation in Florida still undecided.

Catlett was clearly Byrd's No. 1 target, but if he turned down the West Virginia offer the next guy in line for the job was Illinois State coach Gene Smithson, who had ties to West Virginia University president Gene Budig. Joe Retton was a candidate once again, but his apprehension about flying and questions about his ability to recruit major college players eliminated him from consideration.

Byrd even briefly discussed the West Virginia job with Maryland coach Lefty Driesell, but by that time Driesell was firmly entrenched in College Park. "One of the members of the athletic council asked that we talk to him because there was some interest on Lefty's part," Byrd said. "But after about five minutes when I heard his demands about salaries and camps, we both knew that this wasn't going to go too far."

One of the ways the athletic department was able to supplement Catlett's salary was through his statewide radio show. Pictured here is Jack Fleming interviewing Catlett before a game.

WVU SPORTS COMMUNICATIONS PHOTO.

Once Budig signed off on the selection committee's unanimous choice of Catlett, Byrd telephoned the coach in Boca Raton, Fla., and Catlett accepted later that afternoon. Two days later on March 29, 1978, Gale Catlett was flown to Morgantown and introduced as the school's 19th basketball coach.

The 37-year-old Catlett knew well the history of West Virginia basketball and he talked that afternoon about returning the Mountaineers to the glory days of the past when he was a player. However, he offered a few words of caution. "I'm not a miracle worker," said Catlett that afternoon. He was decked out in a conservative three-piece suit (his choice of wardrobe while coaching at Cincinnati was much more flamboyant). "We're going to work hard but there are no secrets; there are no tricks to it. I just think it's a great opportunity at this time to take the job and be the new basketball coach here."

Catlett also answered questions about his willingness to remain at West Virginia. "I have a four-year contract here, and I know I'll fulfill that unless the good Lord has other ideas for me," he explained. "You know this coaching is very difficult sometimes physically and mentally. I think you would be safe in saying this will be my last basketball coaching job."

Catlett spoke prophetic words that afternoon. He served the longest tenure of any basketball coach in WVU history—24 years—and took the Mountaineers back to heights they had reached just once previously, when he was a player during the school's golden era. Catlett had the backing of the entire state, and he consolidated that support by traveling to all parts of West Virginia, speaking at dinners and functions, judging contests at county fairs and riding in open cars in small-town parades.

Catlett's first coaching staff included a pair of assistants with WVU ties: Bob Smith and Gary McPherson.

Catlett helped Smith get into the coaching profession in the early 1960s and later would stay at Smith's house when he was recruiting in D.C. When Catlett was hired at West Virginia he wanted a coach with strong Washington, D.C. ties and Smith fit the bill. "Gale said he would only go back to West Virginia if I came with him as his assistant," Smith joked.

McPherson had served five years on Sonny Moran's WVU staff from 1969–74. After two years at Alderson-Broaddus, McPherson joined Catlett at Cincinnati in 1976 and the two returned to WVU together. The third member of Catlett's first staff was Western Kentucky assistant Lanny Van Eman. Together, this group would return Mountaineer basketball to national prominence.

On the Comeback Trail

The basketball team Catlett inherited from Gardner included key players Lowes Moore, Dana Perno, and Junius Lewis. Despite the late start to recruiting, Catlett's staff was able to sign three prospects, including state products Noah Moore from Parkersburg and Steve McCune from East Bank.

Catlett was confronted with a tough schedule in 1979 that included fourth-ranked Louisville, twelfth-ranked Syracuse and third-ranked Notre Dame. Despite that, he was able to mold this team into a winning one with a 16–12 record that included a second-place finish in the Eastern 8. An exciting 93–92 victory over Pitt at the Coliseum was one of the most talked about games of the year; Moore scored 32 points and Perno came off the bench to add 18 points in a hotly contested game that saw 61 fouls called and six players foul out.

The Mountaineers also had big wins in '79 against Virginia Tech, Rutgers and Duquesne. WVU had the NCAA tournament-bound Scarlet Knights down by 20 before finally winning 68–61. A record crowd of 15,118 showed up to watch WVU put a scare in the Irish by taking a 28–25 halftime lead before falling 70–54 to a Notre Dame team coming off a Final Four appearance the year before.

After defeating Duquesne in the opening round of the Eastern 8 tournament in Morgantown, West Virginia lost in the tournament semifinals to Rutgers 55–52. Daryl Strickland and James Bailey combined for 35 points against West Virginia in helping Rutgers to the Eastern 8 title.

Moore led West Virginia with an average of 17.3 points per game, Perno averaged 12.2 points and Lewis finished his four-year career by averaging 10.5 points and 6.4 rebounds per game. Five times that season the Mountaineers won games on last-second plays.

Catlett's teams played an appealing brand of basketball featuring half-court traps, full-court presses and fast breaking at almost every opportunity. During his career, Catlett was known for constantly changing defenses and utilizing multiple offensive sets. "You had to be pretty cerebral to play in my system," Catlett explained. "I thought because we didn't recruit the greatest

After three ordinary seasons playing for Joedy Gardner, guard Dana Perno thrived during his senior season under Catlett in 1979, averaging 12.2 points per game and shooting better than 53 percent from the field.

WVU SPORTS COMMUNICATIONS PHOTO.

Greg Nance, a 6' 8" forward from Washington, D.C., averaged 8.8 points and 5.8 rebounds per game during his four-year career from 1978–81, including a 12.8 points-per-game average as a junior in 1980.

WVU SPORTS COMMUNICATIONS PHOTO.

players in the world—good players and a lot of players that blossomed when they got here—that the way to beat teams that had these All-Americans and everything was [to confuse them]. You couldn't confuse the coach because all of the coaches knew what they were doing, but you could confuse the players. The players on the court had to figure out when you're playing full-court press; is this a zone? Do I pass against it or do I dribble? Is this an odd front or an even front?"

Catlett soon began outfitting his teams in more colorful uniforms that included blue- and gold-striped warm-up shirts with white collars. He also searched the old Field House for the carpet the team had used when he was a player to run out on during pre-game introductions, reintroducing one of college basketball's great traditions.

Now with a full year to recruit, Catlett's staff went out and signed a class for 1980 that included guards Greg Jones and Diego McCoy, forwards Russel Todd and Gary McIntosh, and junior college center Phil Collins.

Russel Todd stands and waits to greet center Phil Collins during pre-game introductions.
WVU SPORTS COMMUNICATIONS PHOTO.

Assistant coach Lanny Van Eman found out about Jones from a sportswriter he knew in nearby Youngstown, Ohio, and Jones was one of two college-bound prospects at Rayen High School that year. Jones's high school teammate, Joe James, had already signed with Michigan. Wolverine coach Johnny Orr then saw Jones playing in an all-star game and tried to sign him as well. "Johnny Orr goes back to the locker room when the game is over and he wants to talk to Greg Jones," Catlett recalled. "His high school coach said, 'No, no, he's going to West Virginia.' He protected us and if he wouldn't have, the kid would have gone to Michigan. The kid that went to Michigan was good, but he wasn't as good as Greg Jones."

Greg's older brother advised him that he would be better served to go to West Virginia and clear a new path. "He said, 'You've been setting him [James] up for years now so don't even think about going with him,'" Jones recalled. He took his brother's advice and chose West Virginia.

It became apparent right away that Jones was not a typical freshman. The Mountaineers had lost four of their first six games to begin the 1980 season and the players had a long 13-day break for Christmas. Before they left campus, Jones got up in front of the entire team and gave a rousing speech about the importance of remaining focused and getting back on time to be prepared for the second half of the season. By the end of his speech, Jones had everyone in the room fired up—the coaches included. "I said to one of the assistant coaches, 'Can you imagine that coming from that guy?'" Catlett chuckled. "He won me over."

Ten days later when the team was due back to begin preparing to play Xavier, everyone was back on time ready to go—everyone, that is, but Jones. "He called up Gale and told him that he missed the bus in Youngstown," laughed Gary McPherson. "Gale had to suspend him for the Xavier game."

West Virginia's record in 1980 once again hovered close to the .500 mark. There were losses to third-ranked Ohio State, ninth-ranked Syracuse and third-ranked Louisville, and disappointing road defeats at William & Mary, Penn State, Ohio, Virginia Tech, Duquesne and Rutgers. Seven losses that year were by only four points or less.

Marshall, which had lobbied the state legislature to get on West Virginia's schedule, was played twice that season with the Mountaineers winning both times. And, for the first time since 1977, West Virginia swept Pitt in the season series.

West Virginia got hot in the Eastern 8 tournament, avenging a pair of regular-season losses to Duquesne by beating the Dukes 95–87 in the quarterfinals at the Civic Arena in Pittsburgh; Moore scored 26 and Joe Fryz added 25 to overcome B. B. Flenory's game-high 32-point performance. In the semifinals against Rutgers, West Virginia withstood 22 points and 10 rebounds from forward Roy Hinson to pull off a 77–66 victory. Moore was once again at the top of his game, scoring a game-high 27 points, while Collins and Todd combined to score 22 points against a tall and talented Rutgers front line.

But standing in West Virginia's way in the finals was Villanova. The Wildcats defeated the Mountaineers in the conference championship game for the second time in four years. Coach Rollie Massimino's three star players—Alex Bradley, John Pinone and Rory Sparrow—scored 57 of the team's 74 points in a double-digit victory. Moore had 22 points for West Virginia and was named the tournament's most valuable player. He finished sixth on the school's career scoring list at the time with 1,696 points and was taken in the third round of the NBA draft by the New Jersey Nets. Moore played parts of three seasons with the New Jersey Nets, Cleveland Cavaliers and San Diego Clippers.

Shortly after winning the Eastern 8, Villanova left for the Big East Conference. Penn State also dropped out for a brief period of time before returning, and then Pitt left the Eastern 8 for the Big East after the 1982 season. At the time, Catlett was upset with some of the choices the league was making for replacements.

"The original Eastern 8 members were pretty good," Catlett said. "Villanova was in there. Penn State was in there. We had a pretty good league with a lot of good rivalries and then all of the sudden after a couple of years, we started to see some defections.

"There were some pretty rough days," Catlett added. "We used to have a tournament in Philadelphia and then they would move it to Pittsburgh and then back and forth. Rutgers stuck by our side on everything. [Rutgers AD] Fred Grunninger was a great guy, a great athletic

Gale Catlett gives his team some instruction during a 1979 game at the WVU Coliseum.

WVU SPORTS COMMUNICATIONS PHOTO.

A publicity photo of guard Lowes Moore going high above the rim while dressed in a white tuxedo.

WVU SPORTS COMMUNICATIONS PHOTO.

director, and he knew what West Virginia's program meant."

Despite losing his starting backcourt in Moore and Fryz, Catlett was finally putting the pieces together in 1981. Jones, McCoy and freshman Quentin Freeman, though inexperienced, were talented and ready to take command of the backcourt. Collins and 6-foot-8 junior Donnie Gipson formed a workable tandem at center, while quality players Todd, Greg Nance and Dennis Hosey were now experienced forwards. It was West Virginia's deepest team since 1977, and for the first time since their Southern Conference days, the Mountaineers were going to play a full round-robin schedule in league play.

Following early season losses to Marshall, Virginia Tech and Ohio State, West Virginia ran off 10 straight wins to post an undefeated January. Seven of those victories came in Eastern 8 action, including a 55–52 victory at Penn State and an 85–69 win over St. Bonaventure in Olean, N.Y. Against Penn State, Jones scored 21 points and West Virginia was able to overcome 20 turnovers by holding the Nittany Lions to just 38.6 percent shooting. The win over St. Bonaventure in Morgantown, Jan. 14, 1981, was originally thought to be West Virginia's 1,000th victory—one of just 24 schools at the time to reach that historic milestone. Further research concluded that it actually occurred three days later against Massachusetts.

A disappointing loss in the final game of the regular season against George Washington gave West Virginia a 19–7 record heading into the Eastern 8 tournament. However, West Virginia barely got by the Bonnies in the opening-round game in Morgantown before falling in the semifinals to Duquesne in Pittsburgh.

WVU had a miserable start against the Dukes, going scoreless for the first 9:44 of the game before fighting back to tie it at halftime. But Duquesne outscored West Virginia 34–29 in the second half behind the play of Bruce Atkins and Ronnie Dixon to knock WVU out of the tournament.

Still, West Virginia's 20 wins were good enough to earn an invitation to play in the NIT, giving the school its first postseason tournament appearance since 1968. West Virginia drew a first-round home game against Penn and after jumping out to an early 11–2 lead, the Mountaineers had to come back late in the second half on a three-point play by Todd and a long jump shot by Jones for the win.

West Virginia needed more clutch performances in its second-round game against Temple in Morgantown. Backup guard Vic Herbert hit a shot from the corner at the buzzer to send the game into overtime, and Hosey made key free throws in the extra session to help the Mountaineers pull out a 77–76 victory.

Three days later, West Virginia was sent west to face the Golden Gophers in Minneapolis. WVU managed to overcome an early 15–8 deficit to defeat Minnesota 80–69. Jones led four double-figure scorers with 20 points, and the Mountaineers limited Minnesota center Randy Breuer to 17 points and just four rebounds, and All-Big Ten guard Trent Tucker scored only 13 points on 5 of 12 shooting for the Gophers.

The Minnesota victory put the Mountaineers in the NIT semifinals at Madison Square Garden to face Nolan Richardson's Tulsa Golden Hurri-

canes. Paul Pressey scored 20 points and handed out nine assists to lead Tulsa to an 89–87 victory. Jones's long field goal try to tie the game grazed the rim at the buzzer. McCoy played the best game of his brief WVU career, hitting 12 of 15 shots for a game-high 30 points.

"When you shoot 60 percent and out-rebound your opponent you should win," said Catlett after the game. But West Virginia had committed 29 turnovers, including a combined 14 by starting guards Jones and McCoy.

West Virginia dropped the consolation game two nights later to Purdue, 75–72. Todd and Herbert led WVU with 16 points each.

The Mountaineers' 23–10 record was their best in 18 years, and the team was treated to a parade through downtown Morgantown to celebrate their memorable season. Catlett was happy with the performance of his team, but he was displeased with the financial support he was getting from the administration. A department-wide budgetary shortfall of more than $650,000 forced the basketball team to travel by bus for the second half of the season. University financial advisor Ben Tuchi was brought in to determine how bad things were, and even the state legislature got into the act and ordered a complete audit of the books. Eventually, Fred Schaus was asked to return to run the athletic department. The success the football and men's basketball teams enjoyed in the early 1980s straightened out the department's financial circumstances much faster than even Schaus had anticipated.

Back to the Big Dance

West Virginia had the two most important ingredients for an outstanding season in '82—great players and a great schedule. With the exception of Marshall in Huntington, most of the Mountaineers' toughest games were in Morgantown. Plus, West Virginia did not face a single team ranked in the Top 20 until meeting Fresno State in the NCAA tournament's second round in Logan, Utah.

West Virginia reeled off a nation's-best 23-game winning streak that ended with a 74–64 loss at Rutgers to complete the regular season. The Mountaineers compiled an Eastern 8-record 13 regular-season conference victories and outdrew all of the other first-round sites combined during its opening-round conference tournament match-up against UMass.

Key wins came in Morgantown against Ohio State, 73–68, and at Roanoke, Va., against a Virginia Tech team that claimed the Gator Bowl Classic. West Virginia also managed a pair of heart-pumping victories against Pitt.

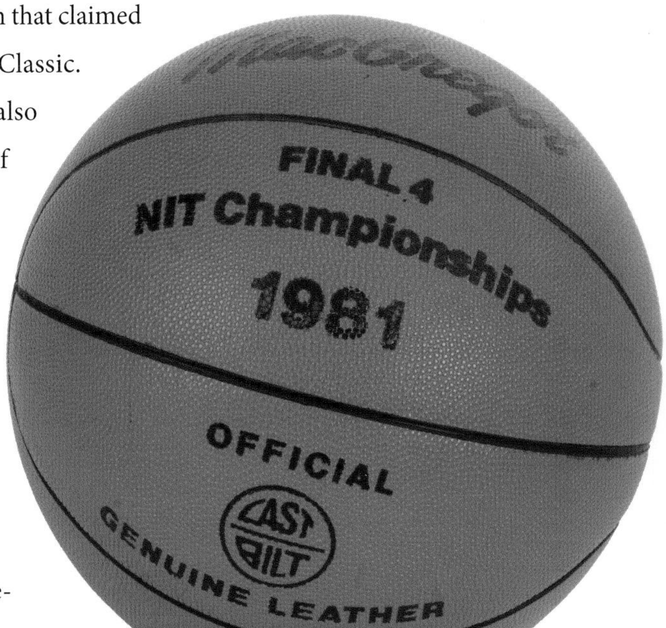

Emotions in the Pitt-West Virginia series were ratcheted to a new level when Catlett returned to West Virginia and Tim Grgurich was still

Bruising center Phil Collins goes up for a jump shot. Collins, a Palos Heights, Ill., native, played three seasons for the Mountaineers from 1980–82, helping the Mountaineers to the NIT semifinals in 1981 and an NCAA tournament appearance in 1982.

WVU SPORTS COMMUNICATIONS PHOTO.

coaching at Pitt. The two had played against each other in the early 1960s.

Joe Fryz remembered getting caught in the middle of the rivalry while playing at Moon Area High outside of Pittsburgh. "Pitt recruited me since my sophomore year of high school and they recruited me very heavily," Fryz said. "[Panther player] Tom Richards was from Moon and everybody just assumed that I would go to Pitt.

"Tim Grgurich never talked to me again after the day I signed with West Virginia," Fryz said. "After a couple of games we'd bump into each other as the teams were leaving the floor and he would never say anything to me. Then, I saw him years later at an NBA game and I said hi to him and he didn't even acknowledge me."

Fryz and Grgurich were gone by 1982, but that didn't keep the Backyard Brawl from once again reaching a fevered pitch. Gale Catlett made sure of that.

"Fred Schaus is to blame," Catlett said of his lightning rod status with the Panther fans. "When I went there as a freshman, we were behind Pitt at halftime. This is a freshman basketball game. Well Coach Schaus comes into the locker room and was pointing his finger and he said, 'I want you to know, we hate these guys. Don't let these guys beat you!' We went back out there and beat them in the second half.

"I didn't know that much about Pittsburgh because of where I was located in the eastern panhandle," Catlett said. "He injected that. From that point on, I took it that you had to beat Pittsburgh."

Another reason Catlett took the Pitt series so seriously was because he wanted to make an impression on the Pittsburgh media because he wisely understood that they were the pathway to even greater press exposure for his program. "That's the closest big city to us so if your program is going to get national recognition you can get it out of Pittsburgh," Catlett explained. "I always wanted to make sure our teams did well against Pitt because you at least had the chance of getting some national coverage."

While Catlett kept the fire burning on West Virginia's side, Mountaineer students discovered someone new to dislike when Roy Chipman took over the Panther program in 1980. Chipman had a patch of white hair and a gap between his front teeth that gave him a distinctive look. The WVU students soon took to calling him "Chipmunk" and they enjoyed watching him go into one of his frequent foot-stomping tirades.

Chipman put on quite a show at the end of a hotly contested game in Pittsburgh on Jan. 29, 1982, when West Virginia was the beneficiary of a late lane violation call in a game that ended with WVU winning 48–45.

The Mountaineers were clinging to a 44–43 lead with 14 seconds left when Steve Beatty went to the free throw line to shoot a one-and-one. Beatty's shot went in, but official Jack Prettyman waved off the basket, claiming Panther forward Clyde Vaughan had entered the lane too early. A heated dispute followed, and Pitt was assessed a technical foul. Jones sank both free throws. After the game, disgruntled Panthers fans rained the court with fruit, beverage cans and just about anything else they could get their hands on.

An unhinged Chipman chased both officials into the locker room. Afterward, he called the lane violation "a Mickey Mouse call." Chipman was still steaming 30 minutes after the game.

"I've coached games for 20 years and I've never seen a call affecting a game like that one did," Chipman said. "Whether or not the kid was in the lane had nothing to do with the play. That was not [Prettyman's] call. He's at midcourt. The guy underneath should be watching the lane. My kids got cheated."

If not for the controversial call, the game would have been forgettable. The two teams combined for 42 turnovers and 51 fouls. West Virginia shot 38.6 percent from the floor and 52.9 percent from the free throw line. Pitt was even worse, shooting 24.6 percent for the game.

A month later, the Panthers and Mountaineers met again in Morgantown before a record crowd of 16,704—almost 3,000 more than the Coliseum's capacity. West Virginia had reached sixth in the polls after first cracking the rankings following a victory over South Alabama on national TV, and West Virginia was a heavy favorite to defeat Pitt, especially since the game was on West Virginia's home floor. However, the Panthers kept the game close. Pitt's bid for an upset ended when Todd's two free throws with 43 seconds remaining gave the Mountaineers a five-point lead. Jones then stole the basketball and fed Tony Washam for a dunk to ice the game.

"To win 23 games in a row is a fantastic achievement," Catlett said after the game. "To win 31 in a row at the Coliseum is a fantastic achievement. I'm not too sure these things aren't happening too quickly for everybody to comprehend."

When the two teams met a third time in Pittsburgh for the Eastern 8 Championship, a volatile rivalry had turned combustible. The Panthers couldn't resist gloating when they eventually pulled out a 79–72 victory at the Civic Arena. Ten days earlier, Catlett had made reference to Pitt's program being "mediocre" when asked by a reporter if he thought the series would continue on a home-and-home basis when Pitt moved on to the Big East Conference in 1983.

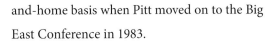

"For a mediocre team we played pretty good," said Pitt star forward Clyde Vaughan after winning the Eastern 8 title. "If we are a mediocre team then what kind of team are they?"

Chipman got in a few digs as well. "I'm going to go back and look in my dictionary and find out what the meaning of mediocrity is," he said.

The West Virginia-Pitt series had reached its apex. Emotions began to cool the following year when the two teams no longer played twice a year. (A decade later, the series would experience another revival when West Virginia also joined

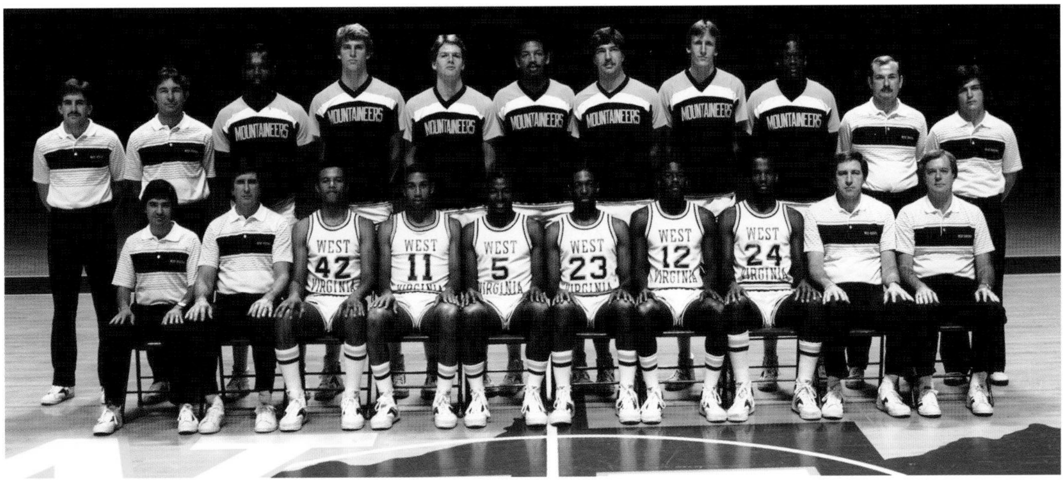

Gale Catlett's 1982 team won a nation's-best 23 games in a row and finished the year with a 27–4 record, ranked 14th in the country.

WVU SPORTS COMMUNICATIONS PHOTO.

the Big East Conference prior to the 1996 season.)

"[Chipman] was a pretty good coach," Catlett said. "The best teams I played against Pitt were probably Paul Evans's, but I will tell you Chipman's teams were very good. They talk about [John] Beilein's 1-3-1, well, Roy Chipman's 1-3-1 and [Temple coach] John Chaney's [match-up] zone were the two best defenses I played against during my coaching career."

Guard Greg Jones, pictured here playing against UNLV in 1983, was one of the most dynamic players of the Gale Catlett era. Jones scored 1,737 points and handed out 430 assists during his outstanding four-year career from 1980–83.

WVU SPORTS COMMUNICATIONS PHOTO.

After beating North Carolina A&T in the opening round of the NCAA tournament, Fresno State outlasted the Mountaineers 50–46. Catlett's slowdown game worked perfectly for 38 minutes until two WVU turnovers and a pair of missed free throws keyed Fresno's nine-point run during the remaining 1:26 of the game.

"We wanted to spread them out because they were cutting off our passing lanes," Catlett explained after the game.

A fantastic 27–4 season had ended. WVU finished the year ranked 14th in the country, returning to the national playoffs for the first time in 15 years. Catlett was named Basketball Times National Coach of the Year and Jones was named the conference Player of the Year.

Four starters were returning for the 1983 season, including Jones, Todd and Washam, the team's top three scorers. Freshman forward Lester Rowe barely missed averaging double figures in 1982 after being inserted into the lineup midway through the season. Catlett had a deep and experienced team, and he chose to upgrade the non-conference schedule with games against Ohio State, NC State, Pitt and a late-season made-for-TV date with UNLV in Morgantown. West Virginia was also playing Marshall on a regular basis, including games in Huntington.

"[Marshall coach] Stu Aberdeen called me and he said, 'Coach, this is not fair to play up there with your officials on your home court all of the time. I've got a job, too.' I said, 'I'll tell you what I'll do, Stu, I'll talk to the people here, but we'll play you in Morgantown one year with our officials and in Charleston next year with your officials. Then back to Morgantown and back to Charleston,'" Catlett recalled.

"The second thing was they got their new place [Henderson Center] and they called and asked us to play home and home," Catlett added. "I said, 'I'm not playing you home and home. I'll play you one year in Morgantown, one year in Charleston and one year in Huntington with neutral officials.' Then I had to sell this to my people."

What eventually came out of those early discussions was the decision to play an annual game in Charleston at the Charleston Civic Center.

"[Then assistant athletic director] Mike Parsons worked hard to work out an agreement that was acceptable to both parties and benefited both schools financially," said Catlett. "That has not always been the easiest of negotiations."

Before the start of the '83 campaign, the Eastern 8 changed its name to the Atlantic 10 and added Penn State, St. Joseph's and Temple to a lineup that also included West Virginia, Rhode Island, Duquesne, George Washington, Massachusetts, Rutgers and St. Bonaventure. West Virginia was the pre-season favorite.

An eight-game winning streak to begin the season was stopped at Stetson, and West Virginia's two-week appearance in the Top 20 ended with a 67–59 defeat against eventual national champion NC State in the Meadowlands in East Rutherford, N.J. Losses also came at Penn State and at Pitt.

West Virginia's 39-game home winning streak was snapped by St. Bonaventure, 64–63, on Jan. 20, 1983, to drop West Virginia's record to 10–5. Another seven-game winning streak following that defeat was finished with another loss to coach Jim O'Brien's Bonnies, 63–61, in overtime. It was one of five overtime games played by the Mountaineers in 1983, including a triple-overtime thriller against Virginia Tech that ended with a 90–86 WVU victory. (At the time West Virginia's only other triple-overtime game also came against Tech in 1972.)

However, the game of the year for the Mountaineers happened on Feb. 27, 1983, when No. 1-ranked UNLV arrived in Morgantown to face the Mountaineers in a nationally televised game on CBS. The Rebels were a wounded team, having already lost earlier in the week to Fullerton, and were playing without 6-foot-7 forward Garland Hudson, who injured his knee that week in practice.

West Virginia was also feeling the effects of a long season. Jones had lost his front tooth in the Virginia Tech win earlier that month as the result of a collision with Renardo Brown while the two were attempting to get into a full-court press.

The first indication that UNLV coach Jerry Tarkanian was taking his team into an ambush came when the Runnin' Rebels arrived in Morgantown and stayed at the Holiday Inn next to the Coliseum. Tarkanian could see from his bus window the long line of students camped outside the gate in 30-degree weather, and then later that night, he could hear them as he unsuccessfully tried to sleep before Sunday's game.

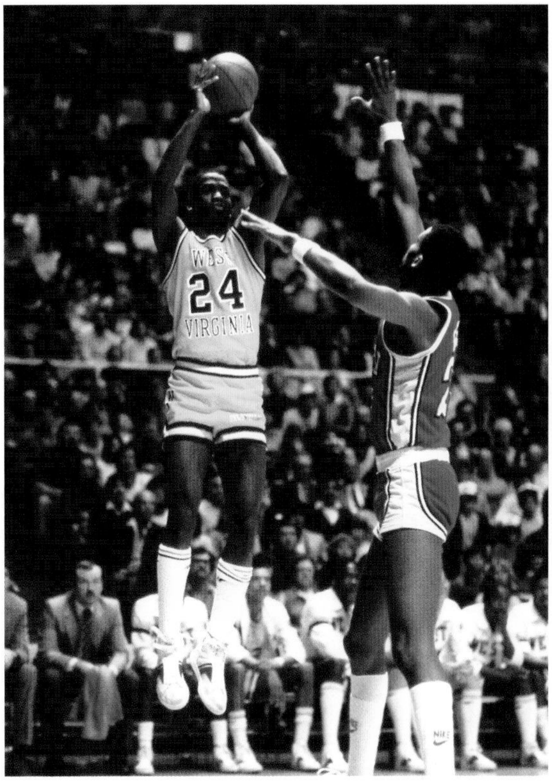

The WVU Coliseum became a very difficult place for opposing teams to play under Catlett. No. 1-ranked UNLV found that out in 1983. Lester Rowe is pictured here shooting a jump shot against the Rebels.

WVU SPORTS COMMUNICATIONS PHOTO.

When a nervous Tarkanian met Catlett at midcourt the next day, he already had one of his trademark white towels draped over his shoulder ready for chewing. "How in the hell did you ever talk me into coming here to play, Gale?" Tarkanian remarked.

West Virginia built a nine-point halftime lead before the Rebels came back twice in the second half to cut WVU's lead to one, 41–40, and then again, 49–48. Both times Jones answered with clutch baskets.

Jones gave West Virginia its biggest lead of the game at 15 points with 2:20 remaining. The senior hit five 3-pointers and finished with a game-high 32 points. When the final seconds ticked off the clock, the students rushed the court and celebrated. Thousands of fans remained in the arena afterward to listen to Catlett's post-game radio show. It was the coach's 100th victory at West Virginia.

"When you try and play a full-court game with Jones, you're crazy," Catlett told his statewide radio audience. "If we could have made some more free throws, we would have been up 18 or 20 at halftime."

The Mountaineers continued their outstanding play in the Atlantic 10 tournament, beating Penn State in Pittsburgh before knocking off St. Bo-

WEST VIRGINIA 87, UNLV 78

Greg Jones was taking a cab ride over to the WVU Coliseum before West Virginia's game against UNLV. The cab driver, not knowing Jones was Jones—the Mountaineers' best player—said he needed to hurry up and drop him off at the Coliseum so he could get back home in time to see the West Virginia-UNLV basketball game on television.

It was at that moment that Jones realized something pretty big was happening on Sunday, Feb. 27, 1983, in Morgantown.

If that weren't enough, when he walked into the arena, there to greet him was a completely full student section. It was 10 in the morning, more than three hours before tipoff. Students had camped outside the Coliseum for more than two days to assure themselves seats for the biggest game they had ever seen in their lives.

"This is a very tough place to play," said West Virginia coach Gale Catlett. "There is some kind of magic about it when you get a crowd like this. It's hard to think."

UNLV was the first No. 1-ranked basketball team to make an appearance at the WVU Coliseum. The Runnin' Rebels were without starting forward Eldridge Hudson, who had injured his knee in practice, and point guard Danny Tarkanian, the son of UNLV coach Jerry Tarkanian, was suffering from bronchitis. Also, UNLV was not going to occupy the top spot in the polls on Monday regardless of the outcome of the West Virginia game because the Rebels had lost to Fullerton, 86–78, earlier in the week. The 15,638 fans who showed up for the game could care less. It was still a game for the ages. Fans were treated to an entertaining session full of fast breaks, dunks and 3-point shooting.

Six minutes into the contest, Jones knocked down a pair of 3-pointers to give West Virginia a 14–8 lead it never relinquished. With the score 23–19, West Virginia ran off 10 straight points to open a 33–19 advantage with 5:55 left in the first half. Russel Todd scored four of those points with Jones, freshman Renaldo Brown, and center Tim Kearney producing two each.

In the second half, UNLV pulled to within two, 39–37, after 3-point and two-point goals by Larry Anderson and an 18-foot jumper by Sidney Green. The Runnin Rebels' then got it to one, 41–40, with 14:56 remaining. West Virginia was clinging to a 51–50 lead with 9:36 to go when the Mountaineers got a big 3-pointer from Jones at the top of the key.

Forward Russel Todd goes up for two points against UNLV during the 87–78 victory over the Runnin' Rebels at the WVU Coliseum in 1983.

WVU SPORTS COMMUNICATIONS PHOTO.

Then a layup and two free throws by Jones made it 57–51. Back-to-back Jones baskets got the lead to eight, 68–60, with 4:23 to go, and a Jones steal led to a Todd basket to put the Mountaineers ahead by 10. The lead swelled to 15, 78–63, with 2:21 remaining and twice more at 80–65 and 82–67 with 1:15 left.

Jones played one of the best all-around games of his career, hitting 12 of 21 shots including 5 of 10 from 3-point range, for a game-high 32 points. He also grabbed seven rebounds, made four steals and handed out two assists. "I didn't think he was that good of a shooter," said Tarkanian. "But he shot the hell out of it."

Kearney scored 15 points and grabbed 10 rebounds, Todd scored 14 and freshman Dale Blaney added 11. The Mountaineers shot nearly as well from the floor (53.6 percent) as they did from the free throw line (56.4 percent).

Green led UNLV with 24 points and 16 rebounds.

It was Catlett's 100th victory in five seasons at West Virginia. "This is a great thing for the state and a great thing for our program," Catlett said after the game. "This has been a really fun afternoon."

Asked if this was the biggest win of his 11-year coaching career Catlett replied, "Well, I'd never beaten a No. 1 team."

naventure and Temple in Philadelphia's Spectrum to capture the A-10 tournament championship. Todd's team-high 23 points, along with a six-point spurt late in the game, gave West Virginia its first conference tournament title since 1967.

West Virginia was a victim of the slowdown game once again in the NCAA tournament. This time it was James Madison who let the air out of the ball. At a press conference before the game, Catlett criticized Dukes coach Lou Campanelli's stall-ball style of play. Campanelli shot back by referencing Catlett's former tenure at Cincinnati when the school was cited for NCAA infractions that did not directly involve Catlett. (Catlett later threatened to sue the NCAA if his name was ever tied to any sanctions. It wasn't.)

James Madison eventually took over a close game down the stretch when Charles Fisher made seven free throws in the final 49 seconds to upset West Virginia 57–50 in Greensboro, N.C. It was the Mountaineers' lowest scoring output of the year.

Catlett and Campanelli did not shake hands after the game, nor did they acknowledge each other during their post-game press conferences.

West Virginia finished the season with a 23–8 record. Jones averaged 22.3 points, while Todd showed averages of 14.3 points and 8.1 rebounds per game. It was the first time since 1962–63 that West Virginia had made back-to-back trips to the NCAA tournament.

Jones was a two-time Atlantic 10 player of the year who completed his career with 1,797 career points. He led the Mountaineers to a pair of NCAA tournament appearances in 1982–83 and an overall record of 88–36. "He is one of the best players to ever play here," said Catlett of Jones.

As Catlett began preparing for the 1984 season, he had a chance to match the man who recruited him, Fred Schaus, and become only the second West Virginia coach in school history to take teams to the NCAA tournament three straight years.

The Success Continues

With Jones and Todd gone, Catlett had his work cut out to get the Mountaineers back to postseason play. At one point in early February, West Virginia was staring at a 10–9 record after a tough 63–61 loss at Rutgers.

Then, the Mountaineers went on a six-game winning streak that included a pivotal victory at Virginia Tech. West Virginia trailed the entire game and had the basketball underneath Tech's basket with four seconds left, down one. Perfectly executing an inbound play designed by Catlett, Michael King found Tim Kearney breaking toward the basket, and Kearney hit a twisting shot ahead of the buzzer to give WVU a 68–67 win. It was West Virginia's third straight victory against the Hokies. "That was a key game for us because it showed that we could go on the road and beat a good basketball team," said Catlett.

Another big triumph came in the Atlantic 10 tournament semifinals in Morgantown. Temple had gone through the season unbeaten in conference play, taking a 25–4 record into the semifinals. Dale Blaney's 13-foot jump shot with four seconds remaining put West Virginia ahead, 66–65, and Kearney's free throw with one second left locked up the 67–65 upset victory over the 15th-ranked Owls.

"We were running through our offense trying to get the best shot we could," said Blaney. "I passed it to Mike King in the corner. I got it back and saw that there were only eight seconds left, so I had to create something."

One night later in the championship game, West Virginia got 13 points off the bench from J. J. Crawl to outlast St. Bonaventure 59–56.

Crawl continued his heroics in the NCAA tournament against 17th-ranked Oregon State in Birmingham, Ala. West Virginia's defense produced 18 turnovers that included three critical Beaver miscues late in the contest. With 19 seconds left it looked like Crawl was going to be the game's goat when he missed the front end of a one-and-one with the game tied at 62. Oregon State grabbed the rebound and called time-out with 13 seconds remaining.

When play resumed, the Beavers were setting up for a game-winning shot attempt when Crawl stole Alan Tait's pass at midcourt and went in to sink the go-ahead basket. A half-court heave by Oregon State fell short of the rim at the buzzer.

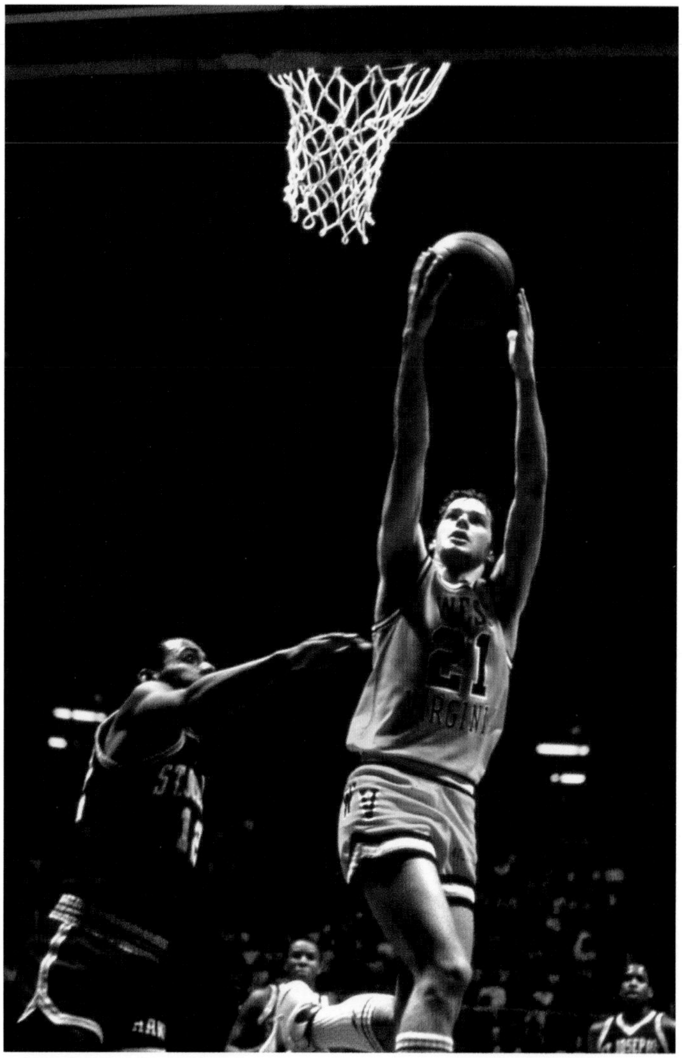

Above West Virginia players Michael King, Lester Rowe and Tim Kearney celebrate the Mountaineers' 1984 Atlantic 10 tournament championship game victory over St. Bonaventure at the WVU Coliseum.

WVU SPORTS COMMUNICATIONS PHOTO.

Above right Guard Dale Blaney's jump shot with four seconds left helped West Virginia upset 15th-ranked Temple 67-65 in the semifinals of the 1984 Atlantic 10 tournament in Morgantown.

WVU SPORTS COMMUNICATIONS PHOTO.

Catlett said later that Crawl's steal was a case of being in the wrong place at the right time. "I meant for him to deny the inbound pass but I'm glad he misunderstood me," Catlett said. It was Catlett's third win against a ranked team at West Virginia and the 250th victory of his career.

Eleventh-ranked Maryland had little trouble with the Mountaineers two days later in the second round, winning easily 102–77. The Terps shot 66.7

ATLANTIC 10 CONFERENCE

Name changes and revolving membership marked West Virginia's 19-year association with the Atlantic 10 Conference. The A-10's roots can be traced to March 2, 1975, when eight university representatives met in Harrisburg, Pa., to form a new basketball league. That meeting and subsequent meetings led to the formation of the Eastern Collegiate Basketball League (ECBL), which began operation for the 1976–77 season. The eight charter members of the ECBL were Duquesne, George Washington, Massachusetts, Penn State, Pitt, Rutgers, Villanova and West Virginia.

"Lester Rowe from Buffalo" works for rebounding position in a game against Pitt at the Pittsburgh Civic Arena for the 1982 Eastern 8 championship. Rowe later served as an assistant coach on Gale Catlett's staff. WVU SPORTS COMMUNICATIONS PHOTO.

"The original Eastern 8 members were pretty good," said former West Virginia coach Gale Catlett.

Just a year after beginning operation, the ECBL became known as the Eastern Athletic Association and then the Eastern 8. In 1977–78, the Eastern 8 added other sports to its championship roster. Former WVU athletic director Leland Byrd served as president and executive director of the league until assuming the role of commissioner in 1981.

"The first thing we joined was the Hoopster Rooster, which was the Eastern 8," said Catlett. "I had no knowledge that Leland Byrd was one of the main guys that formed the Eastern 8, and then he left us and became commissioner of the Eastern 8."

Byrd presided over the losses of Penn State in 1979, Villanova in 1980 and then Pitt in 1982. St. Bonaventure was added in place of Penn State in 1979 and Rhode Island was added in 1980 to replace Villanova. When Pitt departed for the Big East Conference in 1982, the Eastern 8 readmitted Penn State, added St. Joseph's and Temple, and changed its name to the Atlantic 10 Conference in 1983.

"I had too much on my plate to get involved in any conference stuff, although I was on several search committees for new commissioners and different things," Catlett recalled. "I learned a lot from that, especially from the candidates that turned us down. I would ask them what their perceptions of the conference were and what we could do to improve it. West Virginia University was one of the big reasons the Eastern 8 was formed."

West Virginia, Rutgers, Temple and St. Joseph's made up the core of the conference from 1983 until 1995, when West Virginia and Rutgers were invited into the Big East.

West Virginia won five regular-season basketball titles in 1977, 1982, 1983, 1985 and 1989, and posted a 183–94 overall record in A-10 action.

Catlett was named Eastern 8 coach of the year and Greg Jones was named player of the year in 1982. Jones was also named league player of the year in 1983 and Lester Rowe was named Atlantic 10 tournament MVP in 1984.

First Team Atlantic 10 Conference

1977, Tony Robertson (G)
1979, Lowes Moore (G)
1981, Greg Jones (G)
1982, Greg Jones (G)
1983, Greg Jones (G)
1986, Dale Blaney (G)
1988, Darryl Prue (F); Tyrone Shaw (F)
1989, Steve Berger (G); Darryl Prue (F)
1991, Chris Brooks (F)
1992, Ricky Robinson (F)

percent from the floor and had five players reach double figures, led by Ben Coleman's 19 points.

For West Virginia, it was yet another 20-win season and its third consecutive trip to the NCAA tournament. A second golden era was underway.

Catlett's fourth consecutive 20-win season in 1985 was a complete surprise. The Mountaineers were predicted to finish fifth in the Atlantic 10, but somehow Catlett found a way to mold a team with only one senior (Lester Rowe) into the league's regular-season champion with a 16–2 record. Five of West Virginia's nine losses in 1985 came outside of the conference against Maryland, Pitt, Virginia Tech, Auburn and VCU.

Mid-1980s guard Holman Harley entertained Mountaineer fans with his fast break bounce dunks.
WVU SPORTS COMMUNICATIONS PHOTO.

West Virginia managed to produce unexpected victories over Rutgers and Massachusetts on the road. Dale Blaney hit two 3-point baskets to help West Virginia pull out a 76–74 overtime victory against UMass. Holman Harley, who became a crowd favorite with his high-risk bounce dunks, hit a 3-point basket ahead of the buzzer at Rutgers to send the game into overtime. West Virginia eventually won 76–71.

But the most unlikely victory of the season came at St. Joseph's when it appeared an officials' reversal of a call after the game was going to stand. Trailing 50–49 with three seconds remaining, West Virginia had the basketball underneath St. Joseph's basket, and the play Catlett had designed was called "Home Run." Renaldo Brown threw a full-court pass to Lester Rowe at the top of the key. Rowe then quickly spun around and threw the ball to Vernon Odom on the left wing, where Odom fired up a shot that Rowe alertly tipped in as the horn sounded. West Virginia's players and coaches ran off the court thinking they had won the game.

Then, 10 minutes later, officials came into West Virginia's locker room informing the team that St. Joseph's was the winner because Rowe's shot had come after time had expired. "Incredible," was the one printable word Catlett used after Dutch Shample delivered the bad news.

Two days went by before Atlantic 10 commissioner Charles Theokas overruled the decision, stating the officials' jurisdiction over the game had ended the moment they left the floor.

A surprising loss to Duquesne in the first round of the Atlantic 10 tournament relegated West Virginia to the NIT despite the Mountaineers winning the A-10 regular season title and Athletic Director Fred Schaus serving on the NCAA selection committee.

Catlett, armed with a manila folder full of stats and rankings (including several obscure ones), went on the offensive. "When you win a regular season championship in a conference ranked the eighth-toughest in the country by *Basketball Weekly*, you win eight of your last nine games, 16 of your last 19 and play the 11th-toughest non-conference schedule in the country . . . ranked by *NCAA News* last week, you're ranked fifth in the Eastern Cup poll, you win 20 games and participate in the last three NCAA tournaments and not get an NCAA bid, then the NCAA's selection committee has made a tremendous error."

The Mountaineers did not recover from the disappointment of not making the NCAA tournament. In the NIT, West Virginia fell to a .500 Virginia team 56–55 at the Coliseum. Rowe (14.4 ppg) and Blaney (12.3 ppg) were West Virginia's top point producers on a team that had nine different players score more than 100 points for the season.

West Virginia's sixth consecutive 20-win campaign and a fourth trip to the NCAA tournament in five years occurred in 1986. The Mountaineers played another difficult schedule, facing 10th-ranked Auburn and St. John's in the preseason NIT, traveling to Auburn to face the Tigers once again, and then playing St. Joseph's, Maryland and Pitt during a five-day stretch. After that, a loss to 20th-ranked Virginia Tech in Blacksburg put West Virginia's record under .500 at 4–5.

Then the Mountaineers won 10 straight and 14 of their next 16 games. One of the two losses—Temple's 57–51 victory at McGonigle Hall—was played without the game clock working. Afterward, Catlett couldn't conceal his irritation. "It's a shame we're playing for an NCAA berth and a championship for the league and the clock didn't work. It's amazing."

Above Forward Darryl Prue, pictured here against Virginia Tech, hit two key free throws with 1:08 remaining in the game to knock off Temple in the A-10 semifinals. Prue is now an assistant coach on John Thompson, III's staff at Georgetown.

WVU SPORTS COMMUNICATIONS PHOTO.

Above left J. J. Crawl, pictured here in a game at Rutgers, made a steal and a layup to defeat 17th-ranked Oregon State in a 1984 NCAA tournament first-round game in Birmingham, Ala.

WVU SPORTS COMMUNICATIONS PHOTO.

West Virginia finished the regular season with victories over Massachusetts and Rhode Island to tie for second place in the Atlantic 10 standings with a 15–3 conference record.

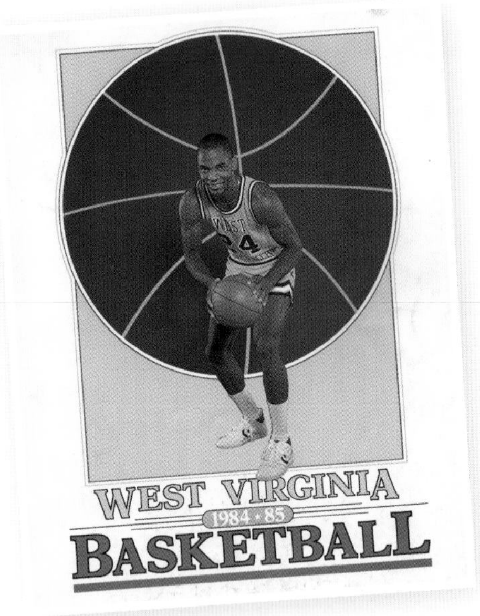

After defeating Rutgers in the opening round of the A-10 tournament, West Virginia managed to overcome a 13-point deficit to defeat Temple 61–56 in the semifinals (with the clock working this time). Darryl Prue's free throws with 1:08 remaining keyed the victory.

The Mountaineers fell in the championship game to St. Joseph's 72–64 in an entertaining game aired nationally on ESPN. The Hawks outscored the Mountaineers 39–30 in the second half after trailing by one at the break. Maurice Martin came off the bench to lead all scorers with 22 points.

Forward Tyrone Shaw, pictured here going up for two against Marshall, was a fan favorite for his assortment of fakes and moves around the basket.
WVU SPORTS COMMUNICATIONS PHOTO.

West Virginia was one of three Atlantic 10 teams (St. Joseph's and Temple the others) to get into the NCAA tournament in 1986—a first for the three-year-old conference. But in a first-round game in Greensboro, N.C., the Mountaineers couldn't hold on to an early lead and lost to Old Dominion 72–64.

Blaney (17.0 ppg), Harley (15.2 ppg) and Brown (10.7 ppg) averaged double figures for the season. Blaney, an overlooked recruit from Hartford, Ohio, finished his outstanding college career with 1,520 points.

Catlett's roster took on a different look in 1987. In the backcourt, in place of Blaney and Harley, were senior J. J. Crawl and the youthful tandem of Herbie Brooks and Steve Berger.

Up front, West Virginia had Wayne Yearwood, Darryl Prue and 6-foot-9 senior center Darrell Pinckney. Six-seven forward Tyrone Shaw came from San Jacinto College where he had helped lead the Ravens to a 37–0 record and the national junior college championship. The resourceful, pump-faking Shaw worked his way into the starting lineup by January.

Sitting out to concentrate on academics was 6-foot-6 New York City forward Chris Brooks, a Parade All-American considered one of the Top 25 high school players in the country, who was recruited to WVU by Ron Brown, the school's first-ever African American assistant basketball coach.

The 1987 squad turned out to be one of Catlett's better defensive teams, holding opponents to an average of 60.7 points per game and 43.3 percent field goal percentage. West Virginia also carried a seven-rebound advantage on the glass.

Key road victories came at Notre Dame and Temple, along with solid home wins against Alabama-Birmingham and Virginia Tech. Crawl held Notre Dame All-American guard David Rivers to just 8 points, and hit a pair of clutch free throws with eight seconds remaining to give West Virginia to a 57–55 victory over the Irish in South Bend.

West Virginia also got an outstanding victory at the end of the season at fifth-ranked Temple. Once again, Crawl played great defense against the Owls' Nate Blackwell, holding the Temple standout to only 8 points in a box-and-one alignment Catlett devised specifically to stop him. Temple made 11 of 35 shots in the second half, and Shaw scored 16 points to lead the Mountaineers to a memorable 64–61 triumph. The victory snapped Temple's 33-game winning streak at McGonigle Hall, but the Owls eventually claimed the rubber match in the Atlantic 10 tournament finals, defeating the Mountaineers 70–57 in their home city.

A poor second half tripped up the Mountaineers in the first round of the NCAA tournament against Western Kentucky; Western won on a last-second basket by Kannard Johnson at the Carrier Dome. WVU made just 7 of 24 field goal attempts in the second half, and some missed free throws down the stretch gift wrapped the upset win for the Hilltoppers. With the score tied at 62 and Western Kentucky positioned to inbound the ball underneath its basket, Johnson managed to slip between Prue and Shaw for the game-winning shot.

"We went to sleep and the kid made a great play," remarked Catlett afterward.

Despite the disappointing ending, West Virginia's 23–7 record put the Mountaineers in an elite class of teams. It was West Virginia's seventh consecutive 20-win season—only North Carolina and Georgetown had a longer string of 20-win campaigns during that period of time. Yearwood (12.9 ppg), Prue (12.6 ppg) and Shaw (11.9 ppg) were the team's leading scorers. West Virginia's seven-year run of 20-win seasons ended in 1988, as did its two-year NCAA tournament streak. With Pinckney gone to graduation, a lack of size was a big issue for the Mountaineers. West Virginia that year started 6-foot-6 Brooks, 6-foot-7 Prue and 6-foot-7 Shaw up front. The Mountaineers hit a rough stretch in February, and their 15–5 record soon became 16–12 when West Virginia dropped seven of eight, including back-to-back games against No. 1-ranked Temple, in a span of five days.

Rhode Island eliminated West Virginia in the semifinals of the Atlantic 10 tournament on the Mountaineers' home floor, and then West Virginia lost 62–57 in overtime to up-and-coming Connecticut in the first round of the NIT to finish the season with an 18–14 record.

Catlett was able to solve his height dilemma in 1989 when 6-foot-10-inch Ray Foster became available for one year because of NCAA sanctions leveled against Cleveland State. Foster was a teammate of Shaw at San Jacinto when the Ravens captured the national junior college title, and Foster became an immediate starter on a front line that included senior Darryl Prue and junior Chris Brooks. In the backcourt, West Virginia once again had Herbie Brooks and Steve Berger. These five started all 31 games for the Mountaineers in 1989.

Experimenting led to a pair of early season losses to Robert Morris and Bradley. After the two-point loss to the Braves, Catlett chose to stick primarily with his five starters while rotating Tracy Shelton, Wade Smith and Shaun Jackson off the bench. Those eight players got the bulk of the playing time as West Virginia started a winning streak against Mount St. Mary's that consumed 22 games and lasted 84 days, during which West Virginia knocked off some pretty good teams.

"That '89 club, I would just kind of say, 'Let's go win by 10 and come back in here.' We could

New York City's Chris Brooks, pictured here blocking a dunk try by Maryland's Brian Williams, was one of the most highly sought-after players ever recruited by Gale Catlett.

WVU SPORTS COMMUNICATIONS PHOTO.

Herbie Brooks runs the fast break during a game at the WVU Coliseum. Brooks finished his four-year career with 1,105 points.

WVU SPORTS COMMUNICATIONS PHOTO.

Darryl Prue drives to the basket against Duke All-America forward Danny Ferry during this 1989 NCAA tournament second round game in Greensboro, N.C.

BLUE & GOLD NEWS / GREG HUNTER.

beat anybody," Catlett said. "They just had a confidence about them. They played together. The secret to coaching is, and will always be, chemistry, and that team had chemistry like you wouldn't believe."

Herbie Brooks made two baskets and grabbed a missed free throw in overtime to help the Mountaineers defeat Pitt 84–81 in Pittsburgh. Brooks scored 16 points in the second half and finished with a game-high 26. Seventeen days later, another Brooks (Chris) scored 19 points to lead West Virginia to a 69–61 win at Maryland. A 17–8 run after Maryland had closed the score to 39–34 was the difference in the game. Then, Steve Berger tallied 19 points to snap Temple's 31-game A-10 regular season winning streak in a 65–63 victory over the Owls at the Coliseum.

West Virginia's winning streak finally ended Feb. 26 at Temple when the 14th-rated Mountaineers fell 74–56 to the Owls. Freshman Mik Kilgore sank West Virginia with seven 3-pointers and 33 points.

West Virginia finished the regular season 17–1 in Atlantic 10 play and was awarded the top seed heading into the tournament in Philadelphia. After an easy 79–59 win over St. Joseph's, the Mountaineers watched Ed Fogell put up 28 points in leading Penn State to a shocking 86–64 upset victory in the semifinals. After West Virginia got to within five, 41–36, Penn State went on an eight-point run. Ironically, West Virginia outscored Penn State by 43 points during its two regular-season victories that year.

"I really thought we were a step behind most of the game, but Penn State really did a nice job," a disappointed Catlett said afterward. "Everything we tried didn't work."

West Virginia's loss impacted its NCAA tournament seeding while dropping its national ranking six spots from 13th to 19th. The Mountaineers were sent to Greensboro, N.C., where a meeting with Tennessee awaited them. The Vols got 22 points from forward Dyron Nix, but little else from the rest of the team. Nix was 7 of 14 in the first half while his teammates were only 2 of 17. That helped West Virginia build a 35–23 halftime lead. In the second half, the Mountaineers expanded their lead to 20. Herbie Brooks scored 22, and Foster added 19 points and 11 rebounds in the 84–68 victory. The Tennessee win set up a meeting with ninth-ranked Duke in the second round before a highly partisan Blue Devil crowd. After a well-played first half, the game essentially came down to a free throw shooting contest in the second half. Duke was 13 of 15 from the line while West Virginia was 4 of 11, including making just 2 of 6 over the remaining 9:07 of the game. Free throw shooting was West Virginia's Achilles heel all season (the Mountaineers came into the game shooting just 58 percent from the line). "We didn't get our best free throw shooters to the line today," said Catlett afterward. "It would have been nice to make a few more free throws."

West Virginia had a 55–54 lead when Duke scored eight of the game's next nine points. The Mountaineers closed to within one (62–61) with 3:01 remaining before Blue Devil freshman Christian Laettner scored a layup and Danny Ferry made two free throws after Darryl Prue was whistled for a questionable blocking call. The foul was Prue's fifth. Duke went on to win the game 70–63 and later advanced to the Final Four, while West Virginia's season ended with an outstanding 26–5 record.

"I didn't know Mike Krzyzewski that well, but he gets me after the game at midcourt and he says, 'You're the best defensive team we've played this year and we were lucky to win,'" Catlett recalled.

It was the third-most victories in school history at the time, and the Mountaineers established Atlantic 10 records for conference regular-season victories, consecutive conference wins and conference road victories.

Darryl Prue finished his outstanding career with 1,426 career points, 865 rebounds and shooting 55.8 percent from the floor. "You know what I think of Lester Rowe, but there was never anyone better than Darryl Prue," said Catlett. "Darryl was number 24 and we had a pretty good run of number 24s there. Rowe was 24. Russel Todd was 24 and Damian Owens was 24. I'll put that up against anybody in the country on four kids wearing the same number. Those were four great kids and four great players that wanted to win for the Mountaineers."

What Catlett's teams accomplished in the 1980s easily makes the decade one of the best in school history. The Mountaineers were 217–95 overall (.696 winning percentage) with six NCAA tournament appearances and two NIT trips. Some of the biggest crowds in WVU Coliseum history were achieved during the decade, the

Above Point guard Steve Berger surveys the floor during West Virginia's 1989 NCAA tournament game against Duke in Greensboro, N.C. Guarding Berger is Duke's Quin Snyder.

BLUE & GOLD NEWS / GREG HUNTER.

Left Catlett's 1989 team didn't lose a game for 84 straight days and finished the season with a 26–5 record before bowing out to Duke in the second round of the NCAA tournament.

WVU SPORTS COMMUNICATIONS PHOTO.

Chris Leonard remains the most accurate 3-point shooter in WVU history, making 41.7 percent of his career 3-point tries from 1989–92.
WVU SPORTS COMMUNICATIONS PHOTO.

Mountaineers drawing more than 10,000 for home basketball games 46 times during the decade. West Virginia's great home support helped the Mountaineers win 84.1 percent of their games at the Coliseum in the 1980s.

The 1988–89 academic year, which also included football's unlikely march to the national championship game against Notre Dame in the Fiesta Bowl, was a fitting conclusion to Fred Schaus's athletic career. Schaus had announced well in advance that 1989 would be his last year at WVU.

Schaus's replacement, Ed Pastilong, had worked in the department for 14 years in various roles. Pastilong, a former Mountaineer quarterback, was one of the few WVU athletic directors since Harry Stansbury (Dick Martin being the other) to have predominantly a football background, but his interest in all sports became apparent in ensuing years. While living in Moundsville, Pastilong frequently hitchhiked to WVU basketball games as a high school student. "I can remember one time on a real cold afternoon getting stranded in Waynesburg for about two hours before we finally caught a ride," Pastilong laughed. "By that time the basketball game was already over."

Six years later, this so-called football guy made a profound impact on the basketball program when Pastilong was able to help steer West Virginia University into the Big East Conference. That was the watershed event in the school's history, transforming West Virginia University into more of a national school.

Big East Bound

Catlett's teams experienced continued success in the 1990s, but not quite the degree that his teams had enjoyed during the '80s. Of course, joining the Big East Conference in 1996 had something to do with that.

A couple of near-.500 seasons started off the new decade for the Mountaineers. In 1990, West Virginia failed to reach postseason play for the first time in 10 years when it posted a 16–12 record and was bounced in the opening round of the Atlantic 10 tournament by Massachusetts. Ten of West Virginia's 12 losses that season came on the road. Sophomore guard Tracy Shelton was the team's leading scorer averaging 17.8 points per game.

A highly touted freshman class that included Marsalis Basey, Mike Boyd, P. G. Greene, Lawrence Pollard, Ricky Robinson and Phil Wilson arrived in 1991, but the Mountaineers continued to struggle away from the Coliseum, losing nine road games on the way to a 17–14 record. One of the most talked about games of the year happened in Morgantown on Feb. 23, when the Mountaineers blew out Temple 91–66. Owls' coach John Chaney was so disgusted with his team's play that he got tossed with one minute remaining in the half. He spent the second half in the locker room telling stories to a West Virginia state trooper.

"We were using multiple defenses and multiple offenses and John Chaney said once, 'Every time I call time-out to change something, we go back out to adjust to them and he's doing something else," said Catlett. "John and I were never real close friends, but at the same time I have so much respect for him because he was a great coach. He had an extra burden on his shoulders, too [with his social activism]. I didn't have to do that."

A 56–53 loss to Temple in the semifinals of the Atlantic 10 tournament led to the school's fourth NIT appearance in 10 seasons. West Virginia defeated Furman 86–67 at the Coliseum in the opening round before falling 85–79 at Providence. Catlett tried nine different lineup combinations that year before settling on a starting five that included Brooks and Charles Becton at forwards, Jeremy Bodkin at center, and Boyd and Chris Leonard at guards. Brooks was the only player to start all 31 games, finishing his senior year with averages of 16.7 points and 8.0 rebounds per game.

Key regular-season victories over Pitt, Virginia Tech, 25th-ranked Massachusetts and a surprising run to the Atlantic 10 championship game helped West Virginia make a return trip to the NCAA tournament in 1992.

Shelton got the Mountaineers on their way by scoring 16 points off the bench to lead six double-figure scorers in an 86–85 victory over Pitt in Morgantown. A week later, Leonard scored 18 points to help the Mountaineers edge Virginia Tech 66–65 in Blacksburg. To begin January, Greene produced 15 points to lead West Virginia to a 76–75 upset of 25th-ranked UMass in Amherst, and the UMass victory started a

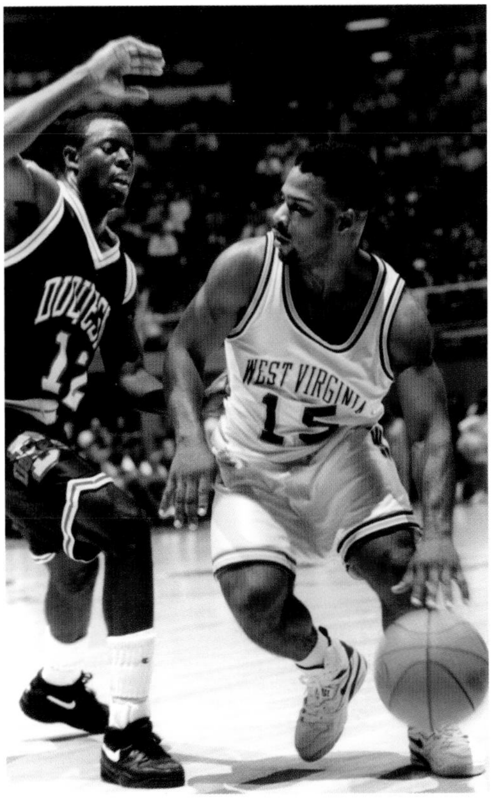

Above Listed at 5′8″ in the program but more likely 5′6″, point guard Marsalis Basey wooed crowds with his tough and determined play. He finished his four-year career in 1994 with 1,168 points and 514 assists.

WVU SPORTS COMMUNICATIONS PHOTO.

Right Forward Ricky Robinson scored 1,373 points and hauled down 746 rebounds during an outstanding four-year career from 1991–94.

WVU SPORTS COMMUNICATIONS PHOTO.

10-game winning streak that eventually ended in Morgantown against Rutgers. West Virginia dropped five of its seven remaining games to finish the regular season with an 18–10 record.

After beating Duquesne 76–69 in the opening round of the A-10 tournament, the Mountaineers clipped Temple 44–41 in the semifinals in Philadelphia despite a 10:46 scoreless stretch in the second half. Temple ran off 11 consecutive points and took the lead, 41–40, on a Mik Kilgore 3 with 6:01 to go. But the Owls never scored again. Shelton gave West Virginia back the lead, 42–41, with 4:30 remaining, and Leonard hit two free throws with 2:08 left for the final points of the game. Leonard scored 20 of West Virginia's 44 points.

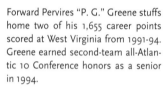

Forward Pervires "P. G." Greene stuffs home two of his 1,655 career points scored at West Virginia from 1991-94. Greene earned second-team all-Atlantic 10 Conference honors as a senior in 1994.

WVU SPORTS COMMUNICATIONS PHOTO.

The league finals moved on to Amherst, where 22nd-ranked UMass pulled out a 97–91 victory in a highly entertaining game. Greene came off the bench to score 21 points to lead the Mountaineers. Later that weekend, West Virginia was one of the last teams to get into the NCAA tournament field of 64 as a 12-seed facing Missouri in Greensboro, N.C.—a familiar site to West Virginia fans.

Things were going well for the underdog Mountaineers in the first half until the lights went out. WVU was leading 16th-ranked Missouri 35–32 when the Greensboro Coliseum went dark because of an electrical storm. A second outage occurred when WVU was leading 38–34. When the lights came back on, Missouri shot lights out, hitting 63 percent of its shot attempts in the second half on the way to an 89–78 victory.

"It was the weirdest game I've ever seen in my 29 years of coaching," said Catlett. "It was a disruptive way to play for the national championship when your players are all pumped up and have a lead, and all of the sudden the lights go out. And then you come out again, you've got a lead, and then the lights go out. Then, it's tied."

The delays were particularly harmful to West Virginia, which planned to try and wear down a Missouri team that used only seven players. Leonard scored 25 for WVU while guard Anthony Peeler led the Tigers with 25. The Mountaineers' final record was 20–12.

The 1993 season had a little bit of everything: close games, leaky roofs, bomb scares and blizzards that made an otherwise ordinary 17–12 season seem quite unusual. Even before the season started Catlett had to deal with an off-season automobile accident that claimed the career of promising center Wilfred Kirkaldy and severely impaired guard Lawrence Pollard for his remaining three seasons in the program.

Nine times West Virginia played games that were decided by four points or less. A 75–74 loss at 22nd-ranked Arizona was typical of how the season went. Mike Boyd had an opportunity to tie the game at the end of regulation, but instead of launching a potential game-tying 3, he inexplicably drove to the basket for a layup at the buzzer. A couple of overtime losses on the road against Alabama-Birmingham and UMass were also there for the taking.

A 79–54 victory over 21st-ranked UMass at the Coliseum Feb. 27 was the highlight of the year. Greene scored 25, Robinson added 15, and West Virginia held UMass' big guns Louis Roe, Tony

Barbee, Derek Kellogg and Jerome Malloy to a combined 6 of 28 shooting.

A bomb scare at St. Bonaventure briefly delayed West Virginia's 82–67 victory over the Bonnies to end the regular season. The building was evacuated, and with no place else to go in the middle of a snowstorm, the two teams hopped on West Virginia's bus while bomb-sniffing dogs were dispersed to check out the arena. The West Virginia players and coaches sat on one side of the bus while the St. Bonaventure players and coaches sat on the other side waiting to return to Reilly Center to finish the game.

Three days later, the Mountaineers suffered their worst loss in A-10 tournament play in the first round to Temple, falling 80–53. Shelton was the only WVU player to reach double figures with 10 points.

It was off to the NIT once again for the Mountaineers, where West Virginia advanced past the first round following an up-and-down, 95–84 victory over Georgia at the Coliseum. Former Oak Hill High teammates Greene and Shelton hit for 22 and 20 respectively.

In the second round, a forecasted blizzard forced West Virginia and Providence to play a day earlier at the Providence Civic Center. The Friars were able to hang on for a 68–67 victory when Phil Wilson's game-winning shot glanced off the rim. Wilson had made it into the lineup when Bodkin was sidelined for the remainder of the year with a stress fracture.

Shelton and Greene each passed 1,000 points for their careers, while West Virginia's 17–12 overall record included a 7–7 mark in Atlantic 10 play.

Another 17-win season followed in 1994, though it was considered a disappointing ending to the careers of West Virginia's touted freshman class of 1990.

At one point in mid-January, it looked like West Virginia was headed for a big year and another NCAA tournament appearance. The Mountaineers won nine of their first 10 games, including an 87–82 triumph at Ohio State and a 49–47 nail-biter at seventh-ranked Temple. WVU reached as high as 19th in the polls after a 20-point victory against Duquesne that boosted its record to 13–2. Then the wheels came off when Boyd suffered a knee injury that limited his effectiveness for the remainder of the season. Losses followed at St. Bonaventure, at George Washington and at Marquette to make WVU's record 13–5. Another three-game losing streak on the road against Duquesne, UMass and Rhode Island left West Virginia at 15–9.

New York City guard Seldon Jefferson brought pizzazz and style to Morgantown during his three seasons playing for the Mountaineers from 1995–97. Jefferson managed to score 1,168 points and averaged 14.1 points per game for his career.

WVU SPORTS COMMUNICATIONS PHOTO.

After that the Mountaineers were upset 70–68 in the opening round of the Atlantic 10 tournament by Duquesne, and a third trip to the NIT in four years ended in the second round with a 96–79 loss to Clemson at the Coliseum. The senior class of Greene, Robinson, Boyd and Basey all scored 1,000 points for their careers, while Wilson became the school shot-block leader at the time with 174.

Left West Virginia's Gordon Malone and Georgetown's Othella Harrington at the center jump for West Virginia's first-ever Big East game at the WVU Coliseum played on Dec. 2, 1995. Georgetown won in overtime, 86–83.

WVU SPORTS COMMUNICATIONS PHOTO.

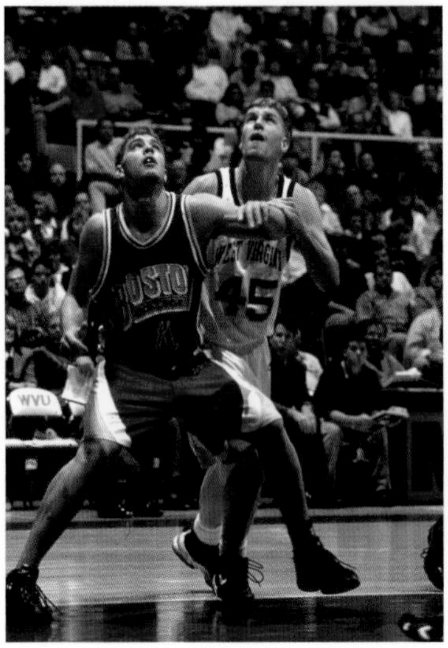

Below left Forward Brent Solheim scored 869 points, grabbed 428 rebounds and shot 53.6 percent from the floor during his four-year career at WVU.

WVU SPORTS COMMUNICATIONS PHOTO.

A major renovation was in store for Gale Catlett's WVU program in 1995 in what was to become the school's final season in the Atlantic 10 Conference.

In the winter of 1994, the Big East began discussing a lucrative long-term football/basketball television deal with CBS. Five years earlier, West Virginia had entered into a football-only arrangement with the conference along with Virginia Tech and Temple. Because Big East football and basketball were configured separately, the football schools were unwilling to represent the non-football schools in the television negotiations. It became apparent to the football schools that the conference could only remain intact by expanding, otherwise, they would have to split up and form a separate all-sports conference. Seven of the 10 Big East members had to vote in favor of expansion to remain together, so in order to finally get the required seven votes, a compromise was reached. West Virginia and Rutgers from the Atlantic 10 would join the league as full-fledged members. The conference would also add Notre Dame in all sports except football. Temple and Virginia Tech did not garner the support needed from the basketball schools to go beyond 12.

The invitation to the Big East would have a profound impact on the entire West Virginia University athletic department. Immediately, it enhanced West Virginia's image nationally. "I've seen a lot of good things happen at WVU in 16 years, but this has to head the list," said Catlett at the time.

Catlett and his coaches no longer had to answer questions from recruits about the quality of competition the Mountaineers were facing in the Atlantic 10 Conference. Now West Virginia could finally go after top-notch prospects it had frequently lost to Big East schools.

Meanwhile, the Mountaineers managed a 13–13 record in their A-10 swan song in '95. Forward Zain Shaw was the only senior starter and he had a fine year, averaging 14.8 points and 6.6 rebounds per game, but the program was already taking on the personality of the younger players such as Damian Owens, Brent Solheim and Jarrod West—three key parts to West Virginia's 1998 NCAA tournament Sweet 16 run.

Before they reached that point, though, the Mountaineers had to take some more lumps in

THE BIG EAST CONFERENCE

Ed Pastilong will state without hesitation that the achievement he is most proud of during his 20-plus years directing the Mountaineer athletic program was the school's invitation into the Big East Conference in 1994. Getting West Virginia University into an eastern all-sports conference was the objective of every athletic director since the days of Harry Stansbury in the 1920s.

Former West Virginia University Director of Athletics Ed Pastilong was the man responsible for getting WVU into the Big East Conference as a full-fledged member in 1996.
WVU SPORTS COMMUNICATIONS PHOTO.

West Virginia came close on two occasions. In 1953, WVU was unsuccessful in its attempt to join the Carolina schools that broke away from the Southern Conference to form the Atlantic Coast Conference. At the time, Morgantown, W.Va., was simply too difficult to get to.

Three decades later, in 1981, Penn State's Joe Paterno came within a decimal point of creating an eastern all-sports league, which West Virginia supported. However, negotiations broke down over revenue-sharing, and Pitt killed the plan when it joined the Big East Conference in 1982.

Seven years later in 1989, when football conferences began expanding to strengthen their television bases, the three Big East football independents—Boston College, Syracuse and Pitt—were in a difficult situation. To survive, the Big East had to extend full membership to Miami and football-only invitations to West Virginia, Rutgers, Virginia Tech and Temple in 1991. The Big East Football Conference began round-robin play in 1993.

A year later, the Big East began discussing a lucrative long-term football and basketball television deal with CBS. Because Big East football and basketball were configured separately, the football schools were unwilling to represent the non-football schools in TV negotiations.

It became apparent to the football schools that the only way the conference could remain intact was by expanding. Seven of the 10 members had to vote in favor of expansion. The four football schools plus Villanova and Connecticut—both contemplating a jump to Division I-A in football—were all in favor of expansion. That left one school to coerce. The matter was eventually turned over to the presidents, and St. John's, fully understanding the long-term implications of remaining intact, became the deciding vote in favor of expansion. West Virginia and Rutgers were added as the Big East's 11th and 12th members, and Notre Dame later became the 13th participant in all sports except football.

Gale Catlett was pleased the Mountaineers got into the Big East, but his heart was always set on West Virginia getting into the ACC. "My frustration with West Virginia University basketball is that we never had the opportunity to join the ACC," said Catlett. "I thought we had more in common with those schools than we did the Big East schools. That's not a put down. We had more in common with North Carolina than we did with Georgetown. We had more in common with Maryland than we did with Villanova because of our total program."

The Big East added Virginia Tech as its 14th member in 2000. Three years later, Virginia Tech and Miami left the Big East to join the ACC with Boston College following in 2004. The Big East in 2005 added Cincinnati, DePaul, Louisville, Marquette and South Florida to make up its present 16-school configuration.

First Team Big East Conference

1998, Damian Owens (F)
2001, Calvin Bowman (F)
2006, Mike Gansey (G); Kevin Pittsnogle (C)
2007, Frank Young (F)
2008, Joe Alexander (F)
2010, Da'Sean Butler (F)

Forward Damian Owens, pictured here driving to the basket against Georgetown, earned first-team all-Big East honors and was recognized as the conference's defensive player of the year in 1998.

WVU SPORTS COMMUNICATIONS PHOTO.

1996. More than 15,000 showed up for West Virginia's inaugural Big East game against sixth-rated Georgetown at the Coliseum. West Virginia saw its 12-point lead disintegrate in the final 3:34, and the Hoyas outscored the Mountaineers 10–7 in overtime to pull off an 86–83 victory. It was a preview of just how tough things would be for West Virginia in the Big East. Losses followed to Pitt, Villanova and Miami, as well as to Seton Hall in the opening round of the Big East tournament—all five coming by five points or less.

The Mountaineers played a total of nine ranked opponents in 1996, or the same number of ranked teams they had faced during the prior four-year span playing in the Atlantic 10. West Virginia's first Big East victory came against 12th-ranked Syracuse on Jan. 16, 1996, at the Coliseum. Sophomore forward Gordon Malone was brilliant, scoring 22 points and blocking a pair of shots in a 90–78 victory. Another fine win came at 20th-ranked Boston College in late February. Ohio State transfer Greg Simpson and Seldon Jefferson scored 23 points each; Owens added 21 and seven boards.

Despite a 20-point defeat at Pitt to end the regular season, and a last-second loss to Seton Hall in the first round of the Big East tournament, West Virginia showed it could be competitive by winning three of its remaining five games in conference competition. After missing post-season play for two straight years, Catlett once again had the players he needed to make another tournament run in '97.

West Virginia's 11–7 Big East and 19–8 regular-season records that season were remarkable in two respects. One, it showed that West Virginia was better equipped to adjust to Big East play than other newcomers Notre Dame and Rutgers (as well as Miami several years before). And, two, it showed that the Mountaineers were still not getting the respect they deserved. West Virginia and Syracuse, both 19-win teams, failed to earn bids to the NCAA tournament. It was the first time Big East schools with 11 conference wins and 19 regular-season victories were left out of the Big Dance. Since 1983 when the Big East began its dramatic ascension, 65 out of 71 Big East teams with at least 17 regular-season victories had made the NCAA tournament. Massachusetts, Texas and USC wound up getting in that year over Syracuse, Southwest Missouri State, Tulane and West Virginia. "Being the first Big East school in history with not only 11 league wins but 19 regular-season wins not to get an NCAA bid is shocking to me," was Catlett's opinion on Selection Sunday.

Catlett had ruffled some feathers a week earlier in New York when he began campaigning for an NCAA bid following WVU's 76–69 loss to Providence in the Big East quarterfinals. The veteran coach went on to compare West Virginia's resume to other Big East schools—the first time anyone in the conference could ever remember a coach doing that at the conference tournament. It was a clear sign to old-timers that the close-knit days of the league were over.

Despite the disappointment of not making the NCAA tournament, there were several impressive victories on West Virginia's resume in 1997. WVU gave Syracuse its worst-ever beating at the Carrier Dome on Dec. 4, 1996, when the Mountaineers ran and dunked their way to a 101–79 victory. It was a meaningful win to Catlett because he had always held Syracuse coach Jim Boeheim in such high regard.

"I've heard all these years about Jim Boeheim just having all this great talent and you know what, Jim Boeheim is one of the smartest guys I know," said Catlett. "First of all he gets in a damned zone and makes you shoot outside all of the time and you can't get it inside. But secondly, his best players take all of the shots. When you get a defense people can't attack and when you get your best players taking all of the shots, well, that's pretty good coaching to me."

Two four-game winning streaks were also impressive for the Mountaineers. The first spanned 10 days from Jan. 22 to Feb. 1, during which West Virginia defeated Rutgers, Notre Dame, Boston College and Pitt. The second came at the end of the season when a non-conference win against Towson preceded victories over Seton Hall, 18th-ranked Villanova and Miami.

West Virginia's inspiring play continued into the NIT. The Mountaineers withstood 38 points from Bowling Green's Antonio Daniels to outlast the Falcons 98–95 in an entertaining game at the Coliseum. On West Virginia's side, Gordon Malone impressed pro scouts with a 24-point, 18-rebound effort.

The Mountaineers followed the Bowling Green win with a 76–73 victory at NC State. Jefferson scored 19 points to pace five double-digit scorers. West Virginia's season then ended one game short of the NIT semifinals with a 76–71 loss to Florida State in Morgantown.

Although Jefferson, center Sandro Varejao, and reserve guard David Liguori were lost to graduation, and forward Gordon Malone surprisingly chose to leave school a year early to enter the NBA draft, Catlett had assembled one of his strongest teams at West Virginia for the 1998 season.

Adrian Pledger scores two of his 10 points to help West Virginia upset ninth-rated Cincinnati in the second round of the NCAA tournament in Boise, Idaho.
WVU SPORTS COMMUNICATIONS PHOTO.

Sweet Success

Catlett had Owens, Solheim and West as three-year contributors and he dipped into the junior college ranks to bring in guards Greg Jones and Adrian Pledger, along with 6-foot-11, 265-pound center Brian Lewin. In addition, a pair of outstanding young players—6-foot-8 sophomore forward Marcus Goree and 6-foot-5 freshman guard Jarett Kearse—gave the Mountaineers a deep bench.

Above Guard Jarrod West was the hero of West Virginia's 1998 NCAA tournament victory over ninth-ranked Cincinnati when his last second shot defeated the Bearcats.

WVU SPORTS COMMUNICATIONS PHOTO.

Right Forward Calvin Bowman became the second player in school history to earn first-team All-Big East honors when he was selected in 2001.

WVU SPORTS COMMUNICATIONS PHOTO.

Connecticut had been the only remaining Big East team West Virginia had yet to defeat since joining the conference.

Then the Mountaineers hit a rough stretch at the end of the year when a worn-down West Virginia team lost its last two games of the regular season to Boston College and Miami, and then was upset in the first round of the Big East tournament by Rutgers. Owens was the one hurting the most. He injured his back during a 73–58 loss to Syracuse and spent the remainder of the regular season trying to play through the pain.

The loss to 12th-seeded Rutgers actually turned out to be a blessing in disguise. It gave Owens and other injured players extra time to heal. When West Virginia was announced on Selection Sunday as a 10th seed in Boise, Idaho, the players were reasonably confident that they could make a run in the NCAA tournament.

They did.

Seventh-seeded Temple, one of West Virginia's old sparring partners from its Atlantic 10 days, was never in the game. West Virginia led 32–20 at halftime and extended its lead to well beyond 20 points in the second half. The much taller Mountaineers destroyed the Owls on the glass, 46–24, and shot an impressive 54.2 percent from the floor en route to an 82–52 win.

"We're veterans who've played a lot of games, and we wanted to make sure it wasn't the last game for us," said Solheim.

That depth was evident right away with a five-game winning streak that included the San Juan Shootout title with victories over Puerto Rico-Mayaguez, Rice and Dayton. West Virginia also ran off consecutive wins against St. John's, Ohio, Robert Morris, Georgia, Virginia Tech and Duquesne. The triumph over 20th-ranked Georgia at the Georgia Dome got the Mountaineers back into the national rankings.

The winning continued against Boston College, Georgetown (on ESPN Big Monday), Miami, Villanova, Rutgers and Providence, along with back-to-back triumphs against Pitt. The best performance of the year came on Feb. 11, 1998, when West Virginia routed sixth-ranked Connecticut 80–62 in a game televised nationally on ESPN. Jones was spectacular, scoring 18 points to lead four double-figure Mountaineer scorers.

The Temple win set up an eyebrow-raising second-round game against ninth-rated Cincinnati, coached by former Mountaineer standout Bob Huggins.

The seesaw game came down to the last seven seconds. Cincinnati, with no time-outs, was able to take the lead 74–72 when D'Juan Baker hit a 20-foot jump shot with 7.1 ticks remaining. Catlett choose to let the game continue on instead of calling a time-out, which prohibited Huggins from having a chance to organize his defense. Catlett's strategy to play worked.

Jarrod West brought the ball down the floor, used a pick from Lewin well beyond the top of the key, and let loose a 30-footer that sailed into the basket with .8 seconds left on the clock—not nearly enough time for Cincinnati to try another shot. The fact that West banked it in from straight on with Ruben Patterson getting a hand on the ball made it even more remarkable—and more difficult for the Bearcat players to accept. "I saw Ruben get a piece of it," said Cincinnati center Kenyon Martin. "I saw a bank shot, and I felt my stomach drop."

It was the first time since Catlett's playing days in 1963 that West Virginia had reached the round of 16 in the NCAA tournament. A week later West Virginia came within three points of reaching the Elite Eight, falling 65–62 to eventual national runner-up Utah in Anaheim, Calif.

"That was about as hard a fought game as we've had all year," remarked Utah coach Rick Majerus afterward. "I'm emotionally drained. I feel very fortunate to move on."

West once again had a chance to make a dramatic 3 at the end of the game. "I thought he made it," Utah center Michael Doleac said. "It hit the front of the rim. Thank God the clock ran out." West Virginia's 24–9 record was its best since its 26–5 campaign in 1989. The Mountaineers set a school record by forcing 649 turnovers; Owens led the team in scoring (16.5 ppg) and steals (97), while three other players averaged double figures. In all, seven players averaged better than 7.6 points per game—a typical trait of Catlett's best teams. Owens became the first WVU player to earn a spot on the All-Big East first team, and he was also voted conference defensive player of the year.

"The '98 club we had some ups and downs, but we took some time off after the (Big East) tournament and we had great leadership," said Catlett. "Jarrod West, Damian Owens, and Brent Solheim were three great kids. They roomed together and they wanted to win. Then you had big Brian Lewin, who was a big puppy dog and just a great kid. And we had Marcus Goree coming off the bench. We had some really talented kids."

Catlett's Final Years

There were other fine moments during Catlett's remaining years at WVU, most notably a respectable 14-win season in 2000 when the team was forced to play all of its games on the road because of asbestos abatement in the WVU Coliseum and a 17-win campaign in 2001 that included another NIT appearance against a schedule that featured games against eight nationally ranked teams.

Goree, junior college transfer Calvin Bowman, and forward Chris Moss led the Mountaineers into the new millennium. Bowman averaged 17.6 points and 9.7 rebounds per game in 2001 to earn first-team All-Big East honors and claim the league's most improved player award.

Forward Marcus Goree gets into position to grab a rebound in a game against Connecticut at the WVU Coliseum. Goree scored 1,183 points and pulled down 675 rebounds during his four-year career in 1997–2000.

WVU SPORTS COMMUNICATIONS PHOTO.

Gale Catlett doing an interview with ESPN's Bill Raftery after a home victory.
WVU SPORTS COMMUNICATIONS PHOTO.

Moss was the best player on a very young team in 2002, averaging 17.5 points and 8.0 rebounds per game.

But a promising beginning to the 2002 season that included last-second victories over New Mexico and Tennessee spiraled out of control following losses to Valparaiso and Pepperdine in the Fiesta Bowl Classic in Tucson, Ariz. A youthful and undisciplined team became unmanageable.

At age 60, Catlett had enough. His competitive nature was legendary. During his later years he would gulp down handfuls of Tums to help digest the painful losses. When it became apparent that the game was changing dramatically—when it became nearly impossible to connect to his players—Catlett chose to resign after a depressing loss to Virginia Tech at the Coliseum on Feb. 13, 2002.

Five games still remained on the schedule, but Catlett simply decided that it was time to go. No press conferences. No formal announcements. Just a simple statement expressing his love for the state and a word of thanks to those who gave him the opportunity to fulfill his life-long dream of coaching at his alma mater.

Catlett's nephew Drew coached the remaining five games of the season. It was one of just three losing seasons Gale Catlett endured in 30 years as a college head coach.

Catlett's achievements were impressive: eleven NCAA tournament appearances, 16 postseason appearances, and an average of 19 victories per season. He became the 45th coach in NCAA history to win 500 career games and the 41st Division I coach to win more than 400 games at the same school.

"When you look at the wins and losses, it doesn't tell you enough about the knowledge Gale Catlett possesses," wrote ESPN's Dick Vitale in 2002. "If you ever sat down and talked basketball with him, he would give you a wealth of information about the game he gave so much to."

Longtime foe John Chaney was also complimentary. The two spent a good portion of their coaching careers trying to pull the Atlantic 10 Conference up by the bootstraps. "He was always a very bright, innovative coach," Chaney said. "He could coach on his feet as well as anyone in the business."

"Gale had great tunnel vision," added McPherson. "It was incredible the way he was locked in on game day."

Catlett remained at West Virginia for 24 seasons. The average coaching tenure at WVU was just 3.8 years when he got there in 1978. For nearly a quarter of a century, Gale Catlett was the face of Mountaineer basketball.

"The reason I stayed for 24 years was because I thought it was the best basketball job in the country—and I still do—for me, my family, and the people I had to work with," Catlett said. "When offers came or people called I didn't have much interest in that because I wanted to stay here and coach the Mountaineers. To be an average player like I was and then to be the coach? Give me a break. I just thank God that I was able to be there for those years and had the chance to be a part of that."

Catlett wasn't perfect. He frequently battled reporters and his candor sometimes rubbed people the wrong way. He could be defiant and combative. But he could also be compassionate and extremely generous.

McPherson clearly recalls Gale Catlett's compassionate side. Back in the late 1960s when coaches had to work summer camps to help pay the bills, McPherson took his young family down to Davidson to work Lefty Driesell's basketball camp. The plan was for McPherson to have a place for his wife and young children to stay for the week while he made a few extra bucks.

When McPherson got there, to his horror, no arrangements had been made for his family. He was frantically trying to find a place for them to stay when Catlett stepped in and offered his apartment for them to use. He had taken an assistant coaching job at Kansas and his wife, Anise, was already back at her mother's house in Morgantown preparing for the move to Kansas. Why not give it to someone in need? "That's just Gale's generosity," McPherson said.

Catlett also constantly sought out ways of providing different educational experiences to his players. "That four- or five-year period they were there—that might develop their whole life," Catlett explained. "I thought we had an obligation to get them started right in life and make them understand the importance of an education."

Once during a summer trip with his team, Catlett went through the trouble of getting State Department permission so his West Virginia players could see firsthand the demilitarized zone separating North and South Korea. When the Mountaineers played in New York City, Catlett would take his assistant coaches, staff and their families to Broadway plays, often paying for their tickets himself. He also made sure the team bus traveled past Ground Zero in New York City after the Sept. 11, 2001 terrorist attacks.

"He not only taught us how to become better basketball players, but he also taught us how to become better men," said Chris Leonard.

"He did many things that people just never knew about," added Willie Akers. "The people of this state will never know all of the kind things he's done in his life."

Even though West Virginia suffered through a very difficult 8–20 season in 2002, the foundation of the Mountaineer program still remained solid. Catlett's successor had problems to deal with, but the journey back to the top of the college basketball world was not nearly as far as many people thought.

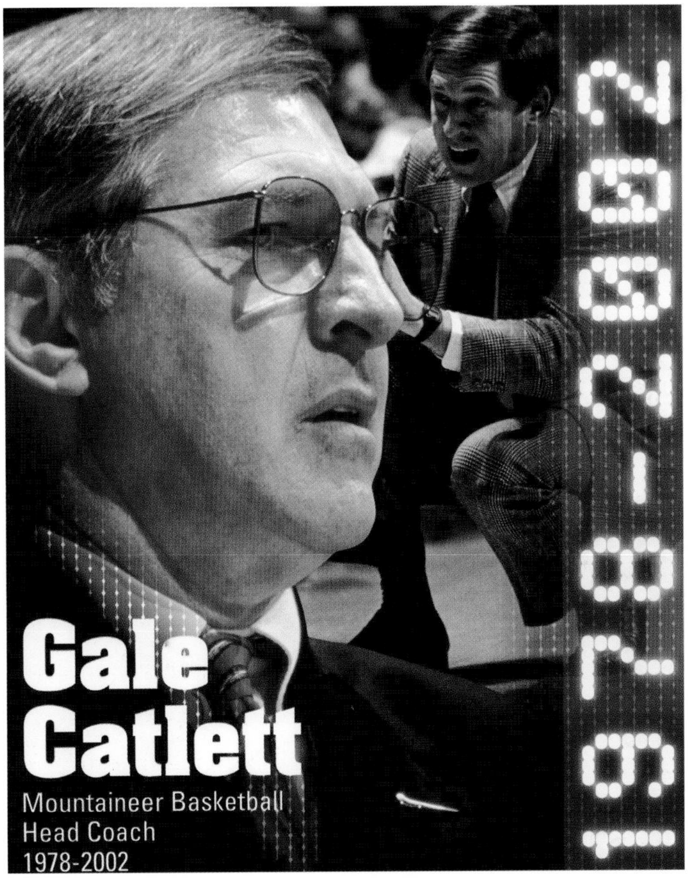

Gale Catlett won 565 games in 30 seasons as a college head coach at Cincinnati and West Virginia from 1972–2002.

WVU SPORTS COMMUNICATIONS PHOTO.

verybody's Bee
ittsnogle
West Virginia
JERRY WEST
LSU
TIGERS
GAME
turday
vember 26,
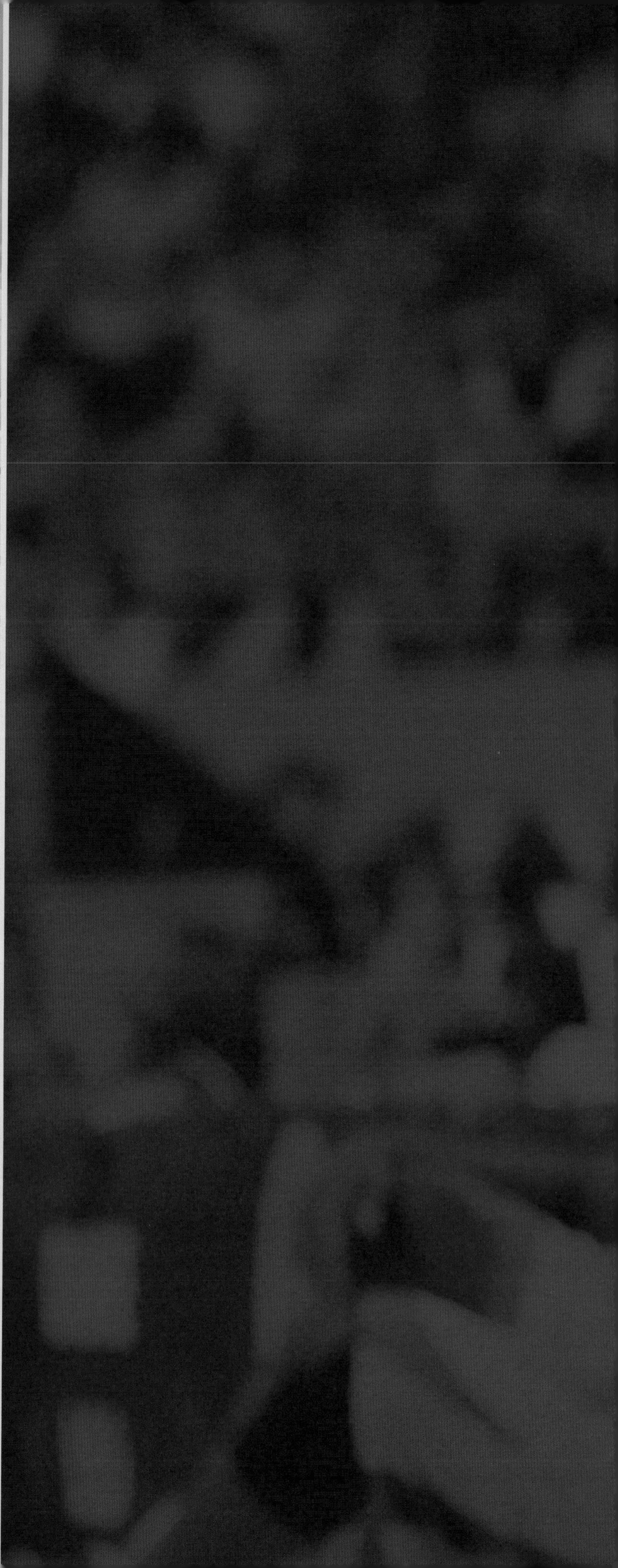

13

Beilein Brings 'em Back

(2003–2007)

John Beilein guided West Virginia to back-to-back Sweet 16 appearances in 2005–06, including an Elite Eight berth in 2005.

WVU SPORTS COMMUNICATIONS PHOTO.

There were two false starts before West Virginia finally hired Richmond's John Beilein on April 18, 2002, to be its 20th men's basketball coach.

Cincinnati's Bob Huggins was the first possibility targeted, but contract terms could not be worked out. Then came Dan Dakich, who agreed to a contract, was announced at a formal press conference at the Coliseum, and stayed a week before returning to Bowling Green. Dakich thought he had uncovered possible violations (the NCAA later ruled them minor), and he came back to the administration with a request that additional money be added to his agreement. The school said the dollars would remain the same, but would consider adding more years to the deal. Dakich said no thanks and asked for his old job back.

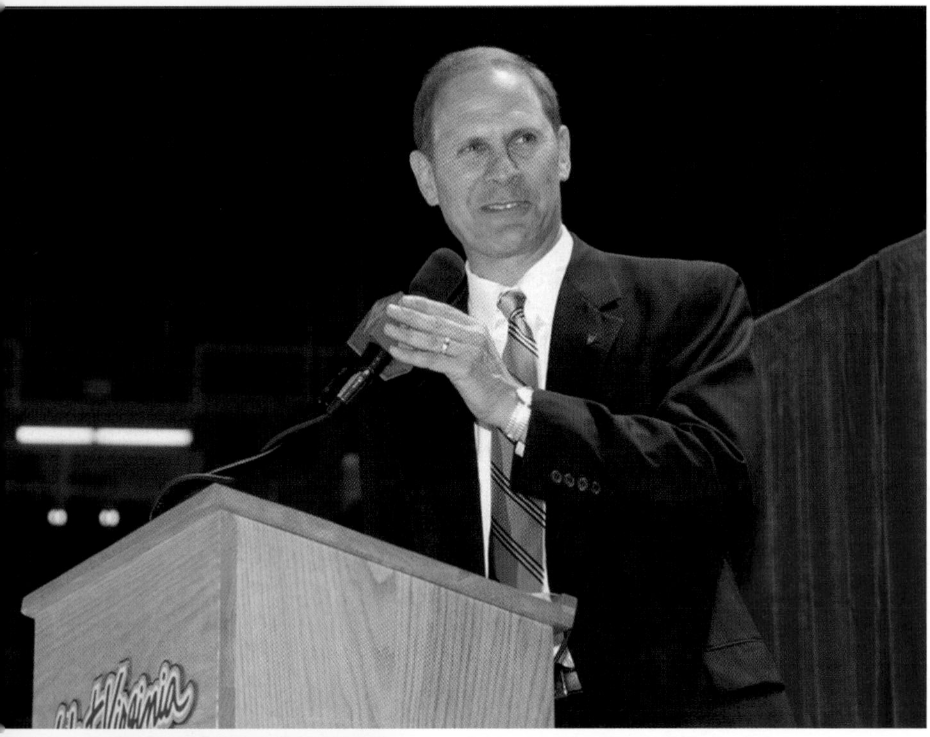

John Beilein addresses a gathering of Mountaineer fans and media members during his introductory press conference at the WVU Coliseum.
WVU SPORTS COMMUNICATIONS PHOTO.

During the week that Dakich was West Virginia's coach, he turned personal workouts into boot camp. "His policy was, if you were on time, you were five minutes late," forward Tyrone Sally said in 2005. "In the weight room, he made me put a 40-pound weight on my legs, with my back against the wall, and my legs bent for an hour. He told me I had to do that to stay in the program.

"It was crazy. I told myself, 'College can't be this bad.'"

West Virginia's unsettling situation did not deter the 49-year-old Beilein, the son of a paper mill laborer from northwestern New York who worked his way up the coaching ladder from junior high school, to high school, to junior college, to Division II and then to Division I.

As a boy, Beilein grew up playing basketball on a snow-covered court on his family's nine-acre farm. His uncle, Joe Niland, coached at Canisius, and Beilein would listen to the Golden Griffins' games on the radio, often charting the team's statistics. Just an average player by his own admission, Beilein went to Wheeling Jesuit as a walk-on where he earned a degree in history.

His college coaching stops were an exercise in patience and perseverance. First it was Eric Community College, followed by NAIA Nazareth (N.Y.) College, Le Moyne (N.Y.) College, Canisius and then Richmond.

Beilein's nine years at Le Moyne College were perhaps the most beneficial to his coaching career. It was at Le Moyne where he came up with his unique two-guard offense that had elements of Pete Carril's Princeton system and Tex Winter's triangle offense in it.

While he was at Canisius, on his first day on the job, Beilein met his three new full-time assistant coaches and asked them what they did all day. Beilein had never had a coaching staff before and was accustomed to doing everything, even the mundane tasks such as organizing team meals and making travel arrangements.

Beilein's five successful seasons at Richmond,

where he led the Spiders to a 100–53 record, one NCAA tournament appearance and three trips to the NIT, put him in a position to land the West Virginia job. During his tenure at Richmond, Beilein was constantly pursued by other schools. First there was St. John's, then Rutgers and Wake Forest. According to the *Richmond Times-Dispatch,* Beilein was contacted by eight different schools during his five seasons at Richmond.

Beilein's decision to accept West Virginia's offer came about quickly. A few days after Dakich chose to return to Bowling Green, West Virginia and Beilein agreed to terms that included a five-year deal that could earn him as much as $725,000 per season if he met all of his incentives.

Beilein said the opportunity to coach in the Big East Conference at a school located in a small college town was very appealing to him. "I have had a competitive drive since I began coaching to try to coach at the very highest collegiate level," Beilein said the day he was hired. "I have an opportunity to rebuild a program that I think has tremendous potential, and I've chosen to do that."

Most saw a West Virginia roster full of players that did not fit Beilein's style—a style that he first developed out of necessity on the small college level. Shooting, passing, unselfish play and intelligence were the four primary characteristics that he looked for in his players. The most important moment in Beilein's coaching career came in 1987 at Le Moyne when the NCAA adopted the 3-point shot. "It was too good to be true," Beilein said. "People didn't know how to defend it."

The 3 turned out to be Beilein's Excalibur. His perfect team, some of his former assistant coaches would sometimes say, would be five interchangeable players—all of whom could handle and shoot the basketball.

A few years after taking advantage of the 3-point shot, Beilein went into his laboratory at Canisius and came up with an unorthodox 1-3-1 zone defense that he borrowed from Roy Chipman. The decision to use the 1-3-1 came out of necessity when his starting center got hurt before the conference tournament. The 3-ball and the 1-3-1 zone would become the two staples of Beilein-coached teams at WVU.

"He's put his own spin on the Princeton offense, and his 1-3-1 zone is creative and tough to get used to," Texas A&M coach Mark Turgeon told *Sports Illustrated* in 2007. "I study his films and try to learn from him."

Beilein was extremely protective of his system, once making a student staff member destroy the notebook of plays that he had been keeping

Johannes Herber hit the winning shot in West Virginia's 2002 upset of eighth-ranked Florida at the Charleston Civic Center.

ALL-PRO PHOTOGRAPHY/DALE SPARKS.

Father John Beilein enjoys a moment with son Patrick as they walk off the floor at the Charleston Civic Center.
ALL-PRO PHOTOGRAPHY/DALE SPARKS.

of Beilein's offense. On another occasion, after letting slip the names of some of his plays (Dirty Harry, Best Play Ever and Double Quickie Potato) while talking to a reporter, Beilein unsuccessfully tried to keep him from using the names of the plays in his story.

There was something else unique about Beilein's teams—he wasn't against recruiting transfers, reasoning that second chances sometimes turned out to be the best chances. Plus, the high school prospects that he did go after were rarely pursued by other Big East programs.

"If we waited on Big East kids we weren't going to get anyway, all the mid-major kids would be gone to Richmond or Butler or somewhere," Beilein reasoned. "We got low maintenance kids who wanted to prove they could play. They're not pampered AAU all-stars. They're just good kids who work like crazy."

Added all up, it was a formula few other coaches in the country ever imagined using.

Building a Winner

When Beilein arrived at West Virginia, some of the players he inherited didn't suit his style and soon departed. Others, such as Tyrone Sally, Chaz Briggs, Josh Yeager and Drew Schifino, stuck around that first year.

One player Beilein was anxious to keep on board was 6-foot-10 Kevin Pittsnogle from Martinsburg, W.Va. Beilein was very familiar with Pittsnogle, having unsuccessfully tried to recruit him to Richmond. Pittsnogle was precisely what Beilein was looking for—a shooting center.

Beilein soon added high school guards Jarmon Durisseau-Collins from Houston, Texas, and Johannes Herber from Darmstadt, Germany. Herber and Collins were originally planning to sign with Richmond, as was Beilein's son Patrick, before changing their minds when the Beileins went to West Virginia. These players would form the nucleus of the team that helped West Virginia make its breathtaking return to college basketball relevance.

Of course there were many obstacles along the way. When Beilein began his first season in 2003, he had just one returning player who started more than 12 games the previous year (Yeager), and only seven players remaining on scholarship. He preached patience.

Beilein also accepted some sound advice from Connecticut coach Jim Calhoun, the same advice Calhoun once received from legendary St. John's coach Lou Carnesecca: stick to your principles. Don't change because you are coaching in the Big East, keep doing the same things you did at Erie, Nazareth, Le Moyne, Canisius and Richmond.

It took four games for Beilein to win over the fans. Facing eighth-ranked Florida in Charleston on Dec. 3, 2002, in what was supposed to be a homecoming game for the Gators' Brett Nelson (a native of nearby St. Albans), West Virginia stunned Florida, 68–66, on a last-second basket by Herber. It was an unlikely victory, given that the Mountaineers trailed the Gators by nine points at one point in the second half. When the game was over, students stormed the court in appreciation.

Beilein was pleased with the victory but was concerned that people were going to get too carried away. "I'm just hoping we don't have any grand illusions that if we played Florida again, the same thing would happen," he said afterward. "We're going to have some bumps on the road as we try to push this program to the right level."

Despite his cautious comments, Beilein pulled off another shocker eighteen days later. West Virginia, after trailing most of the game, defeated Tennessee 65–62 in Morgantown to run its record to 7–1. Drew Schifino scored 28 points, and Pittsnogle added 15 to a winning cause.

The Mountaineers also had UNLV on the ropes at the Jim Thorpe Classic in Las Vegas before finally falling 70–67. There was a five-point win over Miami in Morgantown, followed by a two-point overtime loss at Georgetown. A key victory at Rutgers proved vital in West Virginia qualifying for the Big East tournament, where the Mountaineers lost to Providence 73–50 in the first round.

Added all up, Beilein managed a 14–15 record. West Virginia won five games in conference play, including road victories at Villanova and Rutgers; five of WVU's 11 Big East losses came to ranked teams in '03. It was a remarkable performance for such a young team that was only a year removed from one of the most difficult seasons in school history.

Schifino led the Mountaineers with an average of 20.1 points per game, becoming the first WVU player since Greg Jones in 1983 to average more than 20 points per game for the season. He was named to the All-Big East third team. Pittsnogle also played well, averaging 11.6 points per game and earning mention on the Big East all-rookie team.

Fans stormed the Charleston Civic Center court to celebrate West Virginia's 68–66 upset of eighth-ranked Florida on Dec. 3, 2002.

ALL-PRO PHOTOGRAPHY/DALE SPARKS.

In the summer of 2003, 6-foot-11 center D'or Fischer was added to the roster after starring at Northwestern State, and Beilein went down to Tallahassee, Fla., to recruit overlooked shooting forward Frank Young.

Sitting out that year was St. Bonaventure transfer Mike Gansey. Beilein fell in love with Gansey's game when he was still coaching in the Atlantic 10, once complaining to his assistant coaches that they needed to go out and find more players like Gansey. When the guard eventually became available after an academic scandal at St. Bonaventure, Beilein recruited him like he was LeBron James.

Above Freshman guard J.D. Collins goes up for a jump shot during West Virginia's 65–62 upset victory over Tennessee at the WVU Coliseum on Dec. 21, 2002.

WVU SPORTS COMMUNICATIONS PHOTO.

Above right D'or Fischer goes up for a jump shot over Pitt's Chris Taft in this 2004 game at the WVU Coliseum. Fischer ranked third in the country in blocked shots that year with an average of 4.0 blocks per game.

ALL-PRO PHOTOGRAPHY/DALE SPARKS.

"Pete Carril used to say, 'If you get too many kids with three-car garages, you're not going to win too many games.' Mike is the type of guy, where he's not only a great kid, but he's got that hard nose," Beilein said. "He'll stick his nose in there and really go after it."

"After all that stuff came down [at St. Bonaventure], I was looking for a fresh start," said Gansey. "My parents and I sat down and drew up a list of schools. I was ready to visit West Virginia, Clemson and New Mexico. But I knew Coach Beilein and I liked him. I had played against him in the Atlantic 10 and West Virginia was just three hours away from my home [Olmsted Falls, Ohio]."

The Mountaineers took another big step forward in 2004 by winning 17 games and earning an NIT bid. But once again there was adversity to overcome. Schifino, the team's top scorer in 2003, was suspended from the team following an 11-point loss at Notre Dame and eventually left the program. The Mountaineers also ran into a tough four-game stretch at the end of February when they lost four games in a row to Pitt, Rutgers, Virginia Tech and Syracuse.

However, quality wins were achieved that year against Maryland, Georgetown, Boston College, Seton Hall, Villanova and Miami. West Virginia was also able to pay back St. Louis by beating the Billikens 66–57 in Charleston after St. Louis had routed the Mountaineers by 30 points the previous year.

The Boston College victory, on Jan. 24, 2004, was perhaps WVU's best all-around performance of the season. Sally scored 18 points and Fischer added 12 points and a school-record eight blocks in the 65–62 victory. A 34-point rout of St. John's featured 14 3-point baskets—then a school record.

The team's five-win stretch that began with the Boston College victory solidified its spot in the Big East tournament.

On Feb. 21, 2004, West Virginia's basketball

program celebrated its 100th anniversary with a game against Pitt that featured the team wearing 1959 throwback uniforms. Former players were also invited back to campus to be recognized at halftime. As it did in 1970 when it defeated West Virginia in the final game at the old Field House, Pitt did not cooperate. Chevy Troutman and Julius Page scored 15 points each to lead the Panthers to a 67–58 victory.

In the first round of the Big East tournament, West Virginia battled back after an 11-point halftime deficit to take a late lead against Notre Dame, but Colin Falls nailed a 3 from the corner to put the Irish ahead 65–64, while Joe Herber's last-second shot missed.

At 15–13, West Virginia earned an NIT invitation and was sent on the road to face Kent State in an opening-round game. Sally poured in 17 points and Patrick Beilein came off the bench to contribute 14, leading West Virginia to a 65–54 victory.

Up next was a home game against Rhode Island. West Virginia held on for a 79–72 victory in a tough, back-and-forth contest. Sally led WVU with 17 points while Pittsnogle added 16.

WVU's bid to reach the NIT semifinals ended at Rutgers. The Knights got 26 points from Ricky Shields, and Quincy Douby added 15 in a 67–64 Scarlet Knight victory. Rutgers made 8 of 14 from 3-point distance. Fischer led the losing Mountaineers with 16 points.

Fischer, Sally and Pittsnogle each averaged better than 10 points per game, and all five starters were returning for the 2005 season. Gansey was also now available.

After two years on the job, the pieces were finally coming together for Beilein.

Elite Company

West Virginia won its first 10 games to begin the 2005 season, accumulating quality wins at

A panoramic view of West Virginia's basketball game against Pitt played at the WVU Coliseum on Feb. 21, 2004. The school celebrated its 100th year of basketball that night by wearing 1959 throwback uniforms.

VAN SLIDER PHOTOGRAPHY.

Forward Tyrone Sally scored 1,092 points and grabbed 513 rebounds during his four-year career from 2002–05. Here he is pictured throwing down two against Pitt at the WVU Coliseum in 2004.

ALL-PRO PHOTOGRAPHY/DALE SPARKS.

LSU (ending the Tigers' 56-game home winning streak against non-conference opponents), at home against 20th-ranked George Washington and against 17th-ranked NC State in Raleigh.

Sally scored 22, and Patrick Beilein came off the bench to hit six 3-pointers in an 84–69 victory in Baton Rouge. Against GW, Gansey scored 19 points in front of a sold-out Coliseum to help the Mountaineers to a 71–65 win over the Colonials.

Four days later, Gansey tallied 15 and grabbed 10 rebounds to lead WVU to an impressive 82–69 victory at NC State. It was just the fifth time a non-conference opponent had gone into the RBC Center and defeated the Wolfpack.

The NC State win got the Mountaineers into the national rankings for the first time in seven years at No. 21.

But West Virginia got a heavy dose of reality three days later when Villanova drilled the Mountaineers 84–46, and West Virginia lost five of its next six to make its record 11–6. Three of the five losses were to ranked teams.

The losing streak ended with an 82–78 victory at Providence in what turned out to be a key moment in the season. Sally scored 20, and Gansey added 19, and the Mountaineers shot 55.1 percent from the floor while making 11 3-pointers. A 16-point WVU lead was whittled to four with 2:46 left. "It probably wasn't pretty at times but it was a win and we didn't care how we got it," said Beilein.

West Virginia won seven of its next nine games, including a pair of big wins over nationally ranked Pitt, to put the Mountaineers back into the NCAA tournament picture. Pittsnogle, who became a full-time starter when Fischer missed the Pitt game because of illness, poured in 27 points to lead WVU to an 83–78 overtime victory over the Panthers in Morgantown. A second big victory at Pitt followed 18 days later. Once again, Pittsnogle led the way with 22 points in a 70–66 WVU triumph. The Mountaineers shot 72 percent in the second half including 75 percent (6 of 8) from 3-point range.

"We were probably the only guys who came here and expected to win—and that's what we did," said Pittsnogle afterward. "It was a great feeling and everyone was celebrating."

The Mountaineers split their remaining two games against Rutgers and Seton Hall to finish the regular season with an 18–9 record. Heading into the Big East tournament, West Virginia probably needed at least two victories to get off the NCAA tournament bubble. The Mountaineers wound up getting to the finals, taking New York City by storm.

Pittsnogle hit five 3-pointers and scored 24 points to lead West Virginia to an 82–59 opening-round victory over Providence. Sophomore Frank Young became the hero in the quarterfinals when he had to step into the lineup for Sally, who was sick with a stomach virus. Young hit three long first-half 3-pointers and Gansey scored 21 points to lead the Mountaineers to a 78–72 victory over seventh-rated Boston College. West Virginia led by as many as 25 points in the first half before things got testy in the second half. "We imploded there for . . . I don't know how long it was," said Beilein, "but it seemed like a year."

It was BC's final Big East game before moving on to the ACC. The New York tabloids said it all: "Best Virginia!"; "For Big East, BC is History"; and "Big Money in the Big Apple."

Wrote *Newsday's* Mike Lupica following the win over BC: "We had one of those games that make you pay attention to college basketball at this time of year, and makes you care, and even makes you shout."

The magic continued in the semifinals against 19th-ranked Villanova the following night. Gansey made a ridiculous hanging reverse layup, and then sank the game-winning free throws with 0.2 seconds left to knock off the Wildcats 78–76. This was the same Villanova team that embarrassed West Virginia by 38 points two months earlier.

"I never would have imagined this," admitted Gansey, who scored a team-high 22 points and had his picture on the front of the *Daily News* underneath the title "Mountain Do!"

Inset Kevin Pittsnogle scores two of his game-high 22 points to lead West Virginia to a 70–66 victory over Pitt at the Petersen Events Center on Feb. 23, 2005. This remains the Mountaineers' only victory at the Petersen Events Center.

ALL-PRO PHOTOGRAPHY/DALE SPARKS.

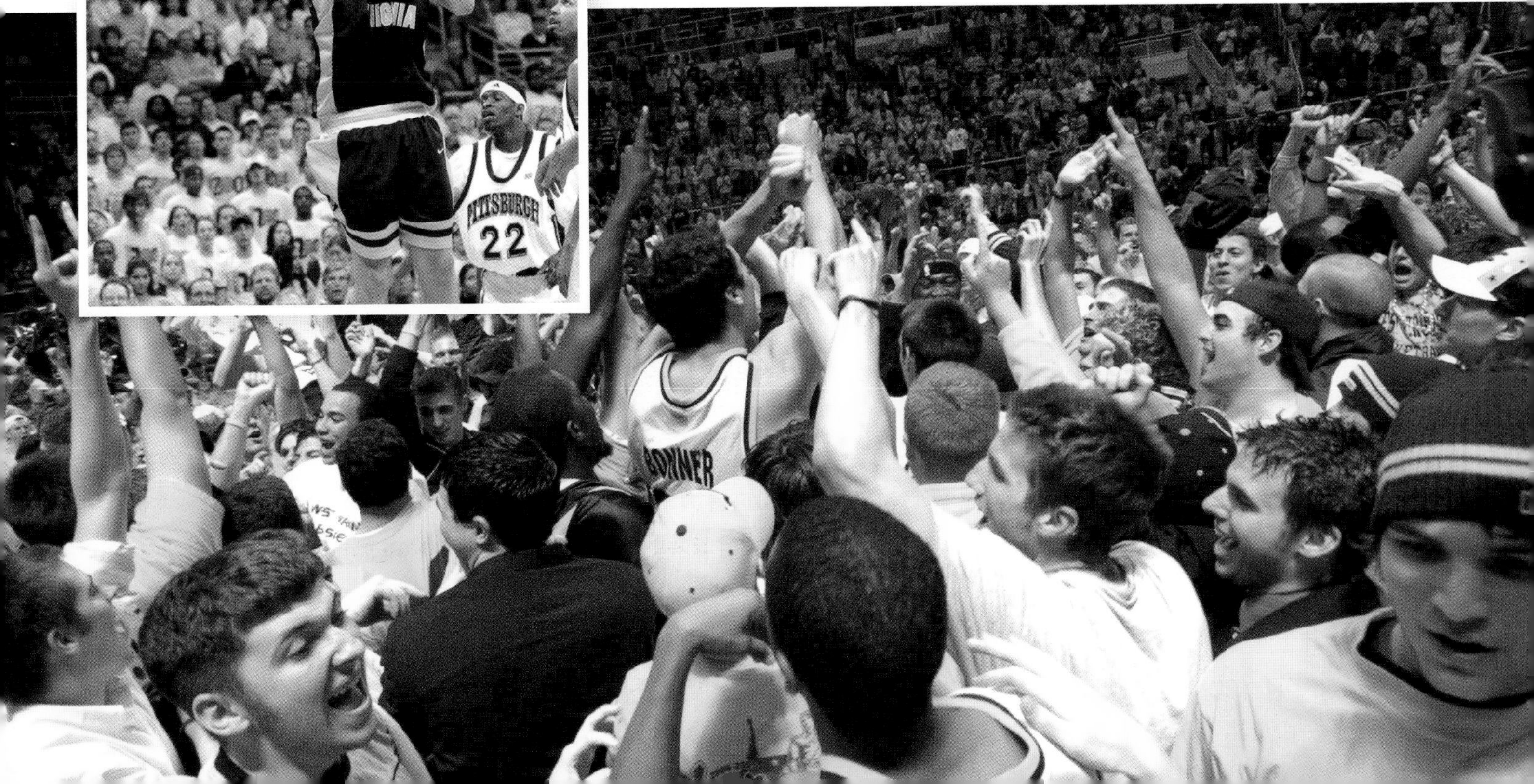

Below Students and players celebrate West Virginia's 83–78 overtime victory over Pitt in 2005 that snapped a five-game losing streak to the Panthers.

ALL-PRO PHOTOGRAPHY/DALE SPARKS.

ORANGE HOLDS OFF UCONN

Warrick, McNamara lead Syracuse past Huskies in physical semifinal: Rubin, P. 54

DAILY SPORTS NEWS

MOUNTAIN DO!

The *Boston Globe*'s Bob Ryan became an instant believer, "Why didn't someone tell me I was going to come down here and fall in love with West Virginia? Why didn't someone tell me how precise and efficient its offense is? Why didn't somebody tell me that West Virginia was a Princeton with talent?"

Wrote *Pittsburgh Post-Gazette*'s Ron Cook: "You don't have to be a West Virginia fan to appreciate what the West Virginia team did last night. But if you are a West Virginia fan? Let's just say a lot of basketball people around America are pretty envious of you and your team this morning."

Even when the glass slipper finally came off against Syracuse in the Big East tournament championship game (West Virginia's first-ever appearance), the praise continued.

"We now know what Cinderella looks like," wrote Dick Weiss of the *New York Daily News*. "It is the fundamentally sound team in blue and gold that is filled with juniors and seniors.

"Forget about whether the Mountaineers belong in the NCAA tournament. This is a team that can make a case to be a higher seed than neighboring Pitt, a perennial power West Virginia defeated twice in the regular season."

As great as this was, the best was yet to come.

The Mountaineers' performance in New York City made them an NCAA tournament lock, and the one place Beilein didn't want his team to go was Cleveland. He thought the pressure would be too great for Gansey playing at home in front friends and family.

"They go through the first pod of teams going to Cleveland, and I thought that was it," Beilein later told *Eastern Basketball*. "I turned to him and said, 'Mike, it's OK. Too many distractions.'

"I was just trying to make him feel better. Then, the second Cleveland pod came up (where West Virginia was sent), and I said, 'Mike, just kidding.'"

Nate Funk certainly was serious, as were his Creighton teammates—West Virginia's first-round opponent. The Bluejays flew out to a 10–0 lead before West Virginia fought back to tie it at 61. With time winding down, Tyler McKinney tried a game-winning shot from the left wing that fell short of the basket. Pittsnogle grabbed the rebound and threw the ball out

Top left Mike Gansey was the hero of West Virginia's Big East tournament semifinal victory over 19th-ranked Villanova at Madison Square Garden in New York City. Gansey scored 22 points and hit the winning free throws with 0.2 seconds left to give the Mountaineers a 78–76 victory.

BLUE & GOLD NEWS /KEVIN KINDER.

Left With starting forward Tyrone Sally out with the stomach flu, sophomore Frank Young stepped in and scored 14 points to help West Virginia to a 78–72 upset victory over seventh-ranked, No. 1-seeded Boston College in the 2005 Big East tournament quarterfinals.

BLUE & GOLD NEWS /KEVIN KINDER.

to Gansey on the wing. Gansey then flipped a picture-perfect pass to Sally, streaking all alone for the game-winning dunk with 2.4 seconds left on the clock. The ball never hit the floor.

"A great play," commented Beilein.

Funk scored 23 for Creighton, but West Virginia was much more balanced with Pittsnogle (17), Gansey (13) and Sally (12) all reaching double figures. West Virginia had survived and advanced.

Two nights later, awaiting West Virginia was second-seeded and fifth-ranked Wake Forest. The Demon Deacons certainly looked the part, jumping out to a 14-point advantage and leading by 13 at halftime. The game turned in the second half when Fischer replaced Pittsnogle at center to guard Wake center Eric Williams, and Gansey got hot in overtime. Gansey scored 19 points in the two extra sessions and finished the game with 29 points.

His 3-pointer with 40 seconds left in the first overtime erased the only lead Wake Forest had in either overtime. Then his two foul shots with 22 seconds to play gave WVU enough room to survive another Wake run to send the game into a second overtime.

In the second extra session, Gansey single-handedly gave WVU a 100–94 lead with a drive to the basket, a 3 from the corner, and two free throws on a play that also ended Wake guard Chris Paul's night. West Virginia held on for a 111–105 victory in one of the best college basketball games of the year.

Kevin Pittsnogle led West Virginia with 17 points and his rebound and outlet pass led to Tyrone Sally's winning dunk against Creighton.

ALL-PRO PHOTOGRAPHY/DALE SPARKS.

Both teams shot better than 50 percent from the floor and combined for 43 assists. Beilein was speechless—literally. He was suffering from laryngitis and had to whisper instructions to assistant coach Jeff Neubauer during the game. That still didn't stop Beilein from drawing a technical foul when he slammed his fist down on the scorer's table to dispute an official's call. "I wish I had a bad hand," whispered Beilein after the game. "Then maybe I wouldn't have slapped the [scorer's] table and got the technical."

Pittsnogle played a key role when Fischer fouled out in the second overtime. He drew a charge on Paul that gave the guard his fourth foul, and he later hit a huge 3-pointer from the corner to give the Mountaineers a seven-point lead.

"I know why I was on the bench," said Pittsnogle. "Eric Williams was just dominating me

Tyrone Sally slams home the winning basket for West Virginia against Creighton in this 2005 NCAA tournament first-round victory.

WVU PHOTOGRAPHIC SERVICES/BRIAN PERSINGER.

inside. And when we put D'or in, that stopped."

Texas Tech was awaiting West Virginia in the Sweet 16. The Red Raiders defeated UCLA and Gonzaga to get to the Sweet 16, and in the days leading up to the game, the focus was on Red Raider coach Bob Knight, now on the back nine of a brilliant coaching career. At the news conference the day before the game, Knight grew tired of answering questions about himself, so he changed the topic and began talking about how well coached the Mountaineers were and what a pleasure it was watching them play. "I throw that out to you guys because you probably wouldn't recognize that," Knight joked. "I'm just trying to help. I've turned over a new leaf. I'm really trying to help the press."

John Beilein acknowledges the crowd after his team's 111–105 double-overtime victory over fifth-ranked Wake Forest in this 2005 NCAA tournament second-round game in Cleveland.

ALL-PRO PHOTOGRAPHY/DALE SPARKS.

Knight was even more helpful after West Virginia's 65–60 win over his Red Raiders. "You don't usually play against a 1-3-1 zone . . . not many people play it," Knight said. "You've got to prepare for that, and, they're an extremely well-taught team at both ends of the floor . . . . They cover well on defense for one another and individually pressured. On offense, West Virginia has really good movement and reads very well.

"Anytime you get to this point, you can't ask for much more. Sometimes your team gets beat.

West Virginia players lock arms on the bench during the Mountaineers' 2005 NCAA tournament second-round game against Wake Forest.

ALL-PRO PHOTOGRAPHY/DALE SPARKS.

WEST VIRGINIA 111, WAKE FOREST 105

West Virginia outlasted second-seeded Wake Forest, 111–105 in a 2005 NCAA tournament second-round game in Cleveland in one of the best NCAA tournament performances in school history. It took two overtimes for WVU to finally come out on top.

Mike Gansey scored 29 points, including 19 in the two overtimes, and senior Tyrone Sally added 21 before fouling out in the first overtime to help lift the Mountaineers to the Sweet 16 for the first time in seven years.

The game began to turn in West Virginia's favor midway through the second half when the Mountaineers used a 7–0 run to reduce Wake's 10-point lead to a 54–51 advantage after Patrick Beilein converted a tough fade-away 16-footer.

A Sally three-point play with 2:16 remaining cut Wake Forest's lead to one, 70–69, and then a Sally backdoor dunk with 1:04 left gave West Virginia its first lead of the game, 73–72.

"They were being aggressive on the wings and Coach (Beilein) was like, 'Take the alley drives.' That's what we did. We were aggressive and attacked it and did a good job of getting by them, sealing them off and finishing," said Collins.

Collins padded the lead with a pair of free throws with 41 seconds left, but a pair of misses by Gansey and Herber opened the door for Downey to sink a 3 from the corner to tie the game with 18 seconds to go.

Collins had a good chance to win it in regulation, but his driving layup grazed off the backside of the rim, and D'or Fischer's stick-back try wouldn't go.

"We knew this game was going to be a matter of runs, it was just a matter of who was going to play defense and get the crucial stops at the end," said Sally.

The ending was in dramatic contrast to the first half when Wake Forest (27–6) played like the team many were predicting to win the national championship. The Demon Deacons were able to use their superior athletic ability and tremendous inside play from 6-foot-9, 291-pound junior center Eric Williams to chase West Virginia out of its 1-3-1 zone. At one point, Wake made eight straight field goal attempts (mostly dunks) to build a double-digit lead.

The scoreboard says it all after West Virginia stunned No. 2-seeded and fifth-ranked Wake Forest in the second round of the 2005 NCAA tournament.

ALL-PRO PHOTOGRAPHY/DALE SPARKS.

With starters Sally and J. D. Collins, and key reserve D'or Fischer all sitting on the bench with five fouls, West Virginia was able to overcome long odds behind the brilliant play of Gansey, who made 9 of 16 field goal attempts and 9 of 12 from the free throw line for his career-high scoring total.

"This is just a dream come true," said Gansey. "Obviously, when Tyrone fouled out, I thought maybe I would put more upon myself to be more aggressive and try and take the game over. In regulation, I missed a free throw that could have maybe sealed the deal, but God was looking down on me today and He gave me all the power."

The Olmsted Falls, Ohio, resident took over the second overtime by scoring West Virginia's first seven points to help the Mountaineers to a 100–94 lead. After a pair of Taron Downey free throws trimmed West Virginia's lead to four, Kevin Pittsnogle drilled a huge 3-pointer from the wing to put the Mountaineers up seven, 103–96, with 2:32 remaining on the game clock.

A key moment for Wake Forest came in the second overtime when All-American guard Chris Paul was called for his fifth foul attempting to draw a charge on Gansey with 3:29 left. Paul finished the game 22 points.

WVU freshman Darris Nichols hit a couple of high-pressure free throws with 1:33 remaining in the second OT to build West Virginia's lead to eight, and Johannes Herber made a layup and added a pair of free throws with eight seconds left to ice it.

We got as good an effort as we could get."

Beilein couldn't believe what he read in the newspaper the next day. Did Knight really say those things about his basketball team? Many years ago when Beilein was courting his wife Kathleen, one of the things he told her was that one day he was going to coach against Bobby Knight. It had finally happened—and he won.

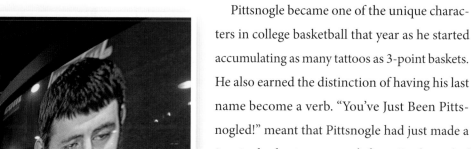

A view of Kevin Pittsnogle on the television monitor while he answers a question during a press conference before West Virginia's NCAA tournament game against Texas Tech in Albuquerque, New Mexico.

ALL-PRO PHOTOGRAPHY/DALE SPARKS.

Pittsnogle scored 22 points and West Virginia hit 9 of 22 from 3-point distance to knock off the Red Raiders. It was West Virginia's deepest run in the NCAAs since the 1959 team reached the finals.

Unfortunately, all that stood in the way of West Virginia reaching the Final Four was a missed shot at the buzzer against Louisville that could have given the Mountaineers a 79–77 victory.

The 93–85 defeat was particularly tough to take because the Cardinals had stormed back from a 20-point first-half deficit. The two teams combined to make an NCAA tournament-record 29 3-pointers, eclipsing the record of 24 set by Loyola-Marymount and UNLV in 1990. "I have never seen such shooting like that in my life—such range," said Louisville coach Rick Pitino.

Pittsnogle scored 25 points, and Sally contributed 11 in his final game at WVU. (Sally was the only scholarship player remaining from the Catlett years.) West Virginia's 24–11 record was good enough to get it back into the national rankings at No. 12 in the USA Today/ESPN Coaches' poll.

Pittsnogle became one of the unique characters in college basketball that year as he started accumulating as many tattoos as 3-point baskets. He also earned the distinction of having his last name become a verb. "You've Just Been Pittsnogled!" meant that Pittsnogle had just made a 3-point basket in someone's face. By the end of his career, "You've Just Been Pittsnogled!" t-shirts were selling better than Jerry West jerseys at the campus bookstore.

Sally was the team's leading scorer, averaging 12.2 points per game, but more pleasing to Beilein was Sally earning his college degree. Beilein had to fight back tears when he was once asked to talk about Sally finally earning enough credits to graduate.

An estimated 6,000 fans greeted the team at the WVU Coliseum upon its return from Albuquerque, N.M. The team spent more than an hour signing autographs afterward.

"One of the greatest regrets I have is that I couldn't experience it the way the fans did," Beilein said. "I hear the stories of this bar in Charleston or this little community in an old mining town where families are all together holding hands and watching the games—or students on spring break taking over a bar to watch the game.

"I wish I could watch the people having fun. I wish I could be on High Street and watch the students celebrate," he said. "You don't see the hugging. I'm watching the Wake Forest game on ESPN afterwards, and I could hear the 'Let's Go Mountaineers' chant going on the whole game. I didn't hear it at all during the game because I was coaching the game."

For Beilein, who had labored so long and so hard to get to this point in his coaching career, the 2005 season was almost a dream.

The success continued in 2006. With Pittsnogle, Gansey, Beilein, Collins, Young, Herber and Darris Nichols returning, the Mountaineers began the season ranked 14th in the country.

Three consecutive losses to Texas, Kentucky and LSU knocked WVU out of the rankings, but those games also showed that the Mountaineers were willing to schedule the best teams in the country. Two of the three losses (to Texas and LSU) were only by a combined four points.

A 92–68 win over seventh-ranked Oklahoma in Oklahoma City on Dec. 22, 2005, got the Mountaineers back on track. Pittsnogle scored 25 points, Herber added 21, and WVU shot a sizzling 66.7 percent (32 of 48) for the game. "We've played as good a basketball game as we've played in West Virginia uniforms against obviously a very good team," said Beilein after the game.

Oklahoma coach Kelvin Sampson was at a loss trying to figure out how to guard Pittsnogle. "We have never played anybody like him," Sampson told *Sports Illustrated* writer Grant Wahl a month later. "He's a two-guard who grew to 6′11″. They hardly ever post him up, and he's always open because it's foreign for big guys to go out and cover him."

That was until two weeks later when West Virginia went on the road to knock off third-ranked Villanova. Now back in the national rankings, the Mountaineers were able to overcome a 58 percent shooting night by the Wildcats by shooting 51.6 percent themselves. Herber led the way with 23 points, while Pittsnogle scored 22 and Gansey 21.

"The way we ended up spreading the floor it was almost a European style," Beilein explained. "Just like the Oklahoma game when people won't hop off of Kevin, well, where's the shot blocker? The shot blocker is outside and we tried to open the floor as much we could."

Gansey was the difference in West Virginia's 60–56 upset victory at 18th-ranked UCLA. The guard scored 24 points and picked Jordan Farmar clean underneath the UCLA basket when the Bruins had a chance to win the game at the end. Farmar fouled Gansey on the play, and Gansey made both free throws to give the Mountaineers a four-point victory.

Left John Beilein and Louisville coach Rick Pitino spend a moment together during a live interview for CBS prior to West Virginia's game against the Cardinals in the regional finals in Albuquerque, New Mexico.

ALL-PRO PHOTOGRAPHY/DALE SPARKS.

"I loved the idea that they came back and we didn't give in," said Beilein.

Two more big wins came on the road at 15th-ranked Georgetown when Pittsnogle scored 25, and at home against 8th-ranked Pitt following another big Pittsnogle performance with 26 points. The home victory avenged a 59–53 loss at Pittsburgh 12 days prior.

"It was a great basketball game and obviously I feel a lot better because we won the game," said Beilein. "The game at Pitt a couple of weeks ago and this game—that's why college basketball is so much fun to attend, to cover, to coach and to play."

After a brief appearance in the Big East tournament, the Mountaineers were heading into NCAA play on a two-game losing streak, dropping their final regular-season game at Cincinnati and losing to Pitt in New York City.

Sixth-seeded West Virginia faced Missouri Valley champion Southern Illinois in the opening round of the NCAA tournament. Pittsnogle scored 18 points, and West Virginia held the Salukis to just 42.6 percent shooting in a 64–46 victory. In the second round, WVU met Northwestern State—first-round upset winners over

Jerry West addresses the crowd at the WVU Coliseum during a ceremony to officially retire his jersey number 44. The ceremony took place on Nov. 26, 2005 at halftime of the LSU game.

ALL-PRO PHOTOGRAPHY/DALE SPARKS.

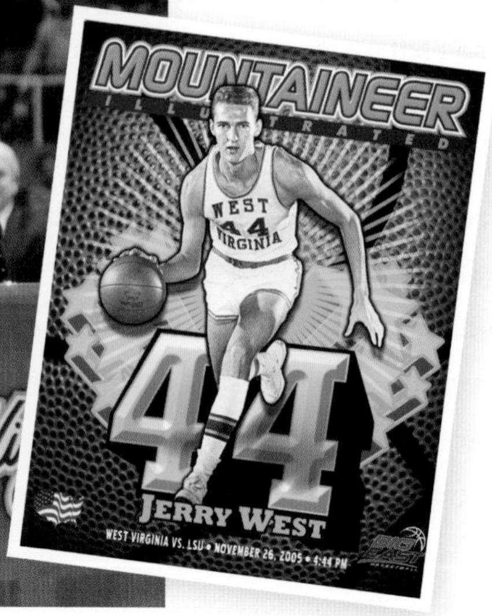

Iowa. Pittsnogle led four double-figure scorers with 14 points in a fairly routine 67–54 victory, taking the team to its second consecutive trip to the Sweet 16.

"To get to this point it's very, very rewarding and I'm very grateful to have this opportunity," Beilein said. "But what I'm most grateful about are some of the guys I've been able to coach because without them this doesn't happen."

The Sweet 16 was a rematch against a ninth-ranked Texas team that featured two outstanding front-line players in LaMarcus Aldridge and P. J. Tucker. Back in November, the Longhorns had pulled out a 76–75 victory over WVU.

Everybody's Been Pittsnogled!

Pittsnogle's outside shooting helped erase a 12-point halftime deficit and his clutch 3 from the top of the key with five seconds remaining tied the game at 71. Unfortunately, enough time was still left on the clock for Kenton Paulino to make his own 3-pointer ahead of the buzzer, ousting West Virginia from the tournament. Tears flowed freely in the locker room after the game.

"With five seconds left after Kevin hit that 3, it's just very hard with their quickness to match up," explained Beilein. "In five seconds you go straight to the basket and I thought we fanned them out enough, but I don't know if there was anything else we could have done."

A 22–11 record closed the final chapter on

Above Kevin Pittsnogle scored 1,708 career points and earned John Wooden All-America honors in 2006 after averaging 19.3 points and 5.5 rebounds per game during his senior season.
ALL-PRO PHOTOGRAPHY/DALE SPARKS.

Left Mike Gansey goes up for a jump shot in this game against Connecticut at the WVU Coliseum on Feb. 18, 2006. Gansey scored a game-high 25 points in an 81-75 loss to the No. 1-ranked Huskies.
ALL-PRO PHOTOGRAPHY/DALE SPARKS PHOTO.

Above Coach John Beilein with his five graduating senior players, from left to right: Johannes Herber, Kevin Pittsnogle, J. D. Collins, Mike Gansey and Patrick Beilein.

ALL-PRO PHOTOGRAPHY/DALE SPARKS.

Left West Virginia's remarkable 2006 senior class pictured on senior day with coach John Beilein. From left to right are Patrick Beilein, Kevin Pittsnogle, J. D. Collins, Mike Gansey and Johannes Herber.

ALL-PRO PHOTOGRAPHY/DALE SPARKS.

WVU's outstanding senior class of Pittsnogle, Gansey, Herber, Collins and Patrick Beilein. "It's sad for these five that have worked so hard and to have it end one day is very difficult for everyone to grasp right now," said Beilein after the Texas loss. "But I'm so proud of them for the way they fought back tonight and the way they have fought back throughout their careers. They can hold their heads high for what they have accomplished."

Pittsnogle averaged 19.3 points per game and shot 40.1 percent from 3 to earn John Wooden All-America honors, becoming the first WVU player to make an All-America first team since Wil Robinson in 1972. Pittsnogle finished his WVU career sixth in scoring with 1,708 points, while Patrick Beilein completed his career by scoring 1,001 points. Gansey averaged 16.8 points and 5.7 rebounds per game, and he came within 24 points of becoming the third player on the team to reach 1,000.

Herber was not only a stellar player, but he was equally outstanding in the classroom where he earned a 4.0 grade point average for his academic career. Herber was recognized by the WVU Foundation as one of its 30 outstanding seniors campus wide.

Rebuilding or Reloading?

With the nucleus of the 2006 team gone, West Virginia was in store for an extensive rebuilding job in 2007. The question for a good portion of the spring was whether or not John Beilein was going to be around to oversee it. NC State's month-long search for Herb Sendek's replacement had also included Beilein, who was previously mentioned in published reports for job openings at Indiana and Missouri.

In late April, Beilein eventually put an end to the speculation by issuing a statement that he intended to remain at West Virginia for a fifth season.

Perhaps Beilein's best coaching effort at WVU came in 2007 when he had to break in four new starters. The group he eventually settled on included Young and sophomore Joe Alexander at forwards, senior Rob Summers at center, and sophomore Alex Ruoff and junior Darris Nichols at guards. These five players started all 36 games that season.

West Virginia ran off a 12–1 record to start the season with its only loss coming against Arkansas in the Old Spice Classic in Orlando. The Mountaineers beat NC State 71–60 in Charleston, and pulled off three

Far left Darris Nichols drives to the basket in this game at UCLA's Pauley Pavilion in 2006. The Mountaineers stunned the 18th-ranked Bruins 60–56.

RICH SCHMITT.

Left Walk-on guard Ted Talkington played a key role coming off the bench when starter Alex Ruoff got into foul trouble during this 70–65 upset of No. 2-ranked UCLA on Feb. 10, 2007.

VAN SLIDER PHOTOGRAPHY.

straight wins in Morgantown against Connecticut, Villanova and St. John's to begin Big East play. Another four-game winning streak followed at the end of January that included a 77–63 win over Marshall in Charleston, which snapped a two-game losing streak to the Herd

Three weeks later, West Virginia managed a surprising 70–65 victory over second-ranked UCLA at the Coliseum. Ruoff scored 18 points and West Virginia held the Bruins to just 38.7 percent shooting in one of Beilein's best wins at WVU. The Mountaineers also got inspiring play off the bench from walk-on guard Ted Talkington, who hit a pair of clutch 3-pointers when Ruoff was mired in foul trouble.

Most pleasing to Beilein was the fact that the Mountaineers were able to knock off a top-rated team at home in front of the fans. "There have been a few times when we've had top-ranked teams come in here and we almost got there," said Beilein. "That's the big thing here—we got the momentum to have people come back."

A 79–65 victory over Cincinnati in Morgantown snapped a two-game losing streak at the end of the regular season to give the Mountaineers a 9–7 league record heading into the Big East tournament.

After easily beating Providence in the first round, the Mountaineers lost a tough 82–71 overtime decision to 12th-ranked Louisville in the quarterfinals. Darris Nichols only scored eight points, but two of them came with 4.3 seconds left on a drive to the basket to give WVU a 66–64 lead. But U of L's Edgar Sosa was the beneficiary of a slow Madison Square Garden clock, giving him enough time to drive the length of the court to make a layup to send the game into overtime.

Despite a 22–9 record that included quality wins over NC State, Villanova and UCLA, West Virginia was denied what would have been its third-straight NCAA tournament appearance. Instead, the Mountaineers were invited to the NIT where they won three straight in Morgantown over Delaware State (74–50), Massachusetts (90–77) and NC State (71–66) to get to the semifinals in New York City.

Nichols hit a fall-away

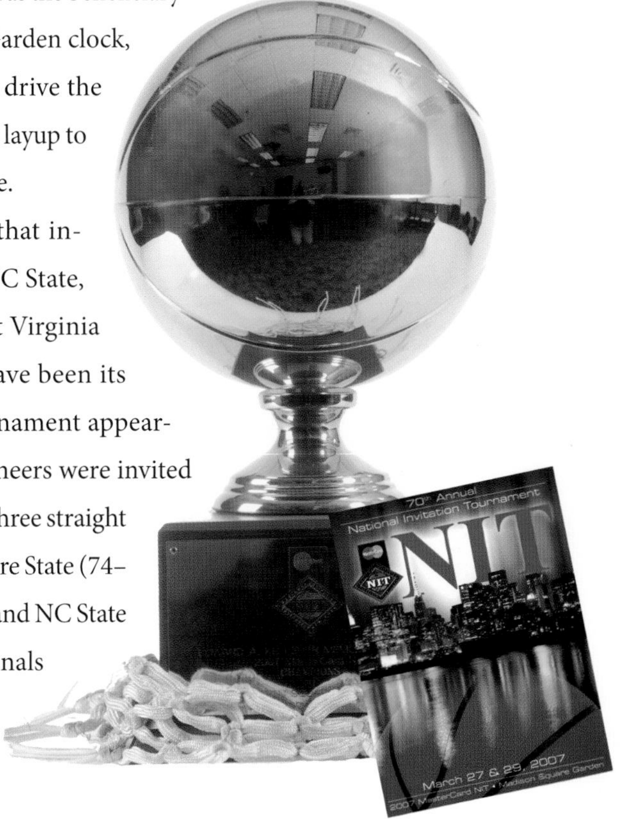

WEST VIRGINIA 78, CLEMSON 73

Senior Frank Young's 24 points helped West Virginia to a 78–73 win over Clemson to capture the 2007 National Invitation Tournament. It was West Virginia's first NIT title since Dyke Raese's Mountaineer team upset Long Island, Toledo and Western Kentucky to win the 1942 NIT championship.

Young was the tournament's most outstanding performer, averaging 22.6 points in five games and shooting 63.9 percent from the floor, including a phenomenal 68.5 percent from 3-point range (24 of 35). In the championship game against Clemson, Young was 7 of 10 from the floor, including 6 of 7 from 3-point distance.

"Frank Young was marvelous the whole game," said West Virginia coach John Beilein.

West Virginia (27–9) used a 12–2 run at the end of the first half to take control of the game. After James Mays's steal and dunk pulled the Tigers to within two, 26–24, West Virginia got consecutive 3-point baskets by Young, and a pair of 3-pointers by Jamie Smalligan and Da'Sean Butler to take a 38–24 lead with 1:10 left in the half.

West Virginia's biggest lead of the game came with 14:53 remaining when Young made his fifth 3 to give the Mountaineers a 49–32 advantage.

Clemson (25–11) made things interesting when Trevor Booker blocked Smalligan's 3-point shot attempt at the top of the key, retrieved the ball and went in for a one-handed slam to pull the Tigers to within 10 at 55–45.

Butler immediately answered with a pretty pull-up jumper, and the freshman added a 3 with 7:23 left to make it a 15-point lead again.

Clemson used a 13–2 run over the remaining 1:05 to make it a five-point game.

"We had a few errors, but we really played to win," said Beilein. "We played to win from the beginning to the end and give Clemson an awful lot of credit."

Frank Young fires in one of his six 3-point baskets against Clemson in the NIT championship game at Madison Square Garden in New York City. Young finished the game with 24 points to earn tournament MVP honors.

ALL-PRO PHOTOGRAPHY/DALE SPARKS.

West Virginia had a 32-to-5 advantage in bench scoring—20 coming from Butler on 8 of 15 shooting. Darris Nichols, who joined Young on the NIT all-tournament team, scored 13 points on 6 of 10 shooting. "If there is a better backcourt in the country [than Nichols, Ruoff and Mazzulla] . . . there might be a few, but they're not juniors, sophomores and freshmen," said Beilein. "That was a pretty good performance by those two and Joe Mazzulla coming off the bench."

West Virginia made 29 of 56 from the floor for 51.8 percent, including 12 of 20 from 3 for 60 percent.

"It's been a lot of fun to play in this tournament, and all the emotions just built up as it went along," Young said. "Of course, we wanted to be in the NCAA tournament. But to win this tournament, all the joy is still there. We're still happy about finishing our season with a win.

"It was gratifying just to see how far I've come as a player," Young said. "The trophy signifies that I did a pretty good job leading this team."

K. C. Rivers scored 18 points to lead Clemson. Vernon Hamilton added 16, Booker scored 13, Cliff Hammonds had 11 and Mays finished with 10.

Clemson shot 47.7 percent (31 of 65), but was just 6 of 22 from behind the 3-point arc for 27.3 percent. "The story of the game is us giving up 3s and them making 3s," Clemson coach Oliver Purnell said. West Virginia's 27 victories were the most by a WVU team since Gale Catlett's 1982 squad posted a 27–4 record. The Mountaineers were 73–31 during John Beilein's final three seasons at West Virginia.

shot from the corner just ahead of the buzzer to beat Mississippi State in the semifinals, and Young poured in 24 points. Freshman Da'Sean Butler added 20 to lead West Virginia to a 78–73 victory over Clemson in the championship game. It was the school's second NIT title.

"Frank Young was marvelous the whole game," said Beilein. "When he was in the first half I was thinking to myself, 'If he gets that third foul I'm going to put him back out on that track.' He hit two 3s and it worked out great."

Young had a fabulous tournament, earning MVP honors, and scoring 17, 31, 25, 16 and 24 points in five consecutive games.

Young was the team's top scorer (15.3 ppg) and 3-point shooter (117), while also hitting 43.3 percent of his 3-point attempts. Nichols (10.9 ppg), Alexander (10.3 ppg), Ruoff (10.3 ppg) and Butler (10.1 ppg) also averaged double figures.

"Sometimes good things must come to an end," Beilein said of his departure.

Beilein's five-year record of 104–60 included a pair of NCAA tournament appearances and two trips to the NIT. His 2005 team was a basket away from reaching the Final Four, and he became the first coach in school history to have teams make back-to-back NCAA tournament Sweet 16 appearances. Beilein's teams were also competitive in Big East play, going 40–40 during a five-year span including a 20–12 mark over his final two years.

Considering the tremendous obstacles that he had to overcome during his first year at West Virginia in 2003, Beilein's ensuing four seasons were truly outstanding.

Pastilong was once again hunting for a basketball coach. This time one of West Virginia's own was ready to come home.

Off to Michigan

Three days after the Clemson win, Beilein resigned with five years remaining on his West Virginia contract to take the Michigan job. A $2.5 million buyout provision in a reworked deal Beilein signed after the 2005 season was eventually settled for $1.5 million, which Beilein agreed to pay in five yearly installments.

"We want to thank John Beilein for his five years at West Virginia University and the success that he has brought to the program," remarked WVU Director of Athletics Ed Pastilong. "Under his leadership, WVU has achieved new levels of national prominence and success within the Big East Conference.

"While we wanted John to remain our coach for the remainder of his coaching career, he has made the decision to leave West Virginia University. We wish him the best in this new chapter of his coaching career."

Coach John Beilein addresses a sea of gold in the WVU student section before West Virginia's game against UCLA in 2007.

VAN SLIDER PHOTOGRAPHY.

Dream Job

Bob Huggins back home again at West Virginia

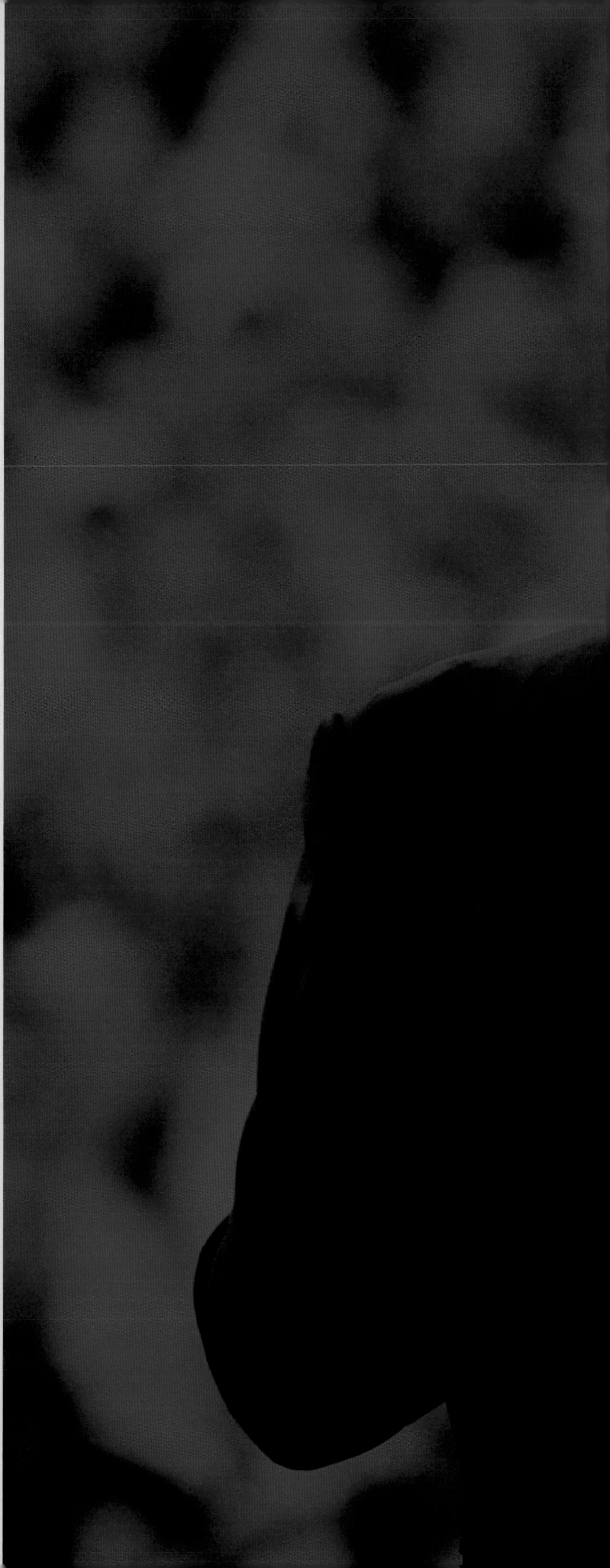

14

Huggs Comes Home

(2007–2010)

Bob Huggins has made 18 NCAA tournament appearances at three different schools, including trips to the Final Four with Cincinnati in 1992 and with West Virginia in 2010.

WVU PHOTOGRAPHIC SERVICES/M.G. ELLIS.

Just two days after John Beilein announced his resignation to take the Michigan job, West Virginia had already identified his replacement: Bob Huggins.

"I've wanted to be here since I was a little kid," Huggins said at the time of his hiring. "Sometimes for whatever reasons, it's not the right time."

Coach Bob Huggins acknowledges the applause during Mountaineer Madness to tip off the 2008 basketball season.

ALL-PRO PHOTOGRAPHY/DALE SPARKS.

But this was the right time. Following a path somewhat similar to the one Gale Catlett took to WVU 30 years prior, it took Huggins and West Virginia two different attempts to reach a workable agreement. The second time, the negotiations didn't take nearly as long, and Huggins joked that WVU Director of Athletics Ed Pastilong wouldn't let him use his reading glasses to examine the fine print on the term sheet he had just signed. "Eddie said, 'It'll be fine, sign here.'"

Born in Morgantown and raised on basketball by well-known high school coach Charlie Huggins in Midvale, Ohio, Huggins was a star player for his father at Indian Valley South High School, where they managed to produce a 26–0 record during Bob's senior year in 1972. Hotly pursued by a long list of schools, Huggins chose Ohio University in Athens over Ohio State. It was a surprising choice considering Ohio State was enjoying a golden era in basketball at the time, winning the national championship in 1960 and claiming seven Big Ten titles during Huggins's formative years from 1960–71.

When Huggs grew dissatisfied with his experience at Ohio University, he decided to transfer to West Virginia where both sets of his grandparents were living. His father had also spent a year at WVU in 1952 before going to Alderson-Broaddus College.

"West Virginia was more my style than Ohio U.," Huggins once said. "The place was different. The players were different. There were more people like me."

As a transfer Huggins had to sit out his first year in 1974, spending that time giving Sonny Moran's WVU players a look on the scout team. A year later in 1975, playing for new coach Joedy Gardner, Huggins won a spot in the starting lineup at shooting guard. In 1976, Huggins moved to small forward with the arrival of standout junior college shooting guard Tony Robertson. And then, during his senior year in 1977, Huggins switched to point guard where he had his best season, averaging 13.2 points and handing out a team-high 109 assists to lead the Mountaineers to one of their strongest campaigns in more than a decade. After a tryout with the Philadelphia 76ers, Huggins started his coaching career as a graduate assistant at WVU in 1978.

Two years on Eldon Miller's staff at Ohio State afforded Huggins the opportunity to get his first head coaching job at NAIA Walsh College in 1980 when he was just 27.

Four years later, including a one-season stint as an assistant coach at Central Florida, Huggins landed his first Division I head coaching job at Akron. Five years after that he reached the big time at Cincinnati, where he guided the Bearcats to a phenomenal 399–127 record in 16 seasons. He took UC to the Final Four in 1992 and led Cincinnati to 10 regular-season conference titles and eight tournament championships. Huggins was a three-time Conference USA coach of the year and was the unanimous choice as C-USA's coach of the decade. In nearly 100 seasons of basketball, never before had West Virginia University managed to hire a basketball coach with a national pedigree quite like that of Bob Huggins.

Happy Homecoming

Bob Huggins had always held West Virginia close to his heart with many of his aunts, uncles and cousins still residing in the area.

"I can't remember whether I was playing here or I was a GA here, but one of the football coaches once came up to me—he was a West Virginian and a great guy—and he put his arm around me and he said, 'Huggs, just remember this: the greatest resource in the state of West Virginia isn't coal. The greatest resource is people. We are the greatest people in the world.' I never forgot that and I've always believed that."

Dream Job

Bob Huggins back home again at West Virginia

COLLEGE BASKETBALL

Huggins: I'm home and happy

"West Virginia people are different than anybody else in the world," added Huggins's WVU teammate Warren Baker. "I'm a West Virginian. I haven't left and I won't because of that. We're very loyal people, and we love people who are dedicated to our program and our cause."

Bob Huggins answers a question during his introductory press conference at the WVU Coliseum on Good Friday, April 6, 2007.

WVU PHOTO SERVICES/BRIAN PERSINGER.

Deciding to return to his birthplace and his alma mater was easy. Telling Kansas State that he was leaving after just one year was not. In fact, it was excruciating. Huggins had developed a strong sense of loyalty to Kansas State during his brief time with the school, and he was leaving one of the best recruiting classes in the country. "I left a great situation at Kansas State with wonderful people who are as close to West Virginia people as you can get," Huggins said.

What West Virginia was getting in Bob Huggins was one of college basketball's best coaches. Huggins had compiled a 590–211 record in 25 total seasons of coaching. He ranked sixth in total victories and eighth in winning percentage among active Division I head coaches when he returned to his alma mater.

"There are good coaches and there are great coaches," said Jerry West. "Bob is one of the greats."

Huggins, who grew up patterning his playing style after West, had developed a strong relationship with him through the years. "The first time I ever met Jerry was at the Final Four in Dallas. I was at the University of Akron and I'm standing there taking it all in— I'm 30 years old and I'm kind of in awe of everything that's going on," Huggins said.

"This guy puts his long arm around me and I turn around and I see that it's Jerry. I had met Jerry when I was here a time or two," Huggins said. "We stood and talked for about as long as Jerry could talk before he was being surrounded by people. He said, 'Here is my ticket number and this is where I'm sitting. Come inside and we'll talk.' He's been phenomenal to me over the years."

Huggins said West's insights were invaluable to him when he was twice offered NBA coaching jobs. "I had the opportunity to go to the NBA a few times and the first guy I called was Jerry to ask him for his advice—what he thought about situations," Huggins said.

In just one season at Kansas State, Huggins revived a dormant Wildcat program—his 23 victories were only two shy of the school record. At Cincinnati, where he made 14 straight trips to the NCAA tournament, his roster of professional basketball players was impressive: Kenyon Martin, Danny Fortson, Corie Blount, DerMarr Johnson, Nick Van Exel, Jason Maxiell, Ruben Patterson, Steve Logan, Kenny Satterfield, Tony

Bobbitt and James White. Huggins's easygoing personality and his relentless work ethic made him one of college basketball's best recruiters.

His style of play was drastically different than the system Beilein utilized for five years at West Virginia. Huggins preferred big, physical players that could get out into the open court. He wanted his big players to be able to get to the rim and his guards to be able to score off the dribble. All of them had to be able to defend.

"I like to play faster. I like to score," Huggins told a gathering of several hundred people at the Coliseum when he was announced as the school's new coach. "You have to guard and you have to do all those things, but you have to score. I like to watch us score. I like to see the ball go in."

Right away Huggins proved that he could be adaptable, starting with a powerhouse coaching staff that included former head coaches Billy Hahn and Larry Harrison, and ex-UC player Erik Martin. The roster of players Huggs inherited from Beilein was assembled specifically to run Beilein's free-shooting, motion-based offensive system. Seven-foot center Jamie Smalligan had transferred from Butler to play for Beilein because he saw what Kevin Pittsnogle was able to do in a system that allowed its 7-footers to shoot 3-pointers. However, playing for Huggins would force Smalligan to learn to play inside.

Athletic 6-foot-8 forward Joe Alexander spent the majority of his time playing on the wing. The same went for Alex Ruoff, Da'Sean Butler and Wellington Smith. Huggins wisely chose to keep the style that fit the players he inherited while gradually working in the things he wanted to do. His very first command was that they all get into the weight room and get stronger. "To me life is about continually bumping up your comfort level. How comfortable are you?" Huggins said.

Fast Start

In 2008, West Virginia got off to a fast start by winning 10 of its first 11 games. The only setback was a 74–72 loss to seventh-ranked Tennessee in Newark, N.J., as part of the Legends Classic. The Mountaineers collected early-season victories

Coach Bob Huggins with his coaching staff in 2008. From left to right: Erik Martin, Larry Harrison, Huggins and Bill Hahn.

ALL-PRO PHOTOGRAPHY/DALE SPARKS.

over New Mexico State, Winthrop, Auburn and Duquesne to crack the national rankings.

After Christmas, West Virginia had several opportunities to defeat Oklahoma in a game played in Charleston, building leads of five points in the first overtime and four points in the second overtime. But both times the Sooners rallied behind the outstanding play of freshman center Blake Griffin (an NBA No. 1 draft pick in 2009). Oklahoma eventually pulled out the game 88–82 in double overtime. Five days later, West Virginia began Big East play with a 69–56 loss at Notre Dame—one of just two times the Mountaineers lost back-to-back games all season.

WVU rebounded with a dominating 79–64 performance against 10th-ranked Marquette. After a couple of telephone conversations with USC coach Tim Floyd and Middle Tennessee State coach Kermit Davis, Huggins decided to use a triangle-and-two defense to slow down Marquette's great trio of guards. The strategy worked better than even Huggins expected. Marquette finished the first half with just 28 points and 11 turnovers. Alexander and Ruoff each had 19 points for WVU.

Another big win came against Syracuse on Jan. 13 at the Coliseum. West Virginia's 20-point victory was keyed by John Flowers's block of a Rick Jackson dunk. The play energized the crowd and led to a 19–9 West Virginia run that built the Mountaineers' lead to 12. Ruoff was the high scorer with 23 points against the Orange.

"I think John Flowers made the play that really got the game going in the right direction when he makes the great block from behind," Huggins said. "It was a big-time hustle play. We get the ball back and it gets the crowd in the game and kind of gets us going."

Far right Guard Alex Ruoff scored 1,420 points and made a school-record 261 3-point field goals during his four-year career from 2006–2009.
ALL-PRO PHOTOGRAPHY/DALE SPARKS.

Above WVU Director of Athletics Ed Pastilong presents Bob Huggins with a framed picture commemorating his 600th career victory. Joining Pastilong and Huggins in the picture are June Huggins and Gov. Joe Manchin.
ALL-PRO PHOTOGRAPHY/DALE SPARKS.

A 77–65 victory at Providence on Feb. 2 snapped another two-game losing streak and put the Mountaineers back over .500 in conference play. Darris Nichols made 7 of 10 from the floor, including 4 of 6 from 3 for a season-high 23 points.

Five days later, West Virginia almost had a big road win in the bag at No. 21 Pitt until Ronald

Ramon hit a buzzer-beating 3-pointer from the wing to give the Panthers a 55–54 victory. Huggins said Ramon was the one Pitt player that he told his players not to leave open.

"We're switching everything," said Huggins. "We switch, we have them covered and we leave their best player for no apparent reason. We just leave him wide open after we switched on him.

"It was a ball screen—we've got them covered; we've got a 5'10" guy covered with our best athlete. We stop them, [Ramon] gives the ball back to the screener who can't beat us and we leave the only guy who can beat us," Huggins said.

WVU was able to overcome the Pitt loss with consecutive home wins over Rutgers and Seton Hall, and another two-game winning streak against Providence and DePaul boosted West Virginia's record to 20–8 overall and 9–6 in conference play.

The emergence of Joe Alexander came in a 79–71 loss at 15th-ranked Connecticut when the forward scored 32 points and grabbed 10 rebounds.

Alexander had one of the more unique basketball backgrounds of any player in WVU history. He spent a good portion of his childhood living in China (his father is president and CEO of the Adelson Center for U.S.-China Enterprise), and when he came back to the States before his junior year of high school in Mt. Airy, Md., most of what he knew about the sport he either learned on his own or from playing video games.

Alexander's two-year career at Linganore High School was remarkable in that it was so unremarkable—his only firm scholarship offer came from Division III Washington College. Believing he could do better than that, Alexander chose to play at Hargrave Military Academy where he was eventually discovered by WVU assistant coach Jeff Neubauer. It was there that Alexander told Neubauer that his goal was to one day play in the NBA. Of course young players say that all of the time, but Alexander said it to Neubauer in such convincing fashion. "He wasn't even starting for his prep school team and I believed him," Neubauer laughed.

Alexander had played so little at Hargrave that he barely averaged a point a game. Neubauer had seen enough of him during open gym, though, that he figured Alexander was worth giving a scholarship. When Beilein finally saw him, he wasn't so sure. "Joe, your teams never win," Beilein told Alexander. To Beilein, simply playing was not enough. A player's intangibles and instincts were just as important as his vertical

Joe Alexander scored 22 points and grabbed 11 rebounds to lead West Virginia to a 73–67 victory over Duke in the second round of the 2008 NCAA tournament.

ALL-PRO PHOTOGRAPHY/DALE SPARKS.

jump. Joe couldn't even name half the teams in the Top 25, but when he got to West Virginia it became evident to his teammates that his work habits bordered on compulsion. Once, when the power was out at the Coliseum late at night, the resourceful Alexander was determined to get a workout so he drove his Nissan down through the tunnel and used his headlights to create enough light to shoot baskets. Another time, his roommates watched in disbelief as Joe went outside to shoot baskets during a lightning storm.

Alexander was soon spending so much time at the Coliseum that he began finding places to keep his stuff. Teammate Joe Mazzulla remembered the time he wanted to listen to his CD player in the locker room and he didn't have any batteries. He began asking around to see if any of his buddies had spares.

Alexander told him to wait a second. He walked out somewhere into the Coliseum, went behind the bleachers and came back a few minutes later with two new Duracells for Mazzulla to use. "He used to hide things in the Coliseum that he would use later," Mazzulla laughed. "Joe is one of the most unique kids I have ever met in my life. If you put him out in the middle of nowhere by himself with nothing, he would somehow survive. That's the type of person he is."

Alexander's basketball career was barely surviving during his first two years at West Virginia playing for John Beilein. Then Bob Huggins arrived and Alexander's career eventually took off, though not without a few hitches at the start.

Huggins once spent almost an entire practice explaining to Joe that he couldn't guard Connecticut's Jeff Adrien from behind. So the

Coach Bob Huggins led West Virginia to NCAA tournament appearances in 2008, 2009 and 2010, his first three years at WVU.

ALL-PRO PHOTOGRAPHY/DALE SPARKS.

first time Alexander ran down the floor he positioned himself directly behind Adrien, who got the ball, scored easily, and was fouled by Joe for a three-point play. After the play, Alexander jogged past Huggins, shrugged, and said, "My bad."

Huggins didn't see the humor in it. Beilein had gone through similar trials with Alexander.

"I remember one day Beilein spent 20 minutes of practice showing Joe the correct way to do a reverse layup," Mazzulla said. "Joe just never got it. How does a kid who is a lottery pick not know how to do something as fundamental as a reverse layup?"

Two days after Alexander's great performance against Connecticut, the forward went for 32 points in a 76–62 victory over Pitt at the Coliseum. He scored 29 points and grabbed 10 rebounds against St. John's in the Garden, though it was Mazzulla's driving layup that sent the game into overtime. West Virginia eventually won 83–74.

"I told [Mazzulla] you're going to have a free lane to the basket, don't rush it because five seconds is a long time. A guy with Joe's speed . . . I just wanted him to get going left-handed. He did a great job and got it at the basket and scored," Huggins said.

The St. John's victory gave West Virginia an 11–7 record in conference play, earning the Mountaineers a No. 5 seed in the Big East tournament.

West Virginia started slow and trailed Providence by as many as nine points in the first half. Later, WVU needed four crucial free throws from Alexander to pull out a 58–53 victory.

In the quarterfinals against Connecticut, Huggins dipped into his bag of tricks and pulled out a point-drop zone defense that proved confusing to UConn's outstanding backcourt. The coaches had detected during film study the night before that Connecticut was bothered by a zone defense Providence had used to beat the Huskies twice during the regular season.

Connecticut shot just 46 percent from the floor and was beaten badly on the glass, 42–26. Alexander scored a career-high 34 points that included a couple of pretty breakaway stuffs late in the game to cement the 76–72 victory.

Alexander turned Connecticut Hall of Fame coach Jim Calhoun into a believer. "Alexander is a terrific player. Our kids feel after he gets it they were going to stop him," Calhoun said. "When he got around 27 or 28 I thought it would be a good idea if they realized that, by the way, he had 32 the first time before they realized he was a good basketball player."

But one night later, Georgetown defeated West Virginia 72–55 in the Big East semifinals. Hoya center Roy Hibbert scored 25 points and grabbed 13 rebounds, and the Mountaineers shot just 40.8 percent in the 17-point loss.

Joe Alexander stuffs in two in this 2008 game played against Marshall at the Charleston Civic Center. Later that summer, Alexander became the first WVU player taken in the first round of the NBA draft in 40 years when he was selected eighth overall by the Milwaukee Bucks.

VAN SLIDER PHOTOGRAPHY.

West Virginia got into the NCAA tournament as the 7th-seed and faced 10th-seeded Arizona in a first-round game at the Verizon Center in Washington, D.C. Arizona chose to double-team Alexander, and that freed up Ruoff to score 21 points to lead West Virginia to a 75–65 victory. Butler scored 19 points while Alexander and Nichols added 14 each. The Mountaineers were

Bob Huggins and Duke coach Mike Krzyzewski shared a laugh at the Verizon Center before the Mountaineers defeated the Blue Devils 73–67.

ALL-PRO PHOTOGRAPHY/DALE SPARKS.

11 of 19 from the 3-range.

"Those are easy shots to make," Huggins said. "When you grow up in your driveway, that's kind of what you do. You shoot step-in shots. Al made some step-in shots and kind of got on a roll."

Inset Guard Joe Mazzulla looks for an opening during West Virginia's 2008 NCAA tournament Sweet 16 game against Xavier at US Airways Center in Phoenix, Ariz.

ALL-PRO PHOTOGRAPHY/DALE SPARKS.

Two nights later against ninth-ranked Duke, West Virginia overcame an early double-digit Blue Devil lead by going on an 18–3 run early in the second half. That run gave the Mountaineers a 47–40 advantage with 12 minutes left in the game. Redshirt freshman Cam Thoroughman, who chose to postpone knee surgery until after the season, came off the bench and grabbed critical rebounds on back-to-back possessions, and then made a layup to give West Virginia an 11-point lead with 3:30 minutes to go. Alexander scored 22 points and grabbed 11 rebounds, but Duke coach Mike Krzyzewski labeled Mazzulla the game's MVP because of his 13 points, 11 rebounds and 8 assists coming off the bench.

"We knew he was good being more of a driver; tough, really good athlete and a tough kid," Krzyzewski said. "But it seemed for a while there he just got so many rebounds . . . like if they played lacrosse he would be the guy on the face off. Whenever there was a loose ball or a scrum, all of the sudden—look, No. 3. And he was the story."

West Virginia advanced to the NCAA tournament Sweet 16 for the third time in four years and had a great opportunity to reach the Elite Eight for a second time, but missed free throws down the stretch enabled Xavier to pull out a 79–75 victory in overtime. Josh Duncan had a career-high 26 points and B. J. Raymond scored all 8 of his points in overtime for the Musketeers.

"We're up six and they beat us down the floor for a basket and we didn't make some free throws," said Huggins. "We had some breakdowns."

Alexander had forced overtime with 14 sec-

Coach Bob Huggins's first team at West Virginia in 2008 won 26 games and advanced to the NCAA tournament Sweet 16 following victories over Arizona and Duke.

WVU PHOTOGRAPHIC SERVICES.

WEST VIRGINIA 73, DUKE 67

Joe Alexander scored 22 points, but it was the tough play off the bench by reserves Joe Mazzulla and Cam Thoroughman that helped West Virginia knock off second-seeded and ninth-ranked Duke, 73–67, in a 2008 NCAA tournament second-round game at the Verizon Center in Washington, D.C.

West Virginia outscored the Blue Devils 44–33 in the second half behind the inspiring play of Mazzulla at guard and the seldom-used Thoroughman playing in place of forwards Da'Sean Butler and Wellington Smith, both forced to the bench with four fouls.

Thoroughman scored a pair of baskets during a key four-minute stretch and grabbed a pair of crucial offensive rebounds with the Mountaineers leading 60–50. Thoroughman's second bucket put West Virginia up 11 at 62–51 with 3:11 remaining.

West Virginia's biggest lead was 13 points at 68–55.

Duke (28–6) couldn't successfully guard West Virginia forward Joe Alexander, who finished with a game-high 22 points while also grabbing 11 rebounds. Alexander took 22 shots, making seven, while also making 7 of 8 from the free throw line.

Mazzulla nearly had a triple-double, scoring 13 points to go with a career-high 11 rebounds and 8 assists.

Above Coach Bob Huggins enjoys a laugh in the locker room at the Verizon Center the day before West Virginia's 73–67 victory over Duke in the second round of the 2008 NCAA tournament.

ALL-PRO PHOTOGRAPHY/DALE SPARKS.

Inset A West Virginia fan displays a "Beat Duke" t-shirt.

WVU PHOTOGRAPHIC SERVICES/M. G. ELLIS.

The Mountaineers punished Duke on the glass, getting a 47–27 advantage that included 19 offensive rebounds.

"We're so small," said West Virginia coach Bob Huggins, "but we've learned to compete."

Alex Ruoff scored 17 points to follow up his 21-point effort in the tournament opener against Arizona, and nailed a falling 3-point basket from the corner with the shot clock at two to tie the game at 37.

Duke scored 12 of its 34 first-half points at the free throw line on 12-of-12 shooting. Included among those free throws were a pair by Jon Scheyer after Coach Bob Huggins was assessed a technical foul by official Ed Hightower during a time-out.

The technical call was right in the middle of a Blue Devil 14–0 run that pushed their lead out to 14–4. Duke also led 18–8 after a pair of Kyle Singler free throws before the Mountaineers began chipping away at the deficit.

Duke got the lead back to seven twice at 24–17 on a Taylor King jumper and then at 28–21 on an inside move by Lance Thomas.

Leading 34–27 with the basketball, Duke had two chances to go up by 10 but 3-point tries by Scheyer and Greg Paulus were off target. The Paulus miss led to a West Virginia breakout that resulted in a pair of free throws by Da'Sean Butler.

Butler could have cut the Blue Devil lead to two, but his 3-point try with 2.8 seconds left in the half glanced off the front of the rim.

Gerald Henderson led the Blue Devils with 18 points. Scheyer contributed 15 and Paulus added 13.

Duke missed 13 straight 3-pointers at one point in the second half and finished 5 of 22 from behind the arc for the game. As irony would have it, the previous time West Virginia lost to Duke in the 1989 NCAA tournament in Greensboro, the Mountaineers were also a No. 7 seed and Duke was a No. 2 seed.

onds left when he hit a pull-up jumper and was fouled during the play. But Alexander missed a chance to put the Mountaineers ahead, and he eventually fouled out with 4:30 remaining in overtime. Alexander scored 18 points and 10 rebounds in what was to become his final game as a Mountaineer.

Xavier was 11 of 19 from 3-point range while West Virginia was only 1 of 11 from behind the arc.

Huggins's first season ended with a 26–11 record. It was the most victories ever for a first-year Mountaineer coach, and it was also the first time a coach had led WVU to the Sweet 16 during his inaugural season. West Virginia finished 17th in the national rankings after facing a schedule that featured 12 NCAA tournament opponents. Huggins's 11 Big East regular-season victories also matched a school best at the time

Alexander chose to enter the NBA draft a year early and was the eighth overall selection by the Milwaukee Bucks, becoming the school's first first-rounder since Ron Williams in 1968.

Ruoff was named an ESPN Academic All-America, giving WVU an Academic All-American in four of the last five years, and nine Mountaineer players were named to the Athletic Director's Academic Honor Roll.

Nichols wrapped up an outstanding career just seven points shy of scoring 1,000. He played on one Elite Eight and two Sweet 16 teams, as

Da'Sean Butler became the first WVU player in 31 years to score more than 40 points in a game when he went for 43 against Villanova on Feb. 13, 2009 at the WVU Coliseum.

VAN SLIDER PHOTOGRAPHY

well as an NIT championship team in 2007. West Virginia's 99–42 record during his four seasons was among the best of any four-year player in school history.

Shortly after his first season, Huggins inked a 10-year contract extension that will take him to his 65th birthday.

Continued Success

Huggins steered West Virginia to another trip to the NCAA tournament in 2009 despite having three freshmen among the team's top six players and no proven scorer.

A 10–2 start to the season was tempered with the loss of Mazzulla to a shoulder injury against Mississippi that he eventually chose to have surgically repaired. A loss to Davidson in the Jimmy V Classic in New York City came without Mazzulla and Ruoff.

WVU's other early season loss was against Kentucky in Las Vegas after the Mountaineers were unable to hold on to an early double-digit lead. A month later, West Virginia's 76–48 victory over 15th-ranked Ohio State was a pleasant homecoming for Huggins and a surprise to the country. With many friends and family at Value City Arena, West Virginia used a strong second half to snap Ohio State's 14-game winning streak. Ruoff led the Mountaineers with 17 points, and they held the Buckeyes to just 31 percent shooting.

"I have a ton of friends and family who were at this game and have spent the majority of my life here [in Ohio]. We needed to play hard against a very good basketball team today," Huggins said after the game. "I have wonderful kids that play hard. I wish they would grow to be 6'10", but these kids do what they need to do to win games."

Another key road victory came on Jan. 22 when West Virginia easily handled Georgetown 75–58 at the Verizon Center. The 12th-ranked Hoyas were no match for West Virginia's smothering defense, making just nine second-half field goals and being out-rebounded by the smaller Mountaineers, 39–31. Da'Sean Butler, emerging as one of the Big East's top players, scored 27 points and grabbed eight rebounds.

"We talked to them at halftime about let's finish the deal," Huggins said. "We were in decent

Freshman guard Darryl "Truck" Bryant broke into the starting lineup midway through the 2009 season and finished the year averaging 9.8 points per game.
ALL-PRO PHOTOGRAPHY/DALE SPARKS.

position at Marquette and we didn't finish it. We didn't finish the Connecticut game, and we really didn't finish the Marshall game or the South Florida game."

Butler's best performance of the year was also the team's best performance of the year—a 93–72 victory over 12th-ranked Villanova at the Coliseum before an ESPN nationally televised audience. Butler scored a career-high 43 points—the third highest ever at the Coliseum behind Austin Carr's 47 against the Mountaineers in 1971 and Wil Robinson's 45 scored against Penn State the same year. Any questions about West Virginia's NCAA tournament résumé were answered that night against the Wildcats.

In the Big East tournament, West Virginia earned double-digit victories over Notre Dame and Pitt. Against the Panthers, Devin Ebanks showed why he made the Big East all-rookie team by scoring 20 points and grabbing seven rebounds. The night before, he pulled down a season-high 18 rebounds against Notre Dame. "Devin has been terrific from the Big East season on," Huggins said. "He's gotten so much better and he's gotten so much better defensively."

WVU's Big East tournament run ended in the semifinals when Syracuse, a six-overtime winner over Connecticut the previous night, needed another overtime to knock off the Mountaineers 74–69. Ebanks sent the game into an extra session with a pair of free throws with three seconds left, and he finished the game with 22 points.

A sixth seed in the NCAA tournament and playing in a favorable bracket against 11th-seeded Dayton was West Virginia's reward for a 23–11

Far right Forward Devin Ebanks had 20 double-figure scoring games and 12 double-double games in points and rebounds as a freshman in 2009.
ALL-PRO PHOTOGRAPHY/DALE SPARKS.

Below Alex Ruoff, pictured here with Coach Bob Huggins, was honored as the Big East scholar-athlete of the year.
BIG EAST CONFERENCE PHOTO.

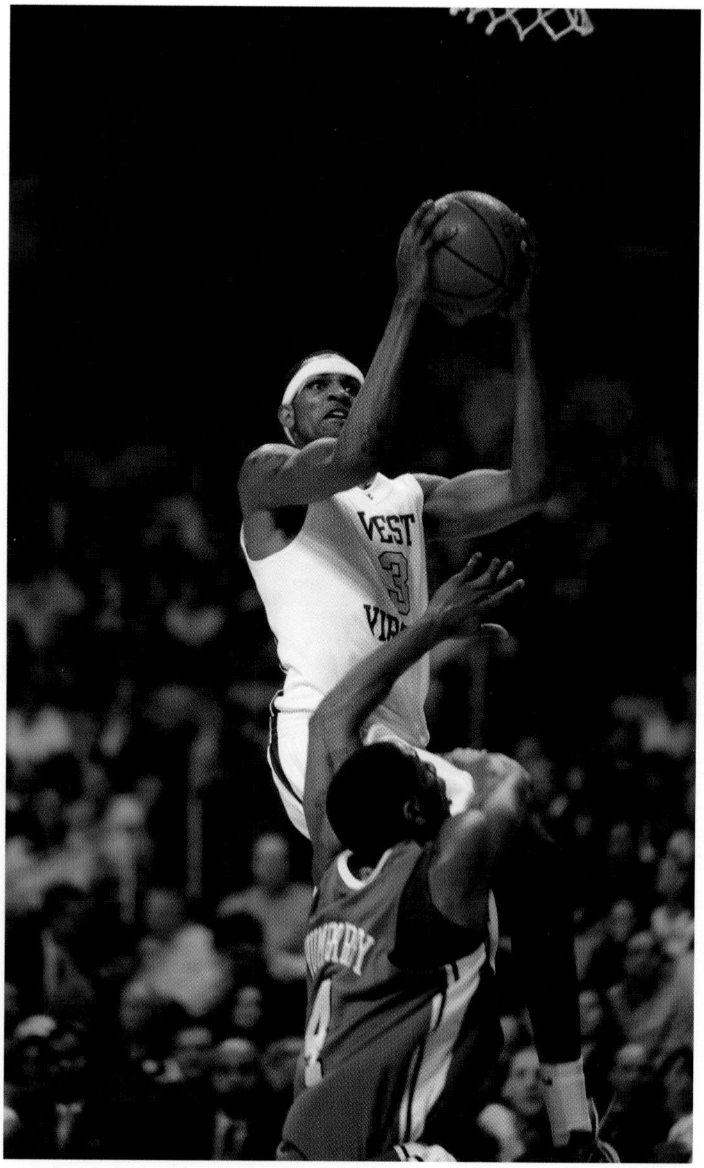

record. But travel problems disrupted the Mountaineers' journey to Minneapolis two days before the game. Mechanical problems with the team's charter plane forced the Mountaineers to remain in Clarksburg for six hours waiting for another airline to pick them up. When the team eventually arrived in Minneapolis in the wee hours of the morning, the total travel time was 11 ½ hours after first leaving Morgantown the previous afternoon.

Even with a mid-afternoon start two days later, West Virginia played like a team half asleep against Dayton. The Flyers pulled out a 68–60 victory, ending the Mountaineers' season in the NCAA tournament first round for the first time since 1992.

"They were really physical with us and they did a good job of taking us out of offense in the first half," said a disappointed Huggins afterward.

Butler earned second-team All-Big East honors, Ebanks was a member of the league's five-player all-rookie team, and Alex Ruoff was recognized as the conference's scholar-athlete of the year. Ruoff finished his WVU career first in 3-point field goals with 261, and ranked among the school's top 20 players in scoring with 1,420 points.

Despite the disappointment in Minneapolis, it was another successful season for WVU. Six of West Virginia's 13 losses in 2009 came to No. 1 seeds in the NCAA tournament, and Huggins became the first West Virginia coach since Fred Schaus to take his first two Mountaineer teams to NCAA play.

On to the Final Four

In late April, just three weeks after North Carolina claimed the 2009 national championship, ESPN's Andy Katz set the bar high for the Mountaineers when he predicted West Virginia would contend for

ESPN's College GameDay comes to Morgantown. From top:

WVU cheerleaders perform on the set of ESPN College GameDay at the WVU Coliseum prior to West Virginia's 2009 game against Louisville.

ESPN's Rece Davis and Bob Knight share a laugh with West Virginia great Jerry West.

Jerry West on the set of ESPN College GameDay on location at the WVU Coliseum. In the background is Bob Knight.

The ESPN College GameDay bus parked outside the WVU Coliseum.

ALL-PRO PHOTOGRAPHY/DALE SPARKS.

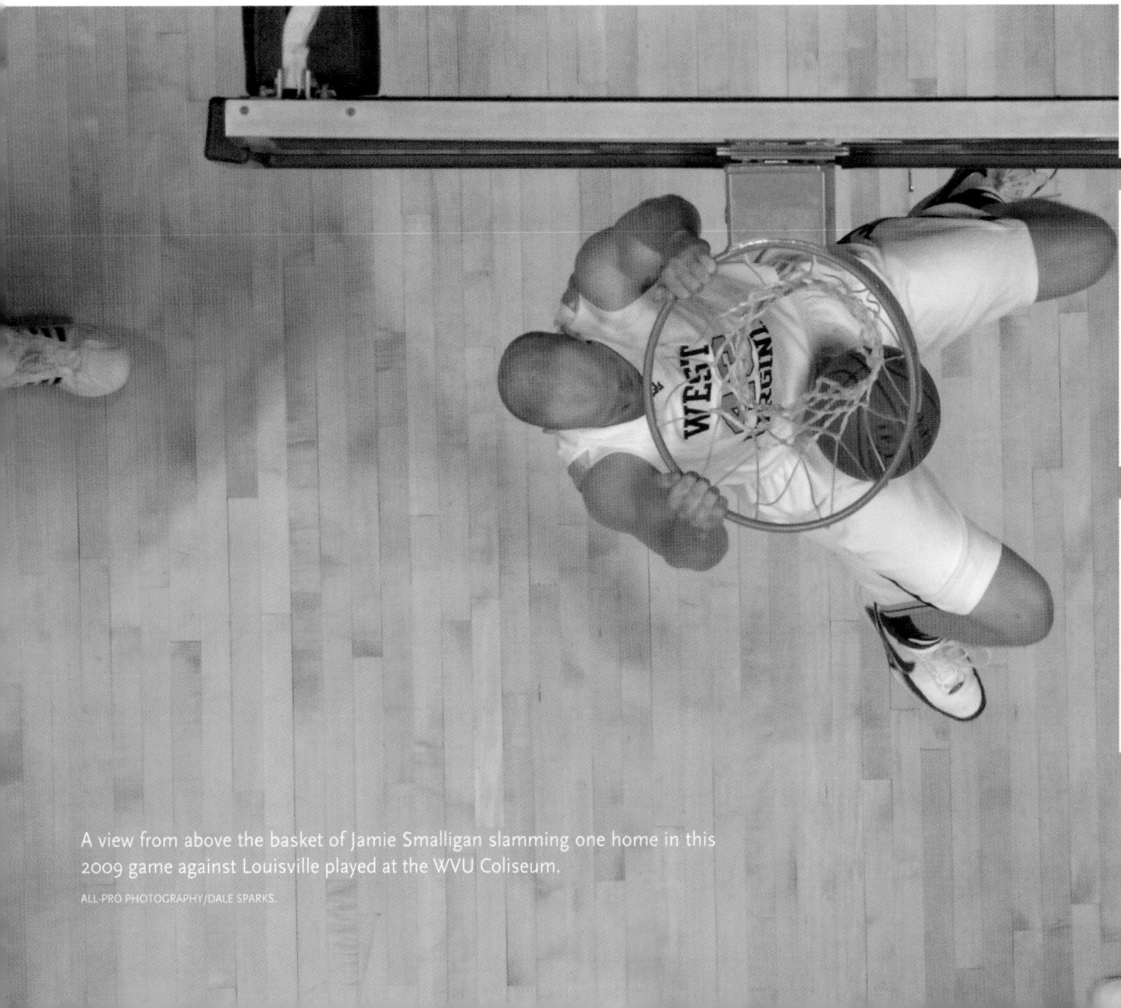

A view from above the basket of Jamie Smalligan slamming one home in this 2009 game against Louisville played at the WVU Coliseum.

ALL-PRO PHOTOGRAPHY/DALE SPARKS.

WVU great Hot Rod Hundley proudly displays his retired number 33 jersey at halftime of the Ohio State game at the WVU Coliseum on Jan. 23, 2010.
ALL-PRO PHOTOGRAPHY/DALE SPARKS.

the Big East title. He also picked WVU seventh in his "way too early" top 25.

Katz and others (*Sporting News* ranked WVU No. 5 in its preseason poll) said it was possible West Virginia could reach the Final Four based on the fact that the Mountaineers were returning four of five starters, including 6-foot-9 sophomore Devin Ebanks, who briefly considered entering the NBA draft after his freshman season.

To get his team prepared for Big East Conference play and a potential run in the NCAA tournament, Huggins assembled one of the most difficult schedules in school history with non-conference dates against Ole Miss, Purdue and Ohio State, and an appearance in the 76 Classic in Anaheim, Calif., featuring a field of annual postseason participants that included UCLA, Minnesota, Butler, Texas A&M and Clemson.

The Mountaineers proved they were worthy of their preseason Top 10 ranking in Anaheim by beating Long Beach State, Texas A&M and pesky Portland to claim the 76 Classic title.

Ebanks made a pair of critical steals late in the game to preserve a 73–66 win over the Aggies in the semifinals, and Butler scored a game-high 26 points to lead West Virginia to an 18-point victory over Portland in the championship game.

The Mountaineers began December ranked No. 7 by AP and No. 8 by ESPN/*USA Today*, and added victories over Duquesne, Coppin State, Cleveland State and Ole Miss to boost their record to 9–0.

Butler and Ebanks shined in an overtime win at Seton Hall the day after Christmas, combining to score 43 points in front of a CBS nationally televised audience. Three days later, Butler worked his magic by hitting the game-winning 3 with 2.3 seconds to lift West Virginia to a 63–62 victory over Marquette. The Marquette win got West Virginia to No. 6 in both polls— the school's highest ranking since Feb. 23, 1982.

Losses on the road at fourth-ranked Purdue and at Notre Dame early in January may have temporarily sidetracked the Mountaineers, but a late-January five-game winning streak featuring impressive wins over No. 21 Ohio State, Louisville and No. 22 Pitt got them back on course.

West Virginia was trailing the Buckeyes by 12 at halftime when Hot Rod Hundley, back on campus for the official retirement of his jersey, electrified the crowd by sinking an impromptu hook shot right after his on-court ceremony. Hundley's hook set the stage for an impressive rally, the Mountaineers scoring 12 of the first 14 points of the second half to get back into the game, and eventually pulling away with a 71–65 victory. Ebanks played another marvelous defensive game, stopping Big Ten player of the year Evan Turner from making a single field goal for the entire second half.

West Virginia had a much easier time of it against Pitt, particularly in the second half, outscoring the Panthers 36–23 over the remaining 20 minutes to record a 19-point victory in the Backyard Brawl. The Pitt game also served as the season debut for freshman center Deniz Kilicli, who was forced to sit out the first 21 games of the season because he had played for a Turkish national team that had a professional player on it.

Three days after the Pitt win, West Virginia needed an earlier wakeup call in a noon game at St. John's, the Mountaineers falling behind by 16 points early in the second half before going on a 26–7 run to register a 79–60 win. Butler was magnificent with 33 points, including a Big East record 7 for 7 from 3-point distance.

The toughest stretch of the season came in mid-February when West Virginia lost back-to-back games to Villanova and Pitt. On both occasions, poor free throw shooting hurt the Mountaineers. West Virginia missed 14 free throws in a seven-point loss to the Wildcats, and three missed one-and-ones late in the game at Pitt helped the Panthers overcome a seven-point deficit with a minute to go to tie the game in regulation. The Panthers eventually won it in triple overtime, 98–95, in one of the classic games in Backyard Brawl history.

One more tough loss at Connecticut that saw Huggins get ejected with 45.2 seconds remaining gave WVU an opportunity to get refocused for the rest of the season. After the game, a disappointed Huggins was in a reflective

Junior John Flowers was an important contributor for the Mountaineers coming off the bench in 2010.
VAN SLIDER PHOTOGRAPHY

mood during his post-game radio show with MSN play-by-play man Tony Caridi, who later began referring to that interview as Huggins's "Hartford Homily."

"I just told [the players] I don't know if they have any idea how much they mean to this state and how much this state rallies around them," Huggins told a statewide audience. "I told them this, 'You have very few times in your life when you are special—very, very few. A lot of people never have a chance to be special.' If we close a couple of games out against some pretty good teams then we're probably top five in the country."

West Virginia slipped to 10th in the AP poll and 8th in the coaches' poll after the loss to Connecticut, but the team took to heart Huggins's appeal to be special.

Wins followed over Cincinnati and Georgetown to close out West Virginia's home schedule.

More than 13,000 showed up for the Georgetown game on ESPN Big Monday to give the Mountaineers the school record for overall attendance (173,281) and average attendance (12,377), besting previous marks established in 1982.

Butler scored 22 points in his final home appearance to help the Mountaineers to an 81–68 victory over the No. 20 Hoyas. Da'Sean was even better against ninth-ranked Villanova, hitting the game-winning shot in overtime to lead the Mountaineers to a 68–66 victory.

A few days before the Villanova game, Huggins wanted to give his team a good laugh by reading them a letter he had received in the mail from a fan complaining about his choice of game attire. The gist of the letter was that the players were not listening closely enough to Huggins's pre-game instructions and they might be more apt to paying attention if Huggs ditched his trademark Johnny Cash look (black West Virginia pullover and matching trousers) in favor of a navy blue suit and gold tie. "I took the letter down to our players and I said, 'If you guys don't start playing better I'm going to have to end up wearing a suit,'" Huggins deadpanned.

Fortunately, the navy suit remained in the closet. West Virginia wrapped up the regular season with 13 conference wins—the most since joining the Big East—and got its first road victory over a Top-10 team in four years with its two-point win at Villanova.

The Mountaineers, tied with Pitt and Villanova for second place behind Big East regular-season champion Syracuse, were the No. 3-seeded team in the Big East tournament, meaning the Mountaineers would have to wait two days before playing their first tournament game. "I don't like the double bye," Huggins said. "I don't like sitting there for two days while people are playing."

By the time West Virginia hit the court for its 9 p.m. Thursday night quarterfinal game against Cincinnati (a winner over Rutgers and Louisville), all three top-seeded teams had been eliminated from the tournament. No. 1 seed Syracuse was knocked out by Georgetown, fourth-seeded Villanova was upset by Marquette and Notre Dame took down second-seeded Pitt.

Da'Sean Butler goes up for the game-winning 3-point basket against Cincinnati in the Big East tournament quarterfinals at Madison Square Garden in New York City. It was one of six game-winning shots for Butler during the 2010 season.

BLUE & GOLD NEWS / KEVIN KINDER.

Despite leading the 11th-seeded Bearcats for most of the game, it looked like West Virginia was going to be the tournament's fourth double-bye victim when Ebanks couldn't convert a basket with the shot clock winding down, giving the basketball back to Cincinnati with enough time to try a game-winning shot.

But Butler pressured UC's Dion Dixon into turning the basketball over near West Virginia's bench with three seconds left on the clock. On the ensuing inbounds play, Da'Sean got the ball well beyond the top of the key, took two dribbles to his left, and hoisted up a 3-point shot beyond the outstretched hand of Lance Stephenson that banked in to win the game for the Mountaineers. Butler said afterward that he called "bank" when the ball was in the air, which Stephenson confirmed.

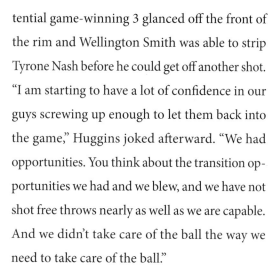

The 54–51 win made West Virginia the highest-seeded team remaining in the tournament. In the semifinals, Butler continued his brilliance, scoring 24 of the team's 53 points in a two-point victory over the Irish. West Virginia saw its 10-point second-half lead evaporate to two when Notre Dame's Ben Hansbrough made a pair of free throws with 47 seconds left. After Butler's 3-point try to ice the game was off the mark, Tory Jackson's potential game-winning 3 glanced off the front of the rim and Wellington Smith was able to strip Tyrone Nash before he could get off another shot. "I am starting to have a lot of confidence in our guys screwing up enough to let them back into the game," Huggins joked afterward. "We had opportunities. You think about the transition opportunities we had and we blew, and we have not shot free throws nearly as well as we are capable. And we didn't take care of the ball the way we need to take care of the ball."

Despite that, West Virginia was making its second Big East tournament championship game appearance since 2005. In this title game against Georgetown, West Virginia overcame another near second-half meltdown to pull out a 60–58 victory over the Hoyas for the school's first Big East tournament crown since joining the league. Butler's game-winner—his sixth of the season—gave him 20 points and he was voted the tournament's most valuable player. During the game, Butler also became just the third player in school history to produce more than 2,000 career points, joining consensus All-Americans Jerry West and Hot Rod Hundley.

Butler's emergence as one of the great players in WVU history will forever serve as a reminder to Rutgers and Seton Hall not to overlook their own. Butler grew up in Newark, N.J., a bicycle ride from Seton Hall's campus and just a short drive down Route 1 to Rutgers. Neither school pursued Butler very hard, and he eventually turned his attention to West Virginia.

Above left Forward Wellington Smith finished his WVU career third in blocks with 163.

BLUE & GOLD NEWS/KEVIN KINDER.

Left Tournament MVP Da'Sean Butler kisses the Big East Championship trophy following West Virginia's 60–58 victory over Georgetown.

BLUE & GOLD NEWS / KEVIN KINDER.

WEST VIRGINIA 60, GEORGETOWN 58

Above A view of the Madison Square Garden scoreboard through the rim (minus the net) after West Virginia's 60–58 victory over Georgetown to claim its first-ever Big East tournament title.

BIG EAST PHOTO.

Left NYC cover boy Kevin Jones celebrates West Virginia's first Big East title.

Da'Sean Butler's floating basket with four seconds left lifted sixth-ranked West Virginia to a 60–58 victory over Georgetown to capture the 2010 Big East basketball championship at Madison Square Garden in New York City. "I came to the top of the key and I had to come get the ball and they kind of switched," said Butler of his winning shot. "I think [Georgetown's Greg] Monroe was on me and I think he had a feeling I was going to shoot a 3. I had a little hesitation, went around him, Freeman stepped up, and had a little hop step and scooped a layup off the glass."

It seemed the Mountaineers were almost destined to win their first Big East title with an all-New York City starting lineup of Butler, Wellington Smith, Kevin Jones, Devin Ebanks and Truck Bryant. Including reserve forward Danny Jennings, West Virginia had six players on its roster from the New York City metropolitan area.

Smith played a fantastic first half, scoring 9 of his personal tournament-best 11 points while grabbing a team-best 10 rebounds. As it had done all season, West Virginia won the game with great defense, tough rebounding and the clutch playmaking of Butler, who joined Mr. Clutch himself, Jerry West, and Hot Rod Hundley in the school's prestigious 2,000-point club. Butler's 2,000th point came late in the first half when his three-point play put the Mountaineers up 24–20.

Georgetown had two four-minute stretches in both halves without scoring baskets, and finished the game shooting just 42.6 percent after carving up top-seeded Syracuse and Marquette in the two prior days of the tournament. However, West Virginia could never quite shake the determined Hoyas, the Mountaineers building leads of six in the first half and then later nine with 12:22 remaining on a Casey Mitchell 3-point basket. That's when Georgetown went to work, getting a 3 from Hollis Thompson and then back-to-back baskets by Austin Freeman and Chris Wright to cut the Mountaineers' lead to two, 43–41, with 10:38 left.

Butler stopped the run with a 3, and added a jumper at 9:02 to take the lead back to seven, 48–41. But as it did two nights before against Cincinnati and again against Notre Dame, West Virginia had to hold on for dear life. Two Monroe free throws with 3:27 left cut Georgetown's deficit to one, 52–51, and the Hoyas eventually tied it at 56 when Freeman nailed a 3 with 54 seconds left. Mitchell unknotted the score with a pair of free throws, and Mazzulla added two more from the line with 27 seconds left to give West Virginia a 58–56 advantage. Chris Wright answered with a basket for Georgetown with 17 seconds left to set the scene for Butler's game-winning heroics.

It was Butler's sixth deciding basket of the season, keying prior victories over Cleveland State, Marquette, Louisville, Villanova, Cincinnati and now, Georgetown.

"It feels good—our familes and our friends are here," said Butler of winning the tournament not too far from his hometown across the river in Newark, N.J. "But we kind of wanted to win for our state first, because the people there love us so much and they support us so much. And I definitely know it means the world to them."

Jones added 12 points and four rebounds for West Virginia. Wright finished with 20 points for Georgetown. After the game, West Virginia fans were treated to "Country Roads" on the Madison Square Garden public address system, a tradition at WVU home games following victories.

When Da'Sean came to WVU, his father, Ira Puryear, gave him a credit card to use for emergencies, and when he received the first bill, there were $750 in charges on it. When his dad examined the bill more closely, he discovered that every single charge was less than $25. "It had every pizza joint in Morgantown on that bill," Puryear told the *New York Times*. When Da'Sean was 11, he once ate so much food at a Chinese buffet that the manager wanted to charge him as an adult. Eventually, with some help and encouragement by strength and conditioning coach Andy Kettler, Butler came to understand that he was going to have to curb his late-night cravings in favor of a more healthy diet. By his senior year, a much more muscular Butler had turned himself into one of the best players in the country.

"He's the third leading scorer in West Virginia history, and if you hang around him, you wouldn't even know it," said teammate Joe Mazzulla.

Right Forward Devin Ebanks was named to the all-Big East third team after averaging 12 points and 8.1 rebounds per game as a sophomore.

ALL-PRO PHOTOGRAPHY/DALE SPARKS.

Freshman center Deniz Kilicli kept West Virginia in this 2010 NCAA tournament game against Washington, scoring 6 first-half points in the Mountaineers' 69–56 win over the Huskies.

ALL-PRO PHOTOGRAPHY/DALE SPARKS.

After the Georgetown victory West Virginia fans were treated to "Country Roads" on the Madison Square Garden public address system, a tradition at WVU home games following Mountaineer victories. Huggins could be seen fighting back tears as he embraced his players on the floor while West Virginia fans serenaded New Yorkers to John Denver's state anthem.

"When you're born and raised in West Virginia and you grow up the son of a coach, and you get to play in Madison Square Garden and I got to play there as a player, and to be able to go coach in Madison Square Garden—and when the game is over with, to hear 'Country Roads' come over the loudspeaker, it's unbelievable," said Huggins.

The school's first Big East men's tournament title was also fitting for retiring athletic director Ed Pastilong, who played an instrumental role in getting West Virginia into the conference as a full-fledged member in 1995.

Following the Big East tournament, West Virginia was seeded No. 2 in the NCAA tournament East Regional in Buffalo, N.Y., where they were to face 15th-seeded Morgan State at HSBC Arena, home of professional hockey's Buffalo Sabres. West Virginia overcame an early 10–0 deficit to defeat the Bears 77–50. Jones scored 17 points and Ebanks added 16 points and 13 rebounds to lead the Mountaineers.

Two nights later against 10th-seeded Missouri, Butler scored a game-high 28 points, including 19 in the first half, to lead the Mountaineers to a 68–59 victory over the Tigers. Guards Truck Bryant and Joe Mazzulla withstood 40 minutes of full-court pressure (Missouri calls it the Fastest 40 Minutes in Basketball), turning the ball over only three times while contributing a combined 7 points. During a 13-minute stretch between halves, West Virginia managed just one field goal but still somehow increased its lead by three points—all on free throws. The Mountaineers were able to close out the victory at the foul line, hitting 10 down the stretch.

The Mountaineers' triumph over Washington in the Sweet 16 was just as taxing. The Huskies forced West Virginia into committing a season-high 23 turnovers with Bryant out of the lineup with a broken foot (suffered in practice two days before the Washington game), but Huggins used a 1-3-1 defense late in the game that proved troublesome for the Huskies. All three baskets Washington managed to score over the remaining six minutes of the game came

WEST VIRGINIA 73, KENTUCKY 66

West Virginia got 18 points from Da'Sean Butler and 17 from guard Joe Mazzulla to knock off top-seeded and second-ranked Kentucky 73–66 in the NCAA Tournament East Regional championship game at the Carrier Dome in Syracuse, N.Y.

Butler kept West Virginia in the game in the first half with the 3-ball—all eight of West Virginia's first-half field goals came from 3-point distance. After Kentucky took an early 16–9 lead by pounding the ball inside, West Virginia discovered its offense from behind the arc, getting back-to-back 3s by Butler and Jones to pull the Mountaineers to within one, 16-15, and another Butler 3 with 5:03 remaining tied the game at 18. West Virginia's first lead of the game came on another Butler bomb with 4:14 to go. West Virginia was also the beneficiary of a technical foul called on Kentucky's DeAndre Liggins for arguing a call that led to two Butler free throws.

An ominous sign for Kentucky came at the start of the second half when Eric Bledsoe missed two free throws right of the bat, and West Virginia responded with a Jones 3, a Mazzulla driving layup and a Flowers 3 from the wing to make it a 10-point West Virginia lead, forcing Calipari to call time-out.

Kentucky got it down to five, 36–31, on a DeMarcus Cousins layup, but Devin Ebanks responded with a jumper and Mazzulla made another drive to the basket that pushed the lead back to nine, 40–31. Mazzulla, who came into the game averaging just 2.2 points per game, scored five points during a two-minute stretch and Ebanks got an easy one on the inside to make it 47–36 with 11:53 remaining.

Layups by Bledsoe and Wall reduced West Virginia's lead to seven, 49–42, but once again it was Mazzulla who answered with a tough drive to the hoop. "What hurts was when we were making a little run and they were hitting layups off those shuffle cuts," Kentucky coach John Calipari said. "Mazzulla just got some layups that were backbreaking."

The 1-3-1 zone that Huggins chose to use for most of the game really bothered Kentucky. The Wildcats missed their first 20 3-point field goal tries and finished a miserable 4 of 32 from behind the arc. "It gets a little demoralizing when we missed the shots that we missed," said Calipari. Kentucky also struggled at the free throw line, missing 13 for the game and going 16 of 29 overall. "The 1-3-1 bothered us," said Calipari. "We've had poor shooting games like this and won, but West Virginia was too good for that to happen tonight."

"We came in thinking we were going to change defenses on them and try and keep them off-balanced," added West Virginia coach Bob Huggins.

West Virginia was out-rebounded 51–36, was 0 for 16 from two-point range in the first half and didn't get its first two-point field goal until a Mazzulla layup with 18:09 left in the game. The Mountaineers also missed 11 free throws.

Top Joe Mazzulla drives to the basket for two of his career-high 17 points against Kentucky in the 2010 NCAA East Regional championship game in Syracuse, N.Y. Mazzulla was named East Region Most Outstanding Player for his efforts.

ALL-PRO PHOTOGRAPHY/DALE SPARKS.

Left Devin Ebanks defends Kentucky guard John Wall. West Virginia's defense held Kentucky to just 4 of 32 from 3-point distance.

WVU PHOTOGRAPHIC SERVICES/M. G. ELLIS.

off of steals. Jones scored 18 points and made three of West Virginia's four 3-point baskets to lead WVU to its first Elite Eight trip since 2005.

In the East Regional finals, West Virginia's victory over top-seeded and No. 2-ranked Kentucky defied the stat sheet. The Wildcats had a 15-rebound advantage on the glass and kept West Virginia from making a single two-point basket in the first half (0 for 16). But Kentucky missed its first 20 3-point shots and went 4 of 32 from behind the arc for the game, helping West Virginia to a 16-point lead with 4:25 remaining. The Wildcats eventually made it interesting when SEC player of the year John Wall banked in a 3 from the top of the key, and Huntington's Patrick Patterson hit two free throws with 41 seconds left to turn it into a two-possession game. But Ebanks put the game on ice when he pulled down Darnell Dodson's missed 3 from the corner, was fouled, and hit two free throws with 13.8 seconds left.

Butler led all scorers with 18 points and Mazzulla finished with a season-high 17—14 of those coming in the second half—to earn East Regional MVP honors. "He just got some layups that were backbreaking," said Kentucky coach John Calipari of Mazzulla.

"The 1-3-1 bothered us," Calipari added. "We've had poor shooting games like this and won, but West Virginia was too good for that to happen tonight."

The 3-pointers Kentucky missed in the regional finals were made by Duke in the Final Four at Lucas Oil Stadium in Indianapolis, Ind. The Blue Devils hit 13 of 25 from behind the arc and Duke's Big Three of Jon Scheyer, Kyle Singler and Nolan Smith scored 63 of its 78 points in a 21-point victory. It seemed like each time West Virginia would make a run to pull closer, Scheyer, Singler or Smith would hit another bomb to answer the run.

West Virginia's comeback hopes suffered a fatal blow with nine minutes left in the game when Butler tore the ACL in his left knee while attempting to take the ball to the basket. Da'Sean collided with Duke's 7-foot-1 center Brian Zoubek, his left knee buckled, and he went to the ground where he lay in pain for several minutes. Huggins walked out on the floor, got down on his knees and hugged his star player.

"I had never felt pain like that in my life and he just got down on his knees, hugged me, and he kept telling me that he loved me," said Butler.

Steady Kevin Jones fires in two during this NCAA East Regional championship game against Kentucky in Syracuse, N.Y. Jones was named to the East Region all-tournament team after scoring double figures in all four games.

ALL-PRO PHOTOGRAPHY/DALE SPARKS.

Wellington Smith finished his WVU career with a team-best 12 points in the Mountaineers' Final Four loss to Duke.

ALL-PRO PHOTOGRAPHY/DALE SPARKS.

Butler had to be helped from the floor and was later taken to the locker room in a golf cart. After Butler's departure, the Mountaineers could only manage to score seven points for the remainder of the game. Senior Wellington Smith was the team's leading scorer with 12 points.

"They played really well," said Huggins of the eventual national champion Blue Devils. "What's really hard is if you try to do too many things to keep the ball out of those three guys' hands, you turn the other two guys loose at the rim to rebound the ball, and I don't think you can let them offensively rebound the ball."

West Virginia's loss to Duke in the national semifinals was just a small blip on what, otherwise, was one of the most memorable seasons in school history. The Mountaineers finished ranked in the Top 10 for the first time in nearly 50 years, produced a school record 31 victories, won their most regular-season games in Big East play and captured their first-ever Big East tournament title.

Butler also secured his place among the greats in school history. He earned first team All-America honors by John Wooden and *Basketball Times*, was an AP second-team All-American, and was the recipient of the Lowes Senior CLASS Award presented at the Final Four to the most outstanding senior student-athlete in NCAA Division I men's basketball.

"I started coaching Da'Sean when he was a

Da'Sean Butler answers a question during a press conference before West Virginia's 2010 NCAA tournament opening-round game against Morgan State.

ALL-PRO PHOTOGRAPHY/DALE SPARKS.

Left Sophomore forward Kevin Jones really blossomed in 2010, finishing second on the team in scoring (13.5 ppg) and rebounding (7.2 rpg) while shooting a team-best 52.1 percent from the floor.

WVU PHOTOGRAPHIC SERVICES/M.G. ELLIS

Below A moment permanently etched in the minds of college basketball fans everywhere—Coach Bob Huggins consoling Da'Sean Butler after his star player injured his knee midway through the second half of the Mountaineers' 78–57 loss to Duke in the national semifinals in Indianapolis, Ind.

WVU PHOTOGRAPHIC SERVICES/SCOTT LITUCHY

sophomore and that was when Joe Alexander had his breakout year," said Huggins. "They told me Da'Sean was just happy being Joe's sidekick. And then his junior year he got 36 or 38 in our first exhibition game and he was in the locker room apologizing that he shot the ball too much and didn't get his teammates involved.

"Well, I was like, 'Come here, man, I need to talk to you. If we're going to have any chance, you're going to have to score the ball for us,'" Huggins continued. "He's done it. If you can be too good a guy, he's too good a guy. He really is concerned about everybody else and getting his teammates involved."

Most gratifying to Huggins was his team overcoming many obstacles to reach the Final Four in 2010. "I think if Deniz [Kilicli] plays a whole year he's a totally different player. That made it difficult trying to get him involved because he is a guy who can score the ball for us.

"Joe Mazzulla not being able to really play for two-thirds of the year hurt. Then Truck goes

Left and below left Architectural renderings of the exterior and practice floor of West Virginia's new $20 million basketball facility, scheduled to be completed in 2011. The facility will be located adjacent to the WVU Coliseum.

down. I think through all of it, our guys did a great job of persevering and working their way through things. They're good guys. They are guys who put the team and the welfare of others before themselves. That's a great character trait to have."

When Huggins returned to West Virginia in the spring of 2007, he explained at his very first press conference how he was going to get the Mountaineers to the top of the mountain. It was a process he used once before when he built

Cincinnati into a national power in the 1990s.

"The first sellout we had at Cincinnati we played Louisville," Huggins remarked. "They said to me, 'Wow, this is great. We have a sellout. People came to see us play.' I said, 'No, they came to see Louisville play.' When they come and see us play and sell it out that's when you've got it going.

"Well, we went to a Final Four and the next year we were pretty good again and we were playing Chicago State. They had suspended their five starters or something and we were going to win the game by 40 anyway, and we sold the place out and tickets were being scalped outside. That's when you know you're pretty good and you've arrived.

"That's where we're going to get to here."

Three years later, Huggins has West Virginia there. Just as it was during the 1950s with Hot Rod Hundley and Jerry West, once again basketball games in Morgantown are the hottest ticket around.

Yes, West Virginia University is in the midst of another Golden Era of basketball.

ALL-TIME WINNINGEST COLLEGE BASKETBALL PROGRAMS

1. Kentucky, 2,023
2. North Carolina, 2,004
3. Kansas, 2,003
4. Duke, 1,911
5. Syracuse, 1,783
6. Temple, 1,740
7. St. John's, 1,703
8. UCLA, 1,686
9. Notre Dame, 1674
10. Penn, 1,663
11. Indiana, 1,651
12. Utah, 1,651
13. Illinois, 1,630
14. Western Kentucky, 1,623
15. Washington, 1,616
16. Texas, 1,610
17. Oregon State, 1,608
18. BYU, 1,608
19. Louisville, 1,607
20. Purdue, 1,594
21. Arizona, 1,584
22. **West Virginia, 1,581**
23. Princeton, 1,574
24. Cincinnati, 1,572
25. North Carolina State, 1,554

845 All DAY
Mountaineer Magic

Bob Huggins ranks fourth among all active Division I men's basketball coaches and 21st all-time with 670 career victories. He has led two teams to Final Four appearances in 1992 (Cincinnati) and West Virginia (2010) and has been named national coach of the year five times during his career.

Afterword

My introduction to Mountaineer basketball came at a very early age. I was born in Morgantown, where both of my parents were raised, and I lived here until I was nine. I can remember sitting on my grandfather's lap listening to Jack Fleming broadcast West Virginia games on the radio, and later when we lived in Ohio, Dad getting up on the roof and turning the antenna toward Wheeling's WTRF so we could watch the Mountaineers on television.

Most of the stories I recall Dad telling me were about Hot Rod Hundley, but I also knew about many of the great WVU players before Hot Rod such as Scotty Hamilton, Leland Byrd, Fred Schaus and Mark Workman. I learned even more about Mountaineer basketball when we used to drive from Midvale down to Morgantown each year to catch the first day of practice at the old Field House. In my mind I can still picture watching Fritz Williams as a freshman in 1964.

Back then the drive to Morgantown was about five hours, and for an 11-year-old, it seemed like an eternity. We took 250 as it cut across the Ohio River at Steubenville, working our way down the West Virginia side until we climbed back up the mountain in Moundsville. Eventually, we snaked our way through Waynesburg, Mt. Morris, and then, finally, Morgantown.

The bond the people have with West Virginia University is like no other place I have ever been. Warren Baker and I have stayed very close. The same goes for Maurice Robinson and Dana Perno. I first met Jerry West when I was a player, but I really didn't know him that well. I also met Hot Rod at about the same time, but I really didn't know him that well either, yet as my coaching career advanced both of them were absolutely phenomenal to me. It has also been great bridging the gap between the older generation players like Buddy Quertinmont and Paul Miller and the younger guys like Darryl Prue and Dale Blaney. Again, it's just an unbelievable bond that we all share.

Pitt has had great basketball but they are not the Steelers. Cincinnati had great basketball when I was there, but they were not the Reds. Mountaineer basketball and football are West

Virginia's pride and joy. I am reminded every day just how much it means to the people of our state to be able to stick out their chest a little bit and say, "That's my team."

We have accomplished a lot in the short time we have been here, but there is still a great deal more to be accomplished. Through the generosity of many, we have one of the best practice facilities in the country under construction, and now it's time to turn our attention to the Coliseum. I don't want to change it and we don't need a new building, we just have to do some fairly subtle things to modernize the Coliseum in a way that it won't disrupt a lot of things. I think people can again walk into our arena like I did when I was a player and say, "Wow!"

My whole goal for coming back to West Virginia was to get this thing rolling and to make us a national presence—to give the guys who follow me the wherewithal to continue to keep it going.

And that is what we are going to continue to do.

Let's Go Mountaineers!

West Virginia native John Antonik received a Bachelor's Degree in Journalism and Master's Degree in Sports Management from West Virginia University. He is Director of New Media for the Department of Intercollegiate Athletics at West Virginia University and author of *West Virginia University Football Vault: The History of the Mountaineers.*

Acknowledgments

The idea for a history of WVU men's basketball was the result of several telephone conversations I had in 2004 with Jim Lewis, Ed Harvard, Bucky Waters and George King following the sudden death of Ron "Fritz" Williams. What was to be a eulogy for a great WVU player and a wonderful human being soon turned into a story about the integration of basketball in the Southern Conference. It was from there that I began to develop a deeper appreciation for the history of Mountaineer basketball.

At the top of the list of those I would like to thank are WVU Press Director Carrie Mullen and West Virginia University Deputy Athletic Director Mike Parsons for making this book become a reality. I would also like to acknowledge the hard work put forth by editor Danielle Zahoran and book designer Than Saffel. Dani and Than always offered the right suggestions at the right times to keep this project on track.

A big tip of the cap to Mickey Furfari, Michael Fragale, Joe Swan, Bryan Messerly, Gary McPherson, Mark Devault, and Tim Goodenow for reading the original manuscript and offering their suggestions. I must also salute Mark Ragonese's hard work on his master's thesis on the history of WVU basketball many years ago as a graduate student working in the Sports Communications Office.

My special thanks to a special lady, Eleanor Lamb, for sharing her personal experiences of more than 50 years working in the WVU athletic department. Thanks, too, to Jay Jacobs, Eddie Barrett, Norman Julian, Sam Scuillo, the late Dick Polen and the late Bill Smith for sharing their leads and stories.

My deep appreciation to all of those who donated photographs and materials for this book including: the family of Dyke Raese, Bob Brown, Greg Hunter, Kevin Kinder, David Tuckwiller, Chuck Virden, James Glenn, Tara Curtis, Dan Miller, Phillip Herron, Warren Baker, Mickey Furfari, Gregg Cave, and Buddy Quertinmont. I would also like to thank the sports information departments at New York University, Manhattan College and the University of California for providing additional photography.

As always I am grateful for the support and companionship from my family, my wife Melinda and our two terrific kids, Sydney and Jack—Melinda for allowing me the time to do this and the kids for moving their toys and playing around my mountain of papers and materials.

And finally, my deep appreciation to all of the Mountaineer players, coaches and administrators that took the time to help me try and get the story right. Space permits me to acknowledge only a fraction of them, but my thanks to the following:

Jerry West, Hot Rod Hundley, Rod Thorn, Dr. Leland Byrd, Ed Pastilong, the late Fred Schaus, George King, Bucky Waters, Sonny Moran, Joedy Gardner, Gale Catlett, Bob Huggins, Bob Lochmeuller, Gary McPherson, Jim Amick, Bob Smith, Jim Sottile, Pete White, Clayce Kishbaugh, Willie Akers, Bob Clousson, Ronnie Retton, Joe Posch, Jim Ritchie, Jim McCormick, Buddy Quertinmont, Jim Lewis, Ed Harvard, Bob Hummell, Wil Robinson, Warren Baker, Maurice Robinson, Tony Robertson, Stan Boskovich, Lowes Moore, Joe Fryz, Greg Jones, Lester Rowe, Chris Leonard, Brent Solheim, Tyrone Sally, Mike Gansey, Kevin Pittsnogle, J.D. Collins, Darris Nichols, Joe Herber, Frank Young, Joe Mazzulla, Joe Alexander and Da'Sean Butler.

I hope this effort matches your superb performances through the years.

John Antonik

June 2010

Bibliography

Articles in Newspapers and Periodicals

Armstrong, Kevin. "West Virginia Star Finds There's More to Life than Pizza." *New York Times*. March 24, 2010. http://www.nytimes.com/2010/03/25/sports/ncaabasketball/25wvu.html.

Baker, Bob. "'Future Bright, I Wish I Could Stay,' Joedy Says." *Charleston Gazette*, March 7, 1978.

Baker, Bob. "Joedy Scared of SAM Missiles But Not WVU Job." *Charleston Gazette*, March 11, 1974.

Baker, Bob. "King Leaving WVU to Take Purdue Cage Post." *Charleston Gazette*, April 8, 1965.

Baker, Bob. "Mountaineers Hope to Shrug Off Criticism, Concentrate on Game." *Charleston Gazette*, March 16, 1968.

Baker, Bob. "Outages Affected WVU More, Coaches Say." *Charleston Gazette*, March 20, 1992.

Bogaczyk, Jack. "Sally; Pittsnogle Remember Dark Days in Mountaineer Program." *Charleston Daily Mail*, March 17, 2005.

Bogaczyk, Jack. "N.C. State and Beilein a New Worry for Mountaineers." *Charleston Daily Mail*, April 24, 2006.

Brady, Erik. "Self-made Coach Lives Out Dream." *USA Today*, March 24, 2005.

Brown, Mike. "Rumors Floating About WVU Coach And Duke Position." *Beckley Post-Herald*, February 16, 1967.

Carey, Jack. "West Virginia Ready to Launch from Anywhere." *USA Today*, March 16, 2005.

Cherry, Mike. "Chaney Recalls Catlett 'Wars': Temple Coach Says He Can Sympathize with Ex-Rival's Plight." *Charleston Daily Mail*, February 19, 2002.

Cherry, Mike. "Imhoff Tip the Stuff of Legends: Accounts of California's Winning Shot Differ from Person to Person." *Charleston Daily Mail*, July 9, 1999.

Cherry, Mike. "NCAA Bursts WVU's Bubble." *Charleston Daily Mail*, March 10, 1997.

Christopher, D. A. "Mountaineers Compiling Great Record In Basketball. Nineteenth Season Drawing To Close. Popular Winter Sports in Charge Of Brilliant Coach." West Virginia University Alumni Quarterly Bulletin, 1928.

Connell, Mike. "'I Guess I Was Lucky . . . '" *Dominion Post*, February 24, 1972.

Constantine, Tony. "Melee is Stopped Short of Full Riot; Coach Apologizes." *Morgantown Post*, February 16, 1970.

Constantine, Tony. Post Scripts. *Morgantown Post*, December 9, 1948.

Constantine, Tony. Post Scripts. *Morgantown Post*, April 28, 1958.

Constantine, Tony. Post Scripts. *Morgantown Post*, March 5, 1970.

Constantine, Tony. "WVU's 1942 Champions Something Special." *Dominion Post*, Panorama, February 14, 1971.

Cook, Ron. "WVU Shines Under Bright Lights." *Pittsburgh Post-Gazette*, March 12, 2005.

Core, Earl. "WVU Teams Attracted Wide Attention." *Dominion Post,* Panorama, February 1, 1981.

Currence, Stubby. "The Press Box." *Bluefield Daily Telegraph*, May 31, 1938.

Derrick, Mel. "Underhand Turnaround Shot Won It' – Mounties' Lentz." *Charlotte Observer*, January 30, 1964.

Donnelly, Joe. "The Destruction (and Rebuilding) of Rod Thorn." *Sport*, March 1962.

Drum, Bob. "Patton-Coached Teams Drive Rather Than Possess Ball." *Pittsburgh Press*, date unknown.

Franke, Russ. "WVU's Crawl Steals NCAA Tournament Victory." *Pittsburgh Press*, March 16, 1984.

Furfari, Mickey. "Catlett Tells His Goals." *Dominion Post*, March 29, 1978.

Furfari, Mickey. "Fan-Fare." *Dominion-News*, March 3, 1970.

Furfari. Mickey. "General, Catlett Ejected for Brawl." *Dominion-News*, February 14, 1963.

Furfari, Mickey. "George King Might Have Been Dentist Instead of Cage Coach." *Dominion-News*, April 13, 1960.

Furfari, Mickey. "KO Mars Furious Battle." *Dominion-News*, February 21, 1963.

Furfari, Mickey. "Player Punches Ref, WVU Tops Syracuse." *Dominion Post*, February 15, 1970.

Furfari, Mickey. "Thorn is Tourney's Top Player." *Dominion-News*, March 18, 1963.

Furfari, Mickey. "WVU Beats No. 1 Rated UNLV 87–78." *Dominion Post*, February 28, 1983.

Furfari, Mickey. "WVU Nips Manhattan by 78–77 on Robinson's Last-Second Shot." *Dominion Post*, February 27, 1972.

Hardman, A. L. "Bucky Ought to Tell All Where He Stands." *Charleston Gazette*, March 7, 1969.

Hardman, A. L. "'Chop 'Em Down' Had Day in Old Field House." *Charleston Gazette*, March 9, 1970.

Hardman, A. L. "Family Man Moran Will Step Down." *Charleston Gazette*, February 18, 1974.

Hardman, A. L. "Hammer Byrd says . . . 'Compete or Quit.'" *State Magazine*, March 26, 1972.

Hardman, A. L. "Hawley Has Done Much to Bring West Virginia to Front." *Charleston Gazette*, February 10, 1952.

Hardman, A. L. "'Honesty and Integrity' Brown's Creed at WVU." *Charleston Gazette*, September 25, 1954.

Hardman, A. L. "The Mountaineer Named Brown." *Sunday Gazette-Mail*, October 31, 1971.

Hardman, A. L. "Prize Pupil of the Old School." *Sunday Gazette-Mail*, January 28, 1962.

Hardman, A. L. "Ron a Little Tense in Debut With WVU." *Charleston Gazette*, December 2, 1965.

Hardman, A. L. "Waters Came Back, Then Left for Duke." *Charleston Gazette*, March 14, 1969.

Henry, Rene A. "Clowning Hot Rod Is Good Team Man." Weekly Basketball Record, February 12, 1956.

Hickman, Dave. "Beilein Coached Without a Voice." *Charleston Gazette*, March 21, 2005.

Hudson, Dick. "'All The World's A Stage.'" *Charleston Daily Mail*, December 11, 1954.

Hudson, Dick. "A Friendly And Fiery Competitor." *Charleston Daily Mail*, March 17, 1964.

Hudson, Dick. "George Didn't Get The Idea At First." *Charleston Daily Mail*, August 22, 1960.

Hudson, Dick. "Lee Patton, A Wholesome Man." *Charleston Daily Mail*, March 7, 1950.

Hudson, Dick. "Stadsvold Death Recalls Another Era." *Charleston Daily Mail*, December 22, 1968.

Hudson, Dick. "Unlucky If We Hadn't Won." *Charleston Daily Mail*, January 20, 1964.

Hudson, Dick. "Waters Wants WVU Invitational." *Charleston Daily Mail*, April 10, 1968.

Hyman, Mervin. "Basketball's Week." *Sports Illustrated*. March 30, 1959.

Johnson, Skip. "Last Second." *Sunday Gazette-Mail*, December 11, 1966.

Johnson, Skip. "Pitt Spoils WVU's Last Game in Field House, 92–87." *Charleston Gazette*, March 4, 1970.

Johnson, Skip. "Two Hassles Mark WVU's 92–81 Overtime Win." *Sunday Gazette-Mail*, February 4, 1962.

Johnson, Skip. "Williams No Cure-All, Says WVU Coach King." *Charleston Gazette*, April 8, 1964.

Johnson, Skip. "Winter of Discontent Ends; Moran Starts WVU Rebuilding." *Charleston Gazette*, March 5, 1970.

Julian, Norm. "Many Ingredients Add Up to Success." *Dominion-News*, December 2, 1970.

Keys, Kevin. "Oh So Close To The Big One." *Front Row Magazine*, February 1988.

Keys, Kevin. "Seeking The Best." *Front Row Magazine*, May 1989.

Longman, Jere. "Catlett Brings Winning Back to W. Virginia." *Philadelphia Inquirer*, February 26, 1982.

Luchok, John. "NCAA." *Front Row Magazine*, April 1986.

Lupica, Mike. "Stunner is West's Best." *West Virginia Daily News*, March 11, 2005.

McHugh, Roy. "The All-Americanization of WVU's Ron Williams." *Pittsburgh Press*, January 27, 1965.

McHugh, Roy. "Pitt Tunes in the Big Noise From Weirton." *Pittsburgh Press*, January 19, 1967.

McHugh, Roy. "Two Friends Looking Down The Barrel." *Pittsburgh Press*, February 8, 1966.

Mossberg, Kerry. "Golden Anniversary." *Front Row Magazine*, February, 1992.

Nichols, Cliff. "Blaney's Jumper Puts WVU in Finals." *Times West Virginian*, March 10, 1984.

Nichols, Cliff. "'My Enthusiasm for WVU Athletics is Sort of Built-In.'" *The Better Times*, May 13, 1981.

O'Connell, Jim. "Big East Woos 2 from A-10." Associated Press, March 11, 1994.

Pinchbeck, Val. "W. Virginia Nips Orange, 99–95." *Syracuse Herald American*, February 20, 1966.

Ramsey, David. "Johnson Becomes Hero." *Post-Standard*, March 14, 1987.

Robinson, Alan. "Catlett in Line as WVU's Basketball Coach, A.P. Says." Associated Press, March 25, 1978.

Ryan, Bob. "This Team's Well-Kept Secret." *Boston Globe*, March 13, 2005.

Smith, Bill. "Boos Help Bury WVU Coach." *Charleston Daily Mail*, February 18, 1974.

Smith, Bill. "The Cat." *Front Row Magazine*, January, 1986.

Smith, Bill. "'Firemen' Hotter Than The Devils." *Charleston Daily Mail*, February 8, 1966.

Smith, Pohla. "Joedy Doesn't Fight?" United Press International, December 15, 1976.

Smith, Pohla. "Pitt Topples Rival WVU To Claim Eastern 8 Crown." United Press International, March 8, 1982.

Tax, Jeremiah. "A Struggle to the Summit." *Sports Illustrated.* January 27, 1958.

Veasey, John. "Takin' It Easy." *Fairmont Times*, February 19, 1974.

Vingle, Mitch. "The Last 7.1 Seconds." *Sunday Gazette-Mail*, March 15, 1998.

Waters, Mike. "'Near Perfect Ending." Eastern Basketball, June 2005.

Weiss, Dick. "Gansey Makes Most of Second Shot and Free Throws, too." *West Virginia Daily News*, March 12, 2005.

West Virginia University. "A Visit to Aurora." Press Release. February 13, 1958. Retrieved January 15, 2009.

Wills, Bob. "Sports and Stuff." *Raleigh Register*, March 19, 1952.

Young, Ed. "Hundley Makes Loeffler Laugh But G.W. Didn't Get The Point." *Charleston Daily Mail*, March 7, 1955.

"All WVU, All the Time." *West Virginia University Alumni Magazine*, Summer 2002.

"College Basketball." *Sports Illustrated*. January 15, 2007.

"Duke Slips Past West Virginia." Associated Press, March 19, 1989.

"Everyone's Been Pittsnogled." *Sports Illustrated*. January 30, 2006.

"Fresno Stops WVU Slowdown." Associated Press, March 14, 1982.

"Glenn Turns in His Resignation at West Virginia." *Charleston Daily Mail*, December 4, 1939.

"Gallant WVU Effort Falls Short in Overtime, 100–98." *Charleston Gazette*, January 28, 1971.

"Hawley Gets Athletic Reins at W.V.U." *Charleston Daily Mail*, July 24, 1938.

"Lane Violation Beats Pitt." United Press International, January 30, 1982.

"Last Game Set Tuesday at WVU Field House." *Sunday Gazette-Mail*, March 1, 1970.

"Martin is Left Behind Team." *Morgantown Post*, Feb. 7, 1922.

"Martin Makes a New Record." *Morgantown Post*, January 23, 1922.

"Marshall (Little Sleepy) Glenn Proves Success As Coach After Playing Career." *Charleston Gazette*, January 21, 1934.

"Mountaineer Basketball Coach Deplores Stalling in Contests." NEA Services, March 6, 1930.

"Mountaineers Face Western Kentucky in Tossup." *Morgantown Post*, March 25, 1942.

"Mountaineers Will Be Honored Tonight." *Morgantown Post*, March 21, 1946.

"Mountaineers Win Praise from New York Observers." *Morgantown Post*, January 5, 1952.

"New York Writers Praise Mountaineers in Defeat." *Morgantown Post*, March 19, 1946.

"NIT Selects WVU, Catlett 'Shocked.'" United Press International, March 11, 1985.

"Penn State Roars Past WVU, 86–64." Associated Press, March 7, 1989.

"Pitt Fans Help WVU, 95–91." *Charleston Gazette*, February 4, 1971.

"Roy McKinley Hawley." *West Virginia University Alumni Magazine*, Spring 1954.

"Scotty Hamilton Draws Tribute of Gotham Scribe." *Morgantown Post*, March 17, 1942.

"Sharrar is 'Most Valuable'; McGuire Puts 'U' With Kan." Associated Press, December 23, 1957.

"Telecast Equipment Set Up For 'U' Game." *Morgantown Post*, February 6, 1959.

"The Country Slickers." *Time*, January 20, 1958.

"They Stole the Show." *West Virginia University Alumni Magazine*, Spring 1942.
"Tulsa Defenses WVU." United Press International, March 24, 1981.
"Two W.VA. Men Sent Back Home." *Morgantown Post*, Feb. 8, 1922.

"University Cagers Play Pitt For Conference Title." *Charleston Daily Mail*, March 18, 1935.

"W.Va. Hailed as Metro Champ." *Morgantown Post*, March 27, 1942.
"W.VA. has a Chance But Misses." Associated Press, March 20, 1998.
"W.V.U. 15, W.U. P. 12." *Daily Athenaeum*, February 25, 1904.
"WVU's 'Cool Hand Stan' Remembered by Pitt Coach." *Parkersburg News*, February 9, 1975.
"WVU Survives, 68–67, on Pitt Timeout Call." *Sunday Gazette-Mail*, February 3, 1963.

Books

Bender, Jack H. *Basketball Log*. St. Louis, Mo.: Valley Publishing, Co., 1958.
Brill, Bill. *Duke Basketball: A Legacy of Achievement*. Champaign, Ill.: Sports Publishing, LLC, 2004.

Caudle, Edwin C. *Collegiate Basketball: Facts and Figures on the Cage Sport*. Montgomery, Ala: The Paragon Press, 1960.

Doherty, W. T. and F. P. Summers. *West Virginia University: Symbol of Unity in a Sectionalized State*. Morgantown: West Virginia University Press. 1982.
Douchant, Mike. *Encyclopedia of College Basketball*. Detroit: Gale Research Inc., 1994.
Douglas, J. William. *The School of Physical Education at West Virginia University: An Historical Perspective 1891–1999*. Morgantown: West Virginia University School of Physical Education, 2000.
Dunnavant, Keith. *The Fifty-Year Seduction: How Television Manipulated College Football, from the Birth of the Modern NCAA to the Creation of the BCS*. New York: St. Martin's Press, 2004.

ESPN. *ESPN College Basketball Encyclopedia: The Complete History of the Men's Game*. New York: Ballantine Books, 2009.

Furfari, Mickey. *Mickey's Mountaineer Memories*. Beckley, W.Va: Beckley Newspapers, Inc., 2008.

Huggins, Bob. *Pressed for Success*. With Mike Bass. Champaign, Ill.: Sagamore, Publishing, 1995.

Julian, Norman. *Legends*. Morgantown, W.Va.: Trillium Publishing, 1998.

Keys, Kevin, and Shelly Poe. *Bring on the Mountaineers*. Morgantown: West Virginia University Department of Intercollegiate Athletics, 1991.

Kessler, Kent. *Hail West Virginians*! Weston, W.Va: Park Press, 1959.

Kriegel, Mark. *Pistol The Life of Pete Maravich*. New York: Free Press, 2007.

Libby, Bill. *Clown Number 33 in Your Program, Number 1 in Your Heart – Hot Rod Hundley*. New York: Cowles Book Company, Inc., 1970.

Libby, Bill. *Mr. Clutch: The Jerry West Story*. New York: Grosset & Dunlap, 1971.

Miller, Stuart. *The 100 Greatest Days in New York Sports*. New York: Houghton Mifflin Company, 2006.

Perry, Michael. *Tales From Cincinnati Bearcats Basketball*. Champaign, Ill.: Sports Publishing, LLC, 2004.

Ryan, Bob. *Hondo Celtic Man in Motion*. Englewood Cliffs, N.J.: Prentice-Hall, Inc., 1977.

Scuillo, Sam. *Pitt: 100 Years of Pitt Basketball*. Champaign, Ill.: Sports Publishing, LLC., 2005.

Interviews by Author and Oral Histories

Alexander, Joe. Interview. June 25, 2008. Morgantown, WV.

Amick, Jim. Telephone interview. Tape recording. June 25, 2006.

Akers, Willie. Telephone interview. Tape recording. November 7, 2008.

Babcock, Al. Interview. Tape recording. February 17, 2007. Morgantown, WV.

Baker, Warren. Telephone interview. Tape recording. April 6, 2007 and March 1, 2008.

Barrett, Eddie. Telephone interviews. Tape recordings. April 3, 2004, March 2, 2005, October 6, 2006, January 20, 2006, November 7, 2008, and March 29, 2010; E-mail interview. January 26, 2009.

Blakemore, Kittie. Telephone interview. Tape recording. October 1994.

Blaney, Dale. Telephone interview. January 16, 2001.

Boskovich, Stan. Telephone interview. October 15, 2001.

Butler, Da'Sean. Interview. Tape recording. April 5, 2010.

Byrd, Leland. Telephone interview. Tape recording. September 25, 2009.

Calipari, John. Interview. Tape recording. March 27, 2010.

Catlett, Gale. Telephone interview. February 5, 2010.

Clousson, Bob. Telephone interview. Tape recording. November 7, 2008.

Constantine, Tony. Interview by Eddie Barrett. Tape recording. September 2001.

Fleming, Jack. Telephone interview. Tape recording. November 17, 2000.

Fryz, Joe. Telephone interview. Tape recording. March 1, 2008.

Furfari, Mickey. Telephone interview. Tape recording. April 9, 2004 and March 2, 2005.

Furfari, Mickey. Interview. January 30, 2010.

Gardner, Joedy. Telephone interview. February 3, 2010.

Green, Tom. Telephone interview. Tape recording. January 11, 2001.

Harvard, Ed. Telephone interview. Tape recording. April 9, 2004.

Huff, Doug. Telephone interview. Tape recording. April 9, 2004.

Huggins, Bob. Interviews. Tape recordings. February 22, 2010, March 6, 2010, March 10, 2010, March 12, 2010, and April 3, 2010.

Huggins, Bob. Press conference. April 6, 2007. Morgantown, WV.

Hummell, Bob. Telephone interviews. January 11, 2001 and January 20, 2006.

Hundley, Rod. Telephone interviews. Tape recordings. March 7, 2005. and January 21, 2010.

Jacobs, Jay. Interviews. Tape recordings. March 2, 2005 and November 7, 2008.

Jones, Greg. Telephone interview. Tape recording, January 16, 2001.

Kimball, Larry. Telephone interview. Tape recording. January 11, 2001.

King, George. Telephone interview. Tape recording. April 9, 2004.

Kishbaugh, Clayce. Telephone interview. Tape recording. March 2, 2005.

Leonard, Chris. Telephone interview. Tape recording. February 14, 2002

Lewis, Jim. Telephone interview. Tape recording. April 9, 2004.

Lochmueller, Bob. Telephone interview. Tape recording. October 6, 2006.

Mazzulla, Joe. Interviews. Tape recordings. June 25, 2008 and March 13, 2010.

McCormick, Jim. Telephone interviews. Tape recordings. February 14, 2002 and October 5, 2006.

McPherson, Gary. Interviews. Tape recordings. January 11, 2001, February 14, 2002, January 20, 2004, April 6, 2007, and September 1, 2009. Morgantown, WV.

Moore, Lowes. Telephone interview. Tape recording. June 21, 2006.

Moran, Sonny. Interview. June 6, 2004. Gulfport, MS

Moran, Sonny. Telephone interview. January 30, 2010.

Neubauer, Jeff. Telephone interview. Tape recording. June 25, 2008.

Parsons, Mike. Interview. August 15, 2009. Morgantown, WV.

Pastilong, Ed. Interviews. February 14, 2002, March 25, 2007 and April 4, 2007. Morgantown, WV.

Polen, Dick. Telephone interview. Tape recording. January 11, 2001.

Posch, Joe. Telephone interview. Tape recording. November 7, 2008.

Quertinmont, Buddy. Telephone interview. Tape recording. October 6, 2006.

Retton, Ronnie. Telephone interview. Tape recording. November 7, 2008.

Ritchie, Jim. Telephone interview. Tape recording. November 6, 2008.

Robertson, Tony. Telephone interviews. Tape recordings. June 24, 2006 and April 6, 2007.

Robinson, Maurice. Telephone interviews. Tape recordings. February 2, 2004 and April 6, 2007.

Robinson, Wil. Telephone interview. Tape recording. March 1, 2008.

Rowe, Lester. Telephone interviews. Tape recordings. January 16, 2001 and January 20, 2004.

Samsell, John. E-mail interview. January 27, 2009.

Schaus, Fred. Telephone interview. Tape recording. March 3, 2005.

Solheim, Brent. Telephone interview. Tape recording. March 1, 2008.

Smith, Bill. Telephone interview. Tape recording. September 20, 2009.

Smith, Bob. Telephone interview. Tape recording. November 7, 2008.

Sottile, Jim. Telephone interview. Tape recording. October 1, 2009.

Thorn, Rod. Telephone interviews. Tape recordings. October 5, 2006 and February 2, 2010.

Waters, Bucky. Telephone interviews. Tape recordings. April 9, 2004 and January 20, 2006.

West, Jerry. Press conference. November 26, 2005. Morgantown, WV;

West, Jerry. Telephone interview. Tape recording. November 8, 2008.

White, Pete. Telephone interview. Tape recording. March 3, 2005.

Media Guides

Atlantic 10 Conference men's basketball media guides, 1983–1995

Big East Conference men's basketball media guides, 1996–2009

Southern Conference winter sports media guides, 1952–1968

Official 2009 NCAA Men's Basketball Records Book

West Virginia University basketball media guides, 1939–2009.

Online Sources

"America at Work." http://memory.loc.gov/ammem/awlhtml/awlwork.html.

Crouthamel, Jake. "A Big East History & Retrospective (Part 1)." *SU Athletics.com*. December 8, 2000. http://www.suathletics.com/sports/gen/2001/history.asp.

Davis, David. "The Man Behind the MLB Logo." *Wall Street Journal.* October 23, 2008. http://online.wsj.com/article/SB122453063968851133.html.

Douchant, Mike. "Smith's Achievement Blown Out of Proportion?" *CBS Sportsline*. March 14, 1997. http://www.cbssports.com/b/page/pressbox/douchant31497.htm.

Goldstein, Joe. "Explosion: 1951 Scandals Threaten College Hoops." *ESPN.com*. November 19, 2003. http://espn.go.com/classic/s/basketball_scandals_explosion.html.

"If West is the NBA Logo, Should He Be?" *FoxSports.com*. http://msn.foxsports.com/nba/.

Taubenberger, Jeffery K. and David M. Morens. "1918 Influenza: the Mother of All Pandemics." Emerging Infectious Diseases. *CDC.gov*. January 2006. http://www.cdc.gov/ncidod/eid/vol12no01/05-0979.htm.

Vitale, Dick. "Retiring Coach Catlett has Given Much to the Game." Dickie V. *ESPN.com*. http://espn.go.com/dickvitale/vcolumn020215Catlett.html

Wvustats.com. http://www.wvustats.com. Accessed January 2009.

Wojnarowski, Adrian. "Who's Joe Alexander? Just ask NBA scouts." *Yahoo! Sports*, June 23, 2008. http://sports.yahoo.com/nba/news?slug=aw-joealexander062308&prov=yhoo&type=legns.

Theses

Colebank, Albert Deahl. "A History of Inter-Collegiate Basketball in the United States with Especial Reference to West Virginia University." Masters of Science Thesis. WVU School of Physical Education, West Virginia University, 1939.

Ragonese, Mark. "Mountaineer Basketball 1904–1993." Masters Thesis. Perley Isaac Reed School of Journalism, West Virginia University, 1993.